WANDERINGS IN
WEST AFRICA

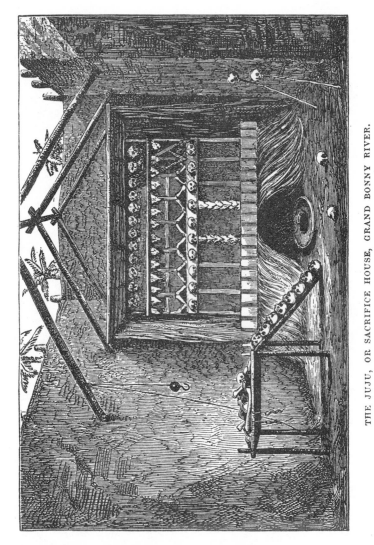

THE JUJU, OR SACRIFICE HOUSE, GRAND BONNY RIVER.

(From a Sketch by the Author.)

WANDERINGS IN WEST AFRICA

Richard F. Burton

Two Volumes
Bound as One

Dover Publications, Inc.
New York

Copyright © 1991 by Dover Publications, Inc.

Published in Canada by General Publishing Company,
Ltd., 30 Lesmill Road, Don Mills, Toronto, Ontario.

Published in the United Kingdom by Constable and Company, Ltd., 3 The Lanchesters, 162–164 Fulham Palace Road,
London W6 9ER.

This Dover edition, first published in 1991, is an un-
abridged republication of the work originally published by
Tinsley Brothers, London, in 1863, with the title *Wanderings
in West Africa from Liverpool to Fernando Po*, and with the
sole author credit "By A F.R.G.S." The foldout map that
originally faced page 1 of Volume I is now attached to the
inside back cover. A new Publisher's Note has been added.

Manufactured in the United States of America
Dover Publications, Inc., 31 East 2nd Street, Mineola, N.Y.
11501

Library of Congress Cataloging-in-Publication Data

Burton, Richard Francis, Sir, 1821–1890.
    [Wanderings in West Africa from Liverpool to Fer-
nando Po]
    Wanderings in West Africa / Richard F. Burton.
        p.   cm.
    Reprint. Originally published: Wanderings in West Af-
rica from Liverpool to Fernando Po. London : Tinsley
Bros., 1863.
    ISBN 0-486-26890-X
    1. Africa, West—Description and travel—1851–1950. 2.
Burton, Richard Francis, Sir, 1821–1890—Journeys—
Africa, West. I. Title.
    [DT472.B85   1991]
    916.604'23—dc20   91-19032
                                          CIP

TO

THE TRUE FRIENDS OF AFRICA

—NOT TO THE "PHILANTHROPIST" OR TO EXETER HALL—

𝕿𝖍𝖊𝖘𝖊 𝕻𝖆𝖌𝖊𝖘 𝖆𝖗𝖊 𝕴𝖓𝖘𝖈𝖗𝖎𝖇𝖊𝖉,

BY

A HUMBLE MEMBER OF THEIR FRATERNITY.

PUBLISHER'S NOTE, 1991

———•———

By 1863 Richard Burton (1821–1890; knighted 1886) had already studied a vast array of European and Asian languages, served on ticklish missions as an intelligence officer in India, entered the forbidden Muslim cities of Mecca (in Arabia) and Harar (in East Africa), attempted to discover the source of the Nile, and visited Salt Lake City (writing at least one book about each experience)—so that it was with considerable archness that he identified himself on the title page of his new work, *Wanderings in West Africa*, solely as "A F.R.G.S. [Fellow of the Royal Geographical Society]."

Wanderings was the first of five books Burton wrote about West Africa as a result of his stint as British consul on a large island off the coast of Nigeria: at the time, called Fernando Po and a possession of Spain; now Bioko and a province of the Republic of Equatorial Guinea. In this 1863 volume, Burton recounts his journey there from England, with particular attention (as he states in his Preface) to the health problems confronting British colonials, present and future, but with a thousand digressions and observations in which his polymathy is given free rein.

Unfortunately, Burton's aggressive imperialism was bolstered by very fundamental prejudices. His unfavorable opinion of black Africans (with some allowances made for Muslims in the north) is expressed throughout *Wanderings* in no uncertain terms, and he finds time *en passant* to attack other ethnic groups as well. After careful consideration, it was felt that this fascinating eye-witness account of nineteenth-century Africa by one of the most remarkable travel writers of all time—a highly regarded explorer, historian, linguist and translator—was nevertheless worth offering once more to a readership who could place it in its proper historical perspective.

VOLUME I

PREFACE.

A NO less authority than Baron von Humboldt has declared, in his "Personal Narrative,"* that, "from every traveller beginning the account of his adventures by a description of Madeira and Tenerife, there remains now scarce anything untold respecting their topography." And after this dictum the great philosopher proceeds to evidence *in propriâ personâ*, the fact that no account can be so correct but that it may be made exacter still.

I was induced to put my notes into the form of pages by the consideration that however well trodden be the path of which they treat, there is no single volume that can be taken with him by the outward-bound. Each separate station of the "African Steam Ship Company" has a small literature of its own : the line however lacks the idea of a handbook. And as for correctness the "West African Pilot" himself requires revision.

In writing these pages, then, it has been my object

* Bohn's ed., Vol. I., p. 48.

to lay down what a tolerably active voyager can see and do during the few hours allowed to him by the halts of the mail packet.

To relieve the dryness of details I have not hesitated to indulge in such reflections as the subject suggested, and to sketch the types, not the individualities, of fellow-travellers.

The reader will observe that I left England with a determination to investigate the subject of West African mortality. My conviction now is, that the land might be rendered not more unhealthy than the East or the West Indies, whereas it is at present deadly, a Golgotha, a Jehannum. The causes of its fearful mortality—principally the bad positions of the settlements—will be found duly indicated.

In taking leave of the gentle or ungentle reader, I may be allowed to remark, that amidst an abundance of greater there is doubtless a crowd of minor blemishes, which those charitably disposed will attribute to the effects of a " single revise."

WEST AFRICA,
  December, 1862.

CONTENTS OF VOLUME I

WANDERINGS IN WEST AFRICA.

CHAPTER I.

OUTWARD BOUND.

A HEART-WRENCH—and all is over. Unhappily I am
not one of those independents who can say *ce n'est que
le premier pas qui coûte.*

*   *   *   *

The day (August 24th, 186—) was a day to make the
Englander leave England without a single sigh. A
north of Europe nor'-wester had set in before noon, a
funereal pall of rain-mist overhung the heavens of Liverpool with black, white sea-dogs coursed and worried one
another over Father Mersey's breadth of mud, the
shrewish gusts tore to pieces the very strongest
showers—

If Britannia chills with tears and sighs the hearts of
her sons home-returning, at any rate, with the same
tenderness she consoles them under departure. Who
ever landed at Southampton in other but the worst
of weather ? Who ever left Dover on a fine clear
morning ?

At 12.15 P.M. the crowded little steam-tender conveyed us from the North Landing on board the A. S. S., *i. e.* African Steam Ship, "Blackland," Captn. English commanding.   Ensued that scene of senseless hurry and confusion in which ticket-porters and passengers —the former professionally, the latter unprofessionally— act principal parts.   However, on this occasion, thus distinguished from many others, I did not lose either box or bag upon the floating pier, nor did my ears suffer from that which usually reminded them of the Avignon portefaix, as he was in the days of Rambling before Railways.

My connection with my beloved native land concluded with a further demand of 6*l.* 2*s.* for baggage.

At 1.45 P.M., when the thirty-five huge mail bags, containing mental pabulum for some score of West-African ports, had come on board, when the two brass pop-guns had announced by the normal hang-fire and horrid ring, that Blue Peter had descended from his eminence, and when the last passenger was put in and the last stranger had put off, we steamed down the Long Reach, past the five miles of dock—the pride of the Liver—past New Brighton—not yet *L'pool sur mer*, but treeless, barren, horrid, hideous—past the North Fort and the South Fort, fine gingerbread-work for Mersey's mouth against Armstrongs, Whitworths, Blakeleys, Dahlgrens, Parrots, and *canon rayés*—past unpicturesque Waterloo, most like a modern barrack, over a bar breaking, to starboard and port, heavily as the Grand Bonny's, past a bit of sandland reminding me of

Araby the Accursed, and—tantalizing contradiction !—
forth into the open sea, heading straight for the North
Pole whilst bound for Tropical Africa.

Now the artificial stimulus of new places and new
faces has passed away, the light gear has been selected
for the cabins, the heavy traps have been sent down
below ; dinner at 4 P.M., and at 7 P.M. tea—with
desiccated milk—are " done." Then comes the first
nightfall on board outward-bound, the saddest time
that the veteran wanderer knows. Saadi, the Persian,
one of the best of travellers, — he studied books for
thirty years, did thirty of *wanderjahre,* and for thirty
wrote and lived in retirement,—has thus alluded to
the depressing influences of what I suppose may philosophically be explained by an absence of Light-stimulus
or Od-force—

> " So yearns at eve's soft tide the heart
> Which the wide wolds and waters part
> From all dear scenes to which the soul
> Turns, as the lodestone seeks its pole."

We cut short the day by creeping to our berths, without even a " nightcap," and we do our best to forget
ourselves and everything about us.

*   *   *   *

But Joy cometh in the Morning. We the gerontocracy
rise refreshed enough. Remembering Mad. Ida Pfeiffer's
saying when shown to her roosting-place—" *Birth* do
you call it ? I fear it will be the death of me,"—we
have slept in the main cabin. The juveniles preferred
the athwart-ship placed paint-perfumed little bunks,

five-feet by two-feet, with the flimsy cushion of compressed horse - hair between back and board, causing
aching bones; and the thin layer of compressed air
between respiratory organs and deck, engendering night-
mares, and chancing broken heads.   We turn out at
6 A.M.—and so shall we do for many a long day—we
" coffee up," smoke the morning cigarette, and prospect
the deck.   The air is clear, the Tuskar lighthouse
uprears its tall thin pale form from the no longer
muddy wave, we peer for "the Smalls," the Saltees
Islands are the last " Singhavolokan" (*vide* H. H.
Wilson); the "Blackland's" head turns S. W. and by
W. half W. (see anything from Norie to Raper)—we
now feel that we are Africa-bound, and we go down to
feed.

> " Hurrah, the bell for breakfast !
>   Hark to the mingled din
> Of knife and fork and hissing chops
>   Stewards are bringing in.
> The fiery skipper's pricking fast
>   His fork into the dish,
> Despatching quickly his repast
>   Of coffee, eggs, and fish.
> In burst the guests, and on they rush
>   Around the jolly tar,
> Who calls on semi-seasick folks
>   To prosecute the war."

And so on all day, concerning which the less said the
better.

Mais qu'allais-je faire dans cette galère ?

Records of travel, I am assured, are interesting in
proportion as the traveller goes forth, not a universal

observer, but with a definite pursuit to a small world of
his own. From the "depths of my self-consciousness"
I had eliminated an idea, that there is some solid substantial reason for the veil of mystery which, like that
of Isis, still shadows the fair proportions of Western
Africa. The old story of deleterious climate, when
statistics prove the "sentimental squadron" to be
healthier than that of the Mediterranean, was, to me,
a by no means sufficient explanation. The perpetual
imputation of "improper indulgences" brought against
Europeans by negro and negroid supporters of the
ridiculous theory, "Africa for the Africans"—*l'Italia
farà da se*—was no reason for overwhelming mortality
in a land which probably is as well fitted for northern
constitutions as India is. Perhaps there might be a
lingering of old tradition: one observes that the public
estimate of a distant place always dates from the last
popular book—say Mungo Park's. Possibly a rich
monopoly, whose deeds are ever best done in darkness.

Such, then, was my "pursuit." I have long since
answered these questions to myself, and if I fail to
satisfy those who do me the honour of reading me, it
will not—it is said with due humility—be my own
fault.

Meanwhile, whilst we cross—in a week—the 1537
deadly-lively miles that separate L'pool from Madeira,
I will *faute de mieux* indulge in a few reminiscences of
steamer travelling, and briefly glance at the history of
the A. S. S. Company which carries the West Coast of
Africa mails.

As most people know, steamers—an invention which outdates almost all now alive—have not yet learned, at least on long-sea voyages, to pay their own way. The Cunard, the P. & O., and the Royal Mail lines—they are named in order of merit—still require large subsidies from Government. On the other hand, commerce has greatly benefited, as the following extract from a Yankee pamphlet may prove :—" The annual increase of British exports to China, Egypt, and India (where subsidized mail steamers were introduced in 1845), since the establishment of steam communication to them, is $39,948,615 ; and this gain is secured at what cost ? Simply by a mail subsidy of but $950,750 per annum, or less than two and a half of one per cent. on the annual increase of exports."*

The A. S. S. Company receives an annual benefit of 30,000*l.* under a contract with the Admiralty, and is understood to pay, besides bonus, seven per cent. per annum.† The reason why this line has hitherto not done more—for something it *has* done—during the last ten years, to develop the resources of the country, must be sought in future pages. One restriction removed would be a boon to the company and the country.

---

* United States and Mexican Mail Steamship Line.   A pamphlet by Carles Butterfield : Hasbrouch & Co., New York.   1860.

† It has secured to itself the advantage of altering the port of embarkation.   It began with Plymouth for passengers, London for specie, and L'pool whence the ships sailed.   London being immemorially connected with Sierra Leone and its adjacent ports, caused a loss, which was remedied by a transfer to the grand northern terminus of the Bights and Oil-River trade.

It is not allowed to trade. It should be encouraged to station a hulk in every river, and its superior facilities of providing the natives, at the earliest convenience, with things suitable to their whimsical fancies would soon break up existing monopolies. Even now it might amalgamate with another company, but it fears the oil merchants, who on their part never give it a gallon of their goods unless compelled by the purest necessity.

The African Steam Ship line was established in January, 1852, mainly by the energy of the late Mr. Macgregor Laird, the second pioneer of Niger explor- ation, and to the end of his days the most enthusiastic, if not the most fortunate, of African improvers. By virtue of certain comma-less articles, the "African Steam Ship Company" binds itself under a penal sum of £2000 to convey mails (and passengers), once every month, " between England and the West Coast of Africa, by means of a sufficient number (not less than seven) of good, substantial and efficient steam-vessels each fitted with a screw-propeller four of such vessels to be of not less than 978 register tons burthen old measurement each and each supplied with first-rate appropriate steam- engines of not less than 150 horse-power and the remaining vessel (to be employed intercolonially only) to be not less than 440 register tons burthen old measurement and supplied with first-rate appropriate steam-engines of not less than 100 horse-power. In- cluding arrival at and departure from England, twenty- two ports are to be visited. Its mileage is a grand total of 10,024 nautical miles, viz., 9434, and 590 of international line. The average rate is to be eight knots an hour, and the return subsidy is fixed at a sum which justifies the African Steam Ship Company's motto "spero meliora." Its device, I may observe, is a negress *agenouillée*, who presents to Britannia of the bare leg a little heap of (typical) "small potatoes," and "some punkins." Freightage *to* West Africa is still 5*l.* per ton of gross cargo (Siam may be made for 3*l.* 10*s.*) ; and by way of encouraging the return of palm oil, *from* West Africa it is thirty shillings less. Sucking officials may spare themselves the trouble of writing on foolscap for contract passages, which reduce 45*l.* to 44*l.* 5*s.* Moreover, there is no difference of passage money between L'pool and Benin River, and L'pool and Fernando Po, which is truly ridiculous. The line was recontracted for in July 1858, six years being the time of expiry. Before that day, however, the merchants of L'pool will probably provide the African Steam Ship Company with a rival. The more the merrier ! And when the present freight prices diminish to half, the export will be trebled, and the fantastic century-old style of oil-exporting will be numbered with things that were.

The line has already, I have said, been beneficial to the West Coast of Africa, and will be more so by encouraging the "tin-pot trader," which in Oil-River-slang means the merchant who has no ship of his own. It may fairly be recommended to the public as one of the great civilising agents of the Benighted continent. It is highly important to invalids who are banished to Madeira, which it at present visits once a month about the first day; and the irregularity in its arrivals and departures, complained of by guide-books, has now made place for the contrary condition. The Island of the Blessed is also to be reached once a month by the "Lusitania," a small Portuguese steamer from Lisbon, and occasionally by an extra packet from Southampton, generally from September to November. The Angola Mail arrives about the same time as the A. S. S. : the Royal Mail has ceased to run there, owing they say to the ridiculous persistency of Lusitanian quarantine regulations; it may, however, resume operations : and every year the vessel homewards bound for repairs touches at Madeira and takes passengers to England about May, the relief steaming outwards in October. The Peninsular and Oriental proposes to send on its Lisbon steamer. Of the Compagnie Franco-Américaine I could hear nothing.* Practically, therefore, the Madeirans receive from Europe two mails per month, on the 17th *viá* Lisbon, and on the 30th direct.

The African Steam Ship line† is cursed, as will be seen, with an Intercolonial of some 400 tons; and woe to

---

* The old brigs are dying out, the "Eclipse" was burned in 1861, the "Comet" was sunk in 1863, and the Portuguese "Galgo" is now the sole survivor.

† The little fleet—may its shadow never be less!—began with chartered ships; it then built the "Retriever," the "Forerunner," the "Faith," the "Hope," and the "Charity." The latter three being large, slow, and fitted with auxiliary screws, failed, and were sold. The next batch was unlucky. The "Candace," on board of which all the watch was asleep, was run into by a Dutchman, near Gibraltar. The "Niger" was wrecked by hugging the iron-bound shore of Tenerife, and the "Forerunner," which carried Dr. Living-

those who travel by Intercolonials, either from Suez, St. Thomas, or the Bonny River. The regularity of the main line yields in the subsidiary to whatever interest demands. It ought to be held to time, but it cannot. It is hard to secure efficient officers for such craft, and harder still to keep them in health. Deck passage is farcically expensive, ten dollars each way : it should be reduced to half. All the African Steam ships are built for cargo, not for passengers; but the intercolonial screw beats all. It will carry eleven, with berths for four. A stewardess is impossible, also a doctor. There is no bath but under the hose. No con-

stone's African journals, was lost on 25th Oct., 1854, close to Madeira. Passing too near the North Point, called in charts the "I. Fora," she ran upon a sunken rock or projection from the island, and went down in forty fathoms. Her gold is still on board—a hint to divers, who, however, have as yet failed. The "Gambia" was sold. The line now (Aug. 186—) consists of the "Cleopatra," Capt. Croft, 1400 tons (she will be disposed of, because too large), the "Armenian," Capt. Wylde, 1000 tons, the "Athenian," Capt. Lowry, 1050 tons, the old "Ethiope" of the second batch, Capt. French, 700 tons, and the intercolonial "Retriever," Capt. Delamotte, 400 tons. The " Macgregor Laird," a fine ship of 1000 to 1100 tons, is still on the stocks.

Since this was written, Captain Croft has taken command of the "Macgregor Laird," and the "Cleopatra," Capt. Delamotte, was lost on the 19th August, 1862, on the Shebar, at the mouth of the Sherbro River, 40 miles out of her course. An engineer and five Krumen were drowned. The crew escaped on rafts ; and the passengers who, though two days on board, had not time to save their watches,— landed in a single boat, three having drifted away whilst laying out a kedge. Mr. Hanson, Her Majesty's consular agent, Sherbro River, was drowned, with his boat's crew, as he came to their assistance—thirteen lives sacrificed by prodigious carelessness. A bad rumour went abroad that the old ship had been purposely lost.

veniences, except through a crowd of kruboys and negroes. In fact, a tour of the Oil Rivers in such a craft would be certain death to a sick man. Cases of the grossest negligence, even touching cargo, are quoted in the out-ports. A little steamer belonging to the Scotch Missionaries, in the Old Calabar, was left in the Bonny River exposed to wind and weather till it sank. The Camaroons mission complain that their boxes and building material have often been landed at the mouth of the river. Fernando Po murmurs because it has only eighteen hours to read and answer its letters, when the Intercolonial might easily give it three days without loss, by returning to it from the Camaroons River before rejoining her consort at the Bonny—the latter being a most unwise measure, which will some day eventuate in the loss of a large steamer. On the other hand, Gaboon is wroth because she is not visited at all, and only finds consolation in the idea, that she is not swamped by negro immigrants from Sierra Leone. I cannot but hope that the eventual terminus of the line will be St. Paul de Loanda, and that its voyages will be weekly instead of monthly.

The little steamer which carries us is now on her twenty-second voyage. She strikes the senses as microscopic, after the usual monsters of long sea voyages. Her engine is of 120 horse-power, and she burns somewhat less than the normal allowance of coal—1 ton to 10 horses. The skipper, however, is allowed 5 per cent. for what he saves, consequently there is little haste and less speed. On the other hand, her builder always quotes

her as his *chef-d'œuvre*, and she has sundry advantages,
—everyone knows that whilst the largest transports are
rarely comfortable, the smaller may be. We have no
mail agent, thus securing the advantageous absence of
a Royal Navy "party," who has little to do, but *fruges
(et Bacchum) consumere*, order four-oared gigs, and make
the master suffer if everything be not "to his liking."
There are no "sea-swells;" even "land-swells" are
scarce, and are hardly appreciated. No "big-bug's"
valet kidnaps the first cup of matutinal coffee. No
learned Theban from the East spins his forty-years' yarn
or acts Triton among the Minnows. We do not always
get a "Purser's answer," ultra-diplomatic as pursers and
soldiers when doing the diplomatic are wont to be. And
the stewards (*mirabile dictu!*) are civil and obliging.
We wear paper collars, steel collars, linen collars, or no
collars. We smoke abaft the mainmast, when crinoline
adorns not the quarter-deck. The feeding is good—
without too much of preserves—and we *can* drink
the beer.

On the other hand, the screw is painfully noisy, and as
to the ladder I must quote from the *West African Herald*.
"It will really," says that amiable individual, "be for
the general good if some governor, or other official of
high standing, will get smashed between the foot of the
ladder and his canoe!" But when will men who make
ships learn to make the steps slope the right way, and a
joint in the backbone of the affair to prevent injuring
boats? Another desideratum, a little less deck-washing
after four A.M. Also, a sad thing for the public,

which is feminine as well as masculine, is the want of
stewardesses: these should be rendered obligatory.*
And we have one solid grievance. The beer and stout
are tolerable, but at this rate will not last; and the ice
may possibly endure to Lagos, the soda-water to the
Bonny. But the wine is dear, and, what is worse,
execrable: the African Steam Ship Company makes
little by it, so we have to pay dear for simple carelessness touching our comforts. The claret is black strap,
the hock is sourish, the champagne all syrup, the
Burgundy is like the house Burgundy of the Reform
Club—meat as well as drink; the Moselle *sent son
perruquier;* the sherry is a mine of bile; and of the
port—the less said the better of such "strong military
ditto." The coffee and tea are not bad naturally, but
artificially; and to distinguish between them requires
a very superior nose. Finally, our berths are, it is
true, uncrowded, but they are capable of containing
more than one, which should never be allowed on board.
I have heard of four and even five human beings stuffed
into one of these loose boxes, and it is not to be wondered at if ladies who have never suffered in Africa,
have been half-poisoned by their cabins when going
home. Why should not the passengers be allowed
legally to claim what is allowed to the denizens of every
hospital, so many square feet of vital air?

At three P.M., on the 30th of August, after a six

---

* Even black women would be better than nothing, if, as I suspect,
white women would not live through the River-tour. At present the
stewardess goes only as far as Madeira.

days' run, we exchanged the North for the South. Off our port bow rose Porto Santo, a long broken line resembling a magnified crater or elongated Aden, which it probably is. The taller cones, especially the Pico de Facho and the Pico de Anna Fereira, strongly suggest volcanic action, and the lower land, which is sandy rather than rocky, hides its fertility from the Atlantic wave. As we sped by it, a single gleam of golden sun piercing the crown of clouds, lit up its ribbed flanks with that picturesque suddenness that delights the eye, and made the surface resemble an expanse of ripening corn.

Porto Santo derives its name from the glorious days of Portuguese history. Prince Enrique o Conquistador of Portugal, third son of Dom João I., by Philippa, daughter of John of Gaunt, and sister to Henry IV. of England, sent in 1418 one João Gonsalvo, whose title became " da Camara," surnamed Zargo, or the " one-eyed," and Tristaõ Vaz Teixeira, to explore the West African Seas. According to some writers the " Zargo " was directed by a pilot who, during imprisonment at Morocco, had heard of the Madeiran group from certain shipwrecked Englishmen: at any rate he is generally supposed to have discovered Porto Santo. The " Monoculous one," who deservedly lies a local hero in the convent Saint Clara, of Funchal, appears to have been made of strongish stuff. The navigators of those days had a tradition that a veil of impenetrable darkness overhung the horizon of the " Holy Port," and that at times a mysterious sound struck the passer by into awe. Some fancied an abyss, others the mythical island Cipango, where Providence had located the Christians that had escaped from the infidel Moors, others the mouth of Gehenna. Zargo, however, after being driven, in 1418, by a storm upon the rugged ridge, which he and his companions named in gratitude the Porto Santo, went straight for the gates of Hell, and two years afterwards discovered its big brother Madeira. Even in the present day the Porto Santians—who are far more African than European—believe in the existence of an island to the westward called San Brandaõ. It is occasionally visible, being probably a mist-land, a Fata Morgana, and if a stranger be seen to use a spy-glass, he is looking, men say, for San Brandaõ. San Brandaõ is also called St. Blandon, Brandon or Borondon, a Scotch priest who flourished in A. D. 565; his island is also seen from the Canaries. It is an old story, doubt-less dating from the submerged Atlantis of Plato, which in the days of Columbus became Antilla, or the Island of the Seven Cities, and formed a midway house between the Old and New Worlds. I shall have more to say about these mystical islands which figure in the legends of all wild and superstitious maritime people; meanwhile I may remark that Ptolemy's Aprositus or Inaccessible Island, with San Brandaõ and Antilla, appear to be the only presentiments of a Western Continent that floated in the Western mind.

Porto Santo, around which lie various barren rocky islets, one of which supplies a fine lime-dirt cheap, is distant twenty-five geographical miles N.E. from Ma-deira; its dimensions are 6½ by 3 miles. It is the second of the five which compose the Erythian group, the others being Madeira and the Three Desertas, and they form a scalene triangle, the Desertas lying to the S.E. of Madeira. The surface is bare of trees, and the population, about 1500 souls, find but few water springs free from brackishness and carbonate of soda. Formerly it produced about 1500 pipes of coarse wine, used for brandying Madeira. When the Italian Cacadada Mosto visited it, in 1454, he saw numbers of Dragoliros, Dragon-trees (*Dracæna Draco*); now not one remains, and even the sister island shows but few. In 1854, its harvest was about 11,000 bushels of barley, and its income was $1154 against an expenditure of $968. At Porto Santo during the last year, the steamer "Ganges," proceeding to India for River Service, happened to break her back upon a spine of Porto Santo. The crew naturally wished to land, they were warned off, however, as not having a clean bill of health. Portugal has been reproached with the flimsiness of her paper laws, here, however, is an instance of authority austere enough.

In the course of the afternoon we sighted, over the starboard bow, the similar form of Madeira, and admired the mass of cumulus gleaming over the topmost heights, Pico Ruivo and Pico Grande. These fine towers soon fell from sight, and with them the wild, grand scenery of the Northern coast, which, according to travellers, far excels that of the South. As evening drew near, we rounded the sharp, serrated line of basaltic rocks, called San Lourenço, the original name of the whole island, not because, like Madagascar, it was discovered on the anniversary of the Saint of the Gridiron, but because the Zargo's ship bore that name. Off this ridge is the submarine outlier, where, in 1854, the African steamship, " Forerunner," was wrecked, and several lives were lost. We then glided by Machico, whose name recalls the tedious tale, old and oft told, of Robert à Machim, or Macham, and the " unfortunate Anne of Bristol." The elopement is well worn, as the heroic end of Major Pierson in Jersey, or the loves of Sassui and Punhu in Scinde; consequently a late authority—in these days there are many scoffers—pronounces it to be a " romantic and probably fabulous narrative." * Our " elbowing island " is determined to lay claim to the discovery, but the tale was probably invented to flatter Prince Henry. There are others again who suggest that the " noble Anna d'Arfet's" name was Miss Darby, daughter of a Bristol trader, and that her elopement was the result of her preferring a juvenile commoner to the elderly peer, her husband. Presently we doubled the bluff tufas and basalts of fantastic Garajaõ, by the northern barbarians called Brazen Head, and we dropped anchor in the Bay of Funchal,—once much noted for fennel, —firing sundry guns, that produced nothing but a fine echo; like the hills of Jamaica, that crash as if about to fall when shot at.

---

* The fatal test of dates has been applied to it. Machim is said to have died in A.D. 1334 : Madeira was discovered in A.D. 1419. If João de Morales, the Spanish pilot, had acted as informant between Machim's people and Zargo, he had been at least forty-two years in prison.

The temperature changed by magic. The usual rough north-easterly breeze of the outside subsided into a luxurious, sensual calm, with occasional puffs of soft exciting westerly zephyrs, or *viento de las mugeres*, formed by the land-wind of night, eddying round the sea-bathed headlands. This charming "embate" is common about Funchal. We could distinctly smell the land, the scent being that of clover hay. Though it had barely struck 10 P.M., the little town lay silent, dull, and drowsy, like the lotus-eaters they are. The scattered *reverbères* told of oil, not of gas; they are fed by the Physic-nut, or Croton (*J. purgans*) imported from Portugal. We felt a conviction that firing our three brass barkers was in vain. The health officer, being an aged senhor, had set out for his Quinta, and *festin a lentè* being the motto of all his tribe, he preferred "Kayf" to giving us pratique that night. The commander of H.M.S. "Griffon," after vainly awaiting permission to board us, at last lost patience, and carried off his mail bag. We were *détenus* on board *nolentes volentes*, for which disappointment the *fainéantisme* of "those Portugooses" suffered due contumely.

I may here remark, that since the "cholera year"— 1856—the pratique regulations of Madeira are arbitrary and exclusive. The quarantine establishment has not been pulled down, but the lazaretto is wholly neglected, and admission to it is taboo'd, because, say the people, there must be all or nothing. When fever is supposed to be on the West African Coast, then bills of health are of no avail. The orders are probably sent from

Lisbon; the local authorities, however, do not object
to money dribbling from the suspected ship into the
town, only the coin must be passed through water.
It is a truly ridiculous spectacle, the old toothless, nut-
cracker-chinned health-officer, quavering with his childish
treble, as he issues orders to his boatmen forbidding any
more daring soul to near the gangway, and depositing
all letters in a deal box, under which he lights a dwarf
spirit lamp. He is naturally subject to abundant
" chaffing," when he waxes wrath and raises his blear
eyes, and declares that he will stop the coaling, which
direful threat procures for him a little peace.

Most of our company retired to rest impatient as
children waiting to see the curtain draw up. Mr. Lyall
("Rambles in Madeira, 1827,") declares, like Baron
von Humboldt, that every traveller opens his quarto with
a short notice of Madeira. Yet, to judge from such
queries as " are there any hotels here? " the public does
not seem to know much about it.

CHAPTER II.

A DAY AT MADEIRA.

31st August.

" I do not know a spot on the globe which so astonishes and delights upon first arrival as the island of Madeira. The voyager embarks and is, in all probability, confined to his cabin, suffering under the dreadful prostration of sea-sickness. Perhaps he has left England in the gloomy close of autumn, or the frigid concentration of an English winter. In a week he again views that terra-firma which he had quitted with regret, and which in his sufferings he would have given half that he possessed to regain. When he lands upon the island, what a change ! Winter has become summer ; the naked trees which he left are exchanged for the luxuriant and varied foliage ; snow and frost for warmth and splendour ; the scenery of the temperate zone for the profusion and magnificence of the tropics ; a bright blue sky; a glowing sun ; hills covered with vines ; a deep blue sea ; a picturesque and novel costume ;—all meet and delight the eye, just at the precise moment when to have landed on a barren island would have been considered a luxury."—*Capt. Marryat.*

I PASSED the long length of a single day and night in and off Madeira, and, consequently, consider myself highly fitted to write a somewhat lengthy account of it. Despise not, gentle reader, first impressions, especially in a traveller. The authors of guide-books for the most

---

* Quoted—the first, but not the last, quotation from "Madeira, its Climate, and its Scenery, a Handbook for Visitors," by R. White, and edited by J. Y. Johnson. A useful volume, and trustworthy in most things, save that necessary over - appreciation of its subject which essentially belongs to the genus guide book.

part excuse their authorship upon the plea of "long sojourn;" of "practical knowledge;" and of "fifteen or twenty years' experience." Such, naturally, deride the audacious intruder, who, after a few hours' stroll and chat, presents himself upon their premises. I am convinced, however, that if a sharp, well-defined outline is to be drawn, it must be done immediately after arrival at a place; when the sense of contrast is still fresh upon the mind, and before second and third have ousted first thoughts. Thus were written such books as " Eöthen " and " Rambles Beyond Railways ;" thus were not written Lane's " Egyptians " or Davis's " Chinese." Except in a New World, where the mind is stunned, observation will, a few days after arrival, lose all its distinctness. The man who has dwelt a score of years in a place, has forgotten every feeling with which he first sighted it; and if he writes about it, he writes for himself and for his fellow-oldsters, not for the public. The sketcher who acts as I propose to do will, of course, make an occasional bad blunder, even as the reverend author of the " Cruise of the North Star " converted the humming-bird house-moth of Madeira into a Trochilus, as Captain Alexander translated Penha d'Aguia, the eagle's wing (for rock); or as the " Rambler in Madeira " rendered Paül de Serra (the " Marsh of the Wild ") " some chapel or shrine of St. Paul." These ridiculous little blots will be " nuts " to the old resident. But, in the main, the *guâche* will be true and vivid. Of course I do not intend my traveller to indite the normal chapter upon the " Manners and Customs of the People," whom he sees in the streets; nor, during his very short sojourn, do I expect that he will neglect to avail himself, as a practised hand always can, of the information derived from those that have learned the place *à fond*. After which preamble, return we to Madeira.

Going "up stairs," as the sex says, at 5 A.M. on the day after arrival, I cast the first glance at Funchal, the place of Fennel. The town is far larger than any at the Canaries, and is said to contain 25,000 to 30,000 souls, one-fourth of the population of the island; it lies at the bottom of a shallow bay, whose arc is five and a half, and whose chord is three-quarters of a mile long from Brazen Head to Ponta da Cruz, and the scattered San Joaõ rocks. Immediately behind it is a curtain of lofty hills, rent on the right by a deep fiumara, a huge gash called the Ribeiro de Joaõ Gomez, which, with other *barrancas* in front and on the extreme left, confines the city to sundry waves of ground radiating from above. Nothing can be more beautiful than this immense bank of vegetation,—this vast pyramid, that looks as if the land had been tilted up at an angle of 40°. Nothing more lovely than the variety and contrast of the greens, for instance, the young sugar-cane a vivid vitriolic hue broken by clumps of dark holm-oak, myrtle, gloomy cypress,—it figures here as in Persia,—and dull bay, with here and there a palm-tree, symbol of the South and East. The multitude of little terraces and dwarf earthbanks in short horizontal lines, with which the ruddy face of the mountain is wrinkled, contrasts curiously with the rounded summits of the upper heights. It yields in the upper heights to clumps of trees and ground bare or sparsely clad with heath, thyme, whortleberry, bilberry, laurel, and various grasses. Eastward lies a tract of barren red land, arid slopes which even joint-stock companies have vainly attempted to irrigate. Westward is another hill-shoulder upon which the south of the city reposes; it is black with basalt, the material of Fernando Po, Prince's Island, and San Thomé,* and red with tufa and argil. The most conspicuous feature is the Ilheo (small sea-holm), by the English called Loo rock, a detached and rugged mass of basalt, which has been walled up and surmounted with a little citadel where signals and continual salutes—the latter becoming happily rare in Europe—vex the English and invalid ear. This fort, which the natives consider a local Gib, was bombarded by H.M.S. "Endeavour," Captain Cook, R.N., the circumnavigator, for an affront offered to the British flag. The incident, which took place in 1768, was expunged by order of Government from Hawkesworth, but was made public by Mr. Forster, who visited the island in 1772. "Loo" has not much to boast of: no submarine tunnel connects it with the Pontinha, or Little Point of the nearer mainland, so that bolting must be made in time. It recalls to me the remark of a Persian friend whom I once escorted over a man-of-war : "Ajab chíz ast mager

* Usually called St. Thomas, and thus confounded with the Danish St. Thomas, in the West Indies, of Dano-Anglo-Yankee-Nigger celebrity.

jáe guríz níst "—" A wonderful affair; but how the deuce does one run away?" Sailing vessels usually lie E.N.E., and east of the Loo rock, with good anchorage in 25 to 30 fathoms. Steamers of course place themselves nearer the shore. Funchal port is evidently a mere roadstead, depending for safety upon the Embate, or westerly wind, which here blows nine months during the year. When, however, as very often happened, especially in the terrible storms of 1803, 1842, and 1848, the wind is from the south or the south-east, ships must slip cables and clear the Points under pain of finding themselves stranded. At the time of my visit the Madeiran fleet was not extensive,—H.M.S. " Griffon," Commander Perry, R.N., a Portuguese revenue cutter, and two or three small merchantmen.

The atmosphere about the town is somewhat hazy. Madeira's veil is thicker even than that of Tenerife. The dew-clouds are slowly clearing off the upper heights— there is not, however, a stain of smoke. The sea is of limpid Mediterranean blue, and the gulls and kittie-wakes—some of these stupids have apparently followed us from L'pool—float like corks upon the lazy tepid swell. The aspect of the buildings is that of the Portuguese colonies generally; the houses are vast, with huge hanging balconies and lanterns, gazabos, belvederes, terrinhas or turrets on the upper stories, where the residents catch the cooling breezes. The colours are various; frequently a bilious yellow, with green or brown jalousies, and the roofs, once flat and terraced, are now steep slopes of home-made tile. Square, staring, similar, and unseemly, these habitations appear from afar like little dens, and, individually ugly, are not so *en masse.* The *rus in urbe* here, as in Asiatic Portugal, is conspicuous. There is a tree for each house; on the east lies the Praça Academica, a formal strip of plantation; in front of the Fortaleza or palace there are more scattered and ragged growths forming the Praça da Rainha, whilst clumps and avenues appear in different parts of the town where the Praças answer to English squares, French boulevarts, and Spanish prados and alamedas. The buildings thin out as they climb the hill. At the first *coup d'œil* I was somewhat struck by the absence of sacred edifices: presently on landing these were found to be not less numerous than in other Lusitanian settlements. The woods from which Madeira, like Kyle,* derived her name, and which according to that dreadful " story " history, when accidentally set on fire, burned for seven consecutive years—one of Clio's pleasant little " desiperes "—have mostly disappeared. In fact, as the old Portuguese chronicler says, the island should now be called da Pedra, not da Madeira—Petrosa, not Sylvania.

The principal buildings in the town, beginning from the right of the charming amphitheatre, are:—The Fort of St. Iago, lying about one mile east of the city, and apparently dismantled. Next the Praça Academica, or Academic groves, thick, sombre, and close to the sea, at the mouth of a great jagged Ribeiro, whose deep

---

* Kyle, in Ayrshire, celebrated by Burns, is derived by some Gaelic scholars from choille, wood; others ignore the derivation.

shingly bed, even down this distance, tells of terrific
torrents. About the heart of the mass the Sé or Cathedral exposes its tall dark tower, with the lower third
whitewashed, and a dwarf poikillated spire capped with
a large gilt weather-cock. Upon the beach stands a
ridiculous column of dark basalt, a tower of Babel, half
finished, and never likely to be done. An English
merchant, Mr. Banger, Benger, or Badger, built this
Folly at a cost of £1350, to unload vessels, and—such is
action at Madeira—when it attained its present altitude
it found itself at a respectable distance from the sea. A
little to the left is the yellow Fortaleza de San Lourenço,
rebuilt in 1803; this palace, fronted by a dwarf promenade, the Praça de Rainha, is a large pile of masonry,
somewhat like those of Goa in her palmy days. Further
left, and overlooking the town, is the Citadel or Peak
Fort (Castello do Pico de San Joaõ), an artless work,
whose vertical fire would, in these days, do very little
damage. The extreme left concludes with a gunless
battery, completing a total of eleven; being *à fleur
d'eau*, it might be utilised; an old convent, a lime-
kiln, and the universal coal-shed; a new consumptive
hospital, of magnificent proportions, since opened, but
closed in consequence of a local squabble; a cemetery
bristling with pyramidal cypress; and a large building
belonging to an English settler, and lately occupied by
Her Majesty of Austria.

At 6 A.M. on the 31st August, we were visited by a
boat containing the post-captain, a stout Portuguese
gentleman, speaking English uncommonly well, and the

health-officer, a very old party, who, after a few silly
professional questions, vouchsafed us pratique. Thereupon the ladder-foot was jammed by a shoal of boats
built after the Mediterranean fashion, broad in the
beam, substantial, treble-keeled and iron-shod to bear
hard grating and to prevent upsetting when drawn up,
painted green for coolness, with a broad stripe of yellow
for beauty, and provided with tall, knobbed posts rising
high at stem and stern for the support of the indispensable awning. The oars are curious contrivances, not
unlike those formerly used in Western Ireland; in place
of rowlocks, a pin fits into a hole in a broadening
surface; the men row well with a long and steady stroke.
We descended with the usual life-and-death struggle, all
for a shilling ahead! passed over the transparent blue
waters, where little Portingals disported themselves in
nature's suit, and turning stern-on backed till we were
hauled by a team of bullocks up the shingle of water-
rolled basalt pebbles. Near the landing-place is a dwarf
caes or pier, a portion of whose cyclopean stones—
concrete would have been better—has been washed
away, and which, as might be expected, has not been
repaired. On the narrow strip of dull brown sand lay
boats, nets, a large store of planks, and other furniture
of a sea-port.

The Entrada da Ciudade, a short street, broad, paved
with basaltic cobble stones, lined with gutters, and shaded
with fine over-arching plane-trees, which, fuel being expensive, are barbarously trimmed, leads to the great square.
On the right, near the water, is the health office and

commercial rooms, where registers and newspapers are found, and an unsightly ruin meets the eye. On the left, with its facing of green promenade, is the Fortaleza, denoted by two sentinels, soldiers of the 1st regiment of Caçadores, with dark-green jackets and white overalls —the appearance of these Light Infantry is soldierly and workmanlike. At this hour we find "Hollway's," the local Long's, dead asleep ; but a small boy is procured for a sixpence to supply us with brandy and soda for comforting the stomach during our long ride. Mr. Hollway, who has been many years upon the island, keeps three establishments—a small boarding-house in the town, a larger one on the Caminho do Meio, and in summer a Quinta near the village of Camacha. The terms for living are 10*l.* 10*s.* per mensem, not including private sitting-room, wines, or other extras. There is a multitude of similar boarding-houses, as Miles', Reid's, Wardrop's, Neale's, &c., &c. Guilletti's is the only hotel properly so called. Besides boarding-houses, there are apartments and lodgings to let from 50*l.* to 200*l.* the season or the year. The town, in fact, is one huge caravanserai, all for hire.

Amongst the eager hungry crowd which accompanied us brawling from the landing-place, we chose two fellows, and struck a bargain for a mount over the Elysian Fields of Madeira, which, by-the-bye, are pretty steep hills. The legal charge for horse, two-oared boat, or covered car, is 300 reis—1*s.* 3*d.* per hour, or $2 per day.* But here, as elsewhere, the stranger pays double

---

* The pataca, or dollar, in Madeira is reckoned at 4*s.* 2*d.* The

by way of penalty; the inevitable visit to Nossa Senhora do Monte will, unless you make an agreement beforehand, cost $2, besides other small coins. The nags were highly creditable, thick-set little Lisbons, eleven to twelve hands high, with tolerable English saddles and bridles; the cost of a good horse is $200, (44*l.*); of a mule, $15—20; of an ass, poor as the English breed, $5—10. Riding-animals are rough-shod, with large oblong nails, and long projecting clamps and claws àt the back of the hoof, raising them like our great-grandmothers'. There are few wheeled carriages in the island, and in 1827 there was not one. Invalids take exercise in covered cars, like the body of a calèche placed upon a sledge, furnished with curtains and drawn by oxen, whence it is called a boi-car, or cow-cart: the invention is attributed to a Major Bulkeley, who, though not a bulky man, excogitated, some fifteen years ago, this contrivance for his family. A less sociable form is the palanquin, half-roofed and cradle-shaped, not box-formed like the East Indian, and the Manchila, or hammock, familiar to Portuguese West Africa, is much used by those who care little for looking or being looked at. Pipes of wine and boxes of goods are carried in the rudest of vehicles: a sleigh formed of two planks, six or eight feet long, pierced at both ends, and fastened together. A perch is attached to the fore part, and a yoke enables the oxen to draw it; when friction is likely to inflame, a cactus leaf or a wet rag is placed under the

coinage is decimal; the testao, or "bit," is worth five-pence, and the dois testaoes, or "pistareen," is ten-pence. Gold is rarely seen.

wood to diminish heat and to render the run smoother. This contrivance, which may be seen on the American plains—*vide* Captain Marcy's "Prairie Traveller"—might be utilised in places by the African explorer, but where the ground is soft it would clog and become unmanageable. The streets of Madeira show hard labour. The slope and the frequency of Fajaas, or land-slips, render it necessary to pave all the highways, which would otherwise be swept into the sea. The material is the inevitable dark basalt. On the smoother passages,—there is hardly an acre of level ground in the island,—cobble stones or round pebbles are chosen, sometimes disposed in a rude mosaic, white lozenges and circles standing out from the black. The extreme angle of these roads is 23° (or 1 in 2½), and 14° (1 in 4), is not much thought of. Where the ascents are steepest the material is angular, and there are raised lines like steps disposed broadways. The result of this superabundant labour is excellent; the rain washes the streets without leaving mud, and consequently there is not more dust than smoke.

Mounting our nags, we—my companion in the Gold Coast Artillery and I—progressed leisurely. There is a fine of $3 for hard riding in the streets, and we had no mind to imitate the "galloping griffins and Pariah dogs," which a gruff general officer described as the greatest of nuisances in Bombay. The first sight was the Praça da Constituçaõ, an oblong with dwarf trees, an unpaved area, where the feet are relieved from stone-treading, and garnished with shady benches and a raised

platform for the band, which here plays twice a week.
On the east is the Sé, or Cathedral of San Francisco,
commenced in 1485, and completed in 1514. It contains some hideous pictures and a fine fretted ceiling of
native juniper (*J. Oxycedrus*), a wood now almost cleared
off the island. The other, or western extremity, is flanked
by S. Francis, an almost ruinous building, whose barred
windows, tall walls, and porcelained towers show that it
was a religious house; the institution which in Christianity has taken the place of the pagan vestal virgins.
It was suppressed and secularised in 1834, when the
island, after the final defeat of Don Miguel, passed into
the hands of Don Pedro, and shared the fate of five monasteries and three nunneries. On the west of the
Praça is the Santa Casa da Misericordia, or hospital,
built in 1834, and next to it the Convente de Santa
Isabel, from whose grated windows female orphans
peep. The former is a large building, with a propor-
tionate staff, a chapel, and a chaplain; but it seldom
contains more than ninety in-door patients at the same
time. It will become a succursale to the grand new
building which overlooks the sea.

Riding through the somewhat intricate streets up the
Carreira, or local Corsa, past the English club, the
college, church, and by the barracks, we found the
houses framed with huge basaltic monoliths. The
windows—many of them built in the old style, glass-
less, and provided with a little wicket in the shutter—
are grated in the ground floor, which is here the only
bank, after the fashion of Southern Europe. The gates

are vast as those in the East, and huge staircases and
double flights of steps spring from the paved and
piazza'd Patio within them.   At times aroused by the
clatter of hoofs, the señorita thrusts her head from the
casement, and speedily withdraws it from the stare of
the strangers fresh from a week on board ship.   Here
may be taken the opportunity of remarking, that though
some fine eyes and hair appeared, I did not see amongst
the lower orders a single pretty face; the every-day
dress is sadly unpicturesque.   Swarthy skins, flat faces,
round, stout contours bon-sens expression, and a wondrous waddle, are here the rule.   The countrywomen
wear uncrinolined gowns of calico and cheap stuff,
with capas or long cloaks, and sometimes red and blue
shawls over their heads.   The peasantry at Madeira, as
elsewhere, is abandoning its highly appropriate local
costume, which now can rarely be seen except in dead
life.   The men are in shirts and long terminations,
or femoralia, of home-spun long-cloth.   Both sexes
have limp top-boots or shoes of buff-coloured goat's
leather, and decorate themselves with the ugly carapuça, a cap whose utter inutility secures for it some
notice.   It is a dwarf calotte of blue broadcloth, some
five inches in diameter at the base or broadest part, so
small that it appears to maintain its place by the exertion
of the frontal and occipital muscles.   The more jauntily
it is worn on one side, to the confusion of the laws of
gravitation, the more " dandified " is the wearer.   From
the apex of the funnel projects a pigtail of the same
material, unicorn fashion, or rather in the style of the

Algerian rats, whom the savants discovered with tails growing out of their noses. Not the slightest use can be assigned to this head-gear, except perhaps the "wild caprice of mortal will," that dictated queues, powder and pomatum to our grandfathers. According to the best authorities, this silly pet of the peasantry was not used during the last century; the horn of Madeira was not then exalted. It may eventually disappear before the foulard and the straw hat. On Fieras the population turn out in much more "dressy" style, with a somewhat violent parure, and, as in India, there are quaint little figures in the shops which illustrate the costumes for the edification of Europe.

Presently we pass the bridge which spans the torrent of Santa Luzia. In former times there were no walls, consequently the three fiumaras that traverse the town have committed awful damage, sweeping away buildings, damaging the harbour by making the water several fathoms more shallow, and on one occasion destroying 400 lives. S. Luzia is a dangerous "wady," with a fearful slope, bone-dry at present, but rolling after rains a fierce and sudden flood, which rises and subsides in a few hours. It is 80 to 100 feet broad, and 20 to 30 feet deep, with rapid slopes. The water pours down it as through crevasses in the Mississippi levées, and the flood has been known to jerk over the walls rocks, which several teams of oxen have been required to remove. The "nymphs of Arethusa," as our soldiers in Sicily called the hideous old washerwomen of that classical spot, here ply their trade, and the larger

boulders are white with sunning linen. Hence the
phrase is *mandar a roupa ao Ribeiro* —" sending linen
to the river : "—and the violent treatment of that linen
reminds me of an Indian dhobi demolishing my Ludlams.
Riding up the left bank shady with planes, we pass in
the gardens a few but a very few vines, with many
plantains, and bananas, which here extend to 1000
feet above sea-level, the Inháme (Koko Kalo or
Colocasia esculenta, a large-leaved esculent, growing
in low and swampy ground,) pumpkins, Chou-chou
(*Sechium edule*), hanging from trellises, and gourds
used like calabashes and trained to little arbours.
A prodigious variety of fruit, consisting of custard
apples, guavas, rose-apples, pine-apples, tamarinds,
maumee apples, mulberries, the common apples and
pears, Longan (*Nephelium longan*) pears, "alligator
pears," walnuts, plums, peaches, figs, apricots, limes,
pomegranates, lemons, citrons, loquats, pitangas, chiri-
moyas, passion-fruits, papaws, and mangoes * is found
scattered about the sunny slopes. Various European
vegetables, potatoes, tomatoes, and greens of all varieties
grow side by side with batatas (sweet potatoes), chilis,
pimentos, arrowroot, ginger, the castor plant, the
bamboo, and that most useful cane, *Arundo donax.*
As we ascend, the effect of vertical action upon the

---

* At Sierra Leone there are good mangoes, especially that kind
called "No. 11." There is also the "peach mango," which assumes
the hue of that fruit on the side next the sun. All the others have
that turpentine flavour which renders them fit only for "fool." At
Madeira the cold is too great for the mango to· attain any excellence—
where "tolerable" it is "not to be endured."

productions of nature is conspicuous. At every few hundred yards the vegetation becomes less tropical; the cactus, banana, Cedar of Goa, yucca, date-palm, rose-apple, Bignonia and Nim, or "pride of India," concerning which the Hindoo sings,

" The Nim, though watered with gur and with ghí,
   Will still remain bitter as bitter can be "—*

give place to clumps and plantations of maritime pine, with chestnuts which supply "polenta," the walnut, the carob or St. John's bread, and forests of laurel. Higher up and above the woody region are bare crags protruding from grass, heath, furze, and broom.† Botanists, however, have dwelt upon the almost complete absence in the most elevated part of the island of Alpine types. The same, as has lately been seen, is the case with the Camaroons Mountain.

The little nags, panting and blowing, did wonders; an English horse would have been dead-beat half way. When the pace is fast, the guide hangs on by the tail, a sensible proceeding, which in these days of rapid evolutions might possibly be applied to the movements of light infantry, chasseurs à pied, caçadores, and others.

* The original is in Brăj Bákhá, the patois of the Braj district. The whole distich is

"Whatever the character is, it goeth not forth from man's life.
   The Nim (*Margosa*) tree will not be sweet if you water it with gur (molasses) and with ghí (clarified butter)."

† According to Bowdich, the vine region here extends to 2700 feet above sea level, though wine is not produced above 2080 : the zone of brooms, pines, ferns, and chestnuts to 3700 ; of laurels and vallíniums to 5600, and of heaths to 6000.

We met at this early hour ox sledges bearing wine
pipes, asses laden with sand and stone, and a few market
mules with tinkling bells. The horns of the animals
were pierced for thongs, and on each forehead hung a
bit of carved bone as a defence against Malocchio.
We passed sundry beggars, propped on alpenstocks—
the land swarms with paupers—whilst at every cottage
a white-haired babe'or black-haired child put forth,
under parental tuition, the hand of mendicancy.
Beggars they are born, and they shall die beggars.
" Bakhshish " is by no means confined to the banks
of the Nile. The dogs, as they will in India, barked
at us from the summit of the walls. The people
were peculiarly civil and kindly; every man touched
his hat, and the women did not object to a " good
morning." Some of the poor devils were hardly used :
their heads were laden with cords of dry underwood, or
huge bundles of fresh grass, and the foucinho (sickle)
hung from their wrists. Men were toilingly carrying
up the hills the sledges which had conveyed merchandise
down the slopes. In one hut by the wayside, we saw a
truly Oriental flour mill. A stream diverted from a
levada or raised watercourse through a wooden pipe,
was working a wheel that turned the upper half of a
pair of basaltic stones rough as trachyte. The population of the island is darker than that of Portugal.
Negro features are not seen, but the mulatto skin is.
They are thieves and pilferers on a small scale, rarely
violent, and reportedly timid. Such is the mildening effect
of climate, that the women rarely scold, the children

rarely cry. They have musical talents, and, like their Spanish and Portuguese cousins, have the organ of language highly developed; even amongst the peasants, improvisation, harmonic conversations and capping verses are exercises common as the æsthetic tea party of the German professor. In conversation they have a kind of nasal drawl or sing-song; the same is the case at Tenerife, and apparently it is a disease common to colonies in general. Capt. Hall compares the lingo to Bermudan English. Finally, Madeira is part of Africa, and the Madeirans are Africans, but they hate to be told that they belong to that ill-starred portion of our planet.

The gutters, as in Salt Lake City, gurgled with cool water, here the primal requisite for cultivation,—fields and gardens fronting the meridian sun cannot thrive without copious irrigation. The upper heights, which attract more rain than the lower regions, afford a few perennial springs, which would course through the rivers to the ocean, but for the industry of man. Watercourses have been built and excavated with abundant toil; each is under a committee or a judge; the distribution is managed carefully, but lawsuits often arise, litigiousness being everywhere part of the peasants' organisation; and heavy sums have been sunk on unskilful levellings. Every garden that can afford it, keeps a tank fashioned somewhat like the mysterious reservoirs of Aden. At this season water is deliciously abundant.

After riding up the steep hill for about a quarter of the way, we, in very pity, breathed the nags, and listened

to the song of the Tintonegro, capirote, or hill-nightin-
gale, that has found its way from the coast of Barbary.
Our guides preceded us; and presently we found them at a
wine-shop, where they tried the usual trick upon strangers.
They asked us to drink, and brought us a sample of the
purest Madeira, composed of caxaça—aguardiente, caña,
cane brandy or rum—and water flavoured with apples,
each element being distinctly tasteable. The custom is
to take a shilling *pour boire,* and then to ask a second,
that the men may refresh themselves. The coin is osten-
tatiously clapped upon the counter, proving thereby that
the payment is *bonâ fide.* The guide drinks standing at
the door, with a low bow to the senhor's good health.
On return he receives back ten pence out of the shilling,
and laughs in his sleeve at your verdancy. The most
cynical thing I could do to the fellows I did. It was
to present them with sixpence. Had nothing been given
they would have been resigned, but the sight of " siller "
tantalised their very souls. Poor devils, they have a
sad life! The island is overpopulated, choked with
some 101,000—the census of 1854—instead of 50,000,
like our Isle of Man. The government most unwisely
lays an embargo upon emigration, by a heavy passport
duty of ten shillings; consequently the people are half-
starved.

I should not have grudged our attendants their
wretched shilling had they put it upon the score of
want; but finessing always arouses a lurking spirit of
opposition.

At length, after a little descent through a thick grove

of Spanish chestnuts, we turned sharp, and came upon
the church of Nossa Senhora do Monte, known to the
English as " Mount Church," and often called by
strangers " the Convent." The building, a tall cinque-
cento, with a domed belfry and steeple at each flank,
is seen glistening from the sea, thrown out in alt-
relief by the dark curtain of luxuriant vegetation that
forms its background : the contrast between the black
basalt bordering and the glaring whitewash is not
without effect. It lies three miles N. N. W. of the
town, and is 1965 feet above sea-level. The lady to
whom it was dedicated has done much for Madeira.
Sailors offer their vows to her before voyaging. About
a century ago, when a famine threatened the island, a
ceremonious procession was made to the church: next
day, in a perfect calm, arrived a grain-ship, drawn
towards the shore, as all saw, by a woman in white.
Moreover, the doll's dress was found to be wet with sea-
water. Such is a small specimen of the gracious deeds
of our " Lady of the Mount," whom under another
name we shall meet at Santa Cruz, Tenerife.

A broad flight of porous basaltic steps, up which the
faithful, especially the fair faithful, are fond of climbing
on bare and bended knee, led to the portico, a thing of
similar materials supported by two columns. The door
was open, and two aged women who looked wickedly at
the intruding Herege Ugnota, composed the congregation. The pavement is of slabs of basalt, covered with
thin planking. Nothing can be more barbaric than the
ornaments of architecture in these lands, where the

cathedral is by no means a pleasant place even in summer. The most sensuous and artistic of races, the people of the Mediterranean, become in their colonies grotesque as Britons. I could not feel commonly respectful with these caricatures around me, in a sacristy containing daubs of an impossible ark and red-winged cherubim, a ridiculous Abraham cutting down an absurd Isaac, angels carrying preposterous grape-bunches slung to a banghy-pole, and other results of talent which at home we see lavished upon the head of George R. or the Ringwood Arms.   To the left was a senhora in a white spangled robe with blue starry cloak, white and blue being the orthodox colours of the Virgin before the Nativity.   Her expression was that of the intellectual-looking wax doll.   The real thing, however, is a little Fetish on the high altar, a small swarthy image like Santa Maria de' Neri at Sorrento.*   She stands upon a silver-like metal, and wears a gold brocade begemmed with precious stones whose proportions in life would be somewhat larger than soup tureens.   A ·jewelled head-

---

* At least she was there in my youth ; but she came, I fear, to grief. During one of the eruptions, when placed before the fiery flood, she was powerless as Knut the Dane to prevent its sweeping down upon her. To punish this excessive ingratitude for numberless wax candles, she was hurled into the lava with a universal '*naccia l'anima tua . . . .!* by her justly indignant votaries. Similarly the Hon. John Byron, in his amusing narrative of his wreck on the coast of Patagonia, saw a Jesuit, who, when the sea was dangerous, " went back into the cabin and brought out the image of some saint, which he desired might be hung up in the mizen shrouds ; which being done, he kept threatening it, that if we had not a breeze soon he would certainly throw it overboard."

dress and a spangled petticoat seem to be the beau idéal
of Roman Catholic beatitude in this world. As has been
shown, she is high JuJu,—great medicine: beating by
a long chalk all the other nozza senhoras in the island.
St Anthony occupies a private apartment off the right
aisle. I know not what he and his pigs have done to
make them popular at Madeira. Sant' Jago Minor is
the city's patron saint.

A mob of boys and youths accompanied us through
the building, pointed out the piscina, exulted over the
single bell in one of the two domed turrets which at
a distance resemble bilboquets, patted the organ, placed
themselves in the confessionals, and showed us the habitations of the priest and the Altareiro, or verger—in fact,
went through the normal course of cicerone-ism.

We were then led to the properer place of worship, a
fountain below the ugly church; a little spring of pure
cold water issuing from the rock and tumbling adown
the slope,

> ' Where all the margin round about was set
> With shady trees."

amongst which the ever-green til and vintratico were
conspicuous.

It was true relief to turn from the pettiness and
tawdriness behind to the magnificent temple of nature
before us. There was a lovely panorama of bold shore,
sea and shipping,—dwarfed to the size of a child's toy
smaller than the kestrel floating in the midway air,—
town and harbour, house and garden, Quinta and
farms and palheiros (thatched huts), shaggy fields,

dwarf plains, tall penhas, watercourses, channels, and dark abrupt ravines with their picturesque voltas. Far to the left lay a comforting sight that relieved the feeling of isolation, the long lines and sharp spires of the blue Desertas—the Desert Isles called by our sailors " the Deserters; " in front the horizon, abnormally high, as if we were in the centre of a bowl, rose brightly marked against a glowing sky; and above us the spicular mountains, and the central ridges of the Erythian Isle, with the thinnest gauze of dew-mist drawn, yeshmak-like, across her brows.

A mile eastward of the Mount Church led us through lanes paved and high-walled to the vertiginous road—full fifty fathoms high—spanning the Curral das Romeiras, " Fold of the Pilgrimesses," which the English call " The Little Corral." It is nothing but the ravine-head from which the Joaõ Gomez Torrent issues, a deep bay in the mountains, whose dizzy depths are broken by a projecting tongue of land, and whose upper heights remind every visitor of Switzerland's

> "hairy sides,
> With forest overgrown, grotesque and wild."

We were fated to descend from the mount by a novel conveyance. The sledge is like a long dismounted dickey, supplied with rollers; externally made of basket-work, and furnished inside with light calico cushions. This *Carro* is guided by a man on each side holding a handle projecting from the dickey, and in the off hand grasping a leather thong attached to what one would call the footboard. It will contain two, but

of course the owner prefers to accommodate one only.
We took our seats together, lit our cheroots, and
presently felt ourselves progressing with a decent
velocity. The distance, two miles, has been made
in seven minutes: we took, however, twelve. The
youths ran alongside of the sledge till they came
to a straiter and steeper pitch, when they hung on
behind as does the guide to his horse's tail, and the
sharp angles are passed by slewing round the vehicle
with the thong nearest the wall. The pace, though not
rivalling that of the Montagnes Russes or the Mont-
morency Cone, is at least exciting: at times, however,
there are accidents. In the town I met a gentleman
who had but lately broken his collar-bone. As is the
rule of the road generally, when a fall is in prospect, one
must never attempt to get out or to protrude a limb, the
only way is to find good foot purchase and to hold
on like grim death. Descending, we passed through a
market-place, at whose neat wooden stalls a motley crowd
had assembled. Fish, of which ichthyologists reckon
186 species, was there in plenty: its metallic glowing
lustre was finer than any feather. We saw cages full of
poultry—the *gallo* is an institution here, well bred, and
a clever fighter; also meat and vegetables in abundance.
The cleanliness of the market was a notable contrast to
Covent Garden.

The usual nasal drawling sing-song Portuguese of
the colonies was varied by the *ca para mim, boi!* and
the *ca-ca-ca-oá* of the ox-drivers, as they ploughed
their way through the crowd, the grumbling of the

Anglo-Saxon, and the villanous English of the touters and curio vendors, who followed us like disturbed wasps. We met in the market-place all our shipmates, surrounded by the hungry concourse. Of the passengers was an *ancien militaire,* a chief constable, going to Sierra Leone; his glance at the mob, and his style of working through by an almost imperceptible movement of the shoulder, told of the practised "bobby." As 9 A.M. was approaching, we returned to Hollway's for breakfast.

The entrance of the hotel was more than usually crowded with man, woman, and child. Every one visiting Madeira is expected to buy at least the following articles :—

1 chair of willow wicker-work, like that of Scinde, price $2 each—to the stranger.

1 pair of buff leather slippers, $0·75 : or shoes, $2 ; or boots, $3.

1 carapuça, or funnel cap, 1s.

1 walking-stick of coffee wood, or other stuff, brought to the island, but proclaimed indigenous.

Also a ruler, a box, a card-case, a paper-knife, and sundry fancy baskets, composed of peeled broomstick— utterly useless all, and by no means ornamental.

If Caius be good to Caia, he will also lay in—

1 shawl, black silk net, £3.

1 white thread   do.   £1.

1 dozen doylies, $1, but more generally 5s.

1   do.   pincushion doylies, 18s.

Feather flowers, any price from 1s. to £1.

And he may invest *ad libitum* in children's frocks, scolloped and belaced, horsehair chains, and gold rings, whose only merit is that three are contained in one very ugly one. The supernumerary waiter will assuredly have a large stock on hand, and look aggrieved, according to the custom of his class, if not patronised. As an old traveller, I avoided him, buying flowers from the nuns, and shawls, with etceteras, from M. A. C. Ribeiro, No. 1A, Rua da Carreira, where there is little doubt the economist was "done," as he deserved.

At the hotel we had an English breakfast, and I find entered in my journal:—"The meal was as good as the island could afford, but 'bad is the best' here. Ah! where shall I fly to escape from that British beefsteak? that British beefsteak which follows me from Indus to the Pole—which will not learn to be *filet*, like its French younger brother, the Biftek, and which still disdains 'fine herbs.' At Madeira it is qualified, however, by the host's remark, that we shall not see another for many a day." But then, you see, I was writing somewhat fresh from the Cabinets of M. Philippe, and remembering the portly form of M. Pascal. Now I remember that beefsteak with feelings of pleasure; what a contrast it was to a leg of old goat, or to the lean, stringy fowls which give men scurvy in introtropical Africa, and how succulent it will taste should Fate ever conduct me once more to Madeira.

The fish was bream—bad;* the figs, green and purple,

---

* This cannot be said of all the fish. The tunny is seldom given to strangers, yet with a *sauca piquante* it is excellent "once in a way;"

were hard and unripe. Fruit is a failure at Madeira,
because it is rarely grafted, and no one cares for
" natural selection."   Apples taste like pears, pears like
cotton made easy. The oranges are tolerable, but thick-
skinned : the little mandarin, here called Tangerine, is
admirable. Flowers are perennial, and, as in California,
they lose their charm : the eye becomes surfeited with
a continual bouquet, *toujours perdrix*. Some, as the
fuchsia, the geranium, and the dahlia, are of species that
have died out of English horticulture for the last twenty
years, at least ever since science took those flowers in
hand and bred them like racehorses. Coffee is grown on
the lowlands near Funchal, and the Portuguese no
doubt drink good *café au lait*; but your Englishman
must imbibe English coffee, with water utterly dispro-
portioned to the quantity of bean. Butter, as in all hot
climates, is utterly vile : I should prefer the graveolent
palm-oil. Milk is poor : cow's milk must be used
by the Anglo-Saxon ; goat's milk ought to be. There
are poached eggs and boiled eggs, but where is the
garlicked omelette ?

We inquired, as travellers will do, about tobacco.
At Portuguese Madeira it is infamous, and the penny
cigars are preferred to the more expensive ; in Spanish
Tenerife it is possible to lay in a tolerable supply.

the sword-fish, despite its name, is not unpalatable ; those who like
conger eels will find them here ; the herring and mackerel are first-
rate ; and never even at Leghorn has man tasted better red mullet.
This "woodcock of the ocean" is small but peculiarly good—by all
means insist on salmonete for breakfast.

Portugal works her way at a snail's pace towards free-trade fare. The manufacture and sale of worked tobacco has been farmed out to a monopolising private company in Europe. Too timid to throw off protection, the government has tabooed the growing of tobacco to Madeira, which might perhaps coin gold by a growth like that of the Vuelta Abájo, Habana; consequently, the Lusitanian lieges are condemned to pay high prices for bad articles. All the civilised world is behindhand touching tobacco. It has, like the Quaker's historical dog, gotten a bad name. One-idea'd hygeists, followers of the "Misocapnic Solomon," have persuaded the world that it is a slow poison, and politicians that it is a luxury, and, therefore liable to unlimited mulct. Even the old statesman will warn his hearers against the tobacco-shop, and—with the history of the East before him—tell them that it is "provocative of thirst" and an "excuse for idleness," which necessarily leads to drinking. "No stimulant, except gin," we hear, "is so dangerously abused" —the last word reads in two ways. Once it was Holy Herb, *herbe à la Reine, Catherinaire,* and so on; therefore, inasmuch as

"Regis ad exemplum totus componitur orbis,"

all followed royal example. Now it is "the weed." King James and Napoleon the Great abused it to mankind, because it did not suit their stomachs: the mighty Conqueror preferred a *bonbonnière* to a *blague.* In England, those who do not "indulge," feel an I-know-not-what moral superiority over, and from their lofty position look down upon, those who do. Legislators,

especially in later life, cut tobacco, and wag the head
at it. Wine is the milk of old age, and old age has
lately, in England at least, greatly reduced the duty
upon its milk: but the tax upon tobacco remains in all
its pristine enormity. France retains her vile *tabac de
régie*, which you must smoke unless you can get on
with bell-ropes or rattans; and her *Bénéfices de la
Régie* are, not including one-sixth for smuggling, some
150,000,000 of francs per annum. Italy also makes it
a monopoly. In England it bears the unconscionable
duty of 3*s.* 9*d.* per lb., producing a wicked item of
revenue, nearly 6,000,000*l.* And why? If tobacco be
a luxury, so is wine, and please let us know where necessaries, comforts, and luxuries show the dividing link. If
free trade in wine be profitable, why this *quasi* Maine-
law for tobacco? Or does a paternal and patriarchal
Government, which could not raise, Russian-fashion,
its revenue by encouraging "useless, superfluous, and
selfish expenses," lay it on so thick in order to prevent
us from spoiling our digestions, like naughty boys,
by too much smoke? If that be the idea, it should
be dismissed; these heavy dues, by excluding a cheap
and tolerable article, give us only a bad and an unwholesome supply. Moderately good Havannahs now
fetch 6*d.*, Manillas, 4*d.*; thus the latter, which cost
in India from forty to fifty rupees per 1000, here
approach that sum in pounds sterling. The fact is, that
those six millions of pounds sterling are enough to blind
the eyes of a budget-maker. But some day will arise a
hard-smoking Chancellor of the Exchequer, who will

quarter the tax, and double his gains by the loss.* Our fraternity will presently become a majority ; one year witnesses an attempt to introduce smoke into all except the coffee-room, drawing-room, and card-room of a club ; another sees a long " writing to the ' Times.' " Let us hope, illustrious smokers and kind brethren of the pipe, soon to see that happy day. " Smoke is great, and it will prevail."

After breakfast we chatted with certain *habitués* of the place. At present there are only the last year's birds, from eighty to a hundred strangers, mostly English, and a first batch of some hundreds is expected in September. There are a few French, and about eighty Germans, whose drawling English is perpetually heard in street and room. The visitors, especially the Anglo-Saxon, do not mix well with the Portuguese. Last year an effigy of Pontius Pilate was, according to custom, hung at Loo rock; that effigy was, I am told, an English soldier in English uniform. The Madeiro-Lusitanians had ascertained that Madam Britannia was at the bottom of the Scourge of Rome's troubles, and adopted that way of displaying a sound, but a somewhat incurious, indignation. These spectacles, now waxing obsolete in France and Italy, are still favourites in these old and crippled colonies. At Tenerife I heard of a late Judas, about the size of a

---

* Since the above was written, the Chancellor of the Exchequer has reduced the duty on what the trade is pleased to call foreign " segars " from 9*s*. 5½*d*. to 5*s*. per lb. ; on snuff from 9*s*. 5½*d*. to 3*s*.; and on other manufactured tobaccos to 4*s*. This is, at least, one little step in the right direction.

mizen-mast, hung in jack boots, with his stomach full of
cats : the especial fun was to watch the action of Gri-
malkin when Iscariot was consigned to the flames.* On
the other hand, St. Peter lashed, like an outrigger
between two boats, walked the waters like a thing of
life—a feat, by-the-bye, in which, if I rightly remember,
when alive he signally failed.

It were a long and intricate subject to investigate the
cause of the Englander's unpopularity abroad. I can but
throw down a little heap of reasons to which everyone
can add as many more. Individually,—of course, this
is not said of the cosmopolitan English gentleman,
who, with perfect tact, everywhere preserves his
nationality, whilst ever respecting that of others,—he
is disliked, collectively hated. He delights in revers-
ing the process upon his French neighbour, whom
he admires collectively, individually despises. The
phenomenon partly arises from the enormous national
self-esteem. " Great Britaine," says old Herbert,
" contains the summe and abridge of all sorts of
excellencies, meeting here like parallels in their proper
centre." And were we not told t'other day at Dover
that we are the first nation in the world? Whilst the
vanity of foreign writers more humanely praises themselves, English pride abuses others. Partly, too, it comes

---

* Mrs. Elizabeth Murray, the authoress of "Sixteen years of an
Artist's Life in Morocco, Spain, and the Canary Islands," declares
that she saw Judas burned on Easter Day, in the Plaza de la Constitucion Orotava, attired in "black cutaway coat, yellow vest and
pantaloons, with Hessian boots." The scene which she describes
is that of " driving out the devil " on the Gold Coast.

from geographical peculiarities. The Englishman is an islander, *toto divisus orbe*, an abscissed joint, like the Jew, of the great human body. He is not like a continental, and he has a sneaking fondness for other islanders. He has his prejudices—unless his blood be very thin,—his eccentricities, his bizarreries, his hobby-horses, his whimsy-whamsies. He is wedded to the homeliness of home. Now he fights for the slave-carrying trade. Anon, in the fury of his emancipativeness, he would gladly convert a garden of sugar, tobacco, and cotton, into a howling waste, a Great Dismal Swamp, starving a million of his own people, and three and a half millions of his congeners. Collectively he is no favourite, because the precedent of his policy is natural egotism, its succedent is success, a worse fault to those who lose by it than his selfishness. We cannot expect our cousins, the irritable Yankees, or the poor devil Germans, to love the rich head of the house of John Bull. We cannot expect rivals, who have striven with us and failed, Spain, Portugal, and Holland—once first rate now third rate powers—to bear our greatness without a look askance. We must not expect friendship from those whom, like the Ionian Republic, we have insulted by benefits. Those who are fighting with us for the world—France and Russia—will not easily pardon our sins of solidarity. Nationally, as long as the Englishman entrenches himself within his own limits, depends upon his own resources, and calls all his neighbours Racha, he is strong and great; he is completely demoralised by the lesson that he, single-handed, is not equal to three foreigners. And not to ignore an important side of the question, the Englishman has been a somewhat noisy though moderate apostle of Liberty, and the father of institutions which, by their success at home, commend themselves to neighbouring nations, amongst whom they would be failures, because lacking the simplicity and the vigour of despotism. By countenancing progress, and by discountenancing political subdivision, he commends himself to the moderate, who are equally opposed to remaining stationary and to sweeping changes in society. Extreme partisans, of course, hold him their greatest enemy, and as they are the loudest speakers, he is abused from Lisbon to St. Petersburg.

Our colloquy ended with a stroll *en masse* about the streets, where the well-to-do population eyed us with no friendly glance. The stranger-mob raises the price, and diminishes the quantity, besides affecting the quality of everything. It spoils the country to the countrymen. A servant who has taken wages from an English family will seldom return to and more rarely abide in a Portuguese Morgado's house. The swells whom we met had the usual Portuguese priggishness and formality of dress and look ; regulation whiskers, dating from Georgius Tertius his day ; back swallow-tails ; "skimpy" waistcoats, and white pantaloons. The ecclesiastics were mostly clad in French attire and the Jesuit cap, not with the vast shovel hat like that of Canada, which made the facetious prelate announce their Spanish eminences as having arrived at the Vatican in their canoes.

They have a kindly look, and I saw none of the offensive jauntiness of the young Sicilian abbate, who can never pass a bonnet without peering Milesian-like under its periphery. It is understood, however, that their morals are no better than they should be; the pretty housekeeper is the rule, and an Englishwoman who, as a Roman Catholic, should deem it her duty to bow to every frock, would soon collect an enamoured tail. The shops are superior to what we expected. At a chemist's I obtained all the materials for making arsenical soap. Another shop supplied excellent photographs; the climate renders them far superior to those of the North. The mystic letters P.V.A.B.—*Paõ vinho aguardiente bom*—upon certain sheds in the Travessas, or cross streets, attracted ours, like other people's, attention. The hens were mostly tied to old shoes, a cock was seen garlanded with flowers, a turkey followed his master like a dog, and the women sat in trellises and arbours staring and taking the air. We met *chemin faisant* one of our Germans at the bottom of a hammock, wrapped up, despite the heat, in coat and shawls; he was dying at railway pace. We had many a gossip, and more than once saw the Caccia del Mediterraneo. We bought the indispensable chaussures from an Italian rascal, a fellow so far gone in cheating that he cheated, as cheats will, himself. Then he cheapened chairs, Carapuças, and grey canary birds, uncivilized animals far dearer here and in the Canaries than in London or Bruges. Madeira wrens (*R. Madeirensis*) are the only birds peculiar to the island

and Machêtes the only instruments. The latter is to the guitar what the piccolo is to the flute. It is, however, tuned in a peculiar way: the two upper strings have, like most Eastern musical implements, intervals of thirds,* whilst the lower have fourths. Like the guitar *raclé* by the Barber of Seville, the accompaniment is composed of simple chords, the words are modinhas, pretty, and affecting. It is peculiar to the small "remains of the submerged continent Atlantis," and is best heard in the Canaries, especially Tenerife.

Tired of marching about the town in brigade, I chartered a youth and set out, to speak Hibernically, *solus.* Passing by the secularised convent, we entered the adjoining street of San Francisco, and called at the office of the agents to the A. S. S. Company, Messrs. John Blandy and Sons, who kindly cashed for me some Bank of England notes, and introduced me to a variety of visitors. I could not but observe that the sane residents long settled at Madeira are thin, pale, sub-green-tinted like East Indians, and wearing the regular tropical look. However fit may be the Madeiran atmosphere for men with one lung or a bittock of a lung, it is by no means so well suited to those with a healthy pair. And the fact is that the English constitution cannot thrive without a winter.

Remained the convent to "do," though not with

---

* Which of course produces the minor key. This guitarette is an especial favourite with the Madeirense, who are said even to talk in it. English visitors sometimes attempt it, but as they expect to be perfect after a dozen lessons—it takes about five years—they rarely succeed.

that morbid feeling which leads the Englishman to the
nunnery and the slave market. Ascending a neat hill,
which seemed to be nearly an angle of 35°, the youth
and I turned to the left, entered a large paved court,
procured a key from the tournoir, opened a door,
ascended a ricketty staircase, and found ourselves in a
whitewashed room. Its long length was garnished with
a shaky table and a pair of poor chairs, whilst a stout
double grating allowed communication with the mysterious apartments within. It was Goa over again. Presently appeared two "fair prisoners," aged ladies habited
after the rule of St. Francis, the founder of the Sisters
of Charity. One was tallish, and showed no slight
remnants of beauty; she was, in fact, a "splendid ruin,"
as a friend of mine terms himself. I had the grace not
to ask her if she was the Sister Maria Clementina, who,
about the time of my birth (See "Six Months in the
West Indies, in 1825," by the brave "Henry Nelson
Coleridge,") was the kindler of every traveller's enthusiasm, the theme of their praise, and the peg to which
they affixed their sentimentalism, upon nuns and
nunneries. The real Clementina subsequently appeared,
spoke pretty Portuguese, and probably would not have
been recognised by the ardent man who wrote "Reader!
if your whim or your necessities should lead you to
Madeira, go for my sake to the nunnery of Santa
Clara," or by the amorous midshipman who, as Captain
Alexander tells us, would kiss her finger-tips.

Flowers of sorts, roses, camelias, fuchsias, jasmines,
and pretty wreaths, were passed through the wicket and

placed upon the table for my inspection. They are
made of feathers, and they constitute, with wax fruit and
sweetmeats, especially candied citron, the industry of the
"poor Clares" of Santa Clara.   I bought a few flowers,
and ended with asking the Sister Clementina about the
state of the house. She informed me that when the
Jesuits were expelled in 1758, the sisterhood was also
suppressed, and allowed to re-enter the world; that many
had returned to their seclusion; that novices cannot now
be admitted; that the order was becoming extinct, and
that in process of time Government will take possession
of the church property.   Meanwhile this and other
"poor Clares" are allowed to spend several months of
the year in their secular homes—a sensible practice which
I would recommend to Bayswater and Birmingham.

Still full of Captain Basil Hall's voyages and travels,
a book which is the delight of most boys' non-age, I
could not leave Madeira without a glance at the burial
ground. Leaving the convent and walking westwards, we
stood upon a plateau under the Quinta Lomellina, below
the Castello do Pico, and enjoyed a fine bird's-eye
view. Here near the sea-level the vine mostly flourishes.
Below us was the English church and chapel, built in
1822, in the Rua da Bella Vista: the laws of Portugal
did not allow it Christian architecture, so it appears in
the shape of an Ionic temple, caricatured and minia-
tured, a truly gratifying national spectacle.   Our
schismatical fellow-countrymen have not failed to
import into Madeira liberty of conscience and right of
private judgment. The residents have naturally been

divided into high church, low church, and no church, and would not worship in the same ten-acre field; whilst those who advocate the "old priest writ large," of course preferred the Free Kirk to the Government Chapel.

A ten minutes' walk led us to the Cemetery, where we rang for admission. The grated door was opened by the wife of the porter, who occupies a hut-lodge on the right of the entrance. A dwarf garden of geraniums, roses, datura, lavender, heliotropes, oleanders, and other strongly scented flowers, led to the Cities of the Dead, which are two in number. The newer or Strangers' Cemetery was bought in 1808, during the administration of General Beresford, to accommodate his 4000 soldiers. It must not be forgotten, that Madeira was a British conquest; and that like Java, Sicily, Goree, and others, it was returned to the original proprietors. And yet, talking of these renditions, a French author is silly enough to say, "*pourtant le léopard fait se faire la part du lion.*" This burial-place is a mere yard, girt, like its right-hand neighbour, by a tall enceinte, which suggests the idea of Spike Island. It is overpopulated like Madeira generally; the walls teem with votive tablets, and the graves are in unpleasant proximity. There are but few monuments with any pretensions to sculpture, and those few are exceedingly bad. An addition to the strangers' ground was bought in 1852 for £2211; it is entered by a neat archway, and is still partially unoccupied. It will not, however, long be empty: out of a floating population of

300 to 500 English the deaths are 12 to 15 annually. Travellers make these places also pegs for their sentimentalisms : to me they appeared inspiring as a cemetery in King William Street, City.

Descending the hill seawards, we passed on the right Laranjeira, the orangery,—the time-honoured tree that bore the golden apples of the Hesperides has disappeared from it,—being the Residents and Merchants' Cemetery. Before 1764, Protestants and other heretics dying at Madeira were either huddled into a hole in the streets or were thrown, as at Maskat, on the dunghill, or into the sea ; and even after that date their funerals required a guard of soldiery. Now there is full toleration, even extended to a people which have not learned to be "tolerant of intolerancy." The very Hebrews, who are much despised by the Madeirans, have a small plot of ground to the eastward of the city on the way to Santa Cruz. It is named the House of the Living ; however, it contains the dead, and a chronograph from Deuteronomy embodies the date—A.M. 5611= A.D. 1851.

I had but little time to visit the New Road, one of the triumphs of local engineering. It is classic ground, leading in the direction taken by the Zargo's boats, and it will after some years abut at Cabo Giraõ—Cape Turn-again—where the old governor's first exploration ended. The cost was about 9000*l*., and the levelness of the line makes it the Rotten Row, as the Carreira is the Regent Street, of Funchal. The most suggestive part is the view of the Telegraph Hill, and the little hummocks of San Martinho, which are so conspicuous from the roadstead. The same formations as those outlying Puerto Orotava and Santa Cruz, Tenerife; they are "parasitic cones" to this pleiocene tertiary volcano, and they open to the south and south-west, showing the prevailing wind to be the north-eastern. Another reason prevented my visiting the "Convento de Bom Jesus," where for $10 per mens. a refractory wife may be confined by her husband,—this exemplary institution may not be openly visited by my sex.

My last pilgrimage was to the spot where Christopher Columbus is supposed to have lived when he resided, probably for health, at Funchal, during the intervals of his trading voyages. In 1851 his house near the Carmo was, like Shakspeare's tree, impiously destroyed; two other localities have claimed the honour, but hitherto with little effect. That in the Rua do Esmeraldo was once a custom-house; but travellers avoid disconnecting it with Columbus, or it would be pulled down. The great explorer married, it will be remembered, the daughter of Perestrello, or Palestrello, one of the early navigators, who subsequently became governor of Porto Santo, and after his father-in-law's death he became possessed of certain charts and pilot's memoranda of Atlantic voyages, which sent him forth to find a new world. His history, methinks, has still to be written, without the "*furor biographicus*,"—the *Lues Boswelliana*, as Lord Macaulay called it.*

---

* A house occupied by Christopher Columbus, when settled before his voyage to the New World, is also shown at Gomera, where he

Returning in red-hot haste to the hotel, I found that the mails had been ordered on board at noon; consequently my companions were in the state of gulls preparing for the annual migration, incapable of a moment's inaction. At Mr. Hollway's I met the Captain-General, *alias* the Governor of Sierra Leone, who had temporarily changed air. A visit in England to the late Governor of Cape Coast Castle, who had spent some seven years upon the Gold Coast and elsewhere, had prepared me for not finding these regions quite so black as they are painted, and here was a fresh proof. I saw a hale and hearty looking man, who could not have been better preserved had he served his time between England and India, instead of between the West Indies and the African coast. The Governor strongly advised me to await three months of acclimatisation before entering upon malarious and laborious travel in the rivers and the creeks. M. Talleyrand's celebrated sentiment, *"mon jeune ami pas de zèle,"* should here be the rule of action; too much activity at first starting leads to grief. But what

refitted the "Nina," reunited his three ships on 11th August, and resumed his cruise on the 7th October, 1492. It was during a previous residence at Gomera that the Andalusian sailor Alonzo Sanchez di Guelva, who trafficked between that island and Madeira, died at his house. The legend is, that he had been carried by a gale to one of the West India islands, whence he returned with the only two survivors of his crew, and dying, communicated his distances and bearings to his host. There is nothing improbable in this, and the accident has happened more than once since. Yet it hardly detracts from the discoverer's fame. The epitaph still speaks the truth :

" A Castilla y Leon,
Nuevo mondo dió Colon."

zealous man can refrain from zeal? I was in the rivers a week after my arrival.

At 1 p.m. the gun was fired, and Blue Peter was run up. With adieus, and without one particle of regret at leaving the "Happy Island," I set out for the beach, escorted by a dwarf curiosity-vendor on my right, and on the other side an old beggar woman, who perpetually did cry, "*Por Amor de Deus!*" and "*Por sua saude!*" A boat was launched, I paid my shilling, and presently found the good ship Blackland's deck bristling with hollow wicker-work chairs. An hour afterwards we were dancing with the breeze outside the harbour, and long before twilight Erythia, alias—

> " Filha do Oceana
> Do undoso campo flor, gentil Madeira,"

had become a fading picture, a memory, a dream of the past.

    *   *   *   *   *

I conclude the subject with a few notes concerning the island, firstly on its value as a Sanitarium, secondly with reminiscences of its deeply regretted, its never-to-be-forgotten wine.

Medical men who have written upon the former subject, and their name is legion, are agreed that the climate of Madeira is excellently adapted for pulmonary and bronchial complaints,—which form rather more than one-fifth, and less than one-eighth of the entire mortality in England,—rheumatism, scrofula, and zymotic diseases, and equally ill-suited for robust health, apoplexy, asthma, hepatic, nervous and dyspeptic affections. Children are said to expect at birth 39 years instead of 19 in England, but those of the English on the island appear degenerate. Instances are known of men who, with an occasional return to the land of their birth, have here outlived for many years maladies that in Europe would have been fatal to them. Raw wind and close sultry weather are equally rare, and Mr. Coleridge pretty justly said that "the seasons are the youth, maturity, and old age of a never-ending still-beginning spring." The dew, abundant upon the upper heights, is unknown near the sea : the fact is there is not cold enough to condense the moisture of the atmosphere. The philo-Madeiran scoffs at the idea of there being humidity in the air of the climate which notably belongs to the damp section. But where a country surrounded by water is 6000 feet high, is profusely irrigated, and moreover lies in the very course of the Gulf of Guinea stream, the evaporation must be great; it is impossible to mistake the sensation of intense humidity at Funchal, or of dryness at Tenerife after Madeira. It lies several degrees beyond the limits of the north-east trade winds; but it has a scirocco or Harmattan,* called Leste, the E., or more correctly the E.S.E. wind opposed to the Embate. This Leste brings from the Sahara and the African interior, birds,

---

* It was long before I could trace the etymology of this word. At length Dr. Horton's "Medical Topography of the West Coast of Africa" (London : John Churchill, 1859), was found to assert that it is derived from the Fanti Aharamanta—from aharaman, to blow, and ta, tallow or grease. But surely the latter element is unnecessary to the sense of the word ; moreover, according to Herr Missionary Zimmerman, aharabata or ahalabata in the Ga language is a foreign word.

insects, and reddish dust. According to M. Ehrenburg the latter is composed of South American infusoria, which others again deny. Usually lasting three days,— it has been known to blow for forty—it is painfully high and dry, even after 300 miles of sea passage, and it disagrees terribly with many invalids. Unlike the coast, however, Madeira seldom suffers from it in spring or winter. The N.E. wind, the young beginning of the Trades, blows for seven out of the twelve months, it is dry and brings fine weather. N.W. is the snowy; S.E. and S.W. the rainy, stormy, squally points. There are distinct sea-breezes and trovadas or land-breezes. As usual upon these mountainous formations, the wind blows from many quarters at once. Dr. Mason says that he has frequently seen three currents of wind affecting the clouds at the same time, whilst the vane indicated a fourth. The maximum difference between the dry and wet bulb thermometers during the Leste has been $22°·50$ (F.). The mercury averages throughout the year $64°$ to $66°$ (F.), and it never falls below $53°$ which becomes uncomfortably cold, requiring fires, which, however, as in Piza of a more ancient date, are not nearly common enough. The annual mean of the barometer corrected for temperature and gravity is $30·092$ inches; the wave is highest at 10 to 11 A.M. and 8 P.M.; lowest at 7 A.M. and 4 P.M.* The minimum fall of rain recorded in books is $22·365$ inches per annum; the maximum in six

* The mercury stands so much higher in many parts of Madeira that the wording of English barometers must be altered.

months has been 41·4, and the average ranges from
29·82 to 30·62. The rains occur in spring and autumn,
when they are sub-tropical, although the island is nearly
10° N. of Cancer, leaving the air bright and genial.
January and February, the latter especially, are the
coldest and wettest, March and April are showery
and windy, May alternately showery and fine; the dry
season sets in from that month to mid-September, when
invalids are recommended to leave England. After
this are the latter rains till the end of December. Snow
rarely descends below 2500 feet above sea-level, it has
at times fallen about the Mount Church, and is not unknown at Porto Santo. Twilight is almost as short as
in the Tropics, and the longest exceeds the shortest day
by only five hours.

Nothing more fickle than the fashion of Sanitaria.
In our fathers' days the Faculty sent its incurables,
despite the fatal *vent de bise* and the *mistral,* to Mont-
pellier. It soon contained 300 English families;
presently reduced to a few wine merchants and econo-
mists. Succeeded Pisa, *vituperio delle genti,* in point
of laxativeness and deadly weariness; and Pau, of whom
her native Bearnais said that the year had eight months
of winter and four of inferno. At present Malaga and
Torquay, which in mean daily range and humidity—the
two desiderata—mainly resemble Madeira, are the reigning favourites; and the great sanitaria of the future will
be Algiers and Egypt. The Isle of Wood began to
appear before the world in the days of Moquet (1601),
who pronounced the air to be very sweet and temperate.

He was followed by various authors, Ovington (1689), Atkins (1720), Forster (1772), Dr. Fothergill (1775), Dr. Gourlay (1811), and Dr. Ruxton (1817). Finally, in 1824, Dr. Heineken—himself a consumptive patient —established its reputation. Dr. Mittermaier thus sums up the advantages of Madeira:—1. Equability of temperature. 2. Purity of atmosphere and freedom from dust and miasmata. 3. The capability of residing on the island throughout the year. 4. The number of comforts and conveniences there procurable. 5. And last, The combination of the chief climatal conditions necessary for the recovery of health. Sir James Clark, a great authority in his day, gave it this high praise, "When we take into consideration the mildness of the winter—20° warmer than in London and 12° than Italy or Provence —and the coolness of the summer—only 7° warmer than London and nearly 5° cooler than Italy and Provence— together with the remarkable equality of the temperature during the day and night, as well as throughout the year,—the mean annual range is only 14°, less than half of that of Rome and Pisa, Naples and Nice—we may safely conclude that the climate of Madeira is the finest in the northern hemisphere."

Madeira, however, has, and ever will have, one terrible drawback besides extensive humidity. The ennui which it breeds is peculiar; it makes itself felt during a few hours' stay. Little islands are all large prisons: one cannot look at the sea without wishing for the wings of the swallow. This, with the usual sense of confinement, combines the feeling of an hospital, or a sick-bay,

and one soon sighs to escape from its dreary volcanic
rocks.   Game is well nigh shot off, except a few
resident partridges and migratory quails in the lower
altitudes, rabbits in the upper brushwood, and waterfowl,
snipe, widgeon, coot, and teal near the shore.   In the
season there are balls, concerts, teafights; out of the
season, nothing.   The theatre is built but rarely speaks;
the opera has to take root; the Turkish bath is unknown; indeed, there is not a bath on the island.
Even the English club-rooms are closed at night.   I
should feel in such a place like a caged hawk ; or,
to speak more classically, like a Prometheus with the
Demon Despair gnawing at my heart.   I could hardly
bear to register meteorological observations for year after
year, or to spend hours in peeping through the telescope
found in every turret; which appears to me the *flaneur's*
only sedentary occupation here.   Nostalgia is a disease
as yet imperfectly recognised.   The Highlanders in
Jamaica died of "Lochaber no more !" and many a
rugged fellow, who would blush at the suspicion, is
pining childlike for home and family.   The only remedy
—preventive there is none—is constant occupation of
mind if not of body, and this Madeira cannot afford.
The *habitués* declare the climate hostile to work.

I must believe that despite vicinity to England—seven
days and nineteen hours of steam, and cheapness of
passage, 20*l.* first class—that Madeira will in the next
generation be deserted for Egypt by all but purely
phthisical invalids.   There is that in the pure dry air
of the Desert of which no green country can boast.

And now of the wine that once delighted the world, so suddenly become an archæological subject—all, alas! food for the antiquarian!

The vine was introduced from Cyprus in 1425, and from Candia in 1445. It was not, however, actually cultivated till the opening of the sixteenth century, when the Jesuits planted the finest cuttings. The Franciscans subsequently carried it to California. There were about forty different kinds used for making wine. The best were the rich and luscious, but uncertain and unprofitable, Malvazia Candida, or Malmsey; the soft and delicate Bual, a Burgundy grape greatly improved; the dry light Sercial, the Amontillado of these wines, unpleasant when new, and made of a Hock grape so unpalatable that the lizards are said to have avoided it; the Hermitage-like Tinta, or Madeira-Burgundy, whose high claret colour was produced by husks or skins fermented with their contents; and finally, the Madeira of commerce. The latter was made from a variety of grapes, light and dark, mixed in the press. When new it was tinted like red wine and water which turned to a light amber hue. Age, heat, and moderate motion improved its flavour: the East and West India Madeira, so called after their voyages, were superior to the "London Particular."

Atkins, in 1720, bought a pipe of Madeira at "Fonchiale," as it was called in Commodore Anson's time, for two half-worn suits, and another for three second-hand wigs. The pipe cost in its palmy days from 25*l.* to 85*l.*, the average being 50*l.*, and the yearly

production amounted to 20,000 or 25,000 pipes, of
which one third was exported, and produced 350,000*l.*
per annum. In 1825 the export was 14,432 pipes: not
bad for a thickly-inhabited mountainous spot, thirty
miles (geographical) long, twelve and a half broad, about
seventy-two in circumference, and not amounting to
240 square miles; in fact, a quarter larger than the
Isle of Wight. The decadence of Madeira commenced
during the Napoleonic wars, when the merchants shipped
inferior growths, which Cettes succeeded in imitating.
Presently, an "illustrious person," a pet of Messrs.
Moore and Thackeray, fearing the effect of Madeira
upon his gout, assented to sherry as a more honest and
wholesome beverage, whereupon his loyal subjects
followed suit. The chief consumer of Madeira was
once England: she was followed by Russia and the
United States, which, however, claim to have taken
the lead. In St. Petersburg it is preferred even to
champagne. In New York I have paid $11 for
a bottle, and have seen men kill its aroma with ice
instead of gently warming it like Lafitte. Under the
sudden infliction of 1852, the terrible *oïdium Tuckeri,*
the energy of the people fell, and in 1854 the export
was reduced to 1860 pipes.

Rather more than a pipe per acre was the average produce of the land, four pipes being the maximum. The
best soils, as at Fernando Po, were the decomposed
basalts, and red and yellow tufas: the worst, stiff clays.
The wines of the southern coast, immediately about
Funchal, were the most highly prized, unequalled in

body, aroma, softness, and delicacy of flavour. The dryness of the soil in the lower regions, where the plant flourished best, made its cultivation peculiarly laborious. The field was seamed with trenches five to eight feet deep, extending down to the moist subsoil, and obviating the necessity of irrigation, even in the height of summer. Vine cuttings were then planted with the refuse vegetation of the intervals, cabbages and potherbs collected in the trenches, and buried as compost. During the second or third spring it was trained along a trellis, and in the north was married to the elm or chestnut tree. For three years there was no produce, and after every twenty years the whole vineyard required replanting. The vendemmia, or vintage, which took place in September, earlier or later, as required by situation, offered nothing peculiar. The picked grapes were foot-trodden in a clumsy wooden trough, or in a rude press ; after a single pressure with the lever, the produce was allowed to drain through a sieve which retained the stalks, and the must was stored in open vats, with an occasional stirring, for four or five weeks. After fermentation it was drawn off into fresh casks, clarified with eggs, gypsum, or bullock's blood, and prevented from acetating by adding to each pipe a gallon or two of Porto Santo, or St. Vincent brandy. Inferior wines were subjected in stores to a temperature of 140° to 150° (F.), which, after six months, forced them to apparent age, but left with them a dry and smoky flavour.

There are still a few pipes of Madeira upon the island, but whether more will be made "*Dio lo sa.*" The merchants declare that the wine will recover, but not in their day. A remedy has, it is well known, been found for the *oïdium*. The vine is washed and cleaned; when the pulverulent white fungus appears, a little powdered sulphur is applied, and the sore is kept healthy by a sprinkling of lime. During the last year several vineyards gave a good yield; but the Madeirans had applied themselves to a new industry, urged apparently by the five sugar-loaves upon the colonial shield, and by the old boast that their island produces the best wine and water, wheat and sugar, in the world. The cane had been introduced in early days from the Mediterranean, Prince Henry sent it from Sicily, but competition with Jamaica and her slave-labour soon reduced the mills from 120 to three. The hope of once more being successful revived, but it is now again decaying. Labour costs thirty cents a day, and the Portuguese does not work like a Louisiana contraband. Sugar cannot be produced under 4*d.* per lb., and the retail price of the native growth is 6*d.* Again, machinery is most expensive, and venture is small. Could it be reduced by half it would pay; now, it will not. The best use would be rum distilling for the people's use. The sugar land is limited; the upper extreme of its cultivation on the southern side may be estimated at 1,000 feet. Finally, the cane exhausts the soil, it requires water, and, what it can seldom obtain, large quantities of manure. It is evident that Madeira cannot compete with Cuba at present, or with the free British colonies, which, in another score of years, must drive Cuba out of the market, force her to import, not to export, her sweets. Another industry is the cochineal insect, for whose growth the cactus (O. Tuna), which overruns the ground, is well adapted. But this branch is decaying even in Tenerife, through the rise of Magenta, which will extinguish cochineal as effectually as Aspromonte did Garibaldi. Yet Madeira, despite all these losses and disappointments, is richer than she was in the days of the wine traffic. The English alone spend some 30,000*l.* to 40,000*l.* per annum in Funchal.

There are still a few pipes of Madeira in the island, I have said. The merchants sell three brands—one at 80*l.*, the other at 100*l.*, and the best at 110*l.* per pipe. The pipe, however, is small measure—92 gallons (= 45 dozen), whilst that of sherry is 108, and of port 115. The bottle, untainted by Cettes, costs $3 to $5.

It is a right melancholy fact—a consideration which I would commend to all " thinkers"—that both wine and tobacco are, unlike other articles of consumption, retrograding rather than progressing in quality, whilst the price is becoming ruinous. We remember good Cognac at 5 francs a bottle; what is it now? If things proceed as at present, what shall our grandsons or even ourselves, as grandsires, drink? What will there be to smoke? With which portentous subject for consideration I conclude the reflections engendered by a day at Madeira.

CHAPTER III.

A DAY AT TENERIFE.

2ND SEPTEMBER.

" No place appeared to her more fitted to dissipate melancholy and restore peace to the perturbed mind than Teneriffe."

Alex. von Humboldt.

" In Tenerife, for a time brief,
   I wandered all around,
Where shady bowers and lively flowers
   Spontaneously abound.

" Where posies rare perfume the air
   In festoons o'er your head,
Brave sheep and cows in pastures browse
   Without remorse or dread."

Lines by a West African Poet.

"From fair Madeira's purple coast we turned," having there left our stewardess and our little band of consumptives. The Madeirans, like the Pisans, complain that strangers expect the climate to make for them new lungs, hence the populousness of the cemeteries. The invalids, being all foreigners, had given us scanty trouble : as a rule, the Madeira-bound English are a bore. The natural national fierceness of the islanders is exasperated by ill health, and bad temper finds a vent upon fellow-passengers. They object to " Palm-oil ruffians " or " Coast lambs," as supercargos and skippers are politely termed, coming between the wind and their

nobility. Though they can hardly treat civil and
military officials, home-returning, quite so cavalierly,
they will complain with all their half lungs that the
ship is made a "sick-bay." They have endless grievances : to mention only one, the proprietors of the
A. S. S. line have been so troubled with correspondence
concerning naked lights and lucifer matches, that it is
hardly possible to obtain fire for a cigar. After leaving
Madeira, our party was reduced to four divisions, viz.,
the official at the first table, and the commercial, the
slaver, and the negro composing the starboard mess.

We were borne from the Isle of Wood with a stiff
breeze, though not yet a trade wind; and the current
usually marked southerly, gave us also westing. We
are still in that branch of the Guinea Gulf stream which
is to Madeira what its Caribbean congener is to Great
Britain. Our coal was composed of comminuted dust,
unmoulded, too, making progress painfully slow;
and decks very unclean. A small dark cloud was
pointed out to us as representing the Salvagens or Sal-
vages. They are three desert rocks between the Purpu-
rean Islands and the Canaries, or more correctly, 100
miles north of the latter, and therefore belonging to
the Canarian group. The largest, which may be from
four to five statute miles in circumference, is called,
from its circular body and conical head, the Grand
Piton, or Screw Ring; the second, one or two miles
round, is, for the same reason, known as the Petit Piton.
The proprietorship is vested in a Funchalese family.
Formerly the larger island was stocked with cattle, it is

now a rabbit warren, and hardly cultivable. The stock having been plundered, the owners gathered orchilla or uzella, useful for litmus, and barilla, which supplies the best alkali; but these also failed. The rocks still support puffins (P. Major, locally called Cagarra, properly meaning a small gull), which afford fat, feathers, and salted meat for the Madeiran market. These, and the islands to the south, were doubtless connected with Africa by low land, and probably with Europe by Gibraltar, till the convulsions which indented the northern shores of the Mediterranean, and drained the ocean for the North African Sahara, submerged those more level tracts that maintained the communication, and converted the rocky headlands into islands. The ichthyology of the seas, like that of the islands, lying north and south of the Salvagens, is interesting and complicated, belonging to the Moroccan coast.

On the afternoon of Sunday, the 1st of September, we sighted from afar the thick dark cloud, whose loom terrified the early voyagers in these mysterious waters, and which we shall meet again at Fernando Po and Camaroons. Here a north-east wind, laden with the vapours of the Atlantic, impinges upon the rocky flanks of Tenerife, and deflected upwards, is condensed in a shroud of heavy mist, though not so heavy as at Madeira. Sailors are mostly superstitious, and magic islands were inventions natural as sea-serpents and Flying Dutchmen. St. Borondon or San Brandaõ* has repeatedly

---

* He voyaged with S. Maclovio or Machutes, vulgarly called S.

been seen, and respectable men, " San Borodonistas "
they were called, have sworn to landing—a storm is an
invariable consequence—on islands as apocryphal as
Tasso's Enchanted Ground, or our less poetical Fiddlers'
Green. The Nubian geographer, writing of the Third
Climate, says:—In this sea is an island of sheep,
which is large, and covered with a dark cloud, in
which island are innumerable sheep, but small, and
their flesh extremely bitter to the taste, and unfit
for food." On the peak of Corvo, westernmost of
the Azores, stood, they say, a mounted man, with
one hand on the pommel of the saddle and the other
ever pointing westward; it sounds like the " Thousand
and One Nights." At the Canary group an eighth
island has been dreamed of, and at the treaty of Evora,
concluded in 1519, Portugal ceded to Spain the right of
conquering *Ilha naõ Trubada,* or *Encubierta,* the " Un-
found Island : " in 1526 an expedition sought it, but
of course in vain. Similar cases are Delos, that never
stood still, the Island of St. Matthew, mentioned by
De Barros, and the Seven Glorious Cities of the Portuguese, founded by the seven Bishops who fled after the
defeat of Don Roderick—one was discovered by a clever
navigator, and the people asked him if the " Moslem
invaders were still in the Peninsula." It is hardly to be
doubted that the mariners were deceived by some effect
of refraction, such as the Fata Morgana, or the Hartz
Mountain Spectre. Moreover, the perpetual gloom

Maló, and they discovered the country by bringing to life the giant
Mildum or Milduo.

hovering over the real islands, especially when wooded, would prepare the curious to see land in any more persistent cloud upon the horizon. We have still mariners in Ireland and Northern Scotland who believe in "San-Borodonisom." O. Brazile, or Hy Brazil,* seen by the people of Arran, and, like Painters' Wives' Island, placed in some unexplored corner of the ocean, is a case in point; and at times a rock, like Rockall, the new cod fishery, is found to exist, which makes us doubt if man has yet exhausted all discovery even in comparatively beaten tracks.

The far-famed Peak is rarely seen from the north-east; at the distance of about fifty miles, it appeared as a lumpy, ogee-shaped cone, in no wise remarkable, but looking like a low triangular cloud, by reason of its whiteness, which is said to be caused by decomposed vitreous porphyritic lava. From the south of the island it may theoretically be seen for 120 miles, but it has lost much of the grand and picturesque aspect which it shows from the Valley of Arotava to the north-east of it, and looks like a flattened dome or block of mountain, with a central jag. We passed at 5 P.M. the historic Anaga Point,† distant five miles from the capital; it is the north-easternmost end of the island, and the beginning of Guanche etymology.

---

* Swift's Tale of a Tub, Section V.

† Benchorro, the Mencey or chief of Anaga, agreed to be neutral and witness his country's ruin when the Spaniards landed at Tenerife. On the 1st May, 1493, they solemnised the Invention of the Cross in the camp of Port Anaga, and presently built there a town, which was of course called Santa Cruz.

As we steamed along, the grisly and iron-bound coast appeared a wall of rock, cut with deep barrancas, and girt with outlying rocks—the skirts of the awful peak. The Ass's ears then stood before us, the lights of San Andres twinkled upon the shore, and the sea was dotted with the flambeaux of the fishermen. About 9 P.M. we had finished the 260 miles that separated us from Madeira, and we cast anchor off the Mole, over the very spot where the cutter "Fox" was sunk, losing 97 men during the ill-judged, gallant and mismanaged attack by "our Nel." in 1797.

The Islands of the Canary group lie about fifty miles from the nearest point of the African coast; they are seven in number*—Ptolemy and Pliny knew but six—are calculated to contain 180,000 to 200,000 inhabitants, and to present an area of 2900 square miles. Professor Forbes believes them to be, like the other three island groups, Azores, Madeira, and Cape Verde, the exposed remains of a continuous and extensive tract that formed the western prolongation of the European and African shores. He points to their identity in geology as well as in botany with Europe, and thus assists us in explaining the old legend of Atlantis. Professor Piazzi Smyth looks upon them "as constituting one enormous volcano, still to arise out of the ocean in all its majesty," and holds "that the African

---

* Including the three Selvagers, the Fortunate Archipelago numbers sixteen islands, of which six are very small—such as I. de Lobos, off Fuerteventura, and La Graciosa, Allegranza, Roque del Oëste, Roque de Leste, and Sta. Clara near Langarote.

continent may one day be ramparted on the west by a
greater than Andean chain of mountains, of which
Madeira, the Canaries, and the Cape de Verdes, will be
some of the most glorious summits." Their names,
beginning from the easternmost, are—First, Lanzarote
or Lancerota, so called in A.D. 1400 by the Norman
knight, Jean de Bétancourt the Great, after some
Lancelot* of his acquaintance.   Second, distant two
leagues, Fuertaventura, in our maps Fuerteventura,
which the French call Fortuite, it is the great supplier
of limestone.   Third, Canaria, called by the Normans,
from the bravery of its people, or because it was
selected as the head quarters, Gran Canaria.   Fourth,
Tenerfe or Tenerife, of which more anon.   Fifth,
Gomera, formerly unknown, but found so named from
its gums by Jean de Bétancourt. Sixth, "Benahoave,"
"my country," called Palma, by the two runaway
lovers from Cadiz, who discovered it.   Seventh and
lastly, Hierro or Ferro of the Fountain tree.   The
natives called this, the westernmost of the group,
Esero, or strong.   " When the Spaniards showed
them iron, they found it exceeding everything in
strength, thereupon they called it Esero ; and when
they began to speak the Castilian language, they
spoke of iron indifferently as Esero or Hierro, which

---

* Perhaps Lancelote Maloysel of whom Bontier and Le Verrier speak.
A Lancerota in A.D. 1446—47 discovered a great river between Cape
Blanco and Cape Verde.   The natives called it Ovedoc; he gave it the
name of Sanaga, or Çanaga, possibly from the Anaga above mentioned.
The word survives in the French Senegal.   In 1487 the same Lancelot
is mentioned as returning to the Canaries.

last is the Spanish word for that metal; so that at
last they translated the real name of the island Esero
into the Spanish one Hierro, which it retains to this
day. But the Portuguese, and some others following
their own dialect, called it Ferro; and some will have it
that the natives call it Fer, though there is no proof
for this assertion." *

The word naturally recalls to my mind a geographical

---

* Book I. " The History of the Discovery and Conquest of the
Canary Islands, translated from a Spanish manuscript lately found in
the island of Palma, with an inquiry into the origin of the ancient
inhabitants." By George Glas, 4to, London, 1764. The translator
should at least have mentioned the name of his author, Father Juan
A'bren Galindo, who resided in these isles in 1591, and who wrote a
history of them, printed in 1632.

George Glas—I know not why some call him Glasse—was a Scotch
skipper, who in the middle century, when "master mariners" were
not over particular, traded between England, the Canaries, and Western
Barbary. Determining to settle in the latter, he freighted a ship, and
with his wife, daughter, and servants landed at the port of Guader,
which the Spaniards had called Santa Cruz de Berberia. Ignoring its
history, he called it Port Hillsborough, in honour of his patron, the
Earl and minister of that name, and made alliances with the Moors
and Arabs. The Spanish ambassador in London reported the case to
Madrid, and the Captain-General of the Canary Islands was ordered to
seize the adventurer. Glas appeared, after some time, at Santa Cruz,
off Tenerife, was imprisoned, and, after an attempt to escape, was
kept *au sécret*. By scratching his name on crusts and throwing them
on the beach, tidings of his detention reached the British consul, who
reported the affair home, and Lord Rochfort, British Envoy at Madrid,
obtained his liberation. The ill-starred Glas embarked with his
family at Port Orotava on board a London-bound ship, the Earl of
Sandwich, richly loaded with gold, dollars, wine and silk. Four of
the crew murdered all on board—the unfortunate mother and daughter,
lashed in each other's arms, threw themselves into the sea. The
assassins were arrested at Dublin, and their trial and execution may be
found in the "Annual Register" for 1765.

grievance, that the petty national jealousies of Europe have deprived us of the benefit of a single point *de départ* in longitude. "The great meridian," according to Mr. Greenhough,* "by the most ancient Greek geographers,† passed through the Fortunate Islands, now the Canaries; thence it was translated by the Arabians to the uttermost part of the western shore. The best of them brought it back again to the Canaries, and placed it on the Peak of Tenerife, the supposed Junonia of Ptolemy."

"Ptolemy as Marinus the Syrian cited by him, and the ancients before them, fixed the great meridian in Hera or Junonia (Canaries); our own countrymen removed it from the Canaries to the Azores, under the idea of this being the magnetic meridian, which it is not; and if it were, the reason would be bad, and the alteration objectionable."

"Stevinus, a Dutch geographer, brought it back to the Canaries, observing that one of these islands should be fixed upon, a change which he terms *exiguus quidem sed notabilis et perpetuus.*"

"Johnson in his lesser globe of 1602, makes the great meridian pass through Corvo and Flores, but in that of 1616, through the Peak of Tenerife."

"The difference of longitude from the Pico to the

---

* Mr. Greenhough's Anniversary Address to the Royal Geographical Society. Vol. ii. p. 74.

† Hipparchus, of Nice, in B.C. 162, established his first point of longitude at Ferro. With the ancient Greeks it was the boundary of space itself.

Arabic meridian is 10° more East according to Abul-
fida,—from Pico to the Island of St. Michael's 9°,—
from Pico to Corvo 15°, and both so much more
west."

Pico or Ferro would be to longitude what the first
point of Aries is to the heavens, and what the equator
is to latitude—0. After an ordinance of Louis XIII.
of France, Cardinal Richelieu, by the advice of the best
mathematicians, ordered, on 25th April, 1634, that the
first meridian as in the days of Ptolemy should be placed
in the western extremity of Hierro. Now there are a
dozen 0's, and not one great meridian; London, Paris,
St. Petersburg, Madrid, Washington are all usurpations,
to use an old chronicler's words, and they confuse the
idea of longitude in the minds of men. One might
as well make the parallel of one's birth-place the 0 of
latitude. The loss of a single position is like that of
the Latin language, in works of general reference, and
those intended for the widely scattered learned of the
world, who must now drudge through half a dozen
dialects.

The variety of derivations adduced by the savans to
explain the term Canaries, may amuse the reader. Pliny,
who informs us that in his day the Fortunate Islands,
which showed vestiges of buildings, were deserted, says
that Grand Canary was named on account of its mastiffs
or large dogs, two of which were presented to Juba, king
of Mauritania. When Europeans visited it they found
no dogs,* but they remember that Pliny mentions the

* Lancerota now produces a fine large breed like the Newfoundland:

Canarii—so called from their dwelling with dogs and sharing with them the bowels of wild beasts—who lived beyond Mount Atlas, near the country of the Perorsi Æthiopians. These may have been the earliest colonists. Ptolemy calls Cape Bojador,* now, or Cape Blanco, Gannaria, or Caunaria extrema; and it has been remarked that the semi-Semitic population on the Senegal River term the country between that stream and Mount Atlas, Gannar. If true, this would give a trustworthy clue. Since the modern formal discovery of the island, authors, though they neglect to inform us what the aborigines called their country, have proposed a variety of wild derivations. The Canaanites had of course a chance. One finds Canaria in the fact that there are large dogs bred there—"Unos afernian ser por muchos canes que en la Canaria hasta hoz se crian"—others that the natives eat, dog-like, quantities of raw meat; others in Crano and Crana, children of Noah—Cranaria

---

the common dogs of the island are like the pariah of the east; there are bastard greyhounds and pets which will presently be noticed.

* In 1412 a ship sent by John I. of Portugal is said to have doubled this Cape (26° 20′ north latitude). In 1415, the Great Prince Henry, his son by Philippa, daughter to John of Gaunt, and therefore half an Englishman, sent two small vessels, but they were driven back. It was successfully explored by Gilianez in 1432-33. In 1440, Gonçalez Baldeza reached Cape Blanco (20° 47′ north latitude), 160 miles beyond Bojador, and brought home the first cargo of seals' skins. After his next journey, 1442, he was more fortunate, and returned with ten slaves and gold dust. The voyage is memorable as being the first incept of the slave export which afterwards rose to such a height. Prince Henry died in 1463. At his death, despite all the national enthusiasm, the Portuguese had not reached Sierra Leone, or one-third of the distance to India.

becoming Canaria—others in the thorny bushes with red fruit, called *Uva Canina*, or dogs' grapes. Others in the devil appearing to the natives, shaped like a shark-dog, as Dr. Faustus saw him; he also showed "in other figures which the natives called Tibicenas." Thomas Nicols, writing in 1526, opines that though there were "dogges" in the island, they only "served the people instead of sheep for victual." He heard from the conquerors that the word Canary was derived from a common growth, "square canes in great multitude together, which, being touched, will cast out a liqueur as white as milk, which liqueur is rank poison." He palpably alludes to the *Cactus*, the *Euphorbia*, or other kind of spurge-wort. Some have derived it from Canna, as canes, especially sugar-canes, are there abundant. Others from Cano, singing birds being abundant; others "because it abounds with an herb called in Latin, Canaria (but in the Castilian language Triguera), which the dogs eat in the spring to cause themselves to vomit or . purge." The application of the word is not less remarkable than its derivation. If it comes from a dog, it has descended to a dance and a wine, now almost obsolete, and to a bird that still exists.*

* The Canary sack which Sir John Falstaff loved is as extinct as good Madeira. The place of export was El Puerto de Orotava. The trade continued till the peace of 1815, after which it never recovered; there were two wines, Canary and Malmsey. The former, made from a large grape, was the *vin ordinaire*, strong and heavy; the latter was made from a smaller berry, and was sweet and agreeable. The favourite sites were the lower two hundred feet of hills with southern aspects; dry walls breast high, and built four or five feet from

From the earliest ages these Νησοι μακαρων have been the subject of enthusiastic comment; and I may here observe that although the Fortunate Islands are not now peculiarly happy, they might, with care and culture, be converted into an earthly Elysium. The group is thus described by Plutarch: " The soil is so abundantly fruitful, that it produces spontaneously plants and fruits, for use and delicacy, sufficient to answer the wants and delight the palates of the inhabitants." Of the climate he observes, "it is firmly believed even by the barbarous natives themselves, that this is the seat of the Blessed." M. Bovy de St. Vincent, in his " Essais sur les îles Fortunées," discovers in Tenerife and its neighbours, the veritable Mount Atlas of Homer and Virgil, the Garden of the Hesperides with their golden apples, the Gorgons under Queen Medusa, the Elysian Fields, the Purple Islands, the Atlantis of Plato, and the cradle of that Atlantic people, which earthquakes, volcanoes, and eruptions of the sea subse-

one another, prevented the earth being washed away. The vines suffered for four consecutive years—1852 to 1856. From Glas we hear that the Guanches had public-houses where they sang and enjoyed the Canario or Canary dance—a short quick measure, long preserved in the islands, and imported into European Courts, Spanish and others, where, however, it has yielded to other novelties. The air or melody was also borrowed from the natives. The canary, the goldfinch, and the capirote are still the principal songsters of the island. The canary bird appears to have been common to the Cape Verde, Madeira, Canary, and Azore groups. Adanson (" Voyage to Senegal ") noticed at Tenerife that the canary bird, which grows white in France, is there grey, and attributes the change to the effect of climate. A further civilisation has turned it yellow.

quently annihilated. As might be expected, the aborigines have been traced back to the Ten Tribes of Israel,
and their extinction is explained by an emigration to
America,* like the Irish of the present day.

The island of Thenerife, Tenerfis, Tenerfe, Tenerife,
or Teneriffe, lies about the centre of the Canary group.
Etymologists derive it from a king, Tehinerfe; others
translate it the White Mountain, from the Palman
word, Thenar, or mountain, and Ife, white; others
make Tiner to signify snow or white, and Ife, mountain; no matter, however, it signifies Mont Blanc. The
shape is that of a leg of mutton, with the end bone
to the north; the extreme length is seventy, and its
greatest breadth twenty-two miles. Its circumference
is not mentioned, the area is 897 English square
miles, according to Humboldt, and the population
64,000 to 70,000 souls, of which Santa Cruz contains,
in books, 15,000 to 20,000, but more probably 8,000 to
10,000. Its history does it honour. In A. D. 1402 to
1406, Gadifer, or Gayferos de la Salle, and Jean de
Bétancourt, or Bethencourt, who in 1403 obtained from
Don Henry III. a grant of the Fortunate Islands, with
title of king, accompanied by 200 Normans and Gascons,
besides seamen in three ships, conquered the "Islas
Menores," Lanzerote, Fuerteventra, Gomera, and Hier-

---

* The theory was that a chain of islets with short intervals, if not a
solid body of land, extended quite across the Pacific and Atlantic
Oceans—a theory not yet disproved by geographers. John de Laet, a
Flemish geographer, explains Pliny by an emigration of the Canarians
to America.

ros; but were beaten off from Canary and Palma. Years
elapsed before proud Tenerife and her sister islands
succumbed to Spanish valour, and after a century and
a half the aborigines were either extinct or blended
with their conquerors. The wars and the policy of the
assailants forcibly remind us of Mexico and Peru ;
Hernan Cortez and Pizarro having been represented
by Rejon de Vera, and Alonzo Fernandez de Lugo.
The latter, a scion of a noble Gallician family, after
fighting against the Moors of Granada, and assisting in
Perdro de Vera's conquest of Great Canary, applied to
Ferdinand and Isabella for permission to conquer Tenerife and Palma. In 1491, he was by them appointed
Captain-General of the Canary Islands and of the coast
of Barbary, from Cape Geer to Cape Bojador. Having
wasted his means of recruiting, he betook himself in his
distress to the High Church of Seville, when an ancient
man of venerable aspect and quite unknown to him,
placed in his hands a large bag of money. Of course it
could be none other than St. Peter himself, of whom
Lugo was all his life a devout admirer. With these resources he equipped three ships, landed at Great Canary,
and recruited his force to 900 men. With this army he
attacked Palma, and, despite the valour of its Amazons,
he defeated the natives in three sanguinary battles; after
seven months from the date of his landing, he proclaimed
the kings of Castile monarchs of " San Miguel de la
Palma," and on the 3rd of May,—the English calendar
calls it, with unintentional *naïveté*, the "Invention of
the Cross," — 1486 or 1492, he built Santa Cruz,

and declared it the capital of the island. The native prince Tanausu, being sent a prisoner to Spain, starved himself to death. Lugo was then made Governor of Palma, whose lands were divided amongst the conquerors and the conquered, the principal actor taking to himself the district of Los Sauces, or The Willows.

Lugo, true to the motto of his race,—" Quien lanza sabe mover, ella le da de comer," the spear supports him that knows its handling—a curious contradiction to something said about the sword—returning to Gran Canaria, collected 1000 infantry and 150 cavalry, with whom on the 31st of April, 1493, he set sail for Tenerife. The eight Menceys were in great alarm. A local prophet had foretold the fall of Quebohi Bencomo, or Benchomo, the Mencey of Taoro, by a great white bird, which would bring with it ruin.* The Spanish ships were probably the fulfilment of that prophecy; others say that white birds preceded Lugo's little army. Having conciliated Anaterve, the Chief of Guimar, and, having planted his cross and celebrated the 3rd of May, the Spaniard on the 4th May, 1493, advanced up the broad pass towards the Vega of Laguna, and met the natives at a place where the chapel of our Lady de la Gracia now stands.

Bencomo, after a Tagoror, or native council, in which great discord prevailed, advanced towards the Spaniards.

---

* Similar prophecies were made by "Ajone" in Hierro, that before his death the god Eraoranhan would come in a white house—reminding us of the Mexican prophecies touching Cortez, and the Kafir's respecting the English.

His mission was peaceful, his manner hostile, and he swore by Echeyde the Peak* and by the bones of his father, the Great Tenerfe, that he would annihilate the invader. He refused all the proposals of the Spaniards, and insisting that they should evacuate the island, returned to council with his brother Menceys. He then proposed a confederacy, with himself at the head. This aroused the jealousy of those who considered themselves safe from the Spaniards, and he of Guimar joined Lugo with 600 vassals.

In the spring of 1494 Lugo broke up his camp at Laguna, and marched westward to attack the enemy. Bencomo detached 300 of his best men to surprise an exploring party that had sighted Arantapala in Taoro, the present Orotava; they manned the rear where the Spaniards had to return through the Pass of Acentejo, and committed great slaughter, forcing the survivors to flee. Lugo advanced to support the fugitives, and did battle for two hours. At length, hearing that Bencomo

---

* According to the older travellers, the Guanches called the Peak Echeyde, a name which survives in the Pico de Teyde of the present day. It was a place of horror to the pagans who placed their bad-god Guayota (opposed to their good-god Acheman) in the centre of the earth or at the bottom of the crater, which would be equivalent to our Hades. They swore by Echeyde; another oath was by the bones— Viera says the skulls—of ancient princes. The last sole monarch of Tenerife was the Great Tenerfe, who died about a century before the Spanish invasion, and his nine sons divided his dominions, forming with a bastard child a total of ten. The descendants of these Menceys or princes were, according to popular belief, secretly sworn by certain elders and near relatives, upon a bone of the Great Tenerfe preserved in a leathern pillow.

was approaching with 3000 men, he prayed to St. Michael, and escaped by a cloud and a panic of the enemy. He lost, however, 600 of his men and 200 allies; the Pass was then called La Matanza, or The Killing, a name which it bears to this day. As only 200 wounded men remained, and his provisions were exhausted, he evacuated the island the 8th June, 1494.

Returning a third time to Grand Canary, the undaunted Lugo was enabled to levy 1100 infantry and 70 horse, by the aid of Genoese merchants, and the third Duke of Medina Sidonia, who sent him from Spain 650 footmen and 45 cavalry, chosen from his tenants at San Lugar. He effected his second landing at Santa Cruz towards the end of the year 1494, rebuilt his cross and tower, and pitched his camp on the plain of Laguna. The Guanches, according to the Spaniards, opposed him with 11,000 men,—impossible out of a total of 15,000 souls. Bencomo, stoutly refusing all proposals, advanced with his men, who suffered much from the fire of the enemy, whilst their leader was himself wounded and obliged to leave the field. Tinguaro, the Mencey of Anaga, was killed in this battle of Laguna, and his head was sent on a pike as a warning to Bencomo, who returned a heroic answer, envying the chief so honourable a death.

Spanish pertinacity broke the spirit of the Guanches. The uncommonly wet season of 1495 and the hardships of the campaign brought on fevers and the terrible modorra or lethargy.* The land was full of corpses

* It is described as a drowsiness accompanied by a profound melan-

whom no one buried or embalmed. The Spaniards, who also suffered from famine, advanced towards the interior, where they were met by the brave Bencomo at the head of 5000 men. After a battle of five hours, he was again wounded, and lost 2000 of his army. The Spaniards pursued the fugitives with shouts of " Victoria! Victoria!" in remembrance of which a village and a church were afterwards built upon the spot.

After this signal victory the Spaniards under de Lugo, who like Hannibal could conquer but could not use victory, returned to Santa Cruz on the 4th January, 1496, where they were recruited and refreshed by the generosity of the Duke of Medina Sidonia. They advanced once more on the 1st July, and established themselves at Orotava. Bencomo, though still in arms on Mount Tigayga, saw that the contest was useless, and proceeded to the Spanish camp. Received by Lugo, he and his beautiful daughter, Dácil, were duly baptized and became subjects of the Spanish monarchy. He

---

choly, which proved fatal in a few days. The present "sleeping dropsy" or "sleepy sickness" of the West African coast—in Fernando Po several Spaniards have died of it—is the true lethargus of the neurotic or cataphoric class, the effect of softening of the brain and generally the result of over-indulgence in certain pleasures. Young girls die of it, and youths of both sexes have induced it at Sierra Leone by smoking "hashish." It is also caused by want, overwork, nostalgia, morose habits, and other mental and bodily depressors. The patient falls asleep even when eating or in the full glare of the sun, becomes emaciated though with a good appetite, and often suffers from shakiness, convulsions, glandular swellings in the neck, deafness, paralytic trembling, a shuffling gait, and sometimes enlargement of the head. The only treatment is instant change of air, scene, and habits.

is said to have died in Venice : she married Gonzalo
Garcia del Castillo. Two of his descendants, the Dean
Don Pedro Josè Bencomo and his brother Don Cristobal
Bencomo, confessor to Ferdinand VII., died in 1828.
The remaining Menceys of Tenerife were carried by
Lugo to Spain, and were presented to Ferdinand and
Isabella. And Lugo himself, after a glorious career as
General of the Coast of Barbary and Perpetual Governor
of the island of Palma and Tenerife, in which he
founded many of the towns and churches, died in 1525.
Thus ends the strange and eventful history of the
Guanche conquest and conquerors. At the end of a
century they were no more, those primitive goat-herds
scattered over a finite tract of some few dozen miles. It
is a sad chapter in the blood-stained annals of the
world.

As we cast anchor the sky cleared and the deep cloud
drew off to the north-east. It being Sunday, and 9 p.m.,
seasons at which Southerns do not usually distress themselves, the health-officer's boat did not put off till our
energetic captain had blazed away half-a-dozen times with
his "resonant smoke-eagles," as modern poetry would
have it, but in prose brass carronades. It was a wonderful
roar, the echo from the rocks, a voice like thunder, a most
Ossianic sound—the spirits of the Guanches seemed to raise
a cry of lamentation from their graves. After a curious
collection of questions, all of which might easily have been
condensed into one, we were allowed *pratique ;* and, hearing of an opera, I hastened on shore. A line of scattered
oil lamps denoted the town, which, situated on the north-

east side of the island, rises from the wave, looking
at this hour and distance like a lurid whitish sheet, un-
backed by hill or verdure.   A red light guided us to
the mole, which the splashing of waves at high tides—
the rise is nine feet—must make at times a ticklish
landing-place. Ascending the steps, and passing through
the gate attached to the castle of San Cristabol, after
a few yards we found ourselves at Richardson's Fonda.
It is named the English Hotel.   I need hardly say that
there is an English hotel everywhere, and is both better
and dearer than its French rivals.

A gloomy, dreary place—by night at least—was that
same English hotel.   A large building, with walls two
feet thick enclosing a *patio,* whose hanging balconies of
massive dark wood-work support llianas and creepers
that must make admirable homes for the scorpion and
the centipede.   In the centre is an old well, and, contrasting with an English pump of bran - new shape,
dating 1857, is an Oriental stand for "monkey-jars"
or water-pots.   They are of light red porous clay,*
sometimes ornamented with insertions of waxy quartz,
which appears auriferous: the form probably dates from
the days of Hanno: others trace in them a resemblance

---

* The Tenerife dripstone, a huge basin of porous sandstone, which
requires only an occasional scraping, is, like the monkey-jars, a good
investment for those going south.   According to Adanson ("Voyage
to Senegal," &c., A.D. 1749), "the water from the mountain springs
at Tenerife being hard and crude, is filtered through a stone very
common in the quarries....It is a kind of lava of the colour of soot,
in a medium betwixt the density of the grey lava and the porosity of
the pumice."

to the Etruscan. Ascending the dark heavy stairs, we found ourselves in a long sombre room, with a heavily-raftered and painted ceiling. A well-worn carpet, a couch, a table, and a few chairs were the only furniture. On the whitewashed walls hung engravings of Majos Toros, East-Indiamen, and other subjects, dating from the year 1810. An English official on sick leave from the Gold Coast had been left, at his own request, by the last steamer in the English hotel. Few, I warrant, but old T—— would have dared to repeat in such a place and at such an hour—

"Mihi est propositum in tabernâ mori,"

—the sentiment which Sterne stole from Leightoun, and Leightoun stole from the jolly old Walter de Mapes. To me the fate of my compatriot appeared truly pitiable.

"A stranger's roof to hold thy head,
A stranger's foot thy grave to tread,
Desert and rock and alp and sea
Spreading between thy home and thee." *

* * * *

After Mr. Purser had ordered for the ship all the delicacies of the season—sheep, potatoes, pigeons, and so forth—we set out in the dry still air for the post-office; and after long knocking, succeeded in lodging the bags and in counting them to the glimmer of a solitary

---

* Since the above was written the Messrs. Richardson have opened another hotel, which yields in nothing to the best Madeiran boarding-houses. It is classic ground : within its walls Peter Pindar wrote his ode to the Canarian fleas.

tallow. The aspect of the place prepossessed me strongly
—but how can Humboldt call it a "neat town?" Tall
houses, most irregularly built; palace alongside of
lodging-hole, with huge balconies and sometimes half
glass windows looking out upon narrow streets and lanes,
by no means so inodorous as those of the Isle of Wood,
gave a *quasi*-Moorish and a most picturesque aspect to
the scene. The soft light reminded one of Malta.
The pavement, however, was of kidney-shaped stones,
like those of Madeira—uncommonly trying to new
comers. The Rambla, the Alameda and the Plaza were
deserted, and we met but one party of Señoras and
Señoritas,—of whom one was pointed out as having thrice
ascended the Peak,—returning, duly guarded of course,
from the bath. The opera-singers had left Santa Cruz
after the season for Cadiz. So we re-embarked on board
the "Blackland," and, with orders to be called early,
retired to enjoy a sleep undisturbed by the *roulis mas-
sacrant*, the clatter of the rudder-chains and the swing-
swong, fore and aft, side to side motions which had
sorely damaged our rest during the last night.

Daybreak, usually so staid and trite,—if the usual
thick mist be wanting,—is a wondrous spectacle at
Tenerife. When Columbus was ordered by Isabel la
Catolica to describe the appearance of Jamaica, he
crushed a sheet of paper in his hand, and partially opening it out upon the table, told Her Majesty that the
crumpled paper would show it better than his words
could tell. The same would serve for Madeira, Tenerife,
Fernando Po, and almost all these outlying islands of

West Africa, which contrast strongly with the flat coralline formations of the eastern coast. But to return to
the dawn.

As the African sky, transparently azure, lights up like
a cheek recovering from mortal faintness, the unrisen
splendours fall gloriously from the blue depths of the
ethereal vault upon the jagged crenellated points and
bristling cones, where the condor and the roc might
build, and which, sharp as the fracture of obsidian, spring
from the volcanic lower levels. Now the sheen creeps
down, with matchlessly brilliant tints, the sides of the
tremendous pyramids, revealing perpendicular or beetling
crags and cliffs, bleak and bare, black and ruddy-brown,
as if still fresh from the action of fire, and rock curtains
rent by deep anfractuosities, grizzly barrancas, narrow
fiumaras paved with water-rolled pebbles and wavy
beds and solid sheets of lava that have remained un-
altered since the days of its creation. Those gnomon-
like peaks, bisected with feathery cloud, throw strange
shadows around them; varying with each half hour,
they so change the view, that nothing but the upper
outline remains to be recognised. Then warmer and
warmer pour the rays over the purple curtains of beautiful Guimar, above which rises a light whitish cone—
PICO GRANDE—over the cultivated lands, bronzing the
heights, the limpidity of the air making all appear upon
the same plane, over the thin surf-line creaming upon
the shore, over the deep blue waters sleeping at the feet
of the cliffs. Such are the peaceful beauties of the scenery.
When the howling wind dashes the waves high up the

rocks, and the rain-mist shows through its rents, the deep sheers and the iron walls that gird this Island of the Blessed, the sight must be truly awful.

On such a morning—the fair, not the foul—I cast my first glance at Santa Cruz de Tenerife; so called after the early fashion of the Portuguese and Spaniards who took possession of the land by planting a cross, and hence have a confusing variety of Santas Cruces. The country looks yellow, shadeless, and barren after Madeira; it never has anything but the thinnest coat of transparent green, yet the beautiful transverse range called the Guimar Hills, gives it a beauty all its own. The town is far more level than Funchal,* though smaller, nor is it outflanked by such a multitude of villas and farm-houses. Beginning at the right, is a breach in a wall of high black rock, to which the roaring of the waves has given the name of Valle de Bufadera. It is a gully, serving as a blowpipe to raise the storm when least wanted. Here " Saint Nelson " first landed his men, and, according to native tradition, attempting to march over the hills, was beaten back with stones and rocks. Beyond it, apparently connected, lie the castles of San Miguel and Paso Alto, from which a Jacob's ladder threads the sides of the tall coke-

---

* Humboldt describes the "little town" of Santa Cruz as lying "on a narrow and sandy beach, whose houses of dazzling whiteness with flat roofs and windows without glass, are built close against a wall of black perpendicular rock devoid of vegetation." Surely the great traveller must have described Santa Cruz as his countrymen, according to Goethe, would describe a camel.

like rocks, where the powder-magazine stands and in whose flanks batteries are said to be concealed. Further on, where there is a stretch of level ground, at the mouth of a now dry fiumara, is the cochineal plantation of D. Manuel Conche, the well-known Captain-General of Cuba. The cactus is favoured by the dryness of earth and air, and constitutes the principal growth of this by no means fertile island. The long white walls of the enclosure—length and straightness of wall are here characteristic features—are garnished with pepper-box turrets; and laden camels, stately and slow, carrying their arched necks with Oriental gravity, zigzag along the dusty roads. Beyond the plantation begin the more modern fortifications, which make already a respectable show. A new citadel that will contain twenty-seven rifled cannon of the largest calibre, with casemates for 1000 men, is rapidly rising. Next to it is the saluting battery—twenty-three fine old brass guns—which sunk the "Fox:" then, not unlike an English martello tower, the fort of San Pedro, which fired the shot that made Nelson a manchet. The castle of San Cristobal,—where the first tower was built,—and its outworks protect the mole, and the south of the city is commanded by San Juan. There are no works on the land side, which can be attacked with all facility. The habitations extend behind the fortifications from north to south, and occupy a low bench, which rises interiorly to Laguna, terminating southwards in a white and sandy plain some three miles long. The houses, which struck me by their

resemblance to those of Malta, are of large square form,
gaily tinted with red, white, and yellow, and the case-
ments are mostly green. Like Madeira it presents the
anomaly of a city without smoke. Here and there a
spire-like cypress or a date-palm gives an Oriental
aspect to the place. Besides the defences, there are but
two conspicuous buildings in the town : on the right,
the church of San Francisco, with its domed and
many-storied tower; and on the left the parish church
dedicated to Our Lady of the Conception, the spiritual
guardian of Santa Cruz. The quarantine anchorage lies
at the other side of the mole. The lazaretto, a low
building, whose red, white, and yellow walls by no means
prepossess one, is close to where we are reposing. The
roadstead, for harbour it can hardly be called, is
open to every wind except the west, which blows the
rarest.

I am informed that Las Palmas, the principal city of
Great Canary, is improving her port; if so, she will soon
effect the ruin of Santa Cruz. The two capitals have long
been rivals, and have agreed to share the dignities between them. The Bishop and the Audiencia, or High
Court, reside at Las Palmas. Santa Cruz is the
residence of the Captain-General, the Civil Governor,
and the Military Commandant; and as the place is,
like Madeira, a part of the Empire, a province, not a
colony, these officers are independent of each other.
The only craft in port were two square-rigged mer-
cantmenh, and four island schooners — cutter-like
craft, not inelegant, nor I suspect inodorous. The

people fish as far as the Moroccan Cape Nun,* and exchange their captures for orchilla and fine Barbary wool ; their crazy and ill-found vessels, hardly provided with ground tackle, occasionally fall a prey to the fierce and treacherous Bedouin Moors.

Landing with the usual difficulty at the mole, we passed through the guardhouse gate into the hotel. The troops on the island are now a single brigade (about 400 men) of Spanish artillery, neatly clad in red caps and white shell-jackets, with overalls to match; a most appropriate habiliment, were it not so conspicuous. The others, with those extraordinary forage caps bearing the arms of Spain, red-faced blue jackets and white trousers, with cartouche boxes supported, after Spanish fashion, by uncrossed braces as well as belts, are the local militia. The islands supply seven regiments, which are liable to service throughout the Canaries. The officers were, but are no longer all indigenous, and the commandant and adjutant are drawn from the line. The men are a fine race, tall and sinewy; their manly aspect contrasts strongly with the half-starved Madeirans. They are not deficient in good looks : handsome is, however, as handsome does, and

* Called Cape Nam, Não, or Non by the Portuguese, because beyond this none had proceeded. It is probably so named from Ras Nún, the Cape of Fish—as Jonas is Zu'l Nún, the Lord of Fish—and was Europeanised to Non or Nom. About 1415, when Prince Henry of Portugal, being twenty-one years old, took up his abode at St. Vincent, the nearest point to Africa, the only portion of the West African litoral known to Europe, was that between Capes Spartel and Nun.

the Canarians, though quiet, orderly, and sober in their own country, have the reputation of "roughs" in Cuba and elsewhere. There is a chronic squabble between the people of Laguna and Santa Cruz : the former term the latter fishermen, and these retort by calling their rivals cooks ;—a diversion which sometimes ends in a stabbing match. In the south of the island there is a population which was as celebrated for landlord shooting as the Irish of the present day. There, too, the aboriginal and semi-Semitic type still peeps out in spare, straight, slim figures, skins of a darker stain, irregular features, piercing black eyes, and high Arab cheek bones.

After performing the duty of ordering breakfast, we sallied forth to imspect the town. Opposite the hotel stands the local Alameda " El Maydan," or promenade, a dusty, high-walled space, like the Florian Gardens of now cockneyfied Malta. We saw there a few fine mimosas, dahlias, daturas, and other wild flowers : a gipsy-like family was boiling the pot in a quiet corner. On the right of the hotel, near the centre of the town and close to the sea, was the Plaza de la Constitucion.* It is an oblong paved with flags, and surrounded by a lower band of cobble-stones and *trottoirs*, with iron pillar'd lamps and queer old stone seats for loungers who prefer the sitting position whilst prospecting promenades.

* Besides the Parliament of Burgos (Castile), which met in A.D. 1169, nearly a century before the Leicester Parliament, and old Constitutions of 1808 and 1821, a statute was issued in 1834, shortly after the death of Ferdinand VII., Queen Maria Christina being Regent. A constitution was generally given in 1837, and modified in 1845 to the form in which it now exists.

Six streets or lanes manage its circulation, and the south-western and south-eastern corners communicate with the sea. Here is the palace of the civil governor, a corner house, with tall white-washed front and long green jalousies. On the other side is the abode of the captain-general, a handsome building, with brilliant window-railings, and guarded by two bell-tent-like sentry-boxes for artillerymen in uniform. The square also contains a Frenchified *café*, whence the *coche*, or omnibus, drawn by four mules or horses, starts twice a day for Laguna; and under the same roof a French hotel,* generally preferred because it cooks well, is obliging, and charges 1*s.* 3*d.* less than the English hotel, which demands $1 50. The other buildings are dwelling-houses, wine cellars, and a shop or two. These establishments, though not rivalling Madeira in appearance, excel them in civility. Moreover, here you have a pretty Spanish dialect instead of a debased *patois* of the debased Portuguese *patois.* The background exposes the lower slopes of partially-cultivated highlands, but, alas! does not afford a view of the "cloud-piercing Peak."

At the upper end of the Plaza, or away from the sea, stands a tall white cross of white marble, to point out the spot where De Lugo, in the bay of Amaza, first planted the symbol of Christianity in Tenerife. The original heavy wooden article is still preserved in the Hospital. Opposite it, and at the other end, is a

---

* It presently came to grief from a suspicion of robbery to the tune of 20,000 dollars from a neighbour.

glaring monument of the same material, "the Apparition of the Blessed Virgin," as she appeared to the Guanche kinglets. Made at Genoa, it is the local Virgin, the San Pilar, the Nossa Senhora do Monte of the island. The Virgen de la Candeleria, so called because the Pagans always visited it on Candlemas-day, rejoices in the following legend, which explains the action of the group. About 140 years before the arrival of the Spaniards, two Guanche shepherds driving homewards their goats, saw at a place called Chimisaya, in the kingdom of Guimar, on the south side of the island, what appeared to them a woman bearing a babe upon her right arm, and all the flock took flight in the wildest terror. Being contrary to their laws to address or even to pass a woman in a solitary place, they made signs to her to depart, and when she would not, one of them proceeded to fling a pebble at her. His arm, at once dislocated at the shoulder, remained immovable. The other shepherd, drawing his tabona, or obsidian knife, approached, and attempted to cut the figure's hands and arms. Instead of succeeding, he wounded himself. The men flying in terror, reported the affair to their Menceyacaymo, who at once visited the place in state. He was astonished at the marvellous beauty of the figure, which was attired in splendid dress, and carried in the left hand a green-coloured taper. The Mencey, determining to do it honour, ordered his nobles to carry it to the palace; but though it was small and light, it waxed— like most miraculous images—of an unbearable weight. The goatherds being then commanded to take it up, their hurts were at once healed, and the burden became a mere feather. It was deposited at Chinguaro in the palace-cave of the troglodyte prince, and all that country-side paid to it divine honours.*

When the Spaniards conquered the island, this image fell into their hands, and in 1539 the Emperor Charles V. committed it to the Dominicans. They placed it on a grand altar in a convent which they had built near the original cave, in a miserable hamlet down the coast called after the Virgin, Candeleria. The order became enormously wealthy, and many a miracle, *teste* the "History of the Canary Islands," by D. Juan Nuñez de la Peña (Madrid, 1676), was performed accordingly. The little image of dark red wood, hardly four feet high† and very mean, though the work of angelic hands—so the Delphic poetry of the God of Verse appeared always dreadfully prosaic—was loaded with pearls, and the green-painted candle was replaced by one of pure gold. Its end was τραγικωτατον. On the 7th November, 1826, a long-remembered hurricane or cyclone burst over the island, sweeping battery and monastery, chapel and image, into the sea; and though long watched for, it has never thought proper to reappear. Most probably it was mortally offended by the dwarfish Demon, Constitucion,

---

* A similar tale is told of the Christ of Ponta Delgada, in the north of Madeira, to which many pilgrimages are still made. One can hardly help envying folk who can content themselves with such a faith of dry bones.

† In the upper and lower folds of the dress were numerous Roman initials, of course profoundly mystic, which caused great discussion, but which were never conclusively provided with words.

which, in 1821, placed in deposit the wealth of con-
vents and nunneries. Melancholy to relate, heretics will
opine, judging from three or four nail holes in the
back of the image, that it was nothing but a ship's
figure-head cast on shore, and say the same of the Christ
found by fishermen off the Ponta Delgada. In the
marble group, which dates from 1778, the Guanches
are very respectably attired in tunics and buskins, after
the fashion of "Moorish" prints in the days of the
"Lettres Persannes:" they have still the usual comple-
ment of noses, although those "dementos," the mid-
shipmen, will mutilate them to revenge the Fox. The
obelisk still bears in large letters Plaza Real, which have
not wholly been obliterated, and the fine monument is
spoiled by mal-position. As regards the Plaza, the
fault of the whole scene is want of verdure. All is dry
around, whilst the cindery aspect of the soil above, the
bronzed appearance of the desolate rocks, caused, I
believe, by some epiphyte, and below, the brown terraces
of bare and sunburnt earth, contrast unfavourably, in
the green man's eye, with the *entourage* of Funchal.
But the land is open, the sense of prison vanishes, and
the yellow hue tells of wholesome dryness.

Leaving the Plaza, we turned to the right, and after
threading sundry shady streets, arrived at the Cathedral
of the Conception. It was of course open, so we passed
through the basaltic portico without other ceremony
than the attendance of a guide and a multitude of
small boys—they are impudent as the London juvenile
and the London sparrow—who think it necessary to

favour the stranger with their company. The cathedral is not remarkable in style—the usual bastard Renaissance of trans-European art, built of basalt, with the round Norman arch, and a nave, two aisles and side, a high altar, a retable, a cushion, a table, and an organloft. But here, as in all other churches of the island, the three walls of the building are plain even to gloom, whilst the altar, the chapel, and the end of the church blazed with gilding and silvering. Piloted by a young chorister in the usual magpie suit of black and white, we first visited the chapel of Iago, on the left side of the church; here, planted against the walls, on each side of the cross, in long coffin-like cases, with glass fronts, are the colours of the British cutter "Fox" and her boats, that came to grief in the memorable affair of 1797. It is some satisfaction for the Englishman to reflect upon the native proverb, "If we don't care for Trafalgar, we don't care"—speaking as an Englishman would of a hundred years hence—"for this misfortune." The other decorations are vile pictures and viler statues. The angels were habited in a golden *juste au corps,* with wings and double tunics to match; their heads were surrounded with wreaths of flowers that reminded me of the latest London ball, when at six a.m. milady returns to her "bower," whilst their legs were ευκνημιδες with Moorish buskins like the Guanches of Candelaria.* Nor less did various Saviours and

---

* The anachronisms are the more unpardonable, as authors distinctly describe the Guanche dress, tight coat of grass cloth extendin₃ to the

Dolorosas suffer atrocious agonies at the painter's hands. The organ-loft was bare, "barring" a piano. The Roman Catholic cathedral must sparkle and dazzle, be splendid and sensuous, at once awe and delight the senses; like a race-meeting or pyrotechnics, to be respectable, it must be upon the grandest scale, otherwise it is a failure. There is nothing imposing in tawdriness and bad art, and the sight of first-rate magnificence induces anything but a "prayerful" tone of mind.*

Before leaving the church I was shown an ex-voto tablet certifying that by the good aid of our Lady of Candelaria a French merchantman escaped a terrible storm. The ugliness of surrounding objects brought forcibly to mind the old satirist's sneer,

> " Nec Deus intersit, nisi dignus vindice nodus
> Inciderit."

And the no less pungent saying of the modern,

> " De par le Roi ! defense à Dieu,
> De faire miracle en ce lieu !"

which should be proclaimed with loudest Oyez ! oyez ! oyez ! in every colony that ever came from the Mediterranean.

---

knees, girt round the waist with a leather belt, an outer cloak of goat skins, and a similar cap of skin taken off entire and so placed that a goat's beard hung under each ear to be tied under the chin, and shoes of raw hides. Some also wear bonnets of skins adorned with feathers.

* Not long ago these seven little islands, hardly equal to seven of the smallest counties in England, had 40 churches, 40 monasteries, and 130 hermitages.

After inspecting the cathedral, we wandered about the streets seeking *l'aventure.* The weaker half of the population is a most distinct improvement upon Madeira: fine eyes, luxuriant hair, clear olive skin, and features which are often regular and sometimes beautiful. For those who admire black anywhere except "in the skin," there is nothing more enchanting than the women of Tenerife. Pretty, however, they never are past the age when the *diable* endows them with fleeting charms; they all become either handsome or dead ugly. In England, on the contrary, there are hundreds of pretty women to one beauty—the latter is far rarer than amongst their southern sisters.

> " J'aime le vin blanc, said Montaigne ; Montaigne's friends
> Consigned him and his wine to all the fiends."

Despite which danger, I will confess, that one soon wearies of black eyes and black hair, and that after a course of such charms, one falls back with pleasure upon brown, yellow, or, what is better than all, red-auburn locks and eyes of soft limpid blue. Nothing, however, truer than *chacun a son goût,* and that " *tous les goûts sont respectables.*" Were like to love like, and not to seek in love that contrast which is generally fatal to friendship, our race would presently split up into pigmy and giant, deformed and transformed, in fact, into all the varieties of its canine friends.

The costume of the peasant population approaches the picturesque. As we left the church we met the dama with the mantilla, that remnant of Oriental

modesty, or the *veo preto,* a long flowing black silk veil—
the peasantry seem to prefer white and coloured stuffs—
hanging behind the head, and invariably armed with the
fan, more fatal than the *cuchillo.* The lower classes of
the town, instead of the *manto y saya,* wear shawls or
large kerchiefs over calico dresses, untanned brogues,
and upon the head a fichu or two. A high-crowned felt
broad-brim, such as belong to men, and often two hats,
placed ole' clo' fashion, protected, as amongst the
Welsh, the market women and the gude wives from the
ardours of "that indecent sun." The males had huge
sombreros, shirts and jackets half concealed under a
manta or blanket-poncho, whose embroidered or leathern
collar suggested the burnous, short breeches like Indian
anghirs of brown stuff, or white soutanelles of cotton,
like knickerbockers, and gaiters bandaged up the leg like
the classical Italian brigand, or curious leathern gaiters
like those of Mexico. The priest wore his decent,
womanish robes,—surely the petticoat, like tobacco, has
been adopted in Europe by the wrong sex!—and the huge
antique tile, like a bit of tree trunk, with a hole for the
head. The beggar looked as if one might make a good
sketch of him in his rags, and there was the usual
Spanish nobility in the manta, even although it came
from Manchester. It is the Arab's aba and burnous, the
Roman toga, the Irish cothamore, the Scotch plaid, the
American buffalo hide and poncho, the European cloak.
The dog of the old Spanish masters—which in breeding
lands appears an invention—slunk about the gutters.
The rest of the tableau was filled up with heavily-laden,

ill-begotten, and ill-conditioned camels, ponies, mules, oxen, and half-starved asses, shrinking from a cruel goading with the garote or alpenstock, which has been bequeathed to the Tenerife man by his predecessor the Guanche.

On a rising ground where formerly stood the convent of San Domingo, now stands the market-place, a substantial building like the Sotto Borgo of Pisa. It was late, and business was consequently slack, confined to a few fruits and vegetables; the crowd, though noisy, was small. My companion, a Gold Coast artillery-man, affected to recognise amongst the listeners a gentleman of slaving celebrity. Near, but separated from the market-place by a narrow lane, is the theatre, a neat building bearing the name of Isabella II. The language of the streets was a Spanish, non-explosive as the Chilian, which avoids gutturals, and the women, when not bawling, articulated with a pleasant languid drawl. The sun became hot—the mercury showing 79° F. in the cool house—but the heat was dry, and dry heat never yet injured a sober man.

Returning to the hotel, we breakfasted, *à l'Anglaise*, with tea and coffee, on bream and boga (*Bux vulgaris*), mutton chops, very " skimpy," from a lean goat, and bad fruits; apricots hard as potatoes, figs unripe, and over-ripe pears —the prickly pear, which one learns to admire in the fiery Mediterranean, is here used, but neglected down the coast. The wine was Malaga, unsupportably strong, like cheap port. After feeding we returned to business —the gratification of our wants. Some required cigars.

At the time there were no good 'Havanas in the place, but cigarettes are an excellent investment for those going down South; a stranger can buy eight bundles for two pezetas or twenty pence. Dogs, but not mastiffs, which, if they ever existed, are extinct, form another local article of trade. That preferred is a small white animal, with black nose, apparently broken, like the little pug-" dawgs" sold in Regent Street, and the silky curly hair of a spaniel; they clip the circumoral region and trim the feet of this bastard poodle like his European legitimate brother which the French so often call " lion." The principal merit seems to be the great charm which M. Michelet and his school find in the Parisienne: it consists in being always maladive. The price is about $5. The vendor begins by asking 10, the purchaser by offering 2, and they meet half way. Tenerife also boasts of good "bussocks," which resemble rather those of Egypt and the East than those of Madeira and England. The price varies, according to age and size, from $8 to $12. Mr. Distin had warned the Fernandian Consul that the Canarians are cunning in concealing a disease of the frog. He consequently left £10 with Mr. Richardson, and a request that specimens might be forwarded to him. It was an unwise investment : asses never outlive the year at Fernando Po, and generally they die much sooner. There, as at Accra, it may be truly said that the climate is fatal to a horse, a donkey and a white woman. Mules at Tenerife were found to be much more expensive than their half-brothers the "mokes." When good they

are rarely to be bought under $120, and are pre-
ferred by many for riding. The camels, originally
from Morocco but now raised at San Cerota especially,
fetch the price of mules. They are badly bred beasts,
and very snappish; a muzzled camel-fight is a favourite
amusement. We did not fail to provide ourselves with
Gallos de Pelea, to while away the "similar hours" on
board. The general colour of the birds is dark, with
red or yellow hackles, clear eyes, and bright golden legs.
They showed uncommonly good blood: one was killed,
and the other fell a victim to the cruel climate of Fernando Po. The price is according to fancy; these cost
£1 per bird.

My labours at Santa Cruz concluded with a visit to
Mr. Parkinson, then Her Majesty's acting consul; and I
was accompanied to the beach by Mr. Bartlett, son of
the consul that preceded Mr. Murray. Both were
obliging enough to be catechized as travellers will.

The produce of Tenerife was, in 1812—15, from 8000
to 11,000 barrels of wine, before the wine disease fell
like a blight upon the island. There were eight or
nine kinds, but all inferior to those of Madeira. The present exports, which are trifling, comprise corn and various
cereals, goats and cattle, cochineal and orchilla. There
is a good printing-press and two newspapers, the Eco do
Comercio and the Guanche. Three English families
only are permanently settled in the place: Messrs. David-
son and Co.; Messrs. Hamilton, agents to the African
Steam Ship Company; and Messrs. Richardson, of the
English Hotel. Either this island or its neighbour, Gran

Canaria, may look forward to better days,—if, at least, they consider an influx of strangers to be a blessing. At present Tenerife is connected with the mother country by a weekly vessel from Cadiz;* of these visitors two proceed onwards to Havana. It is also connected with England by two lines, the English African Steam Ship and the North African Companies, each of these monthly.† About every six weeks there is a merchant steamer from Marseilles. And there is an extra colonial vessel which carries strangers to the neighbouring islands.

I should greatly prefer Tenerife to Madeira. Madeira is a prison, and a cockneyfied prison: a prison in which you meet "Town" to boot. Guide-books may expand themselves in the gorgeous guide-book style, upon excursions, rocks, and sailings to Cama do Lobos, Homem em Pé, Porto Santo, and Deserta Grande,—all places within or almost within cannon-shot. But even the guide-books cannot deny that there is an ennui in the Isle of Wood which passes show. Tenerife also is quiet and dull, with a witness. There are many old Spanish families, descended from the victors and settled in the island since the days of its conquest. Unhappily the *sangre a zul*, though gifted, according to no easily

---

* The Spain and Canary line leave Cadiz on the 7th and 27th of each month, and leave Tenerife on the 14th and 29th: the voyage occupies four days. The Havana steamers touch at Santa Cruz on the 15th and 30th, when outward bound, but do not touch on return.

† The steamers start from London, *viâ* Lisbon, Gibraltar, Mogador, and Grand Canary, reaching Santa Cruz on the 20th of each month: during yellow fever they are not sent.

pleased witness, with graceful courtesy and a kindly absence of etiquette, rarely mingles much with the *petite noblesse,* or the less-aristocratic strata of society; and it has, I need hardly say, learned to stand aloof from the tourist. The common people are by no means so polite, but they are more independent, and are a finer race than the Madeirans. Santa Cruz does not yet, it is true, possess any of the comforts and conveniences of her northern neighbour. *En revanche,* she has the charm of semi-orientalism, perfect liberty, and an utter absence of Bond Street and May Fair: good enough in their place, but sadly misplaced outside the White Cliffs. In the Canaries there is less confinement; the neighbouring island can always be visited; and during the three summer months, June, July, and August, there is the Pico do Teyde,—the world-known Peak.* The dripping cavern near Ycod,

---

* During the other months it is closed by ice and snow, with which it supplies the island. Its altitude, 12,176 feet above sea-level, wants little of the line of perpetual snow, in that latitude 12,500 feet; yet in places, as for instance the Cueva de Yelo, or Ice Cave, 11,085 feet above sea-level, congelation lasts through the year. The routine ascent is made in two days, the travellers sleeping at an estancia *en route.* It is easy, as the road can be ridden along for the greater part of the way, and can show little danger, as the ladies of Tenerife have often succeeded in climbing it, and in singing songs on the topmost Piton. Like the Camaroons Mountain, it still slumbers, but it is not dead.

Of course there remain only details of exploration, where MM. Webb and Berthelot have done the general, and M. Arago the social science; where Mr. Piazzi Smyth (1856) laboured at photography and astronomy, and which is constantly visited by enterprising men. The Peak, it will be remembered, was the opening scene of Humboldt's labours in 1799, and suggested to him laws touching the geographical

said to connect sea and peak by a tunnel 8 miles long, and 11,000 feet of rise, still calls for exploration. In fact, the whole cluster teems with varied beauties and curiosities. As for climate, the air of Santa Cruz is drier, brighter, and therefore more wholesome for consumptives, than that of Funchal, and the average heat in summer does not exceed 90°, nor does wintry cold fall below 60° (F.). At Santa Cruz there are thirty to thirty-six days of rain to seventy-one at Funchal: Tenerife, moreover, has many climates, enabling the consumptive patient to escape the vicinity of the sea, which often makes him wretched. Every one remarks its elasticity, purity, and invigorating properties. The vale of Orotava, known by its Dragon-tree, if by nothing else, lying on the northern side of the island, has an average of 5° warmer than Madeira, whilst Santa Cruz is about 3° less than Orotava. But before invalids can resort to Tenerife, much must be done. Beyond being a free port, Santa Cruz offers no inducement to strangers, who, after being worried and cheated in all directions, find an utter absence of all the comforts of life. To establish an hotel on a proper scale would ruin any individual: it could only be undertaken by a company; and I am not sanguine that even this would succeed. The Spaniards seem not to court the influx of strangers.

distribution of plants. His admirable descriptions sent forth clouds of scientific travellers to all quarters of the globe. Here the geologist, Von Buch (1815), developed his "magnificent" theory of craters of elevation. In botany, also, the "gifted Swede," Christian Smith, succeeded Humboldt, and fell a victim to the ill-fated Kongo exploration.

It would hardly be gracious to leave Tenerife without some notice of its old inhabitants the Guanches. *En passant* let us remark that the sentimentalist who cries shame upon the ethnologist for theoretically " wiping out at his caprice whole nations of brother men," can here find many traces of a race completely extinct. The term Guanche is erroneously applied by the uninitiated, the Rev. Thos. Dubary (Notes of˙ a Residençe in the Canary Islands, etc. London : 1851), Dr. Pritchard (Researches into the Physical History of Mankind, book 3, chap. 2, etc.) included, to the natives of all the Canary Islands.* The earliest and most correct writers limit it to the people of Tenerife. Secondly, it is generally supposed that the islands all spoke one language : this is the theory of old Clavijo, and in later years of M. Berthelot, who opine that a great number of common and proper names, as well as local denominations, beginning in Te, Che, and Gua, were equally used in various islands and even in the entire Canary group ; whereas, on the contrary, their dialects, according to ocular witnesses, were mutually unintelligible. Thirdly, the theory is that the Guanche language

---

* The people of Tenerife, according to Glas, called themselves Vinchune, which the Spaniards corrupted into Guanche. Etymologists explain it thus : ''The inhabitants of Tenerife called themselves Guan (the Berber wán), one person, and Chinet, or Chinerf, Tenerife. So that Guanchinet meant a man of Tenerife, and was easily corrupted to Guanche." In Glas we find mentioned a "Captain Artemis," who defeated De Bétancourt. By adding Guan (*i.e.*, wán) we obtain the word Guanarteme, a chief ruler. Clavijo's vocabulary contains only forty-four words.

was Berber.* I cannot but think, despite the high authorities in favour of such hypothesis, and the peculiar formation of the feminine in the names of ancient and modern places, that it was a somewhat less distinctly marked Semitic tongue, like those prevailing in the corresponding latitudes on the eastern coast. Had it been decidedly Semitic, the Spaniards, of course, would have understood it; but a Meccan cannot comprehend the romances of old Himyar on the eastern coast of Arabia, much less an Abyssinian or a Galla. In the Canarian we have Sesette, Satti, and Tamatti, signifying 5, 7, and 8: these are Semitic, but less near the original type than the Berberan, Sedis, Set, Tem.† Again, in

---

* See Royal Geographical Society's Journal, vol. ii. p. 172, "Ethnological Remarks on the Original Languages of the Inhabitants of the Canary Isles. By Don J. J. de Costa de Macedo, Perpetual Secretary to the Royal Academy of Sciences at Lisbon;" with a learned terminal note by the Editor.

† In the paper above quoted (p. 181) M. de Macedo remarks, "Among the numerals of the Canary language there are some that resemble the Berber and the Shulúl; but there are others also that are entirely different ; and that is sufficient to show the disagreement of those languages. If the identity of two languages could be formed by a resemblance between some of their numerals, the Portuguese and the German might be shown to be the same." Did the learned Secretary forget that Portuguese and German are the same in origin, —cousins german, both branches of the great Indo-European family ?

I differ also *toto cœlo* from the author who asserts that " Languages do not change their physiognomy, and are not corrupted except by contact with other languages and by an augmentation of the wants and commerce of the people who use them." The manifold dialects of Upper Hindostan, all descended palpably from one stock, and the confusion of tongues in East Africa, prove how powerful is isolation and a total want of communication in modifying man's speech. Even the English factories can teach this lesson.

Tenerife, we have many words beginning with al and ben, as Almogaren,—El Masjid, — Bencomo, — Bin Kaum—the latter a proper name. In the case of Benicod, or Benycod, it is only fair to suppose that it means Son of Ycod, probably the chief who founded the present town of that name in Tenerife. The Canarian Faycan, Faycag, or Faycayg, again, meaning priest, is palpably Fakih : whilst Kabeheira appears to be Kabír.

There is much of interest in the life-like accounts left by the earlier Spanish writers of the poor Berber goatherds, the doomed race that passed away four centuries ago. They were forward savages, who knew how to cook meat, avoiding our modern European abomination—gravy. They held it base to injure the women, children, and houses of worship of the enemy : their form of marriage was polyandry. They had a nobility that never had condescended to cook, or to tend, milk, seize, steal, or kill cattle, or to insult the weaker sex. They had, like most barbarians, a constitutional government, holding Sabor or councils in the squares before their caves, called Tagoror.* They were fond of fatness in women, and crammed their hides with gofio, the Moorish Kuskusu; leanness, I may remark, is a sin never forgiven by southern men. They tried causes

---

* In Glas, however, "Tagaror," and in Clavijo "Tagoror," we are informed by M. de Macedo, is a Tenerife word signifying properly not a place of council or punishment, but an assembly, tribunal, or ajuntamiento, whereas *sabor* was applied to the "supreme council of state," where important affairs were determined upon, and criminals tried and punished. Clavijo, however, uses "Tagoror," also, as the place of meeting.

before a jury of twelve, and they fought duels, or
rather prize-fights, with obsidian bowie-knives, till the
spectators cried *Gama! Gama!*—" Hold! enough!"
They had ordeals, nuns (Magadas), and nunneries
(Tamogantin Alkorak, *i.e.*, houses of God), and they
recognised the right of sanctuary. Helotage, cuissage,
prelibation, and pucelage were not unknown. Their
treatment of the corpse shows a queer but interrupted
connection with Egypt, even as the Camaroons and Fer-
nandian peaks are cognate in point of botany with the
Abyssinian highlands.* "Ganigos," or pots of milk,
were placed for the use of the dead. According to the
islanders, there were as many as 200 mummy caves,
and specimens are still found in malpaises, the desert
parts of the island. I heard of a peasant who lately
discovered the body of a child, beautifully sewn up
in kidlike mortuary-skin, and beat it to pieces, not
knowing that its value was at least $50. But my limits
warn me that it is time to refer the reader to the fountain-
head : Pierre Boutier and Jean le Verrier, Ca da Mosto,
Viera y Clavijo, Nicols, Gomara, Galindo, and Nuñez de
la Peña.

---

* The Guanches wore a peculiar cylindrical coral-red, black, or
other coloured bead. If this prove similar to the Popo or Aggri bead
of the Gold Coast and Bight of Benin, it is another Egyptian peculiarity, inimitable to all other races. It is said (but I believe erroneously) that clay pipes, like those found in the Irish kistvaens, have
been met with, proving that the aborigines smoked tobacco or some
succedaneum. The Dragon-tree (*D. draco*) of Orotava is generally
derived by naturalists from the East Indies; but why go so far when it
is to be found in Morocco upon the Somal Coast and on the islands of
the Socotra ?

Before leaving Tenerife I have still something to say —historical and literary.

The city of Santa Cruz is now much stronger than it was in A.D. 1797. How three or four martello towers that could have been shelled with ease, and a wretched sea-wall that trembles with salutes, whilst the whole southern seaboard affords the readiest means of disembarkation, could have given Admiral Lord Nelson so complete a "whipping," it is hard to explain. The reader will remember that the great sailor, after an attempt upon the treasure-ships off Mexico, attacked Santa Cruz with four ships of the line, three frigates, and the "Fox" cutter. The Commandant, General Gutienez, was about to yield, when Captain Troubridge, landing to the south of the town, marched to the Dominican monastery, which he seized. According to local statement, Gutienez was persuaded to resist by a young sergeant, Manuel Cuera. Captain Bowen, R.N., who was to act as guide, was killed whilst disembarking at the Mole, Captain Troubridge was permitted to retire, and Nelson was obliged to withdraw, after losing his colours, his arm, his boats, and some 250 of his best men. The attempt on a stormy night, when the surf broke fearfully, was ill-judged in the extreme; yet it brought the hero—who expected, by the bye, utter ruin—1,000*l.* per annum, the Bath, and the freedom of the cities of London and Bristol. The only gratifying consideration in the affair is the gentlemanly behaviour of both the enemies after the battle. The Spaniards, with whom we are ever on better terms in war than in peace, gave every Englishman a loaf of bread and a bottle of wine; and Nelson took home for General Gutienez a despatch informing the Spanish Court of the victory which their soldiers had won over himself.*

The life of Nelson, like that of Washington, has still to be written; but who will do it? Who dares to set before the public a faithful portraiture of all the frailty and meanness, vice and folly, greatness, splendour of spirit, and high superiority over the herd of men which characterise a Napoleon, or even a Nelson? And *cui bono?* say many. Here is a man who has taken official rank as a British naval hero—has not his life been written in classical English by Robert Southey, Esq., LL.D., Poet Laureate, etc., etc.? Better *quieta non movere.* Has not the book been published by John Murray, Esq., of Albemarle Street? What the deuce would you do more? For my part, I would know the truth; I would see published the copy of verses written after the battle of Copenhagen, and hear more of a journal lately printed. Lord Holland,•Captains Hunter and Foote, Miss Williams, and Mr. Ruskin, wrote at a season when no one could hope for an impartial hearing,—who could then demolish a popular "sea-king" that died exactly at the right moment? The worst of these conventional biographies is, that the world derives from them no moral hints. So it is with History. Although *quocumque modo scripta delectat,* I have lived long enough to see *that* is written; and to the best I prefer, with the learned Frenchman, the mere novel, because that

* Santa Cruz has thrice beaten the English. In 1657 Blake lost 500 men before San Cristobal. In 1706 Admiral Jennings also failed.

splendidè mendax pretends to be true, whereas, with equal claims to veracity, this owns itself to be fiction.

There are two literary works which caused no small excitement in, and amusement to, the island. The first is that of a *savan's* brother, M. Jacques Arago, " *Voyage autour du Monde.*" "I had almost said the wisest literature in Europe"—Mr. Thackeray's dictum touching French authors—certainly does not apply to the works of this *littérateur.* As is his people's wont, he kept his right eye upon Paris, and, *naso adunco,* he looked out upon the world with his left, whilst his intense Miso-Albionism made him often blind of the mental optic. The speeches and dialogues are mythical as those of the Homeric heroes; and he does not hesitate to falsify History and to sacrifice Truth upon the altars of patriotism and prejudice, picturesqueness and *couleur locale.* His adventure on board the pirogue "Espagnolo" is a caricature; his amourettes with *une trentaine de jeunes filles* is a farce; his conquests here, there, and everywhere, are a Gallic dream. The Spaniards naturally deride the following conversation which took place between M. Arago and the Consul de France at Tenerife :—

"M. le Gouverneur (D. Pedro de Laborias) ne sait pas écrire," says the traveller.

"Non," replies the Consul.

"Et son secrétaire ?"

"Il ne sait pas lire."

"C'est différent ! De pareils hommes représentent une nation!"

A little further we find a prophecy too false for a Tangier Jew. "Ténérife m'offrit bientôt un spectacle plus effrayant encore (than Gibraltar). C'était toujours une Espagne, mais une Espagne sans avenir, parcequ'elle luttait sans énergie contre les maux présents qui l'écras aient. Ténérife mourra vaincu par un brick de guerre; ou écrassée sous une colère de son volcan. On s'échappe de Saint Croiz comme on fuit le cadavre d'un reptile a demi-putrifiée, et Saint Croiz pourtant est une capitale." With respect to Nelson's failure, M. Arago sagely remarks, "Qu'un de nos amiraux y soit envoyé; il n'y laissera ni ses vaisseaux, ni ses soldats, ni ses drapeaux, et nous aurons l'île." I am not aware that French admirals usually succeed when Englishmen fail: in fact, there are some cases to the contrary. If I remember right, the French admiral, Du Guai Trouin, landed, in A.D. 1711, at St. Vincent, and was beaten back by the unarmed inhabitants with stones; and, of course, M. Arago, when proposing a gun-brig to capture Santa Cruz, forgets a certain place called Saragossa, where the flower of the French army was

" Foiled by a woman's arm before a broken wall."

And now—after this galimatias raisonné—of the other work, which caused even more excitement than the former.

It is called "Sixteen Years of an Artist's Life in Morocco, Spain, and the Canary Islands."* Unfortu-

---

* In two vols. London : Hurst and Blackett, 1859.

nately there is very little of art in it, and the places visited
are only Tangiers, in Morocco; Gibraltar, Cadiz, and
Seville, in Spain; Tenerife and Grand Canary, in the
Fortunate Islands. It is hard to write a book upon
such trite paths. "A vagabond from a baby," the
authoress left, without date, England at the age of
eighteen, stayed nine years at Tangiers, and quitted it
when her husband was appointed Vice-Consul at Tangiers, August 30 of 1841. Positive ideas are easily
formed at the age of eighteen, but even ladies should
be expected to correct them a little later in life. The
characteristics of the book are a fine appreciation of
neighbourly shortcomings: all "catch it," Moroccans
and Spaniards, French and English; and attempts at
speculating upon abstruse subjects which call to mind
the old lines,

> "What a pity that beautiful women
> Talk of what they don't understand;"

or unpolite Dr. Darwin's definition of feminine communication,

> " Hear the pretty ladies talk,
> Tittle tattle, tittle tattle;
> Like their pattens as they walk,
> Pittle pattle, pittle pattle."

And the pity is greater when, as in this case, and
that of Mrs. C. M., an Anglo-Indian authoress ("Six
Years in India," Bentley, 1857), the unfortunate person
least concerned in the book—I mean the husband—has

to endure all its pains and penalties. One year after the publication, the authoress was transferred to Portland (Maine) ; and her enemies, left to tell their own tale, declare the book was written to punish those who had been backward with their hospitality.

We learn, however, from it a few things. That the beauties of Morocco are "generally idle, good-natured, gossipping, and frivolous, possessing—in fact, all those small peculiarities of character that distinguish women in our own Christian country." That "in Spain generally, and in the Canary Islands, the religion which thinketh no evil, and that delights in doing good, is unfortunately at a very low ebb." After a glimpse at Cadiz and Seville—where the time seems to have been spent in a low boarding-house—and a more extensive experience of Tenerife, the lady pronounces upon Spain and the Spaniards, their character, customs, religion, and institutions. This is what the foreigner does who judges England by the standard of Leicester Square and Sierra Leone. We are told that the Government employé is a perfect pest, besides being no better than he should be — besides, does he not despise trade, commerce, merchant-princedom? That "the Peak of Tenerife is more than 15,000 feet above sea-level." That "the faith of the people in various absurdities of divination is irresistible ; " as if united Europe would not show ten times as much superstition !—as if the lady had never heard of Halloween and Co. ! That the "primitive people of the island is a race of beastly savages." That every girl has a novio or lover; and that the authoress was tempted to rebuke one who denied the soft impeachment with "tell that to the horse marines !" That a " disgraceful system of peculation, of oppression, and of robbery has long been the disgrace of Spanish officials." I think we will stop at this point.

Returning on board about noon on Monday, 2nd September, we banged a gun, shook hands with the strangers, and stood out for blue water. Passing southward we saw the wash of the waves at a place where, on the 12th June, 1857, the African steam ship "Niger" was wrecked. Beyond it lies the Castle of San Juan, with the lazy little Spanish windmills guarding that entrance to the town. The low ledge of seaboard now showed an inclination upwards to a ridge, distant about three miles, and some 1500 feet above sea-level. It is crowned by Laguna, the abbreviation of San Cristobal de la Laguna, for three years the capital of Tenerife. The tall spires and white houses leading to this Citta Vecchia glistened in beautiful contrast with the blue waves at our feet. A ribbon denoting a broad road ran straight up the acclivity through a land of corn-fields, and cactus plantations, with occasional quintas and an old fort. Nothing green there met the eye save shrubs standing singly or in small clumps ; but we were in the depth of the dead season. Beyond this ridge of yellow wavy ground were alternate "backs" and gullies with serrated edges, an iron land, in long perspective, visible only when we had placed some distance between us, with intervals denoted only by tints, blue-brown below, blue-pure above, less and less distinct. Here there

was none of the scene-painting flatness which the
limpidity of the air usually gives to such views. Fore-
shortened to the eye from our ship's quarterdeck, the
Guimar Hills rose above one another till they culminated
in the shoulders of the Atlantean Peak. Apparently
upon, but situated behind the dome, is a dwarf projection distinctly visible: a mere inch represented a
basial circumference of more than two geographical
miles, and 537 feet in height : — few would suspect
that in this smooth inch they see that mighty mass at
whose base the toil-worn traveller pauses, and after
surmounting four-fifths of the mountain, finds his heart
quails at beholding a " 'Pelion upon Ossa piled,' so
stern, so stony, and so steep !"

As the afternoon advanced, wreaths and fillets of
fleecy pack, like the purest lambs' wool, floated upon
the head of Nivaria, which rose steeple-like above the
huge ridge representing its church—a wintry land in
this sub-tropical summer — whilst upon the waving
stream-like lava beds, once liquid now solid sheets of
rock, and destined to be the sites of fertile fields, the
burning sun poured its unclouded rays in a prodigal
shower of light and colour, and purple became blue,
and blue, a cerulean stone grey, till distance hid from
our eyes one of the masterpieces of Nature's work,
one of the world's great landmarks, and a pyramid of
condensed vapours looming out of the sea, upon the
verge of the northern horizon, was all that remained to
us of Tenerife.

CHAPTER IV.

9TH SEPTEMBER.

" The grave,
Dark and untimely, met my view."

Leyden.

TUESDAY and Wednesday were stormy days. We
had passed out of the south-west, which becomes a
surface-current somewhere about 40° north lat., and
had entered the region of the north-east Trades : they
at first appeared in unlovely guise, or rather they
yielded to the southern blasts. The sea had the long
roll of the ferry-line between L'pool and Boston, U.S.
Mother Carey's chickens—who is the old party, and
where does she roost ? — flitted about our wake, the
rain drizzled from time to time, and Æolus took liber-
ties with our mizenmast. On Wednesday, the 4th, the
Trades assumed their wonted aspect—a hot sun, contrasting with a crisp cold wind, that caused Neptune's flocks
to gambol over the long ridges rising from the cool
green plain. The firmament appeared high above our
heads—as we enter the tropics it will be lowered, and
the sea will exchange its present bright and lively
aspect for the eternal monotonous roller of the Atlantic

Ocean. We had reason to believe that we had quitted the parallels, north of which, according to the Sons of Albion, health and comfort have made their homes. Noon of the same day saw us abreast of Cape Blanco, to Northern what Cape Negro is to Southern Africa. The only remarkable events in its life are its being named Ganaria Extrema by Ptolemy, and its being re-discovered by one Gonçalez Baldeza in A.D. 1440.

We are now plunging deep into the tropics, and on Thursday night we had our first tornado. It is seldom found in these latitudes at this season, but it had been brought up by late southerly gales. There was nothing new in it but the name. The phenomenon is absolutely the same in Eastern as in Western Africa,—an embryo hurricane, but of shorter duration and inferior violence. The word is corrupted and usually derived from the Portuguese *tornado*, "returned," alluding to the sun reced-ing from the tropic of Cancer; others deduce it from the Spanish *torneado*, "thunder," or *tormenta*, "a storm," in Portuguese *trovão*, or *trovoada*. I should rather deduce it from some bastard Italian word, making it synonymous with the cyclone, or circular storm of modern days. Its most remarkable feature is its returning over head, or walking round and re-attacking from the oppo-site quarter. The usual time is before and after the rains, when the electrical conditions of earth and air undergo important changes. The tornado season shares with the African year, the rains, the smokes, and the dries. Its greater frequency near and upon the ocean, and the fact that it generally appears after hot sunny weather, reminds us of the old electro-chemical theory, that storms arise from the disengagement of electricity by the evaporation of sea-water. On the other hand, the aspect of the atmosphere, and the swiftness of the movements, suggest that the high tension of rolling wind-driven clouds, disengages electricity by friction. Very distinct warnings appear, sometimes for hours, in a suffocating sultriness—a deep stillness and silence, as if Nature was preparing for the fray. This is easily felt, and forms the best guide. Barometer and aneroid are here, unless scientifically observed, of little use—so uncertain, that the severest atmospheric derangements hardly affect them to the extent of half an inch. During the paroxysm the mercury and the aneroid hand move with little tremulous jerks up and down, and at the end there is a slight rise. Meanwhile a dark cloudbank settles upon the horizon, perhaps opposed to a sun burning in clearest air, and there are dark flashes of lightning, so distant, however, that their reports are inaudible. Some remark that this gathering is more frequent at the turn of the tide. Now is the time for making all snug on board. It may be too late when the arch has distinctly formed, and however threatening be the aspect of the heavens in other directions, it must be borne in mind that the tornado invariably sets off the land. I have never seen the " ox-eye," as the older travellers call the nucleus of the storm. It always appears to me to rise from the horizon in the form of a rugged arch, outliers of unattached cloud, and dark pendent edges, which, however, become more regular as they draw nearer. At this stage there is often a peculiar haziness not unlike a fog in the atmosphere. As the huge arch, often 100° long, rises towards the zenith, occasionally setting backwards and forwards, the vista of sky which it discloses, showing the want of depth in the cloud bank, is of a ghastly yellow hue, or sometimes a pale dead grey. Presently there is a cold blast, the arch moves forward with portentous speed, the sea shows a line of black or steely blue where it passes, and all know the tornado is "down upon them." It sometimes bursts so suddenly, that boats cannot take in sail. A few more such gusts, often quick and successive, accompanied by many-hued lightning, rosy, yellow, red, white, and blue, and either zigzag or globular, bring on the crisis. The firmament is now a sheet of vivid flashing fire, with chains of electricity which seem to shoot into earth or sea. In one case I distinctly observed the direction of the zigzag to be from the earth upwards. The crushing rolling thunder sounds unearthly, like the clash of brazen clouds or the encounter of huge metallic bodies, without half a second's interval from the parent flash, and incessantly repeated to the terror of all creation. Meanwhile the ears are deafened by the rush and roar of a mighty wind, perhaps the most awful sound that awful nature knows. The trees are twisted sideways like natural vanes as it were. There is a curious correspondence in the number of *rafales* or gusts; another peculiarity is that there seems to be no shelter from the tornado; even under a tall cliff it will blow as if the place were

exposed to it. And that nothing may be wanting to
the terrors of elemental war, a big drop of rain announces another presence; another and another succeed,
and in a minute, before cloak is ready, rattling torrents
of tropical downfall—now

Blown all aslant, a driving, dashing rain,

then, like a falling wall of water,—beat down the
highest waves, or flood the surface of earth. After a
pleasant twenty minute, the fury of the fiery element
begins to subside; the rumbling sound, distinctly perceptible along the ground, ceases, and the livid sulphu-
rous flickerings, like a huge furnace, are apparently ex-
tinguished by these water-pots of the Danaids. Heavy
sullen rain, a pitiless pelting, with occasional gusts and
long pealing thunder-claps, often solitary, and totally
unlike aught heard in temperate regions, ensues, and
after a total of forty minutes, there may be a dead calm.
One draws breath after such scenes; perhaps trees are
torn, houses are unroofed, mud huts are thrown down,
bells are cracked by sudden contraction and expansion,
and vessels are driven from their moorings. The phenomenon appears to be very local,—hardly perhaps five
miles in breadth,—and in some places tornados will be
seen to blow in different directions, both well within sight.
Often also, after working round to the opposite or fair
quarter, they re-form upon the horizon, and once more
extend to the zenith. They are sometimes double, one
following the other from the same direction, as if the
first had not thoroughly exhausted itself. They are not

without danger. During my first year in West Africa I was on board a ship when she was struck by lightning; on another occasion I had a narrow escape from the fluid; and on the third, the wind blew down a large tree top, that fell close to my sleeping hammock. Those that occur at night in the height of the tornado season can hardly be described without an apparent exaggeration. They must be seen and heard to be understood.

Our first tornado, however, was mild. During the fury and acme of the outburst the waters boiled as if an earthquake or a volcano had shaken them, and compelled us to put in the deadlights, under peril of swamping. The thunder and lightning were not worse than many storms that I have seen in England ; nor was the rain at all remarkable. On the next morning, however, all was still, the sky cloudy, and the atmosphere damp and warm like a steam bath, and this appears to me to be the rule. According to Dr. Madden, a tornado has sunk the mercury 10° F., others have observed 20° F. It was probably only a temporary change caused by wind and rain. Our initiatory specimen afforded none of those " exquisitely delightful sensations " which, following these battles of the elements, render them at Sierra Leone a matter of hope rather than of fear. Perhaps however, they are more beneficial on the outskirts of the tropics than near the equator.

About noon on Friday, the 6th of September, we sighted in the offing Ovedec, or Cape Verde, rightly so called,—the discovery of Diniz Fernandez, A.D. 1446. It is the Trafalgar, the westernmost point of Africa, 17° 3′,

from the meridian of Greenwich. At first appeared the
Two Paps, upon the taller of which the authorities of
Senegal have erected a lighthouse. Presently, from
beneath the horizon emerged dots which formed a long
low line of green vegetation. As we approached, the
true Cape appeared, with its outline the Almadies rocks
—a ledge mostly sunk, but here and there rising above
the foam in wicked-looking diabolitos, or black masses,
of which the largest is a die-shaped slab. The Two
Paps are brightly green and well wooded; their sea-
wall is a precipice, which apparently drops sheer into
the wave, and in places patches of yellow sand line the
base. We are now on the threshold of tropical luxu-
riance, which in Western Africa extends South from
the Senegal river (N. lat. 16° 30'), whereas in the east
the arid region of the coast reaches to nearly the
equator.

The distance was of course too great to sight on the
right hand the Cape de Verde Islands, which, according
to some, are the Insulæ Beatæ, beyond which the
ancients had no certain knowledge of Africa ; others
make the Cape the Hesperian Keras, and apply this description to the island :—" Contra hoc promontorium
Gorgonis insulæ narrantur Gorgonum quondam domus
bidui navigatione distantes à continento." (Plin. lib. vi.
c. 36.) D'Anville places them among the Bissagos.
This, then, was the austral extreme of the world, of
the whole world to civilized man 450 years ago. The
islands are salient points in the geography of the eastern
Atlantic, sterile, grim, with serrated ridges and isolated

peaks sometimes 8000 feet high, and their formation points them out as continuations of the great Sahara. As we advanced we were visited by birds and butter-flies, wasps and mosquitoes, from the humid regions around this Green Cape, the western Prasum Promontorium. We then steamed by the little green-capped rocks called the Madeleines, and after another hour a curtain of coast, opening before us, disclosed the red citadel and the subject town of Goree, the Gibraltar of West Africa. It lies twelve hours from Bathurst, and was once a mail station : presently however it ceased to pay. The site is a volcanic island, ditched and defended from the shore by the respectable Dakar Strait, some 3000 yards broad. At our distance we could see but four vessels lying in the excellent roadstead to the north-east of the settlement. It has a semaphore, a good quay, and fine stores, principally built by French soldiers, who receive extra pay. Its garrison is 600 marine infantry. The governor ranks below him of Senegal, but he reports direct to the minister at Paris.

The word Goree is clean forgotten in England ; per-haps even the humorous and talented gentleman who penned the following passage would have difficulty in telling you exactly its whereabouts.

" Here is a placid-looking little old man, trotting briskly down John-street, Tottenham-court-road. He is about seventy, apparently, but walks erect. He has a natty little three-cornered hat, a well-brushed black suit, rather white at the seams, grey silk stockings, and silver buckles in his shoes. Two powdered *ailes de pigeon*

give relief to his simple good-humoured countenance,
and his hair is gathered behind into a neat pigtail,
which leaves a meandering line of powder on the back
of his coat. His linen is very white, so are his hands,
on one of the fingers of which he wears a ring of price.
He lodges in a little street in the neighbourhood I have
mentioned, pays his rent regularly, has frequent friendly
chats with the bookstall-keepers, to whom he is an
excellent customer, and with whom he is highly popular;
pats all the children on the head, and smiles affably at
the maid-servants. The neighbours set him down as a
retired schoolmaster, a half-pay navy purser, or, perhaps,
a widower with a small independence. At any rate he is
a pleasant body, and quite the gentleman. This is about
the close of his Day. Would you like to know his Night?
Read the Old Bailey Sessions paper: ask the Bow-street
officers, who have been tracking him for years, and have
captured him at last: who are carrying him handcuffed
to Newgate, to stand his trial for murder. His double
was Governor Wall, Commandant of Goree, who was
hanged for the murder of Sergeant Armstrong, whom
he caused to be flogged to death; very strongly adjuring
the negro who inflicted the torture to cut the victim's
liver out."

A mystery clothes the place—even the 'cute Mr. P.
of Philadelphia has failed to explain it. In 1831 it was
in miserable condition, now it is in first-rate order. It
is an outpost of the colony of Senegal, where the French,
agreeably to their custom, have organised a powerful
military force of 2500 European soldiers, and 8000

native auxiliaries, with a squadron of thirteen steamers, to ensure mobility, many of them Crimean gunboats, and highly effective for river navigation. The object is of course to shake hands with Algeria, to link the North African possessions with their future conquests south of the Sahara, and eventually with the rich mineral lands lying eastward of Senegal; and already the territory almost equals Algeria in extent, with a directly subject population of 100,000 souls. Goree connected by an electric wire with St. Louis of Senegal, the head-quarters, is of use to vessels delayed by the river bar; and Senegal will, of course, be the first base of all operations intended to work northwards and eastwards.*

The English hug themselves in the idea that the French are bad colonists—much on the principle that one Briton can always beat three Gauls; if so, France, like China, is improving. Algeria, Senegal, and Siam ought somewhat to modify our opinions. She has still one grand fault—an excessive bureaucracy, which of course engenders a rage for over-government; this is transient. In the days of Louis XIV. the principle of non-interference in commercial affairs was recog-

---

* The Senegal river is navigable, even during the dries, for 200 miles above the military posts, Richard Toll, and Daganna. One hundred and thirty French leagues in straight line from the mouth lead to the Fort St. Joseph de Galam, whose palmy days will be now renewed. It was founded in 1697 by the Sieur de Brue, Director-General of the French factory. He ascended the river 600 or 800 miles, and on return offered with 1200 men to annex the mines of Bambúk, which had so profitably been worked by the Portuguese. The French Government refusing, stout-hearted De Brue applied himself to the gum trade.

nised, and will be recognised again. She now requires a fleet, which will always keep up the colonies, and an outlet for her army—Madagascar or Mexico—which will ever provide fresh conquests. She begins on the right principle by sending her best men, naval and military, to her colonies. She shows her force, and impresses the natives before proceeding to treat ; she educates the children of the chiefs, and compels her lieges all, under a penalty, to speak French.* This warlike imperial colonial policy contrasts strongly with our Quaker-like peacefulness ; about Gambia the natives have sneeringly declared that they will submit to the French, who are men, but not to us. And the large establishments at Goree and St. Louis have, of course, drawn away from us the Gambia trade. France now extends her arm to the falls of the Senegal river. She first beat the Fulas, once so bold, and then she organised and gave flags to them. She has checked the incursions of the Moors upon the gum-gatherers of the Sahara. This new policy was inaugurated in 1854.

St. Louis, the capital and centre of this warlike colony, lately commanded by that distinguished soldier Colonel (now M. le Général) Faidherbe,† is not fortified,

* The "Ecole des Otages" was founded at St. Louis about 1855. It instructs some twenty youths, the sons of the principal native families ; after two or three years, they receive command of a canton, or, if they distinguish themselves, they may complete their education— as did the son of the last Queen of Walo—in France. There are many primary schools for children of all classes, and the marabuts, or learned Moslems, are bound to send their pupils once a day to these French institutions ; a measure not yet extended, I believe, to Algeria.

† This officer has commanded six years in the Basin of the Senegal,

but it boasts of fine buildings, of which the most remarkable is the military hospital. The city contains 15,000 souls; as many as forty ladies, the wives and daughters of civil and military officials, have been seen at a single ball. The works are superintended by French soldiers, who can labour where an Englishman would drink himself to death. The colony has a perfect little army. The commandant can take the field with 2500 troops, armed with double-barreled rifles, and 1500 will appear upon the Champ de Mars. The force consists of one regiment marine infantry, one corps black Voltigeurs, and two French batteries of light field artillery, 6-pounders, drawn by mules, whilst 100 spahis, mostly convicts, are mounted as lancers, and dressed in fez and burnous. Besides these, are the trained native auxiliaries.

Since 1854, under undue competition, the trade of this colony has greatly fallen off; nor will it recover till there is less of protection and of interference. At present the revenue of Senegal and its dependencies is—

Customs (2 per cent. ad val.)   . . . £12,000

Other sources   8,000

and has published in the "Annuaire du Sénégal pour 1861," an account of his proceedings, beginning with the early hostilities in 1854, and ending with some twenty treaties of peace, concluded between the strangers and the natives. During his government, admirable surveys of the country have been made, and French travellers have penetrated to the Western Sahara, the mountains of Ardran, the oasis of Tagant, the Brakna and Bambûk countries, Futá-Jalo, and the sources of the Senegal river. English and French commerce are now running a race towards Timbuktu. We may hope to reach the goal *viâ* the Niger, our rivals *viâ* the Senegal; but unless something more be done we shall lose the day.

Giving a poor sum total of £20,000 against a yearly expenditure of £160,000. The yearly exportation, according to the *Journal des Debats*, is upwards of thirty millions of francs.

The exports from Senegal are ostrich feathers, ivory, and gold (in 1860 equal to £2450), hides, horns, and live cattle, wax, palm-oil, gum Senegal, which has declined from 40 to 18 sous per lb., and ground nuts— better than those of the Gambia, because cleaner, being handpicked and not threshed. Of the latter article, Bathurst exported in 1860 about 10,000 tons; Senegal some 1588. But the former was or became principally French property, and the next year told a different tale of proportion. Cotton grows spontaneously, and the people collect it for their own use. The local "Admininistration" offered in 1860 some forty centimes per kilo for uncleaned stuff—an excessive price. There were some hopes of inducing English capitalists to embark in the affair; but, as the *Journal des Debats* justly remarks, "Ils se sont retirés, probablement pour la même cause qui ferme nos colonies aux étrangers : la difficulté d'y fournir des établissements agricoles, et de gouverner leurs affaires comme il leur plâit, en se conformant aux lois générales."

Ninety miles beyond Cape Verde, and a total run of 950 knots, placed us at the mouth of the Gambia river. We are now about to land in the Guinea region.

The word is *sub judice*. According to Barbot, it is derived from Ginahoa, a province north of the Senegal, and the first Negrotic region discovered by the Portuguese, who then extended the name to four-fifths of the coast; but is there any such place? Others propose Ghana or Ghina, the modern Kano, an Arabo-Sudan Empire, which was wholly unmaritime. Others advance the claims of Jenne, Jennah, or Jinne, the Moslem commercial emporium south of the Niger. It is called by early travellers the Land of Gold, which was there brought by the Mandengas and the Moslems of Bure. Others take it from Jenna, a coast town, once a place of note governed by an officer under the king of Gambia. There are objections to all these theories; but, at any rate, the word is a reality. In 1481-2 D. John II. of Portugal assumed the style and title of Señor de Guine, and the English applied its name to a coin.

As the West African coast has few barriers or distinct divisions, the limits of Guinea are laid down apparently arbitrarily by every writer. Its utmost bounds have been from 20° north latitude, to 20° south latitude, afterwards the extent of Sierra Leone jurisdiction, bounded, in fact, by Senegambia and the southern coast regions. In the fifteenth century it seems to have comprised the country between the mouth of the Gambia river, north latitude 13° 30′, and Angola 10° south latitude; yet an old map in my possession, dating 1558, restricts it to the region immediately north of Cape Palmas.* Bosman (1700), describing Guinea, begins

* Fac-simile. "Africa, extrahido do Atlas MS. feito por Diogo Homem em 1558, existente no Museo Britannico: publicando pelo condo de Lavradio em 1660."

with the west of the Gold Coast, and leaves his reader
at " Cape Lopez di Gonsalvez " as the uttermost point
of Guinea and its gulf, Angola beginning south of it.
Others divide the coast into North Guinea, or Nigritia,
between the Senegal and Gambia rivers, where the
Daradi- Æthiopes occupied the lands of the present
Mandenga ; South Guinea Proper to the Jamoer or
Camaroons river, or according to others to the Fernan
Vaz river or Cape Lopez, the lands of the Achalinces
Æthiopes, and lastly, Western or Lower Æthiopia, the
country south of Cape Lopez, and belonging to the Hes-
perii Æthiopes. For Ethiopia, which originally signified
all Africa south, south-east, and south-west of Egypt,
has been extended by the moderns to the whole south;
eastern Ethiopia bordering on the Indian Ocean,
Western Ethiopia on the Ethiopic or South Atlantic
Ocean. In our maps Northern Guinea is the name
still given to the region bounded west by Liberia, east
by the Camaroons mountains; Lower Guinea from Cape
Lopez to S. Paul de Loanda.

The limits mostly adopted by modern writers, who
divide Guinea into Proper or Upper, and Lower, are as
follows :—The former, the northern, extends from Cape
Verga in 10° 19′ north latitude, with a coast-line of
2000 miles, to CapeLopez in 0° 36′ south. This would
comprise the various divisions of Sierra Leone ; the
Three Coasts—Grain, Ivory, and Gold—and the three
bights, Benin, Biafra, and Pannava or Pannavia.
Others, with more correctness, prefer to Cape Lopez
the Camaroons mountain in 4° north latitude as the

southern limit; that gigantic pile forming a barrier between lands greatly differing in geological formation, population, and polity. This reduces the coast-line to 1500 miles. Lower or Southern Guinea thus commences either at the Camaroons mountain or at Cape Lopez, and stretches to Benguela in 16° south latitude. It is also known as Southern Ethiopia. Popularly, the three Bights are excluded from Guinea, which would thus consist only of Sierra Leone and the Three Coasts, a line of about 1800 to 2000 miles. No one has attempted to lay down an average inland depth for Guinea. It is inhabited by a number of tribes still little known; and in these days it is a word of little use; rather a name of literary curiosity than one of convenience. There is no such kingdom, and there never was; moreover, the term is utterly unknown to the natives. In modern naval parlance, the littoral is portioned out into three divisions—the northern, from the Senegal to the Bights of Benin and Biafra; the Bights division; and the south coast, from Cape St. John, in 1° 9′ 7″ north latitude, to 20° south latitude.

The annals of European and English progress upon this coast present little of interest beyond a succession of dates and names—perhaps the only reliable part of history. Suffice it to say, that the first settlement by white men was, according to general belief, the Castle and Fort of St. George, afterwards called Elmina, built in 1481, and made the head-quarters of the Gold Coast. For about fifty years the Portuguese monopolised the field; and, to use the quaint language of Bosman,

" served for setting-dogs to spring the game, which, as soon as they had done, was seized by others." Such is popular history, copied by one author from another. At a future time I will discuss the subject of French priority of claim to discovering this coast, and the counter-arguments of Portuguese writers.

From sunrise the sea had changed its blue for a dull, dirty, muddy green; and the leadsman ever sang out, " by the mark, nine," and " by the deep, ten." Low land loomed on both sides, with tufted mangroves, often based apparently upon the waves, showing that we were entering an estuary; and the channel soon narrowed from seven miles to three. " Gambia " is said to mean clear water, surely a misnomer, it is as muddy as the Mersey. As we approached the land, the sun burst through the thick yellow swamp-reek and the dew-clouds with a sickly African heat. Far to the right, in the Port St. Mary, stood a whitewashed building upon a dwarf red cliff. On our left, the river's proper right bank, was Fort Bullen, an outpost on a tongue of land dead-green as paint, and scattered with tall Ben-tangs (*Pullum ceiba*), or bombax trees. This silk-cotton differs greatly in shape from its congener in Eastern Africa. The bole is thorny, the buttresses are larger, several trunks rarely anastomose, the branches seldom stand out horizontally, nor are the leaves disposed in distinct festoons. It is everywhere, however, a noble tree, useful for shade, and supplying the people with canoe materials and a poor cotton. At Fort Bullen, which is about one hour's row from Bathurst, there is a

detachment of one officer—alias Commandant and Governor of the Queen's Possessions in the Barra country—
and seventeen men. The place is by no means wholesome,* and there is no high ground within reach.

Another half hour placed before us Bathurst in full
view. It suggested somewhat the idea of a small
European watering-place, and contains barely 5,000
souls. The site has none of those undulations which
render a place picturesque; everything is horizontal,
straight-lined, and barely above sea level. Beginning
from the westward are a few detached houses, a colonial
hospital, a military ditto, the Governor's quarters, large
barracks—upon whose turret floated, or rather depended
the flag of St. George, the market, the slaveyard,
and the esplanade, behind whose line of trees lay the
mass of the settlement. The houses might be those of
Byculla, Bombay—in fact, they date from the same epoch
—large uncompact tenements, washed glistening white
or yellow, with slates, tiles, or shingles, which last curl
up in the sun like feathers. Further on are heaps of
native huts, like beehives, or a crowded rickyard, rising
from swamp and sand, and terminating abruptly up the
river. There is an Octagon, not a concert-room or chapel,
but a coal depôt, and there are two one-gun martello
towers at the angles of the fort looking towards the

---

* Capt. Hewett ("West Africa," chap. xvi.) says it is the most
healthy spot in the river, but that is not much. I like Capt. Hewett's
book, though critics and reviewers have treated it badly : it tells the
truth bluntly, especially upon such ticklish subjects as the liberated
Africans and the slave trade.

town, which may relieve the view, but which look anything but dangerous. A nearer glance shows the house walls stained and gangrened with mildew; a fearful vegetation of Guinea grass, palms, plantains, cotton trees, and caoutchouc figs, which at a distance resemble whitethorns, occupies every inch of soil, and the inundations of the river sometimes find their way into the ground floor. In fact, the island and settlement of St. Mary (of old a cemetery) seem to be selected for unhealthiness, for proximity to mud, mangrove, miasma, and malaria.

The island is an elbow about five miles long by two broad, bounded eastward by Oyster Creek, a lagoon-like branch of the Gambia River; westward by the main mouth of the stream. It is an island within an island; the latter, also called St. Mary, is the northernmost of that mass of continental islands which, formed by the Gambia and the Cacheo River, extend south to the Rio Grande.* It is, in fact, the delta of the Gambia, and is marked in most maps as the "Combo," "Forni," and "Feloop" country. St. Mary-the-Less is a mere strip, a sandpatch, which potent heats and tropical rains clothe with a vivid and profuse vegetation. Water may everywhere be found three feet beneath the surface, but it is brackish and bad. There is hardly any versant,—in places the town is below the level of the river;—excellent brick sewers have been built, but the rains prefer to sop the soil. And lest the island be

* Explored about 1446 by Tristaŏ Nunez, who was killed, probably for kidnapping.

gradually carried away, there is a penalty for removing even a pailful of sand from the beach.

Bathurst was unknown in the days of Park, when traders went up the river to Jilifri, nearly opposite Fort James, and Pisania. The site was bought from the Mandenga chief of Kombo—a small annual tribute, still paying,—together with the land called the English "mile." First called Leopold, and presently Bathurst, after the minister of that name, the actual town was built in 1816, under orders of Sir Charles Macarthy, after whom an island in the upper stream has been christened. The settlement, designed for the use of liberated Africans, was erected by Lieutenant-Colonel Brereton and Captain Alexander Grant. In 1821 it was made, like Cape Coast Castle and the Gold Coast, a dependency of Sierra Leone, whose jurisdiction, after the last of the African companies was abolished, extended from 20° N. to 20° S. Now it is an independent government. Like all European settlements of that date, the site is execrable and the buildings excellent.

We anchored off Brown's Wharf, one of the dwarf stages of woodwork whose principal use seems to be that of affording standing-room to the juvenile piscators of Bathurst. When the mail bags were gone, we received a visit from the Postmaster, who, in default of the sick health officer, allowed us pratique. We reflected severely on the excessive "cheek" of questioning the health of new comers from Old England, when the chances are that all the Bathurstians are dying of dysentery and yellow fever. A facetious second mate,

who always spoke of his eye as " she," pointed out to
me with a grin a small gathering of bullocks and buffaloes—the latter word used here for all cattle with
humps—declaring that he had never seen so much meat
at a time, a pig and a pumpkin being the usual supply
in the Bathurst market. He also recounted how a
friend, having employment and salary here, had left the
place after a month on account of the indecent size and
fullness of the cemetery. Near us lay H.M.S. " Dover,"
a neat little steamer, which had lately been repaired,
almost at the expense of a new investment : theoretically,
she carries the monthly mails to Macarthy's Island;
practically, she is found more useful at head-quarters.
Certainly no settlement on this fatal coast should be left
without the means of ready escape. The old " Albert,"
of Nigerian celebrity, and immortalised as one of the
ill-starred three which brought Captain Trotter's expedition to grief, lies in a ruinous state on the left bank of
the river. After her palmy days she was bought by
Government for colonial and mercantile purposes, and
an annual allowance of 2000*l.* was granted for repairs.
She died probably of grief from the abuse heaped upon
her by the Rev. Mr. Poole.*

The wind was rough, and the Bathurstian sharks are
vivacious ; as usual, the knowing beasts will not touch
feather nor rise at bait in harbour. We proceeded

---

* Life, Scenery, and Customs in Sierra Leone and the Gambia. By
T. G. Poole, D.D., Colonial and Garrison Chaplain of Sierra Leone.
London : Bentley, 1850. The grant alluded to above will be found in
vol. ii. chap. 6, and those following it, describing Mr. Poole's ascent
of the Gambia in the ill-starred "Albert."

hygienically to lay in provaunt before landing, and whilst thus engaged we were visited by sundry officials —Dr. Martin, superintending surgeon; Dr. Sherwood, colonial surgeon; the military store-keeper, Mr. Keane; Mr. Deputy Assistant-Commissary-General Blanc, together with his aide, an old *compagnon de voyage* of "the consul's," Mr. Fryer. Mail days are holidays at Bathurst, as in other places " down coast :" these gentlemen breakfasted with us, and hospitably invited us to their quarters on shore. It was drizzling rain; this, however, did not prevent us. At St. Mary's the seasons are simplified to two—wet and dry. The former, which is considered the more unhealthy, especially in the towns, begins in June and ends about mid-October ; November being a fine month. The latter rounds off the year. As usual in Africa, the most dangerous period is during the drying up of the waters, when the vegeto-animal matter deposited in the swamps and hollows by rain and river is being distilled into miasma. The wettest months are July, August, and September. On the 9th August, 1861, there fell in twenty-four hours 9·12 inches, measured by pluviometer, and half the island was under water; on the 22nd July and the 4th September, the fall was 3·50 inches. The lowest temperature is 62° (F.), but only when the high, dry harmattan, or east wind, blows from the Desert. The hottest months are March, April, and May, especially the latter, when the thermometer in the shady upper gallery of the hospital will show a maximum of 99° (F.), very near the point—100° (F.)—when a man has a right to begin complaining of heat. For nine

months in the year the wind blows from the west, with
some northing and southing; yet "windward" at Bathurst means N. N. E. All throughout the coast there
are periodical clearings off of the white population. In
1859, about six months after Sierra Leone had lost half
its number of Europeans, all died except those that
could and would run away. And, after looking at the
settlements—no wonder!

We transferred ourselves from boat to shore upon the
miserable wharf, shaky piles driven into the sand and
planked over. We walked up the main street or esplanade, a broad promenade, with avenues of trees and
drains of masonry, rendered necessary by the deep loose
sand. There are several streets, upper and the lower—
which run parallel with the beach—and they are connected by cross lanes. The decayed look of everything
around, except the vegetation, impressed me painfully.
The multiplicity of useless walls, the clumps of trees,
and the greensward faintly suggest the idea of a semi-
deserted single-regiment station in Western India. Our
first visit was to the Commissariat, a roomy and substantial edifice of stone and lime, with large open verandahs, here called piazzas, lofty apartments, galleries, and
in fact all that an African house should be. Billiard
tables and other comforts and conveniences are not
wanting. I remarked Elands and Koodoo's horns, and
learned that they came from the upper country, where
there is everything of venery, from the sandpiper to the
lion—which is common—the elephant and the hippopotamus. The sport around Bathurst is reduced to water-

fowl, partridges—larger, stronger, and more finely pen-
cilled than the European—a few antelope and "harness-
deer." The town abounds in the natural scavenger, the
galinazo, or turkey-buzzard, and a large species of the
same kind. Our gallant captain bought a fine specimen
of the true Egyptian ibis for a dollar. Here and there
the tall, ill-proportioned Maraboo crane, moping, melancholy, and with shoulders hunched up, ugly as a
pelican, but wearing precious feathers on his back,
squatted upon his leg joints, and looked particularly
stupid.

After a few minutes of "second breakfast," as it is
locally called, at the Commissariat, we walked through
the drizzle to see the town and the townspeople. The
latter at once attracted my attention, and I found no
difficulty in distinguishing at first sight Moslem from
Kafir. The principal tribes, besides the Gipsy-like
Fula, and the wild, half-naked pagan Jolu, are the
Mandengas and Wolofs. The former, anciently called
Mandingo, is a race of gentlemen and horsemen. I was
surprised by their points of likeness to the Somal, who
dwell about the same parallel of latitude on the East
African Coast*—the long limbs, especially the fore-arm,
tall lithe figures, high shoulders, small heads, and semi-
Caucasian features. There is the usual African pecu-
liarity in the toilette,—no two men are dressed alike. The
costume is picturesque : a Phrygian bonnet, glengarry, or

---

* The Mandengas inhabit a triangle, whose base is the line from the
south of the Senegal to the Gambia, and whose apex is the Niger, even
extending to near Timbuktu.

liberty cap, of dark indigo-dyed cotton, and sometimes
the kan-top, or ear-cap, of India and Hausa, surmounts
their shaven heads. When travelling, they wear, as
usual all down this coast, "country umbrellas," like the
Malabar fishermen's hats, a thatch of plaited palm
leaves, shaped like a parasol, with a central swell and an
umbo or boss for coolness and dryness. The body dress is
a long kamis (shirt) of white or blue longcloth, and wide
but short trowsers, like those of European women.
Over all is thrown a sleeveless burnous, or half-sleeved
Tobe, garnished with a huge breast pocket. It is seldom
white, more often indigo-dyed, with broad and narrow
stripes of a lighter tint than the ground-work. An essential article is the taawiz, or talisman, locally and barbarously called gri-gri; a Koranic quotation or
mysterious diagram enclosed in a roll, or in a small
square of morocco leather, hung round the neck, and
attached to various parts of the body. Of these pro-
phylactics, which answer to the little cross and the
medals blessed by the Pope, a serious person will wear
some dozen—a whole volume disposed about his
limbs. Contrary to the rule of Moslems generally, they
honour workers in iron and leather; the king's black-
smith and cobbler are royal councillors. So the barber
of the "Great Mogul" was a personage of exalted rank,
none other being worthy to be entrusted with the imperial nose and throat. Most of the men carried knives,
daggers, and crooked old sabres in leather sheaths—a
practice which should never be permitted in Africa;
natives entering a military or a civil station, should

always be compelled temporarily to leave their weapons with the policemen at the nearest guard-house. The Mandengas returned a ready w'alaykum el salaam to my orthodox address. The Wólof, as M. Koeller writes the word, anciently spelt Joloff, Wolof, Yaloof, and Yaloo, respond Jammagam to the Tobaubo, or white man's Jammagam. They are more like the Abyssinians than the Mandengas are, and are remarkable for good looks, ringlets, and tasteful toilets and ornaments. This small maritime tribe is interesting and civilisable ; many have been Christianised, especially by the Roman Catholic missioners.* They are excellent sailors, and have acquired the title of "Jews of West Africa," a distinction which belongs rather to the rascally Akus or Egbas. A Wolof woman afterwards came on board the steamer, clad in a horrid semi-European cotton gown ; she curtseyed, instead of salaaming, spoke a little poor French, and amused herself with spelling out a missionary tract. Their country lies between the Gámbia and the Senegal, and is divided into sundry petty kingdoms, Senaar, Saulaem or Salem, and Ballagh or Baa.

The scene as we approach the neat market, "Albert," and dome with zinc or iron roof—built by Governor O'Connor—becomes amusing. Men and women sit under the tall cotton trees and the stately banyans,

---

* Usually three priests and five Sisters of Charity—a number now greatly reduced. They keep a school, principally for Wolof children, and are very evangelised. Captain Hewett declares that the Wolofs are "seldom or ever converted to Christianity." I believe the contrary to be the case.

selling oranges, limes, and papaws, vegetables of all kinds, especially the Bhendi of India (*Hibiscus esculentus*), here, as in the Southern States of North America, called okra or okros, and making the best thickening for soup; tomatoes, which grow wild upon the coast as in the interior, and form an admirable corrective to the climate, yams, batatas or sweet potatoes, and baskets of ground nuts, with which up the river even the pigeons are fed. There are kola nuts (*Sterculia acuminata*), both for retail in baskets and packed in bundles with bamboo matting—here they are imported and become costly. The live stock consists of a few geese and turkeys, Manilla ducks, the hardest and the most insipid of their tribe, and the poultry, amongst which is the kind with inverted feathers, lately described under the name of arripiada by Dr. Livingstone and by travellers in Eastern Africa. Some of the crowd are spinning and weaving, all, daddies, mammies, and piccaninnies, with an incessant flow of tongue; many are reading what the ignorant but self-sufficient Kafir will tell you is the Koran, but which are really extracts and prayers written in the square semi-Cufic Maghrabi character, which would take a learned Meccan a month to learn; whilst others, I regret to say, polluted by a licence which calls itself liberty, are shamelessly gambling with little sticks stuck in the ground—may their graves be browzed upon by donkeys! Now and then fighting-looking fellows ride past us, with the Asiatic ring-bit and the Mandenga saddle, a heavy demi-pique. The nags are ponies, about ten hands high, thin and angular, but

hardy, and, like most of the equines in this part of
Africa, vicious and quarrelsome. They have no pace
between a lazy lope and a hand-gallop. Yet, with all
their shortcomings, I should prefer them to the diminutive
bastard barb, here called an Arab, which costs from 20*l.*
to 40*l.* : the latter generally dies early from chills, colds,
and checked perspiration, that brings on "loin disease,"
i. e. paralysis of the hind parts, or from the fatal swelling
of the stomach, which is caused by bad food. A dance is
also going on. The M.C., a wild-looking mumbo-jumbo-
like negro, dressed in savage and fantastic habiliments,
scanty pagne or loin-cloth with red streamers, and strips
of long-haired skin dangling from his limbs, prevents by
his superintendence the lookers-on from breaking into
the circle.* The performers are non-professional ; at
times a lady outsider becoming excited, throws herself *en
évidence,* putting "life and mettle in her heels," and with
the upper person to the fore and the lower person
wonderfully disposed backwards, enacts a part which it
it is difficult to ignore and impossible to describe.
Dancing, in the vapid quadrilles, unmeaning minuets,
and romping waltzes and polkas of civilisation, has
lost, it is evident, all its meaning ; for instance, the
cachucha, which the Portuguese borrowed from the
Kongo in West Africa, has been parodied by the
Spaniards and refined by the French into utter insig-
nification. A few boats and some hides cumber the

---

* The mumbo-jumbo of the Gambia is called, as in books, "Horey."
There is also a regular profession of bards and M.C.'s here as in
Senegal, termed Griote or Guriot.

sand, and amongst the heaps stray pretty deer-shaped goats of small size, and gaunt pigs, sharp-snouted and long-legged as the worst Irisher.   We do not enter the market-place, which swarms with both sexes in blue; African indigo affords a beautiful purple dye, but one soon learns to prefer the white clothing.   Dr. Martin, my kind host and guide, warns me that philanthropy is the order of the day in this corner of the white man's cemetery.

Quæ caret ora cruore nostro !

I can read this in the face of the *casimir noir*, alias the "black diamond."   The liberated Africans, principally Akus and Ibos, have begun the "high jinks," which we shall find at their highest in Sierra Leone. They have organised "companies," the worst of trading unions, elected head men who will become their tyrants, effected strikes, and had several serious collisions with the military.   They are in missionary hands, which disciplines and makes them the more dangerous.   The Mandengas, whom Mungo Park characterised as a "wild, sociable, and obliging people," are now spoken of as turbulent and unruly.   And this is to be expected; a race of warriors must be ruled by the sword.   They would themselves prefer military law to all the blessings of a plebiscite.

Under charge of Dr. Martin I visited the military hospital on the west of the town, close to the swamp. The place is murderous.   There is a sick ward upon the ground floor !—one night on the ground floor is certain fever in most parts of Tropical Africa,—and that ground floor is, like the latrinæ and other offices, frequently under water. In the first story the beds are crowded together, each patient having 800, whereas 2000 feet of air should be the minimum. Moreover, in these regions no first story is thoroughly wholesome, unless a free current of air flows beneath it. Jalousies or shutters take the place of glass windows. On the second floor are the quarters of the medical officers, within pleasant distance of an atmosphere fraught with small-pox and dysentery, typhus, and yellow Jack. This caution of a hospital is built to "accommodate" 23, at times it has had 32, and the average may be set down at 12; when I visited it there were 18 fever and dysentery cases. Amongst them was a Malabar Cooley in the last stage of phthisis, and a Bombay native Christian, who, after exhausting the West Indies, had engaged himself as a bandmaster. I was not astonished after going the rounds to hear of 92 deaths out of 96 admissions, and that at times *el vomito* "improves off" everybody. Reports after reports have gone home, but hitherto without effect. Nadir Shah should have sent his director-general, or whoever the "boss" of that department may be, to pass a season there.

After liquoring up—and such is Gambian hospitality that this genial rite forms part of every visit—we again issued forth, to call upon the Colonial Secretary, Dr. Robertson, then in temporary charge of the place during the absence of H. E., who found it advisable to pass the sickly season at Madeira. Thence we proceeded to the barracks, and after passing through pools with which the spouts had invested what in hot weather is loose burning sand, we found Captain Ivey, the commandant of the troops, surrounded by piles of newspapers. The buildings are substantial, of weather-stained stone—a long flat-roofed range of galleried upper rooms, built on arches over the soldiers' quarters, and commanded by a quadrangular tower, which bears the flag and an old weathercock. You enter the doorway and find on the left a black hole, once called an orderly room, now the Brigade Office; the inner part is a patio or yard. There is a bell in a dwarf cupola over the portal, and a clock so artificially disposed that the soldiers for whom it is intended cannot see it without going outside. This and the loopholes have been standing jests at Bathurst. The latter reminded me not a little of the Aden style of fortification, where, after a hard morning's great-gun exercise, the only accident that occurred was the death of our Bhisti by a rebound of the ball. The loopholes look from the road into the barrack-yard, kitchen, and cellar; the enemy will find convenient shelter whilst firing down upon the former, and the friend concealment during his pilfering the latter. Not far from the barracks, and between a battery and a room once, I believe, used as a church, is the powder-magazine, guarded by a solitary sentry, and boasting none of the precautions, moat, *chevaux de frise*, or tall wall, usually adopted when combustibles are heaped together. A little practice enables a people to forget it, even when the air is full of electric fire, and further south the traders have the pleasant habit of storing kegs by hundreds in their bamboo houses. At the moment I write there is half a ton of gunpowder within stone-throw, in a zinc house, with negro fires not twenty paces from the walls. In Africa, as in Asia, circumstances force a man to become a fatalist.

The garrison at Bathurst now consists of three companies (304 men) of the 2nd West: they are thus distributed. Bathurst has 212, Macarthy's Island, 41, Cape St. Mary's, 34 invalids and convalescents, and Fort Bullen, 17. It has been a favourite theory that the Jamaican negro and others withstand the heat and miasmata of Africa better than the white man; the contrary is probably the case.* The semi-civilised African dies of phthisis much more readily than the Englishman; and if exposed to hardship, he becomes, to use a homely but forcible expression, rotten after the first year. In enduring the fatigues of actual warfare he is, I believe, inferior to the acclimatised European. Although negroes have a singular immunity from yellow fever—none were attacked at Sierra Leone during the five epidemics from 1837 to 1859—the small-pox is a scourge to them, and they die like sheep of dysentery and bilious remittent. Recruited too often among the

---

* The "African Regiment," a condemned corps of 800 men once stationed here and at Sierra Leone, died, it is true, in a few months. But they were "the greatest rascals under the sun, the offscourings of the army, and were drunk day and night, sleeping in the dews and drinking new rum, old palm wine, or anything they could lay their hands upon." The officers were "equally reckless and insubordinate," says Captain Hewett.

loafers of the West Indies and the idle vagabonds of
Sierra Leone, the men, though fine sturdy-looking fellows, and, for blacks, well set up, are troublesome
and litigious. Like the Indian Sepoy, they are very
far from being brave. In the late " Badibu expedition,"
the English sailors and marines lost no opportunity of
showing their contempt for them. They wear the
Zouave dress, than which nothing can look better or be
worse. The fez, though aided with white cover and
curtain, defends neither from sun, wind, nor rain. The
thick cloth jacket is a perpetual poultice. The knickerbockers are heavy, clumsy, and thoroughly unfit for
walking through walls of thorn, guinea-grass, and
matted bush. The costume was intended for the latitudes of Morocco, where there are no such obstructions :
it is wholly misplaced here, except on the parade
ground. And even there it might advantageously be
changed for jackets, and continuations of warm dungaree, with turban and curtain outside a stiff felt cap
—cylindrical, if the helmet is considered out of keeping.
At the time of my visit the troops were suffering from
want of clothing, and had to eke out their toilette with
queer succedanea.

After an excellent lunch of pepper-pot, we mounted
for a " marooning" gallop to the old convalescent-house
at Cape St. Mary's, the local sanitarium and out-station
for invalids. Our road lay westward along the ribbed
sea-sand, the only ride in the place. At certain times
of the tide, however, a four-in-hand could be driven
along its hard, smooth surface. I recognised with plea-

sure on the dwarf ledge above the action of the waves an old friend, the familiar convolvulaceous creeper (an Ipomœa), with its bright green fleshy leaves and beautiful conical pink flowers, which everywhere greets the stranger landing on the dazzling white sands of tropical Africa. Presently we passed the burial-ground, concerning which so much has been said. A few tombstones, mostly without inscriptions, are scattered on the sand and in the bank, and they are so near the shore that corpses and coffins have been washed into the sea. If New Orleans be a wet grave, this is dry with a witness, the depth and looseness of the sand making the excavation a mere hole. Three governors are buried in the sand-bank. But matters of climate are becoming too serious to make us linger long about such places or subjects. *Par parenthèse* I may remark that, whilst the French have at Bathurst two or three missionaries, and the same number of Sisters of Charity, and the Wesleyan chapels and schools * muster strong,—whilst there is a fort, a military square, and other such carnal appurtenances; the Established Church of England—even here, to say nothing of Macarthy's Island—has no house of worship, except what was once an officers' mess, and nothing but a colonial chaplain, who knows to *briller* by his absence. After a hand-gallop of about three miles along-shore, we turned abruptly to the left, where a sign-post directed us, and dashed into bush and wood-

---

* The Wesleyans have two chapels, two European missionaries, and a large school at Bathurst, to which Government allows 100*l.* per annum.

land. The road was heavy and deep with sand, which in the dry season must be painfully loose; the rains and decayed vegetation have clothed it with a coat of green. The Guinea-grass,—lower down the coast it will range from eighteen to twenty-one feet high, and each stalk thick as a walking stick,—already assumes tropical proportions; the bush is lush and tall, and the mangrove, though more stunted than Russian birch, which it resembles in leaf, form, and colour, is thick and juicy. Here, as elsewhere, the shortness and obliquity of the grain, and the excessive hardness of the heart, render this wood fit for nothing but fuel. There are three kinds of palms—the cocoa, the date (which, however, does not bear), and the bamboo, or toddy-palm (*R. vinifera*), the latter so abundant that considerable profit, it is believed, might be made by its distillation.* Further on we shall see the noble palmyra. I recognise another familiar form, the baobab or calabash (*A. digitata*), locally called monkey-bread: it is rather man's bread. The people of the interior prefer it to grain, and the flour mixed with milk is extensively used in curing dysentery.† Here, however, the baobab lacks

---

* The experiment has, I believe, been tried, but it failed for want of sufficient supply of the wine. Palm brandy is much used in Zanzibar, and known by the name of Mvinyo. Mr. Poole does not regret the failure, because "we do not require any further addition to the stimulants, which are found to be quite answerable for the purpose of destroying thousands of souls and bodies." But is he not rather a benefactor to his kind, who invents a new kind of enjoyment?

† Mr. Poole, vol. ii. p. 206, is "at a loss to know why these trees bear the name they do." The people of Sierra Leone have a superstition that it attracts lightning, and never build their houses near it.

the huge proportions of the Central African monster,
and its foliage is ragged and irregular, wanting that
parachute shape which it presents on the Eastern coast.
Coming to swampy ground we drew rein; it is full of
crabs, and their holes are dangerous. Some years ago,
as the local legend tells, a doctor happened to lie down,
probably not "impransus," upon this muddy bed, and
in the morning it was found that the crabs had eaten
his eyes. A similar story is told of a merchant skipper
who was devoured by the dogs in his nighting place,
one of the gutters of Constantinople.

Another mile of bush and woodland, here opening out,
there closing in very thick, carried us to Oyster Creek,
the western outlet of the Gambia river, whose fork
forms the Island of St. Mary. Here we found a
small thatched house of lumber, not very clean, but
almost entirely without furniture; it is a kind of Star
and Garter to the Bathurstians, who make Saturday
their great marooning day. We were welcomed by a
"Mammy," that is to say, a fat, middle-aged mulatto
woman, bred and born at Bathurst, and speaking
"Blackman's English." Mammy, the great synonym
for madam, ma'am, mother, wife, is more prettily and
Frenchfully, but ignorantly, written ma'amie; whilst
Daddy, *i.e.*, sir, master, husband, father—at Fernando
Po they call their consul Big Daddy—is turned by polite
authors into Daaie. Around the Oyster house lay piles
of shells, showing that the native meets with appreciation. But in these lands oysters lose half their
significancy. There are two kinds, the little native

oyster, very sweet and wholesome, and the Mangrove oyster, growing upon trees, a phenomenon which, if lengthy description and facetious remark be a test, mightily tickles the fancy of every African traveller. At certain seasons it is believed to be almost poisonous, and old hands always prefer it roasted. The branch is cut off and exposed to the fire, and this not only cooks the animal, but renders knives unnecessary. The Mammy supplied us with fire and water, and we breathed the nags till the ferry came. Oyster Creek is not 100 yards in breadth, nor is it very deep, but the number and ferocity of the sharks forbid swimming this Styx. Presently appeared the boat, a large flat-sided punt, with hand paddles, worked by a Charon and two acolytes. We were accompanied by men and boys returning to their homes on the mainland, and all armed with old sabre blades in elaborate leathern sheaths. We disembarked at last upon the true African continent, which my foot had not pressed for—years. It felt like a return to *dulce domum.*

The scene at once improved : it illustrated on a small scale how much better is the heart of Africa than its epidermis. The last three miles lay over sand and through the usual *mélange* of bush and woodland ; the former, however, thinned out : the swamp disappeared, and as the ground rose, the *coup d'œil* assumed that "park-like" appearance which every traveller, from Bruce to the latest tourist in Africa beyond the coast, has remarked, all using the same word. Herds of fat, round-bellied cattle were browsing upon the luxurious grass : as we passed them on the gallop they scampered away, dislodging from their backs and sides the brown and red "tick-birds" that were rendering them important services. The lovely black Whydah thrush, or widow bird—as vicious a little animal, by-the-by, as any widow that fancy of jilted spinster authoress ever conceived— fluttered her long tapering tail-feathers over mimosas, all golden balls and emerald leaves. Then followed a causeway of cockle shells and a bridge of tree trunks, spanning a younger brother of the Oyster Creek, for which the colony is indebted to the energy of Colonel O'Connor, the governor preceding him now in power. A few late columnar palms, the *Palmyra nobilis*, unerring herald of a finer land and superior healthiness, frequently appeared; and leaving behind us the dreary plain of arid sand and mephitic jungle forming the Island of St. Mary, suddenly, in a most unexpected manner, a turn of the road round a little rise of ground showed us the quarters at the Cape St. Mary. The distance was a total of about eight miles.

We had passed on the road the assistant-surgeon in charge of invalids, and he had told us to make ourselves at home. We therefore proceeded at once to his quarters, where we found whisky and water, and whilst reposing amused ourselves by teazing a little Ambriz monkey, with a blue face and pretty figure; it was gentle and mild tempered, a very angel among the *Simiadæ*. The Health House, or Cape House as it is generally called, is built upon the top of the cliff, ready to catch all the breezes that blow across the broad Atlantic. The

"muster" is that of the barracks and the larger
houses in the town, but though no expense seems to
have been spent in building it, the neglect of a few
timely repairs seems to have brought it to untimely
grief. I was charmed with the site after the horrors of
St. Mary's Island. A wonderment seized me—how
long will it be before the Europeans of the settlement
remove to it *en masse?* Those opposed to such change
—and such a man there will be in every place, probably
even in Inferno—declare that the roadstead is bad ; bad
however as it is, all own that those of Cape Coast Castle
and Accra are as bad, and that the bays of Lagos and
the "Oil Rivers" are twenty-fold worse. They comment
upon its dullness, the difficulty of obtaining provisions,
and the want of books, which can be procured only from
the Military Library. But were the barracks established
here, dullness would disappear, at least as much as from
the town, provisions would appear, and it is easy to
subscribe to Mudie's—a proceeding which, apparently,
has not been dreamt of by a soul save myself in the
slow lands of Western Africa. All is still redolent of
the times of Adamson, Phil. Beaver, and Mungo Park.
Madras is called the benighted Presidency of British
India. I propose for West Africa—where all things,
ideas, living, literature, commerce, are at least half a
century behind other colonies, from old Newfoundland
to new New Zealand—the *sobriquet* of the Dark Coast.
I begin to think that the antiquated horror of Western
Africa, which methinks is really but little worse than
Western India, will soon pass away from the memory of

the British public, which is wax to receive and marble to retain such prejudices.   Then, as a consequence, hygienic science will readily discover fitting residences for the white man; and then, but not till then, the mines of African wealth, from which we now content ourselves with picking up the fragments, will be effectually and thoroughly exploited.

Leaving the convalescent quarters, when Jocko's temper could stand it no longer, we proceeded to inspect the vicinage.   Our first visit was to a tattered old Bungalow, which Dr. Martin had, upon his own responsibility, hired to accommodate six privates and a sick officer—after the fashion of the Crimean nurses, I put him last—half-dead with fever from Macarthy's Island.   This butt-end of the habitable world, a swamp, six miles by four, derives its name from the late Sir Charles Macarthy, whilome governor of Sierra Leone, who in 1823, by the mistake of his ordnance-keeper in bringing up biscuits and macaroni instead of ammunition, was beheaded by the Ashantis at the battle of Assamacow, and whose name is still sworn by on the Gold Coast.*   The island in

---

* The native account of this event may be read with amusement : it is extracted from Mr. Zimmerman's "Sketch of the Akra or Gu language.   Stuttgart, 1858."   It is a fair specimen of the Gold Coast histories, and was probably published because it gives but a poor account of the English General :—

"*The War of Asamangkao* (*Assamacow*).

"Wherefore the Ashantis with MacCarthy (Governor of Sierra Leone) made war the reason is this : it is said, that an Ashanteman came to Cape Coast to buy things; and when he went to the market, he saw a woman selling stink-fish, and he said unto her : 'Thy fish, how much one ?' And she showed him the price.   Then the

question is situated some 180—200 miles up the
Gambia,—our charts give a direct distance of 110,

man said unto her (saying) : 'Take some off for me !' And the
woman said : 'I do not take off.' — In that time the Ashantis
ruled over the Cape-Coast and Akra-people. Then that same man
said unto her : 'I do not pay thee any more at all, but I take
it by force !' And the woman said unto him : 'Then thy master
which is in Ashanti, he buys the fish for me' (*i.e.* he will pay it).
Then the man said unto the woman : 'Why sayest thou so ?' Afterwards the man began to scold her, saying : 'Thy master who is in
Europe, Osei (King of Ashanti) says of him : He shall come and ——'
And the woman also told him : 'And also thy master who is in Ashanti,
the King says : He shall come and ——' Then the man said : 'Why
sayest thou so ?' and he began to swear that the woman shall be caught
and brought to Ashanti. And the woman ran off to the fort and told
all the things which the man had done unto her. And the man went
off to his town and told it ; and Osei let him be caught and killed,
saying : 'Wherefore he let himself not be killed there ?'

"And Osei sent his messengers down, that the woman may be delivered unto them ; and the Cape-Coast Governor also did not allow
that she was delivered. When this thing happened, the Governor
wrote to Europe, saying : 'Well, this matter has happened !' And the
King also wrote a letter to the Danish King ; and this also wrote a
letter to the fort here, that powder and lead may be given out. And
the English King also despatched a vessel with warriors and captains.
Their chief-captain was called MacCarthy. When MacCarthy came, he
had thousand soldiers ; these all were good warriors. He went off to
this war, and when he went he met with an old woman in the way, and
this old woman told him : 'Master, I beg thee return first ; for the
warriors thou leadest are not enough ; rather return to seek some more
to them ; for the Ashantis are too many.' MacCarthy expressed himself, saying : 'Oh ! these my warriors fit me, that I will fight with
them.' And he went off and fought with them. When they had
fought a long time, then MacCarthy's powder was done. And
the Fantis which had gone with him to war, when they saw that
their powder altogether which they carried was done, they began
to cry, 'Our powder is out !' And as the Ashantis and the
Fantis all have one tongue, they could hear what the Fantis said in
their camp. Then the Ashantis got strength and destroyed them as

and an indirect of 170,—a river so tedious and slug-
gish that the tide can be felt for 170 of its 300
miles. It is, however, the key of the interior, and a

clay. Now if MacCarthy looks how the Ashantis deal with him and
that also his powder is done, he with all his people draws the sword
and meets the Ashantis face to face for a long time. Afterwards,
when there was no more, then he wrote a letter and gave it to one of
his servants to bring it to Cape-Coast Castle, that they may give him
powder ; but when the messengers returned, and the boxes were opened,
they were full of pieces of meat and biscuits. The reason of this was :
those to whom the letter was given were in a hurry when they gave
the things to those who had given them the letter. Afterwards, Mac-
Carthy sent again, and the same was brought. When MacCarthy be-
held how the Ashantis were fighting with him, and that also he did
not get powder, he said unto his Captains and all whom he had gone
to war with, saying : 'Our powder is done, and the Ashantis also are
fighting with us in this way, therefore whosoever wish it may help himself.' Then he himself withdrew himself backward, leaned against a tree,
drew with his hand a pistol and killed himself. So he had the pistol
in his hand and leaned against the tree. And while he leaned there,
if the Ashantis were coming near him, they were afraid, because they
thought he is alive; but at last they perceived that he was really not
alive, but dead. And they took him up, and cut off his head and brought
it into their camp, and took out the brains, and the skull which was
left they sewed into his uniform and filled it with gold, and himself,
the whole body, they roasted and brought him to Ashante. The fat (of
him) they boiled into a lump, and his heart they divided and ate. In
this same war they caught MacCarthy's trumpeter, and upon fear they
commanded him to blow, then he blew, and when he blew, the soldiers
who were not there when MacCarthy shot himself ran and came to the
Ashantis, thinking that their captain was there, and were killed. And the
head which they brought to Ashante has become their fetish which they
worship till this very day.

"And MacCarthy himself of whom we speak here, he stood on the
place where he had stood till the time when his powder and provision
was done, and he did not flee at all until his death."

N.B.—There is no proof that Sir Charles Macarthy shot himself;
but under such cases suicide would be considered by the natives the act
of a man of honour.

depôt of trade, without which Bathurst would soon see an empty market. Consequently we maintain there, in the most tattered of forts, two officers, two assistant-surgeons, and forty-one men. In 1837 and 1839, bilious remittant deepened to yellow fever at Bathurst and Macarthy's Island; in 1860, the medicoes died off in rapidest succession, and the non-professionals, out of decency, followed suit. A " place of wealth and beauty "—as the local poet calls Bathurst—and a hot-bed of disease, like Macarthy's Island, require a Sanitarium, and the only one within reach is Cape St. Mary. Let us therefore hope that the medical big-wigs will not wig Dr. Martin, or deduct from his pay abstracts the rent of the little hovel.

We descended the green and grass-grown cliff by a winding path, which once more reminded the Consul of a previous landing at Mbuámájí, in the land of Ham. By the wayside was a deep well; the water, however, had turned out brackish. Standing below upon the smooth white sandstrip—the shelving of the shore keeps sharks at a distance, and allows a delicious bath—we could discern the formation of the cliff. The facing was a red sandstone conglomerate, about seventy feet high, and large fragments, which had slipped within the action of the waves, had been sunburnt, and honey-combed into the semblance of laterite. The little bay had a shallow depth, and the further horn was covered by a ruined pile. No fear of pythogenic fever here! It is open to the westward, with 200 miles of ocean to purify the gale which hence passes on to unhappy Bathurst, laden with the miasmata of the intervening swamps. Finally, "the Doctor," as they call the morning sea breeze in these lands, is regular and strong, whilst the dangerous land breezes of night are rendered almost innocuous by the rise.

Under the guidance of my indefatigable host, I then proceeded to inspect Bakau, or Bakhs, the Mandenga hamlet adjacent to the Cape House. The country was nobly wooded with the baobab and the palmyra, and from several of the trees hung those hollowed logs which the African still finds the best of beehives. There was a less pleasing suggestion from the number of deserted ant-hills that cumbered the ground. Usually the settlements are strongly palisaded with an outer *chevaux de frise* of stout pointed sticks, firmly fixed in the ground, and at an interval of some feet there is an inner row of upright paling—defences equally needed against the leopard and the two-legged marauder. Here, however, under the shadow of the Cape House, no such precautions are necessary. From the bush we passed directly into a network of little lanes and alleys, a labyrinth formed by the hut walls and the stakes of the compounds. The habitations are of haystack shape : the thatched roof neatly finished off above with a kind of top-knot, and descending to within two feet of the ground, forms ample shady eaves; and the cylindrical body of the abode is either of red tamped and sun-burnt clay, the neatest bamboo basket-work, or split tree-trunks. The entrance, sometimes single, at others double, is always low and narrow, that the

interior may be too dark and cool to invite the mus-
quitoes and land-flies which infest the houses of Europeans; the door is of stakes or canes, a mere make-
believe.

Everything in the building was familar to the
African traveller—the central fire upon the floor, the
rafters shining with smoke, the calabashes, and the
raised bench and mats which form the sleeping appa-
ratus. The venerable matron upon whose privacy we
had just intruded was spinning yarn, like a good old
English lady in the good olden time. By her side
stood a sturdy boy *in naturalibus* cleaning cotton; the
stuff was of poor quality, but not so short-stapled as
the East Indian, which Humbug seems determined to
force upon us, despite the conviction of its valueless-
ness. In the compound—a rectangle, fenced with
stakes, five or six feet high, with transverse sticks and
split stalks between—was a slave girl pounding grain,
with a pestle like a verandah post, in a mortar composed of the lower trunk of a palm. The material was
Guinea corn—Panicum, the Indian Bajri—locally called
"Kus;" the larger Guinea corn, Holcus Sorghum, or
Jowari, is also used. Europeans have learned the use
of these grains, as the favourite "coos coos luncheons"
of St. Mary's prove.

We then proceeded to the house of Tappa, an aged
chief, who has some repute in these parts. Everything
in the village was known to me, as though I had been
born in it. Here is the mosque, circular, of wattle and
dab, with extinguisher roof of thatch and tassel at the

top. There is the Bentang-tree*, where, as in the English pot-house, the elders of the village meet and lay together their wise heads. I almost expected to be asked for a "saphie," to see a "coffle" of slaves enter the village, to pity a "poor Nealee affeeleeta," or to behold Mumbo Jumbo issuing from the bush. Truly great is the power of genius! But who wrote those wonderful travels, Mr. Park or Mr. Bryan Edwards? If the former, how is it that his second journal shows no trace of such power? True, it is unfinished; but so is Lord Byron's Swiss journal, which afterwards contributed to Manfred.

The "dooty" Tappa was sitting on his threshold, in a very *dégagé* toilette. I shook hands with him, and addressed a few Arabic phrases, to which he listened with intelligence, but which he, being no "bushreen,"† manifestly did not quite understand. A few verses of the Koran followed; he then brought for me a MS. of prayers, which were read out greatly to his admiration. A friendly clasp was the result, and he welcomed me to the brotherhood of El Islam. Pity 'tis that Park, Laing, and other travellers, have taken away the bloom and beauty from this "line." In a month I could learn sufficient Mandenga for practical purposes,

---

* So Park calls the Bombax.

† A Parkian word, probably from Mubashshir, one who brings glad tidings. Europeans at St. Mary's divide the Mandenga moslems into two classes—the Marabút, who does not drink, and the Soninki, or Sonaki, who does. The word Marabút (Mullah) is very loosely used; one hears of whole villages of Marabúts who seem to correspond—in the European mind—with the Fetish men of the Gold Coast.

and armed with, not an umbrella, like foolish Mr.
Petermann's Dr. Krapf, but with sword and dagger, a
koran, and an inkhorn, reeds, and a few sheets of paper,
I could pass an honoured guest through the country
where those before me travelled as Pariahs. But I
should not appear in the costume preferred by poor
Park, black beaver tile, and blue coat with brass buttons,
with shoeless feet,—what peculiar perverseness there
was in such proceedings, a perverseness only equalled
by the admirable perseverance with which the wanderer
condemned himself to insult and injuries, and his readers
to a thorough misconception of the people's character!
So far from being treated barbarously by the "Moors,"
an Arabicised population, Park and Caillié fared remarkably well, considering their obstinate kufr, their
inaccessibility to the Truths of a Higher Law, their
ghastly whiteman's faces, and their shocking civilised or
badly worn attire.   Conceive how a negro gentleman,
habited in a crown of eagle's feathers, a grass cloth round
his loins, and a large spear in hand, also travelling on
foot, would have been received in the country parts of
England in 1780. Also imagine that, if he had lived
through the madhouse to tell his tale, what a picture
he would have drawn of the English for the benefit
of the African *badaud* and *gobemouche,* who of course
would never have heard the other part. Mungo Park
was unhappy even in his death. He lost life by firing
upon the kind-hearted people of Busa (Boussa), who
meant him no harm till his violence made them fancy
his boat the advance of the Fellatah army. We shall

presently see what are upon this subject the deductions
of half-reasoning Europeans.

After shaking hands with my new friend and Moslem
brother Tappa, we resumed our walk through the
village, where all looked upon us with cordiality and
good humour.   The men wore the oval pieces of pierced
and strung amber, which their *quasi-periæcii,* the Somal,
call Mekkavi.   The women carried on their heads large
light-yellow calabash gourds, neatly sewn, capped with
a bunch of leaves to prevent splashing, and a bit of
floating wood to warn when the balance is going wrong.
Returning to the Cape House the country, on either
hand, despite a certain sameness, appeared positively
beautiful, after the foul swamps of St. Mary's Island ;
stubble of Guinea corn, loved by quails, a velvety green
expanse of grass, sloping inland, with here and there a
goodly palmyra, more beautiful than the columns of
Baalbek, palms necklaced with wine-calabashes, and in
one part a glade of baobab and other trees, cabled with
the most picturesque lianas, where gorgeous birds sit
and sing.*   And yet there are men who would prefer
the fever haunts of Bathurst.   How strong is the spirit
of contradiction in the British brain!   I would willingly
have lingered in these homely haunts, these pleasant
scenes, these " sylvan shades," for hours and hours ; but
sunset was drawing nigh, and we had eight miles to
gallop before dinner time.   The agreeable afternoon
ended with an equally agreeable evening, when, with

---

* They are sold here as *tie-tie*—twine, rope, cords.

tales of travel and with *bonne chére, non sine aliquo mero,* we managed to make exile anything but a bitter potion. Before resting, however, I have something to say touching the ethnography of this part of Africa.

With Mr. Luke Burke, I hold, as a tenet of faith, the doctrine of great ethnic centres, and their comparative gradation. I believe the European to be the brains, the Asiatic the heart, the American and African the arms, and the Australian the feet, of the man-figure. I also, or let me say we, opine that, in the various degrees of intellectuality, the negro ranks between the Australian and the Indian— popularly called Red—who is above him. From humbly aspiring to be owned as a man, our black friend now boldly advances his claims to *egalité* and *fraternité,* as if there could be brotherhood between the crown and the clown! The being who "invents nothing, originates nothing, improves nothing, who can only cook, nurse, and fiddle;" who has neither energy nor industry, save in rare cases that prove the rule!—the self-constituted thrall, that delights in subjection to and in imitation of the superior races. The aboriginal American has not been known to slave; the African, since he landed in Virginia, A.D. 1620, has chosen nothing else, has never, until egged on, dreamed of being free. He has a fatal respect for the Asiatic, and the European has ever treated him like a child. And yet we—in these days— read such nonsense pure and simple as "Africa for the Africans." *Datur digniori* is the fiat of Fate where such mighty interests are concerned. When the black rat expels the grey rat, then the negro shall hold his own against the white man.

As these pages will prove, there is a striking similarity between the races of Western and Eastern Africa. The former, however, will probably be found superior in disposition and more cultivated than the latter; those have had 300 years of European intercourse, these hardly one. In the west there are no such warlike and terrible tribes as the Shoho, the Somal, the Wamasai, the Makuá, and the Landeens. The King of Dahomey wages war for conquest, like a European monarch some centuries ago; and Andrew Battel's "Giaghas" have long been an affair of history. I remember being much astonished when asked by an eminent, but exceedingly testy, home geographer, if it was really my opinion that the Africans were dangerous to travellers laying open Inner Africa. Presently I recollected that his studies had been almost entirely confined to Western Africa, where, except in very few places, the European may go where he pleases. He had better not do so in the eastern regions.

Every ethnologist divides the population of Africa according to the light that is in him. It appears to me that there are but two great families, with a number of branches, and certain abnormalities like the South African bushmen, which are however too small and unimportant to notice.*

* I altogether discard such divisions as Æthiopians in West Africa, when Æthiopia was north of Abyssinia, Negritians that have never heard of the Niger; and Nilotics, so called because they have

1st. The noble race, or great North African family, which shows everywhere signs of increase, insititious negroid, semi-Semitic, in fact, Mulattoes and Asiatic Æthiopians. Of these are the Abyssinians, Gallas, Nubians, the numerous tribes comprised under the name of Moor, the Mandengas, Fulas, Haussa men, Kaniki of Burnu, and others not yet Moslemized, as the people of Yoruba and Nufe. These races, many of whom show little more than quadroon blood, and have long bushy beards, are possibly Arabs, expelled their country in the days of Yoarab bin Kahtan, and driven by slow degrees westward,* long before the " Saracenic " invasion of the Sudan in the tenth century. In the Sudan and Guinea again, there is a class of black-whites, *i.e.*, a sable people with intelligent and quasi-Grecian casts of countenance, heavily bearded and robust, in fact " black but comely." Some travellers suppose them, from the absence of effluvia, to be produced by a blending of semi-Semitic with pure Negro blood.

2nd. The ignoble race, or pure breed, the aboriginal and typical African, exceptionally degraded in Guinea, and improving as he descends southwards and blends with the true Kafirs, who may be a people of mixed

nothing to do with the Nile. Those who propose in West Africa a ternal division—viz. :—1. Senegambia ; 2. Northern Guinea ; 3. Southern Guinea—have not seized, I apprehend, the more salient points of difference which direct to a different distribution.

* They have lost their language, it is true. But so have the 3,500,000 Negroes in the " United States," and so would, after the second generation, a colony of British settled in East Africa. Captain Burton has, I think, well explained this absorbing peculiarity of the South African dialects in the Lake Regions of Central Africa.

blood.   In his lowest organisation he is prognathous, and dolicho-kephalic, with retreating forehead, more scalp than face; calfless, cucumber-skinned, lark-heeled, with large broad and flat feet; his smell is rank, his hair crisp and curly, and his pile like peppercorns.   His intellect weak, morale deficient, amiability strong, temperament enduring, destructiveness highly developed, and sensibility to pain comparatively blunt.   It is not wonderful that the Caucasian man taught himself by a fabliau to believe that this race had been cursed to be "servants of servants."

The growth of El Islam continues in West Africa. Here however it has long been established.   It is supposed to have begun under a Mandenga warrior in Bambûk, about A.D. 1100.   The Moslems of the west still point to Fúta Jálo and Fúta Toro, as the earliest cradles of their faith; these places are now held by the great Fula race, which, issuing it is believed from Massina, near the Niger, overspread the circumjacent regions.

The ill treatment to which the earlier travellers— Caillié especially, whose fancy was far more forceful than his frame—subjected themselves by their obstinacy and prejudices, produced grievances and misrepresentations which in popular works outcrop up to the present days, I will take the last, Rev. R. M. Macbriar's "Africans at Home" (p. 394), a compilation by a Wesleyan missionary, whose brief residence at Macarthy's Island is not yet forgotten in the colony.*   "All these people—

---

* London : Longman and Co., 1861.   I wonder that a respectable firm could be found to publish a work which borrows from Dr. Living-

Moslems—are capable of civilisation, perhaps not of the highest type, but at least of a respectable form. It must be a Christian civilisation. Mahommedanism has injured their tempers when it has improved their manners; and *it has not benefited their morals.*"† This is about equivalent to asserting that Christianity in England has clothed and fed the people, at the same time that it has degraded them; if this dictum be true, so is that. Mr. D. J. East, in another schoolboy compilation called " Western Africa,"‡ asserts that " these evils—polygamy and the slave-trade—have derived from Mahommedanism fresh vitality and a permanency of strength which they never had before." Yet (in page 272) he quotes Mr. Hutchinson, writer to the mission conducted to Santi or Ashanti by Mr. Bowdich in 1817, who says naïvely of Kumasi, the capital, "This place now presents the singular spectacle of a Christian and a Mahommedan absenting themselves from human sacrifices and other abominations." It is tolerably imprudent for the race that fought about the Asiento contract, and who worked Jamaica, to throw slavery in the teeth of the Moslems; and it is equally ridiculous to fancy that human sacrifice is less abominable to a " Mahommedan" than to a Christian. Rev. M. Bowen—of whom more at a future time—the gentle shepherd who proposes *horresco referens !* to "invade tropical Africa

---

stone—to mention no others—some thirty pages *literatim.*   After this, what is plagiary ?

† The italics here and below are mine.

‡ London : Houlston and Stoneman, Paternoster Row, 1844.

with swarms of missionaries," thus, in his "Central Africa,"* p. 190, shows, à *priori*, his knowledge of El Islam :—"After the venerable Mahometan priest had retired some of the villagers told me he was accustomed to say, 'It is not the Mahometan or the Heathen who will be *saved* (!), but the man who serves God in his heart.' I was not prepared to hear such a doctrine in a suburban village at Illorin." Puerile surprise of gross ignorance! Eight pages afterwards we hear of a Futá named Absolom (!!),† and a footnote informs us that "such names as David, Mary, &c., are common in Sudán." *Proh pudor!* Have these people ever read Sale's Koran?

In opposition to all such assertions, I would record my sincere conviction that El Islam has wrought immense good in Africa; that it has taught the African to make that first step in moral progress, which costs so much to barbarous nature; and that it thus prepares him for a steady onward career, as far as his faculties can endure improvement. What other nation, what other faith, can boast that it has worked even the smallest portion of the enduring benefits done, and still doing, to Africa by El Islam? Granting that ill temper, polygamy, domestic slavery, and the degradation of women ‡ are evils; yet

---

* Charleston, 1858. It is a "powerful" work—the composition of a Texas ranger who became a missionary, who wielded a good rifle at the Dahomian attack on Abeokuta, who received all manner of courtesies from the English in Africa, and who went home and abused them :—*sic itur ad astra*—in America.

† Probably Abd él Salam.

‡ The last charge is utterly unfounded. Nowhere do women hold a higher position, or enjoy such true liberty, as in Moslem lands; and it

what are they to be compared with the horrors of cannibalism and fetishism, the witch tortures, the poison
ordeals, and legal incest, the "customs," and the murders of albinos, of twins, of children who cut their upper
teeth first, and of men splashed by crocodiles ?   Surely
the force of prejudice cannot go beyond this !

Meanwhile the Mandenga † and other Moslem visitors
have proselytised many of the liberated Africans at
Sierra Leone, have built two mosques, and regularly
keep their Ramazan. They are to be met with at Accra,
they are numerous at Lagos, and they are gradually
extending upon this coast towards the southern hemisphere.

I have touched upon the propriety of removing

is curious to hear the assertion made in England, where by statute a
man may beat his wife moderately, force her by law to submit to his
loathed companionship, and dispose of her property as well as her person. A real Eastern, for instance, Mirza Abu Taleb Khan, who travelled
in England between 1799 and 1803 (Longman, 1814), is aghast when
he hears this most ignorant deduction, that a woman is a slave because
she may not sit barefaced in the society of strange men. In Timbuktu
we are told—to quote no other Africo-Moslem instances—the weaker
sex holds a very high position. Women are described as the "soothers
of man's woes, softeners of his grief, and partners of his joys." Can
England say more ?—or as much ?

† To the extensive family of the Mandengas, who occupy the coast
from Gallinas River to Cape Mount, belongs the Vai, Vey, or Vy branch,
who invented the only West African alphabet. It is a small tribe, not
exceeding 100,000 souls. The example of their Koran-reading brethren,
and a considerable Caucasian innervation, prevent our considering
their coarse and semi-symbolic alphabet strong enough to "silence the
cavils and sneers of those who think so contemptuously of the intellectual
endowments of the African race." The fact is, they are no more
Africans than the Mexicans are "red Indians.'

Europeans from Bathurst to a higher and healthier position. "To render Africa a salutary residence for European constitutions," says the prospectus of the Society for the Extinction of the Slave Trade and for the Civilisation of Africa, "may be a hopeless task." The Fellows of the Royal Geographical Society, and Sir Ranald Martin, if consulted, might give a different opinion. When prophylactic hygiene shall become associated with proper therapeutic treatment,—when the lands shall be cleared, locomotion facilitated, provisions made plentiful, and houses comfortable, and especially when only the stations above fever level shall be used by Europeans,—I suspect they will find themselves as much at home in Africa as in Southern Europe. A movement for removing the English soldier in the East from those fatal low-country stations, which in the last half century have wasted, without reckoning invaluable life, some 10,000,000*l.* of English gold, has now been inaugurated. We may not live to see the day, but our sons will.

Another change in prospect for all our foreign possessions is the increased necessity of economy, and the low estimation with which the home-dweller has learned to hold his brother the colonist. Let us see what Dietrichsen and Hannay give as the "Civil establishment" of a place which contains about 7000 inhabitants :—

1 Governor, 1200*l.*

Colonial secretary, 600*l.*

First writer, secretary's office, 300*l.*

Chief justice, 500*l.*

Collector of customs and superintendent of pilots, 475*l.*

Clerk of customs, &c., 200*l*.

Tide surveyor, 150*l*.

Colonial chaplain, 400*l*.

Auditor-general, 200*l*.

Colonial surgeon, 400*l*.

Assistant ditto, 200*l*.

Colonial engineer, 400*l*.

Clerk of councils, 100*l*.

Clerk of crown, 70*l*.

Clerk of police, 100*l*.

Postmaster, 80*l*.

Besides coroner and registrar.

The salaries belong to the days when the officer on the main-guard, at the Fort Gate, Bombay, was not permitted whilst on duty to sell fish. Their tenuity necessitates pluralities which engender heartburns, and even pluralism is not valuable enough to prevent absenteeism. Might not the establishment be reduced by as least one-half? The military surgeon might act at colonial, with proportionately increased allowances. The civil police should be placed, as in India, under military officers. The chief justice, clerk of councils, and clerk of the crown, might *aller se promener ;* police magistrates' courts suffiice for Europeans, and a military superintendent of the native "palavers" would soon make this cheap judicial engine valuable as the Indian Panchàyats. To the latter system I have as yet seen nothing superior, when worked as it was wont to be by an English official, who by his presence kept under and disallowed over-severity. There is nothing that Asiatics and Africans admire so little as British civil courts,* with their trains of lawyers and native hangers-on. And there is nothing more difficult than to explain "the why" to the home-made Englishman. Asiatics and Africans, both litigious races, whose great pleasure in life is a "palaver," a lawsuit, or an indemnity claim, care little for unbought justice; especially when purchased at the somewhat exorbitant price of delay, difficulty, and uncertainty. They are happy when they can approach the judge with something in their hands, and each, knowing that the highest bidder wins, draws the lottery as it were in the dark. The few Anglo-Indians who have spoken candidly, from Sir John Shore downwards, are unanimous upon this point; they are also somewhat doubtful of the good which our civil institutions have conferred upon these uncivil peoples.

But Bathurst has now done its work. The commerce of the place consists principally of the ground-nut (*A. hypogœa*), hides from the upper country, ivory, and beeswax. Gold is still brought down, but the quality is by no means of the best.† The French at Senegal have

---

* A regard for the due development of constitutional government demands for this mighty Gambian empire of 7000 souls an Upper House, under the name of Executive Council. It consists of His Excellency the Governor as President; the Colonial Secretary, the Collector of Customs, the Queen's Advocate, and the officer commanding the troops, as members. An Upper House demands a Lower, and this is found to exist under the name of a Legislative Council, in which seven resident merchants meet for "legislation." We must go further down the coast before we find those sensible institutions, the Court of Equity and the Chamber of Commerce.

† The precious metal has been found in some of the red clay hills on

drawn away the ground-nut : they have squeezed the orange, and they have left us the peel. Those "lively parties" have lately annexed the fine coffee-lands from the Pongo* to the Nuñez rivers; and the treaty of 1845, binding the high "contracting Powers" to refrain from "territorial aggrandisement," expired in 1855. Whilst the English Gambia is now almost monopolised by the French,† the French Gaboon is wholly in the hands of the English merchants. Why not exchange the two? When nations are so decidedly rivalistic, surely it is better to separate *à l'amiable*. According to the best authorities, the whole of the coast north of Sierra Leone might with profit be transferred to the French, on condition of all the coast south of the Kongo River, except what belongs to the Spanish and Portuguese, Dutch and Liberians, being left open to the English. Those who oppose the idea are revolted by the thought of parting with an old and effete colony, and by the reflection that the French will, as is their wont, "seal it up." And who would wish it reopened? I should like to see

the Gambia River near Macarthy's Island, but not pure nor sufficient to pay for labour.

* The word is variously written Ponga and Pongas. It lies in about 10° N. lat, some 50 miles south of the Nuñez, and it is remarkable that the coffee-tree flourishes or rather originates about the same parallel in East Africa.

† There are but four English merchants in the Gambia, Messrs. Goddard, Brown, Quin, and Chown. They export ground-nuts in French bottoms to French ports—English would not pay. The cultivation of the Arachis dates on the Western Coast of Africa from thirty years, and produces per annum forty millions of francs—more than equal to the palm-oil trade.

every more distinguished abolitionist in England and Yankeedom qualify himself for talking sense by a six months' spell down South at "niggers' work;" possibly his opinions touching the feasibility of white labour would be modified. And to those who would retain the Gambia, I wish nothing worse than a year's residence, or, rather, confinement there.

At the time of our arrival Bathurst had had her little war. It arose from what possibly might have been avoided—an armed interference in a commercial squabble, and from what necessarily required to be punished—the plundering of British vessels. The people of Badibu owed a few £ s. d. to Messrs. Chown and. Quin of Bathurst; and the Mandengas, after a few acts of piracy, convinced by the comparison of Gambia and Senegal that the English are "a nation of shop-keepers," had challenged us to "come on." In February, 1860, H. M. S. S. "Arrogant," Commodore Edmonstone, "Torch," Commander Smith, and "Falcon," Commander Heneage, under the command of the first-mentioned officer, steamed up the river. The land force consisted of 400 sailors and marines, eight companies (about 800 men) of the 1st and 2nd West Indian Regiments, and some 600 black auxiliaries, militia,* and volunteers, led by his Excellency the Governor. A French military officer was also present and showed all the courage of his nation. The place to be attacked was a strong and well-made stockade

---

* According to Capt. Hewett, the colonel of this gallant corps is the proprietor of a grog shop.

twenty miles up the river, three up a creek, and one of marching. The little "Dover" carried the Europeans to the attack every day and brought them back to sleep on board their ship. The enemy, besides manning their defences—which, though attacked with howitzer and rocket, resisted till taken in the rear—had a fair force of cavalry, and behaved with true Moslem gallantry. The chiefs, bearing Korans, rushed to the front, sabre in hand. Four of the "King's" sons were slain, and after losing the first fight the Mandengas recklessly challenged our men to a second. Of the "Arrogants," one officer and three men were killed, and twenty-one were wounded. The West Indians lost but one. N.B. Always go by the "casualties."

At Bathurst we shipped on board, besides a young cynocephalus and two niggers *—the latter coming off without money or ticket, were summarily sent to work— a remarkable party of Mandengas, bound for their distant homes. They were probably "gold strangers," as the local idiom calls those who traffic in the precious metal. They were armed with muskets, sabres, and knives; and for victual on the road they secrete rude gold rings, the best form in which the precious metal usually appears, and thus claims more than an equivalent for its weight in dust.

---

* In West Africa, nigger means a slave. It is an actionable word, and, as the reader will soon find out, a negro can recover damages by civil suit from any white man who uses language technically denoted as tending to "a breach of the peace."

Formerly these people used to walk the way between Bathurst and Sierra Leone, and then strike inland towards their country. They now save themselves the first half of the journey by paying $18 for a deck passage; yet a long trudge remains for them. Five in number, they are of moderate stature, with slender and lightly made but muscular limbs, uncommonly thin beards—almost lacking the whisker part—and faces like the Semiticized negroids generally, Arab in the upper and African in the lower half. All are of the Maliki school. They are not, however, strict Moslems. Like Rajpoots and Maharattas, they eat, I regret to say, the wild boar. Salt, according to them, is the best vendible in their country; and,—they knew the Kwara, or Niger,—gold can everywhere be washed near the rivers. I found them kind, obliging, and manly in demeanour: a great contrast to the Christianized African, who is either sheepish and servile, or forward and impudent. One, an old, purblind man, who sat with a clove of garlic up each nostril, called himself El Sharif Mohammed bin Salman, and shook hands with me whenever I proposed an Arabic sentiment.

The Mandenga language is soft and pleasant. I could not make much out of Mungo Park's vocabulary, and Mr. Macbriar's grammar* was deep in the hold. It

---

* A Grammar of the Mandingo Language, with Vocabularies, by the Rev. R. Maxwell Macbriar, translator of the Gospels into Mandingo, &c. London: John Mason, 66, Paternoster Row (printed for the Wesleyan Methodist Missionary Society).

It is regretable that the author should write verb and pronoun in one, as anyanta in paragraph 66 ; akimota, par. 29, and abettea, par

appears very easy to learn : the syllables are distinct, the sounds easy, and twenty-one Roman letters (six vowels, and fifteen consonants) express them all. When these Moslems write their own tongue they use the Arabic character, which is highly unsuited : for instance, most of their nouns end in *o*, and the vowel *e* is constantly recurring. In the Arabic languages and alphabets there are no such sounds or symbols. The abstract words are as usual borrowed from the learned tongue. The general impression which it leaves upon the mind is that time and distance have changed it till few indications—but those are important—of its original African framework remain.

The morning after our arrival was fixed upon for departure from Bathurst. We breakfasted at the Commissariat Quarters, and greatly enjoyed the favourite meal of the coast. It resembles rather the *déjeûner à la fourchette*, the Scotch heavy *früh stück*, or the substantial spreads of our Elizabethan ancestors, than the puny affair of toast and tea now used in England. Men rise early—a pleasant but pernicious practice, for which the only excuse is an old proverb and a more antiquated prejudice. After four hours of walk and work, they require at 9 or 10 A.M. fish, flesh, fowl, and eggs, especially the glowing West Indian pepper-pot and *côtelletes en papillotes*, fruit and vegetables, bread or biscuit,—in fact, a dinner, lacking only the soup

89 ; still more that he should join pronoun, adjective, and verb, as abbettebata, par. 25. Are hyphens and commas things so scarce and rare ?

Claret, or pale ale, are the staple drinks—I have tasted hermitage—followed as they should be by a cup of tea, coffee, or chocolate. And digestion cannot proceed without a pipe or a cigar.

The gun sounded a signal soon after breakfast. We sauntered to the shore, found the boat waiting, and, aided by the tide, soon transferred ourselves on board the "Blackland." A parting drink, a warm hand-shaking, and hearty thanks to our kind and hospitable hosts concluded our visit to what the French call Sainte Marie de Bathurst.

After leaving Bathurst our voyage was not pleasant. The clouds began to bank up in grey and massive heaps, and the rain to dash upon us, now in huge drops, then in a permanent drizzle. I know not which look the more wretched on board ship in rainy weather—the people or the poultry. *Pour comble,* one of our "lady-passengers" was laid up with what the doctor emphatically termed chicken-pox, and what the passengers, for unknown reasons, determined to be small-pox. Her husband was a full-blooded Ibo, of a truly ignoble aspect, despite his gorgeous attire, "like a perambulating rainbow surmounted by a black thunder-cloud," and "jealous as Othello, the type of all jealous men." The facetious mate before alluded to proposed to cut the b—— tongue out of him and sell him for a gorilla. After reading Mr. Poole, the trick it will be found has already been played with some modifications upon strangers.

After quitting Bald Cape, we passed about sixty

miles south of Bathurst the long low shore distinguished only by the Casamanza River, a French settlement, which has lately been surveyed by M. Vallon, as
the Senegambia has by M. Braouïzec, and the Bay of
Arguin by M. Fuleraud—all officers of the Navy and
the Engineers. Our course then lay along the Islands
of Bijougas and Bulama, some 350 miles from Sierra
Leone. This colony, so unfortunate under the redoubtable Captain Phil. Beaver—in the eighteen months, only
six remained of 269 souls, including 122 women and
children*—in 1792 was abandoned, and is now to
become an outpost, seeing that it can afford annually
60,000 bushels of ground-nuts. A party of fifty
men will be sent there from Sierra Leone, with
orders to locate themselves on a hill in the western
or seaward front of the island, not, as before, near
a swamp on the eastern or inland site. It is also
proposed to purchase the "Eyo Honesty," a little
steamer built by Mr. Laird, of Birkenhead,· and intended for the King of that name "down coast," or
South.

Again the weather changed to the normal north-east
trade, cold and violent as if we were in England: the
day was clear, but a zone of pinkish haze, 10° deep,
and raised 5° above the horizon, warned us to expect
pitching and rolling; nor was the warning a wolf-cry.
The passengers took to their berths, and the crockery
fell to breaking: the cook lost his cunning, and, sitting

---

* African Memoranda, Baldwin, London, 1805.

after dinner, became a bore.   Altogether, we were not comfortable, and we looked forward to arriving at " Sillyown," or " S'a Leone," as the above-mentioned pretty Mulatto lady called it, and as I shall do for the future in remembrance of her.

CHAPTER V.

"I have travelled east, I have travelled west, north, and south, ascended mountains, dived in mines, but I never knew and never heard mention of so villanous or iniquitous a place as Sierra Leone. I know not where the Devil's Poste Restante is, but the place surely must be Sierra Leone."

I QUOTE memoriter from Captain Chamier's "Life of a Sailor," which was in every mouth on board the "Black-land." Here, however, as elsewhere, the saying may hold good that a Certain Person may, perhaps, not be so black as he is painted.

Our only amusement during the hours before retiring had been to watch the Sargassa, or Gulf weed, floating with torn stalks, and to speculate upon the mysterious cause which brought anything here that might go elsewhere. These floating prairies—which, by-the-bye, are supposed to give a name to the Ilhas Verdes, or the Cape Verde Islands—are so misplaced that one can never get over the peculiarity of their appearance. At 6 A.M. it was announced that we were off the Ilhas de Los (Loss), or dos Idolos (of Idols), a triad of volcanic islets, Tamara or Footabar, Factory Island, and Ruma, or Craw-ford, not to mention bare rocks and outlying reefs. Our soldiers, for we had whilome a garrison there, found the two former healthy, but inferior to the Bananas, whilst the third was deadly : the largest is five miles by one. Being still inhabited, they supply beef and vegetables, fruits and plantains, and sundry attempts have been made to overgrow them with the ground-nut. Shortly afterwards we were off the Scarcies River, where at seasons there is an awesome bar, some seven miles broad. We made southing, and shortly after noon a lump of mountains to starboard—I had been long looking over the port bow—suggested S'a Leone. The name was given to " Romarong " of the natives by the Portuguese explorer, Pedro de Cintra, in 1467, because they found the King of Beasts, or rather the leopard confounded with the lion, troublesome, or because they thought, as in the case of the Lion of Bastia, that the range had a certain resemblance to a lion couchant.* Imaginative voyagers approaching from the west still see the beast's crest in the Sugarloaf Mountain, the head to the north, and the rump fining away, and dipping to the south. A mass of warm water-laden frowsy nimbus—the Sugarloaf is rarely unclouded— prevented our distinguishing the outline. Some suppose that Tierra Leoa was so named by the Portuguese, from the leonine roaring of the thunder through the valleys on the setting in and at the breaking up of the rainy season.

* Capt. Hewett says in "about 1480—nearly a century previous to the discovery of the Cape of Good Hope" (!), and relates the tradition that a lioness was the scourge and terror of the Portuguese colonists.

Far to our right, or west-south-west of S'a Leone, and opposite Cape Shilling, lay the Banana Islands, like thicker clouds at the bottom of the rain mist; they consist of two lumpy islets, and one rock, apparently volcanic, and they are to S'a Leone what the Isle of Wight is to Southampton. False Cape—truly false to many coming from the north and south,—with its two trees perfectly simulating the S'a Leone or True Cape,—stretched apparently to meet them. Here elephants, in small herds, are said to linger. Due west of Cape S'a Leone, and distant about five-sixths of a mile, lay Carpenter Rock, so called, not from the mechanic that might expect to profit by it, but from the luckless individual who ran his ship's nose upon it. The dangerous wash, with curling rollers charging furiously down upon it, suggested the idea of a school of spouting whales. It is celebrated for its excellent rock oysters, which are brought up in quantities by the divers. Perhaps pearls may be found on this part of the coast, which is not far removed from the parallels of Ceylon and Panama; but who would take the trouble to fish for them? As we neared Cape S'a Leone, two pilot-boats, with flags flying, advanced to the attack. One fell to leeward—perhaps the "Blackland" may have altered her course a wee bit. The more fortunate—Mr. Johnson—hailed us, climbed on board, grinned an African grin a the misfortunes of his rival, who had once "lawyered " us, and secured the pilotage, 3*l.* 10*s.*

"One summons at least!" quoth the gallant Captain English.

Presently a lighthouse, seven miles distant from the town, appeared on Cape S'a Leone, round which the sea runs at times like a mill race. Attached to the red-tipped tower is a bungalow belonging to Government, where invalids resort for fresh air, and derive strength from bathing in a pool, below which a breakwater defends from sharks. On this western face of the mountain mass the play of the sea-breeze is strong and regular, and it is clear, in fact far too clear, of forests. One is tempted to give the site a preference over the Hong-Kong-like hole into which Freetown has been thrown. Unfortunately, there is no harbour for shipping, and—a major consideration—it is backed by a swampy lagoon, over which the night-breeze passes. Freetown will probably not be removed to this black western shoulder; but it will, ere long, have bungalows high up the Leicester Mountain.*

The run in was picturesque, wanting little of being beautiful. Opposite was the estuary of the Rokel, or Rokelle, the S'a Leone River, in places seven miles broad, flowing calm and smooth, and mingling with the ocean between Leopold's Island and Cape S'a Leone. The lowlands at the base of the ridges were broken and dinted with little bights and lagoons of great variety. Pirate's Bay, the first, is a fairy scene, with its arcs of dark red cliff, bespread with the brightest green, and its beach of fine yellow sand, over which waved the feathery head of the cocoa palm. One or two old wrecks still

---

* Some years ago a settlement was tried here: it failed, but chiefly because it was a new clearing.

crumbled there ; the place derives its name from olden
times, when the smoothness of the water and the abundance of fish and fruit tempted the jolly filibusters to a
reláche; and there is a local tradition, that Drake cast
anchor in its blue waters. Beyond it, and separated by
a well-wooded point, lay Aberdeen Bay, a long reach
extending far into the interior, and, after heavy rains,
making this portion of the lowland

   " Both land and island twice a day."

The whole site of S'a Leone is quasi-insular. Bunce
River, to the north, and Calamart, or Calmont, usually
called Campbell's Creek, from the south, are said to meet
at times behind the mass of mountains, and at all seasons
a portage of a mile enables canoes to go round the
colony by water. This conversion of peninsula into islet
is by no means uncommon in the alluvial formations
further south.

 Aberdeen Bay abounds in sunken rocks, which do not,
however, prevent a ferry-boat crossing the gut. Scattered settlements of low thatched huts, like haystacks,
called mostly after the islets upon which they are built,
crown the dwarf cliffs, and hardly emerge from the gorgeous tropical growth. Murray Town and Congo Town
brought us, after passing King Tom's Point, where there
is a 3-gun battery, to Kru Town Bay : here we cast
anchor, banged our guns, and lay awaiting the health-
officers. We are about three cable lengths * from the

   * Ten cables = one sea mile = 6075·5 feet.

shore, and we command a front view of harbour and settlement.

St. George's Bay, as the anchorage is called in books, lies a little westward of the town.   This roadstead—for it is no harbour—is open to the north-west winds, which make it dangerous : it would be almost useless but for the Middle Ground, a large sandbank, in parts, perhaps, rocky, which breaks the seas.   The difference of tint, and the play of the dancing seas upon these sands, is a pretty sight.   The north bank of the river is the low Bullom shore, so called from the tribe its tenants—a long flat line of mud and mangrove, where all the Fevers hold their Court.   The dot beyond it is Leopard, anciently Leopold, Island, where it is said a leopard was once seen ; it is, however, a headland, connected by a sandpit with the most leeward point of the Bullom shore.*   On our right, facing Freetown, and in front of us, is the mass of highland that buttresses the southern side of the Rokel's *débouchure*.   The range is unconnected with any other : its shape is triangular, extending along the coast from Cape S'a Leone north-west, to Cape Shilling south-east, twenty-one miles and a half, and of inland breadth about twelve.   This would give it an area of 250 square miles, or about the size of the Isle of Wight, with thirty miles to spare.   The peninsula is supposed to be volcanic, and sundry shocks †

---

* Bullom, or Búlum, is said to mean low land.   The people are wild as wild can be, but they have always received Europeans with kindness.

† Particularly in 1858 : it extended to the Gold Coast, and was a precursor to the ruins of 1862.

have occurred of late years, arguing that the subter-
raneous fires are not yet extinct. Its appearance, however, is rather that of a sandstone region, softly rounded
contours, with here and there a lumpy cone, a tongue
of land, and a gentle depression, showing the action of
water. If volcanic, the fires must have been for long
ages extinct. The high green background is the *fons
malorum* arresting the noxious vapours of the lowlands
and of the Bullom shore opposite. The Sultan of the
mountains is Sugarloaf Peak, an apparently volcanic
upheaval 2300 feet above sea level; it is rarely our
fortune to see more than its foundation. The Wazir
is Wilberforce, which supports sundry out-stations and
villages, deep-set in dense dark groves. A few reclaimed
patches in natural shrubbery appear widely scattered :
the unsophisticated African is ever ashamed of putting
hand to plough, and the autumnal fires have destroyed
much valuable timber and produce ; for instance, tallow-
trees and saponaceous nut-trees, especially the Pen-
tadesma Butyracea, which once covered the land from
S'a Leone to the Niger.

Nothing can be viler than the site selected for
Freetown ; the fifteenth century would have chosen a
better. This capital of the unhappy colony lies on the
north coast of the S'a Leone Peninsula, on a gentle
declivity, a narrow shelving ledge of diluvium washed
from the higher levels, and forming in places dwarf
facets and little basins. The sandstone is so soft and
friable, that it readily absorbs the deluging torrents of
rain, and as readily returns them to the air in the shape

of noxious vapours. The lowest houses are besprinkled by the wave-spray; the ground, however, rises gradually from the sea to the Arthur's Seat of Freetown, "Tower Hill," whose elevation was variously estimated to me at any number between 300 and 500 feet. At one time the S'a Leonites thought of building a health house on Station Hill, where a signal staff announces the approach of vessels. The tenement rose to nearly its first story, where it stopped short for want of funds. On the heights above the settlement, there is doubtless room for cool and healthy country seats, where the European exiles might be comparatively safe from dysentery and yellow fever. A white lodge peeping from a densely-wooded mountain flank was pointed out to me as Carnes' Farm, called "Mount Oriel," probably for "Oriole," by the lady tenant who has described it. Though not 900 feet above sea level, the climate about this eyrie is said to be wholly different from that of the lower town. But the effects of original sin in site are terribly lasting in these lands; they descend from generation to generation. It is far easier for the Tropics to build than to unbuild, which involves re-building. The great gift of Malaria is utter apathy, at once its evil and its cure, its bane and its blessing. Men come out from Europe with the fairest prospect, if beyond middle age, of dying soon. Insurance offices object to insure. No one intends to stay longer than two years, and even these two are one long misery. Consequently men will not take the trouble to make roads, nor think of buying a farm, or of building a house upon a hill. They might have

every comfort that Europe and Africa afford, but who
cares to write or to collect subscribers for them? They
might have American ice for 1*d*. per lb., and with ice
would come fruits, game, and other comforts, but who
would raise a company or disturb his mind with reflecting
about an ice-house?

We will now cast an eye upon the straggling town,
which seems to be three or four miles in circumference.
At a distance it is not unpicturesque, but the style of
beauty is that of a Rhenish Castle, ruinous and tumble-
down. Bathurst, which I thought an aged fogy, is
young and strong compared with decrepit old Freetown. A week ago the gable end of a huge house
overhanging the wharf fell into the sea, exposing the
anatomy of the whole interior, and last night's rain
washed down part of a chapel. These people consider
not the ways of the white ant : instead of hurrying like
the Termes to repair, they simply abandon the *débris*.
There is no marine parade, and, as in Eastern ports, the
habitations crowd towards the sea, thinning out behind.
The colours of the houses are various : plain white is
rare; blue, gray, light yellow, dark yellow, ochre, red,
dirty brown, brown, black, and especially greens
somewhat flashier than fresh grass, and set off by darker
shades of different depth, are preferred. But all are the
same in one point, the mildewed cankered gangrened
aspect of the decadent Europeo-Tropical settlements,
which contrast so unfavourably with the whitewashed
cities of the Arabs. The principal buildings are placed
to catch the sea breeze. Here, as at Zanzibar, the

temperature becomes unendurable where the wind cannot reach. Those that strike the eye, beginning from the right, are as follows : near King Town's Point is the Wesleyan College, a large building with apparently shingled roof, upper jalousies and lower arches, with a band of verdure in front, defended from the waves by a dwarf sea wall. Some few trees are scattered around it, and in unpleasant vicinity to it are heaps of coal, which is supposed in the Tropics to produce by its exhalations dangerous fevers. Certain it is, that in places like St. Thomas (West Indies), the vicinity of the coal-shed is more fatal, without apparent reason, than sites further removed from it. Beyond the college, and separated by the Upper Town or Kru Town—heaps of little thatched hovels divided by remnants of bush—lies the gaol, a large barn-like structure, faced by a plain black wall. The Colonial Hospital, a kind of bungalow, fronts King Jimmy's bridge, a long causeway through whose single central arch a rivulet of sparkling water finds its way to the sea. At the mouth of the little ravine lies the crowded fish-market, upon a sandy turf scattered over with boats and canoes. On the left of the bridge is a mass of tall buildings, stained and corroded by the rain, with the gaunt Police Court and its ragged flagstaff forming the apex. The next remarkable building is the neat brick bazaar, with dead arches in the long walls, and surmounted by a flying roof with glass windows. Then comes the huge ancient store belonging to Mr. Charles Heddle, one of the oldest residents and the most enterprising

merchant in S'a Leone. Like all the houses immediately upon the sea bank, the frontage is a clear fall of
80 feet, whereas from the street behind it appears below
the average height. Below Mr. Heddle's are warehouses
still to be finished, the bricks not having yet come from
Marseilles. A contemptible jetty, which the boatmen
call after a certain acting Governor, "Dougan's Wharf,"
is the usual landing-place, and a puny lighthouse directs
the disembarkers in the hours of darkness, when the
whole settlement can hardly show an oil light. Freetown sadly wants the comforts of Mauritius—several
and distinct wharves for lighters, watermen's and ship's
boats, which now all hustle one another. But even in
slow-going England, Father Thames shall have a
Boulevart on each side of him long before this "great
Emporium" of Western Africa shall be provided with a
landing-place where shins are seldom broken. Above
the pier, and a little to the left, are the Commissariat
Quarters, also a long low cottage seen from the land,
and a tall grim structure like a bonded warehouse
when viewed from the sea. The bank against which it
is built is here so steep that it must be ascended by
steps. Between the warehouses, but on a higher level,
having a little grassy square between it and the seabank, is St. George's, once a church, but now promoted
to a cathedralcy. It is the usual Protestant place of
worship all the tropical world over—a single tower,
with useless battlements pinning down a long ridged
back not at all unlike a barn. Its interior is plain
whitewash and pew; the exterior weather-stained, light

yellow, and the order is called, I believe, Neo-Gothic.
Fas est ab hoste doceri. Cannot these people take the
hint from the mosques of the lands adjoining them, and
spare us the sight of all these architectural deformities?
The cost was 150,000*l.*, not including a statue of
Buxton, which, somewhat uncharacteristically, has shrunk
into a shady corner. The " Cathedral " is the only
place of worship which attracts the eye. Chapels, however, there are in foison. My gallant anti-Negrophil
friend, whom I shall quote at a future time, informs me
that their name is legion, numbering 175. I suspect
he prefixed the 1, yet the Frenchman's melancholy
exclamation, " What! a hundred religions and but one
sauce!" (here, however, it is "palaver sauce," not melted
butter) is thoroughly applicable to S'a Leone. The
chapels are mostly methodistical, and the schools Lan-
casterian or Monitorial. Beyond the Commissariat, lies
another mass of building where a splendid Bombax,
sole survivor of a once large family, lingering upon the
sea bank, adorned the town with its majestic proportions.
It yielded to fate one bad day and slipped down the
cliff seawards. Running the eye to the left, you see
successively the quarry, where unamiable-looking blacks,
with CONVICT upon their shirt backs, are cutting out
a light red sandstone, the harbour-master's wharf, the
bathing-place—a bit of sea enclosed with heaps of
stones—and a dark dingy wall, with a few old guns *en
barbette,* Fort Falconbridge, one of the chief fortifications in the place. I need hardly say it would fall after
half an hour before the mildest of gunboats. Yet the

place might, at the expense of some 6000*l.* to 8000*l.*, be respectably defended. The three main points, King Tom's, Fort Falconbridge, and Government House, should be strengthened with heavy guns, and outside the barracks a work containing a single large Armstrong would render the others untenable when taken. Of course all this has been proposed, of course no notice has been vouchsafed to the proposal.

The back ground is a green curtain of grass and fruit trees, amongst which predominate the dark prim mango, somewhat like an orange multiplied by two or three, and palms, never absent from the seashore in equinoctial lands. The ground rises gently, but decidedly, with a grassy esplanade, cut by red paths to the Barracks that crown the crest of a lumpy hill. Half way up the ascent is Government House,— in old charts, Fort Thornton,—whose roof but tops the thick vegetation of trees and shrubbery that confine it. On its left is a black bastion, barely supporting a single cannon. On the right, at some distance, is the Military Hospital, whose site at least contrasts favourably with the wet graves, called wards, at Bathurst.

The scene in the roadstead is not lively. There is an awning'd coal-shed, three or four dismantled merchant-men,—dreary-looking as the settlement, and reminding one of old Rotten Row in Sidney Harbour,—with schooners and coasters, which ply to Sherbro Island, and other neighbouring places, and an oil-ship from Marseilles. Hardly, however, had we anchored, when, flying upon white wings,—I spare the albatross, this time—entered

all the Northern Division, H.M. Sloop Falcon, and H.M.
Gun-vessel Torch, the latter having lately justified her
name by setting the Liberian coast on fire, of which
more anon. It was mail-day: home letters are very
acceptable on this coast; but such pleasant meetings
must be "nuts" to the slave exporter, who of course knows
everything that is going on. Before we left the harbour
La Ceres, a goëlette of war, from Fernando Po, bearing
the red and yellow colours of Spain, entered with a hole
through her stern cabin.

We parted with our consumptives at Madeira, we
leave our Africans at S'a Leone. For this race there is
a descending scale of terminology—1. European, 2. civilised man, 3. African, 4. man—the Anglo-Americans say,
"*pussun*"—of colour, 5. negro, 6. darkey, 7. nigger—
which last I have said, is actionable. Many a 5*l.* has
been paid for the indulgence of *lese majesté* against the
"man and a brother;" and not a few 50*l.* where the
case has been brought into the civil courts.* Our
Africans, two in number, were no favourites. One was
a Jamaican shop-keeper, gifted with the usual modicum
of intelligence, and a superior development of "sass,"
justifying the eccentric Captain Phil. Beaver in declaring
that he would "rather carry a rattlesnake than a negro
who has been in London." An Englishman in his position
of life would perhaps have felt that he was of a social
station a shade below his neighbours, and would have
been slightly uneasy accordingly. Not so Mr. Hazel-

* Captain Hewett's "Western Coast of Africa," chap. 9, will confirm this.

face, into whose soul or countenance " *soggezzione*," or shame, never yet entered,—for was he not of the A'mighty negroes? And shall not the most dishonest of negroes in these days stand before kings? The second, our Gorilla, or Missing Link, was the son of an emancipated slave, who afterwards distinguished himself as a missionary and a minister. His—the sire's—name has appeared in many books, and he wrote one himself, pitying his own " poor lost father," because, forsooth, he died in the religion of his ancestors, an honest Fetishist. Our excellent warm-hearted ignorant souls at home were so delighted with the report of this Lion of the Pulpit, that it was much debated whether the boy *Ajái* had not been providentially preserved for the Episcopate of Western Africa. The amiable Miss T——, one of the "prettyfiers" of Africa, prefixed to her little volume a telling scene,—a personal interview " at the Church Missionary House, Salisbury Square," between the "boy" and his deliverer, a gentleman who, in the Indian navy, bore the sobriquet of " old onions." The Episcopal scheme was perfectly *en règle*,—did not Lord Camelford threaten the House of Commons with his negro footman for a fellow member?—it fell through only when all the white shepherds loudly professed intentions of throwing up their crooks. "'Hanged if I would take orders from him!" said one of their calling to me. The son has been two years at King's College, and is of course well posted upon every *res scibilis* : his peculiar vanity at present is to be one-third quack, one-third general trader, and the rest ground-bait for gudgeons. Upon the strength of

the latest humbug—the Cotton "Plant" in West Africa,*
—he has extracted some hundreds of Manchester pounds
sterling; less lucky only than another individual about
here, whose 50*l.* cheques upon the London and Westminster Bank were then flying about the coast.

These individuals are out of their *assiettes.* At home
they will devour, perforce, kankey and bad fish, washing
them down with Mimbo and Pitto—native palm wine,
and hop-less beer—here they abuse the best of beef, long
openly for "palaver sauce" and "palm-oil chop," and find
fault with their champagne. *Chez eux,* they will wear
breech· clouts and Nature's stockings—*ecco tutto.* Here
their coats are superfine Saxony, with broadest of silk vel-
vet collars. The elongated cocoa-nut head bears jauntily
a black pork-pie felt, with bright azure ribbons, and a rainbow necktie vies in splendour with the loudest of waistcoats from the land of Moses and Son; the pants are tightly
strapped down to show the grand formation of the knee,
the delicate slimness of the calf, the manly purchase of
the heel, and the waving line of beauty that distinguishes
the shin-bone. There are portentous studs upon a glorious
breadth of shirt, a small investment of cheap, gaudy,
tawdry rings sets off the chimpanzee-like fingers, and
when in the open air, lemon-coloured gloves invest the
hands, whose horny reticulated skin reminds me of the
scaly feet of those cranes which pace at ease over the
burning sand, for which strong slippers are not strong

---

* I do not at all deny that Africa can bear cotton ; quite the contrary,
it might produce enough for the world. But I doubt that it will, and
as things are now I am certain it will not.

enough; whilst feet of the same order, but slightly superior in point of proportional size, are tightly packed into
patent leather boots, the latter looking as if they had
been stuffed with some inanimate substance,—say the
halves of a calf's head.

It is hardly fair to deride a man's hideousness, but it
is where personal deformity is accompanied by conceit.
Once upon a time we all pitied an individual who by
acclamation was proclaimed the ugliest man in the
B—— army, which is not saying a little. "Poor
E——!" his friends would exclaim; "it's no matter
if a chap's plain, but he is revolting," and they com-
miserated him accordingly.   Once, however, he was
detected by his chums looking into a shaving-glass, and
thus soliloquising : "Well, E——, I declare you'd be a
deuced handsome fellow if you had but a little more
nose." The discreet chum of course spread the story,
and from that moment our compassion departed.

Both our Africans are married to wives,—one is
pretty, and *tant soit peu* coquette, consequently the
husband is terribly "mad,"—and the wives are the
better and far the more agreeable halves.   The men dis-
please me because they kick down, as the phrase is, the
ladder by which they rose. *Par parenthèse,* no man
maltreats his wild brother so much as the so-called civilised negro—he hardly ever addresses his kruman except
by "you jackass !" and tells him ten times a day that
he considers such fellows as the dirt beneath his feet.
Consequently, he is hated and despised withal, as being
of the same colour as, whilst assuming such excessive

superiority over, his former equals. No one, also, is more hopeless about the civilisation of Africa than the semi-civilised African returning to the "home of his fathers." One feels how hard has been his own struggle to emerge from barbarism. He acknowledges in his own case a selection of species, and he sees no end to the centuries before there can be a nation equal even to himself. Yet in England, and in books, he will cry up the majesty of African kings;* he will give the people whom he thoroughly despises a thousand grand gifts of morals and industry, and extenuate, or rather ignore, all their faults and shortcomings. I have heard a negro assert, with the unblushing effrontery which animates the negro speechifying in Exeter Hall, or before some learned society, that, for instance, at Lagos—a den of thieves—theft is unknown, and that men leave their money with impunity in the storehouse, or on the highway. After which, he goes home, "tongue in cheek," despising the facility with which an Englishman and his money are parted.

Our Africans left the ship without, on our part, or probably on theirs, a single regret. Not so with the Mandengas. The honest and manly bearing of these Moslems—so wonderful a contrast with those caricatures in pork-pie and peg-topped broad-cloth—had prepossessed me strongly in their favour. We shook hands, and in broken Arabic bade each other a kindly Allah-speed. Then they disappeared in a canoe, laden

---

* Mr. Crowther's Niger Diary will explain this.

with their pots, pans, and parcels, besides about a dozen muskets, whose stocks, like the Eastern matchlock, were fancifully inlaid with metal plates. The poor fellows are accused at Freetown of sometimes kidnapping a child, and of making too free with the women of the Kafirs; but they never summons white men.

To end this long digression upon the subject of our black fellow-passengers. It is a political as well as a social mistake to permit these men to dine in the main cabin, which they will end by monopolizing: a ruling race cannot be too particular about these small matters. The white man's position is rendered far more precarious on the coast than it might be, if the black man were always kept in his proper place. A European without stockings or waistcoat, and with ragged slops hanging about his limbs, would not be admitted into the cuddy; an African will. Many of the fellows come on board to make money by picking a quarrel. And what does one think of a dusky belle, after dropping her napkin at Government House, saying to her neighbour, " Please, Mr. Officer-man, pick up my towel," or of such a dialogue as this? The steward has neglected to supply soup to some negro, who at every meal has edged himself higher up towards the top of the table, and whose conversation consists of whispering into the ears of an adjacent negro, and of hyæna-like guffaws.

" I say, daddee, I want *my* soop; all de passenger, he drink 'im soop; *me* no drink *my* soop: what he mean, dis palaver ? "

The words are uttered in a kind of scream; the steward cannot help smiling, and the nigger resumes :

"Ah, you laff! And for why you laff? I no laff; no drinkee soop!"

Here the dialogue ends, and the ladies look their acknowledgments that travelling does throw us into strange society.

Succeeded to the health-boat a swarm of visitors— soldiers, marines, merchants, missionaries, one coloured and two uncoloured, but with terrible faces, and a variety of. darkies. The latter seem to be of three classes at S'a Leone. First, the merchant, an honourable name, assumed by all who can buy half a dozen cloths and sit behind them on 'change, chatting and doing little else all the day. Second, the tailor, whose wife is certainly a washerwoman. The work suited to the ninth part of a man in England, is here a great favourite; it gives the hands something to do whilst the body is unworked, and the unruly member is free to run its course. Third, the missionary, of whom the least said the better. One youth, whose complexion wore unmistakeably the "shadowed (to deep mourning) livery of the burnished sun," had crowned himself with a scarlet smoking cap, around which—the light of day was not over-intense, but his skin was doubtless of most delicate texture—he had wound a white gauze veil. Our European visitors were sallow as East Indians after the hot season; in not a few the livid lips, vacant looks, and thinned hair, told of severe fever; and

wherever a healthy face appeared, it proved to be that
of a new arrival.

There is " dignity" in S'a Leone; it wants the rough-
and-ready welcome of Gambia. Finding some touch
of *noli me tangere* in the whites, I turned to the blacks
pour passer le temps. Not the least amusing of our
visitors were the washerwomen; here an influential class,
because this is the only place upon the coast where
linen can be purified in three days. On the West
Atlantic coast it would be done in three hours. They
drive a roaring trade. Threepence a day enables a
person to live; sixpence, to live comfortably. At Freetown, the charge for washing is 3*s.* 6*d.* per dozen—
it is 1*s.* 6*d.* in London where necessaries are somewhat dearer; but by hard bargaining and enduring
a little " sass," you may compound for English prices.
The nymphs of the washtub were exceedingly familiar
—not pleasant when woman is plain. Their dress
was a bright *foulard* of striped cotton, bound like
the anatomy of a turban round the head, and garnished, as our grandmothers' nightcaps were, with
huge bows; gaudy shawls, over white cotton jackets;
and skirts—I believe they call the things—of bright,
showy, calico stuff, making them more gaudy than
any parrot or cockatoo; the ornaments are large gold
earrings and not small necklaces of beads or coral.
Mammy Paradise was recommended to me as capable of
all the duties of a washerwoman; I did not, however,
trouble Mammy Paradise. We also received a visit
from " our Marianne," who has a monopoly of greens,—

literally, I despise puns. She has the reputation of
being, or rather of having been, a beauty, and, like her
race generally, she can say impertinences, which, issuing
from a barbarous mouth, in a peculiar *patois*, pass for
wit amongst those who are not particular about the
quality of the article. Freetown, it may here be observed, is the great source of blackman's English, which
runs down the whole coast, except about Accra, where
the people have learned somewhat better, and amongst
the Krumen, whose attempts are even less intelligible
to the Englishman. "Enty" means indeed; "one
time," at once; "puss," or "tittie," girl, perhaps
pretty girl; "babboh," boy—whence do they derive
these improvements?—"hear," is to understand or
obey; "catch," to have; "sabby," to know; "lib," to
live, to be, or to be found; "done lib," is to die; "tote,"
to carry; "chop," to eat; "yam," food; "cut the cry,"
to end a wake; "jam head," or "go for jam head," is
to take counsel together; "cut yamgah," to withhold a
payment; "make nyángá," to junket; the metaphorical
heart is, "tummack;" all writing or printing is "a book;"
any gift, or baksheesh, "dash;" a row or palaver, "bob."
They always answer "yes " to a negative question, thus
conveying an affirmative,* and, like the American
Southerners, they put the sign of the vocative at the end
of the word—*e. g.* Daddy, oh! Mammy, oh! All bulls
are "cows;" when you would specify sex, you say "man
cow," or "woman cow;" so the fastidious American,

---

* *E.g.*—"Didn't you find water there?" Ans. "Yes, Subaudi, I
did not find it"—meaning "no."

when driven by sheer necessity to make invidious distinctions, must euphuise bullock into "gentleman cow." These peculiarities are not stolen forms of speech; their grammar and etymology were originally literal translations from African dialects which remain, whilst the mother tongues are clean forgotten. The vocabulary might be prolonged *ad infinitum,* but it would be as interesting to the reader as the New Testament translated into blackman's English—and in very shame altogether withdrawn by its patron society from circulation—would be to any save a bibliophile.*

From the moment of our arrival, "negro palaver" began. A *cause célèbre,* which will be referred home, had just been brought to a close. Mr. M——, a civilian official in the colony, after thrice warning out of his compound a troublesome negro and a suspected thief, had applied a certain *vis à tergo,* and had ejected the trespasser, not however with unnecessary violence. In England the case would have been settled by a police magistrate, and the fine, if any, would have been half-a-crown. At Freetown, the negro, assisted by his friends or "company," betakes himself to a lawyer. The latter may be a mulatto, possibly a pettifogger, certainly a moneyless man who lives in a wretched climate for the pure purposes of lucre; his interest is of course to promote litigation, and he fills his pockets by what is

---

* For amusing specimens of amatory epistles the reader may consult Mr. Consul Hutchinson's Ten Years' Wanderings among the Ethiopians, p. 19, &c. ; and Residence in Sierra Leone, by a Lady. London : Murray, 1849.

called sharp practice. After receiving the preliminary fee of 5*l.*, he demands exemplary damages. The consequence was that Mr. M—— was lightened of 50*l.*

These vindictive cases are endless; half-an-hour's chat will bring out a dozen, and, as at Aden, the Sons of the White Cliffs have nothing to do but to quarrel and to recount their grievances. A purser of the African S. S. Company, finding a West Indian negro substituting dead for live turkeys, called him a "tief." The "tief" laid an action for 1000*l.*, and the officer was only too happy to escape with the retainer, three guineas. The same, when a black came on board for a package, sent him off to the quarter-deck; the fellow became insolent, when a military man present exclaimed, "If you gave me that cheek, I'd heave you overboard!" The negro put off, took two of his friends as witnesses, procured an affidavit that the white man had threatened him, and laid an action for defamation of character, &c., damages, 50*l.*—a favourite sum. Despite a counter oath, signed by two or three English officers, one of them a colonel, to the effect that no bad language had been used, except by the plaintiff, whose insolence had been unbearable, the defendant was compelled to make an apology and to pay 15*l.* costs. Another told me that for raising a stick to an insolent servant, he was "actioned" for 50*l.*, and escaped by compromise for 12*l.* When the defendant is likely to leave the station, the *modus operandi* is as follows. A writ of summons is issued. The lawyer strongly recommends an apology for the alleged offence and a promise to pay costs,

warning the offender at the same time that judgment
will go against him if absent by default. Should the
defendant prudently "stump up," the thing ends; if
not, a *capias* is taken out, and the law runs its course. A
jury is chosen. The British Constitution determines
that a man must be tried by his peers. His peers at
S'a Leone are perhaps a dozen full-blooded blacks, liberated slaves, half-reformed fetishmen, sometimes with
a sneaking fondness for the worship of Shángo,* and if
not criminals in their own country, at least paupers clad
in dishclouts and palm oil. To see such peers certainly
"takes pride down a peg," as the phrase is; no use to
think of that ancestor who "came over" with the Conqueror, or that barony lost in the days of the Rebellion.
The excuse is that a white jury cannot be collected out of
the forty or fifty eligibles in Freetown. The jury—model
institution—becomes here, as in the United States, a
better machine for tyranny than any tyrant, except a
"free people," ever invented. It is useless to "challenge,"
for other negroes will surely take the place of those ob-
jected to. No one raises the constitutional question,
are these half-reclaimed barbarians my peers? And if
he did, justice would sternly answer "Yes!" The witnesses will forswear themselves, not like our posters, for
half-a-crown, but gratis, because the plaintiff is a fellow-
tribesman. The judge may be "touched with the tar-
brush," but be he white as milk, he must pass judg-

---

* An Egba deity, the god of fire, &c. Hence Mrs. M—— informs us
that "many of the liberated Africans worship lightning"; and Captain
Hewett asserts that the "Acoo" (Aku) is a fire-worshipper.

ment according to verdict, and when damages are under
200*l*. there is no appeal.*

S'a Leone contains many sable families,—Lumpkins,
Lewis, Pratt, Ezidio, Nicols, Macarthy, are a few of
their patronymics,—against whom it is useless for
a stranger to contend and come off scot and lot free.

---

* I am unwilling to let the reader think that the above is exaggerated.
The only proof in my power is the following extract from the "Sierra
Leone Weekly Times" (June 18th, 1862), the sole paper of any note
in the colony :—

"And what, we may ask, is its last resort when the engine of intimidation will not effect its purpose ? A British Jury. This is the
real instrument of its power. It would matter little to allow the Aku
chiefs to decide questions in their societies, were they not able to tell
those who oppose them, ' Go, then, and see what verdict you will get.'
Let the jury be abolished, and the Aku chiefs and their myrmidons
would soon feel that their vocation was gone. In no other way can an
effectual check be put upon their increasing power.

"Is it just, is it reasonable, to permit this clan to domineer by means
of a British jury ? We know of numerous cases where legal men have
refused to take up causes until assured of the neutrality of the Aku
chiefs. And can this be otherwise when we see with what relentless
and ceaseless persecution they pursue even individuals of their own
tribe who venture to resist them ?

" To leave the jury in their hands is a denial of justice to the rest
of the people.

"Through it they are the tyrants of the law, and every man is at
their mercy.

" Societies of this nature cannot be judged of by their rules. What
can be more seemingly fair and candid than the rules and principles
put forward by many of the European societies ? And yet they have
not shrunk from committing the darkest deeds. And can we in calm
judgment expect better things here ?

" In solemn earnestness we call upon the people of this colony to
unite and rid the country of this redoubtable power, and they will
deserve the gratitude of those great and good men who have been, and
who still are, the benefactors of the African race."

Besides these there are 17 chief and 200 minor tribes, whilst 100 languages, according to M. Koelle,—150, says Bishop Vidal,—are spoken in the streets of Free-town. All are hostile to one another; all combine against the white man. After the fashion of the Gold Coast, they have formed themselves into independent republics called "companies." These set aside certain funds for their own advancement and for the ruin of their rivals. The most powerful and influential races are the Aku and the Ibo. The Akus, or Egbas, known by their long necklaces of tattoo, are called the Jews of Western Africa; they are perfect in their combination, and they hesitate at no crime. They will poison with a pitiless readiness. The system of Egba "clanship," as the local papers call it, is a favourite, sometimes an all-engrossing topic for invective with the press. This worst species of trades-union is characterised, on account of its propensity to intimidate, as the "Aku tyranny" and the "Aku Inquisition." The native proverb speaks the native sentiments clearly enough,—

> " Okàn kan li ase ibi, ìkoko li ase ìmolle
> bi atoju ìmolle tàn, ke atoju ibi pella, bi
> aba kû ara enni ni isin' ni."

"A man must openly practise the duties of relationship, though he may privately belong to a secret club: when he has attended to the secret club, he must attend to the duties of relationship also, because, when he dies, his relations are those who must bury him."

The Ibos are more divided, still they cleave together on especial occasions. This large tribe, whose head-quarters is Abo, at the head of the Nigerian delta, muster strong at S'a Leone, where they are the

Swiss of the community. It is popularly said the Aku will do anything for money, the Ibo will do anything for revenge. Both races are intelligent enough to do harm—their talents rarely take the other direction. If the majority of the jury be Akus, they will unhesitatingly find the worst of Aku criminals innocent, and the most innocent of whites, or Timnis, guilty.*

Surely such an outrage upon reason—such a caricature of justice—was never contemplated by British laws. Our forefathers never dreamed that the liberty and the institutions for which during long centuries they fought and bled, would thus be prostituted—be lavished upon every black recaptive, be he assassin, thief, or wizard, after a residence of some fourteen days in a dark corner of the English empire. Even the Irishman and the German must pass some five years civilising themselves in the United States before they are permitted to vote. What a curious contrast! and how little it speaks for our *savoir faire!* Free the slaves if you like, and strike the slaver to the ground with his victims' fetters; but ever remember that by far the greater number of the liberated were the vilest of criminals in their own lands, and that in their case exportation becomes, in fact, the African form of transportation. If the reader believes that I have exaggerated the state of things at S'a Leone, he is mistaken; the sketch is

---

* "Aku constables will not, unless in extreme cases, take up their delinquent countryman, nor will an Ebo constable apprehend an Ebo thief, and so on through all the different tribes."—*Residence in Sierra Leone*, p. 269.

under, rather than over drawn. And he will presently see a confirmation of these statements in the bad name which liberated Africans bear upon the whole of the western coast.*

* The subjoined extract from the pen of the African editor to the "Sierra Leone Weekly Times" (July 30th, 1862) will at least show that I am not singular in my opinions. The reader will excuse this diffusiveness of refutation. The contrary idea to that advocated above is still ruling in England. It will die out because it is based on ignorance, but we would all of us fain be in at the death.

" England's policy has been to allow the unformed mind free scope to choose its own views and principles from among the many opposing influences surrounding it, without any effort at coercion or direction ; and it is not to be wondered at that the savage and untutored mind of the African, imbued, like most other barbarous races, with great astuteness and cunning, should have very soon adopted the form of civilisation, when it became aware that it would answer its purpose as well as the reality. Herein lies the difficulty of forming a correct judgment of the effects of our policy of freedom upon the African character. And yet what greater proof can be required of the superficial nature of our teaching, and of its want of depth and reality, than the well-ascertained fact that very few instances can be adduced of aliens, thousands of whom are resident, being converted to Christianity or reclaimed from barbarism ? Nothing takes root in a vigorous and rich soil without extending its influence ; and something radically wrong must exist when exertions as disinterested as ever guided a nation in its efforts to benefit another, have produced such barren results. Many who have studied the African character will bear witness to the truth, that the African is a far more innocent and natural creature when he has never been brought within the range of civilised life. But the fault lies not in any natural incapacity for civilisation, but in our method of imparting it.

" We shall not be considered as decrying the African race when we say that it is not fitted, without a guiding hand, to exercise the privileges of English citizenship. We are aware that the opposite opinion will have more adherents, such is the infatuation that exists upon African questions ; but we have only to point to this colony to obtain convincing proofs that we have merely stated a particular appli-

Evening gathered black and heavy upon the brows of
the hills. This is the *finale* of the rains, the Elephanta,

cation of an universal law—the gradual development of the human
mind. By adopting a different opinion, and by following a course
dictated by opposite views, we have formed a race alike incapable of
valuing the coarse but instinctive efforts of their forefathers, or the
refined and purifying elements of civilised life. The next generation
will give further and more convincing proofs of the correctness of these
views ; for, with few exceptions, the liberated Africans are far superior
to the rising generation—in energy, in talents, and in honest principles.
Our policy of allowing entire freedom in the choice of good or evil is
answerable for a large share of the evils which exist, and it accounts
for the want of success which has hitherto attended all the efforts of
the Imperial Government. England had it in her power to guard this
chosen band of Africans from the pollution of clanship and the corruption of idleness. Laws of labour may be out of place in England, but
in Sierra Leone they would have saved an entire population from trust-
ing to the allurements of a petty, demoralising trade,—they would
have saved us the sight of decaying villages, and a population becoming
daily less capable of bearing the laborious toil of agricultural industry.
To handle the hoe has now become a disgrace ; and the people have lost
their manhood by becoming gentlemen. We exhibited a farce to the
civilised world when we appointed learned judges to explain the laws
of evidence, and the complicated details of civil actions, to juries of
ignorant Africans just rescued from the bondship, and when we were
guided by their decisions. A Court of Summary Jurisdiction, presided
over by men of honour and probity, would have been far more suitable to
their wants and to their understandings. The chief judge need not have
held a less dignified position—for purity of justice requires our judges to
be placed above the possibility of temptation. No one can pretend that
English criminal jurisprudence is administered with success in Sierra
Leone ; and latterly less so than formerly, on account of the increasing
power of Aku clanship. In saying this, we cast no slur upon the
Bench. The Bench is far above the criticism of any journal, and we
refer to it merely to reprove the insolence of the Aku apologist who
accused us, not long since, of such pretensions. The Queen's Bench
itself would be powerless before the stolid indifference to the sanctity of
an oath, and the blind obedience to the mandates of chiefs as powerful
as they are unscrupulous. An English judge has but one duty to per-

as it is called by the Hindu, after a certain lunar asterism ; and whilst this southerly wind and cloudy sky do endure, uncomfortable and unhealthy weather will persecute us. Raffales coursed down the Lion's flanks, and the rains discharged their batteries with a fearful energy and perseverance. So the many who had " a hint to stay away" from the station, spent a lively evening on board, collecting under the bit of quarter-deck awning, as Maître Aliboron and his friends gather together for society under some more impervious tree.

On the Wednesday morning, which was tolerably clear, though mists were rolling over the highlands, I landed with the consul of Fernando Po in the captain's gig. At breakfast we had been duly primed with good

form : to follow the strict rules of law, and the terms of his commission. Only the ignorant can boast of the extensive freedom we have given to the African. Freedom, indeed, we should have given, but it ought to have been qualified to suit their capacities. Let the men who advocate the expatriation of the American remember that those whom we brought to this colony are fading from the scene, destroyed by the policy which transferred them to an enervating climate, and then left them to the corrupting influences of an emporium of trade without industry or manufactures. In their stead have arisen the liberated African, and that policy which gives them civilisation without industry, must bring upon them the like consequences. This blind adherence to precedent has allowed the chiefs of the Aku clan—the predominant tribe of liberated Africans—to introduce the most degrading system of secret tyranny known on the African continent. Aku clanship destroys every manly virtue, and neutralises the well-meant but ineffectual efforts to form a people which might kindle the ardour of civilisation and Christianity among their heathen brethren. Arrest that evil in its onward course, and with the commencement of a policy more suitable to the wants and to the capacity of the people, Sierra Leone may yet redeem the hopelessness of failure."

advice, viz., not to notice negro impudence and to turn
our shoulders—the severest punishment—upon all who
tried their hands at annoyance. We rowed to the
Government landing, a ricketty, slippery flight of
wooden stairs, which is positively dangerous at night or
when the waves dash against the jetty. We were
careful to carry no luggage; porters fight for the job,
and often let the object of emulation drop into the
water. One of our mail-bags received this *baptême de
S'a Leone* last night. On such occasions a push or
poke is a forbidden luxury; the man might fall down—
you have certainly injured him internally—you must pay
exemplary damages. Passing through casks in rows we
ascended a short steep path leading to Water Street,
the long broad line which runs along the upper bank.
Here loud—

> " Sounds the oath of British commerce and the accents of
> Cockayne,"

mixed with fearful language on the part of the
"African." A guide presented himself in the person
of Jumbo, a well-known character; and when we
engaged him, he triumphed over his great rival,
" General Jackson," with the true negro laugh, ending
in a chuckle. Our wish was first to post homeward-
bound letters. *Chemin faisant* we entered the establishment of a Mr. Sibyl Boyle, so-called from a ship and
its skipper; it is the regular colonial store, containing
everything from a Dutch cheese to a gold ring, and the
owner, an honourable exception, was civil and honest.

Passing the cathedral, we were shown on its south-west a bit of ground appropriated to the " Wilberforce monument ;" a piece of folly number one, for which 3000*l.*, it is said, have been subscribed.   It is to contain a lecture-room and a library, two of the last things wanted in such a colony.   S'a Leone once had a fine collection of books ; of course it was allowed to go to the bad. Half way up Gloucester Street, the main line leading to Government House, we found the post-office, rank with struggling negroes fighting fiercely for " Mas'er 'um book."   A native policeman, seeing envelopes in my hand, motioned me towards a door, which the black clerk sensibly but sternly shut in my face.   I handed the epistles to Jumbo, who, after contending manfully for half-an-hour, returned with the stern order to come back after noon.   The negro postmaster, whom I afterwards met in the streets, as sternly confirmed the fact. Having thus time to spare, we walked to the top of the street, which might be 150 yards long, and found it arched with sticks and timbers.   This memorial commemorates the auspicious occasion when the colony first looked upon a live Royal Highness, a real white Prince ; it is to be commemorated by a marble *arc-de-triomphe,* for which 700*l.* have been subscribed ; but as 1500*l.* are still wanting, there is not much chance of the present architecture undergoing a change.

Upon this highly interesting spot we stood awhile to remark the peculiarities of the place and its position. The soil is a loose clay, deep red or brown, and impregnated with iron, cold and unfertile, as the spontaneous aloe shows. The subsoil is a rude sandstone, also ferruginous : soft and working well under the axe when first quarried, it soon hardens into the semblance of laterite, and thus weathered, it forms the best of building materials. Imbedded in the upper loam are blocks and boulders, apparently erratic, dislodged or washed down from the upper heights, where similar masses are seen. Many are scattered on the surface, as if by an eruption ; others lie like slabs, or dwarf domes, upon the shore. The shape is usually spheroidal, and the formation primitive hypersthene (close-grained bluish granite), or greenstone, blackened externally by the sun and weather. In the few cuttings of the higher levels I afterwards remarked that detached "hardheads" are thickly puddinged into the more friable sandstone, but nowhere could I see or hear of granitic masses protruded from below. The boulders are cleared away by ditching and surrounding with a hot fire for forty-eight hours ; water, not vinegar, is then poured upon them, causing the heated material to contract and fracture, when it can easily be removed. Magnetic iron, it is said, is also found, but veins of the metal have not yet been discovered.

At the future arch four roads meet : that to the left leads to the old cemetery, now deserted for the new burial-ground on the hill side behind the barracks. There are books which suggest a visit to this spot, and which promise interesting monuments ; *expertus*, I say, with Mr. Punch, in his world-famous advice to people about to marry, "Don't." Under Jumbo's orders we soon found the place, but the gate was closed and the guard absent. After a decent delay, we scaled the wall —not a pleasant operation for crinoline, nor agreeable in small-clothes, on account of snakes. The tombstones are gloomy, heavy parallelopipedons of dingy sandstone, which seem better adapted for a press-yard than a church-yard; and there is no abuse of epitaphs; after the fashion of the tropics, the name is generally considered *de trop.* Intermural sepulture is now forbidden at S'a Leone, as in London; yet there were several fresh graves.

The weak sex, we were told, here musters strong; a curious discrepancy, when they are to the rougher half of humanity about one to ten. It is supposed that women, being less exposed than men, can better resist the climate of S'a Leone. I believe the fact to be the contrary; in many cases the German missionaries have lived, whilst their wives have died. Here lie three Spanish consuls who in four years fell victims to a climate which has slain five captains-general, or governors, in five years. A deserted cemetery, without flowers or whitewash, is always a melancholy spectacle. This was something more. The grass and bush grew dense and dank from the remnants of mortality, and the only tree within the low decaying walls was a poisonous oleander. Another sense than the eye was unpleasantly affected; we escaped from the City of the Slain as from a slave-ship or from a plague hospital.

Our walk had furnished us with a tolerable idea of the settlement's plan. Fronting the north-west, it is built

like all the cities of the very old,* the new, and of the
antipodean worlds, after the fashion of a chess-board,
in squares and blocks; the longer streets flank the sea,
and the shorter run at right angles up the hills behind
the town. Both are of bright red, always edged, and
often more than half overgrown with ribbons of green.
The grass preferred is the American or Bahama, fine,
silky, and creeping along the ground, which it is said
to clear of other vegetation; it forms a good substitute
for turf, and is used to stuff mattresses. When first
imported it was neglected, cut away, and nearly died out;
but it is now encouraged on account of its keeping down
the bush, and its velvety plots greatly relieve the glaring
red surface. The dilapidation of the houses surprised
me. Some are tumbling down, others have tumbled
down; many of those standing are lumber, or board
shanties—"quarter frames" and "ground floors" they
are called; and the few good abodes appeared quite
modern. But what can be expected from a place where
Europeans expect to stay but two years, and where
Africans, who never yet worked without compulsion,
cannot legally be compelled to work?

From the narrow houses of the dead we turned
towards the vegetable market, the neat building with

---

* For instance, the oldest Athens, from the days of Theseus to those
of Hadrian, was like modern Boston—a mass of narrow, tortuous alleys,
on a plan laid out, according to the Americans, by a wandering cow.
The newer Athens was rectangular and parallelogramic, like modern
Washington, but for another reason. The temples of the gods, themselves parallelogramic, like that of Meccah, required broad, straight
avenues, not the *entourage* of a St. Paul's Cathedral.

blind arches and flying roof. Externally stone and
internally brick, this bazaar has half its floor paved and
the other half expecting to be. The roof is of iron : grass
is everywhere too dangerous, palm mats and bamboos are
hardly better, tile is too heavy, slate too dear, so shingles
are here mostly used when they are procurable. After
a rainy season they become grey, and are with difficulty
distinguished from more expensive material. In climates where extremes of heat follow heavy rains, they
curl up and become chronically leaky. The market—it
contained some tailors—was full of fat, middle-aged
negresses, sitting at squat before their "blies" or round
baskets, which contained a variety and confusion of heterogeneous articles, of which the following is a list as
disorderly as the collection which it enumerates. There
were pins and needles, yarn and thread—in the wilder
parts, a thorn and a fibre suffice—needle-cases, with all
kinds of small hardware, looking-glasses in lacquered
frames, beads of sorts, cowries and achatinæ, from which
an excellent soup, equal to the French snail, is prepared;
poor and cheap ginger,—at times the streets are redolent
of it,—dried bats and rats, which the African, as well as
the Chinese, loves; reels of cotton, kolas—here worth
about one halfpenny, and at Bathurst a penny each—and
shea-butter nuts, country snuff-boxes of a chestnut-like
nut, from which snuff is inhaled, *more majorum*, through
a quill; bluestone, colcothar, and other drugs; physic
nuts (tiglium or croton, a favourite but painful native
remedy), shalots, dried peppers, red and black ; horns of
goat and antelope, smoked and dried fish, preferred when

high, to use the mildest term; ground pig—a large
rodent that can climb, destroy vegetables, and bite hard
if necessary—skewered for a *rôt ;* ground-nuts, which the
French have called *pistaches,* very poor rice,* and feathers of the plantain bird. To the walls were suspended
dry goods, red woollen nightcaps and comforters, leopards' and monkey skins, and the spoils of an animal
that might have been a gazelle. The fruits were sweet
sop—the East Indian custard-apple,—soursop (*A. muri-
cata*), citrons, oranges, grown in the mountain districts,
sweet limes, bananas, a finer kind of musa, and plantains,
—which are the horse plantain of Hindostan,—pineapples,
mangos terribly terebinthine,† bitter oranges, unsweet-
ened guavas,‡ the " monkey-plum," or " apple," and the
" governor's plum." The avocado, which the English call
alligator pear (*P. gratissima*), is inferior to the Mexican ;
those fond of it compare the fruit to the flavour of the
finest filberts; I detect in it an unripe melon freshly
taken out of Harrowgate water. The granadilla is not
unlike a papaw,§ the flesh is neglected, whilst the seeds

* There are three kinds of grain :—1. The large Mandenga. 2. The
red rice of Sherbro, which is easily husked : this is rarely grown at
S'a Leone. 3. A liliputian variety, about the size of mignionette,
said to grow in light rocky soils. The natives call it *fundi fundungi,*
or "hungry rice." As a rule, the rice at S'a Leone is dark, but it
is superior in flavour to the Indian.

† It is a common trick to hack the Mango trunk when the fruit
begins to appear : the flavour is improved by the gum flowing off, but
the produce is diminished.

‡ The guava is made to lose its strong medicinal flavour by opening
he trunk, and by inserting with a brush a little honey or sugar and
water.

§ The reader who possesses not the wrinkle, is strongly advised to

and their surroundings are eaten with sherry and sugar; here, however, they are far inferior to the South American. The consul preferred it to all those of Panama —perhaps for reasons best known to himself. The only enjoyable fruit that I tasted at S'a Leone was the strawberry guava, as it is locally called: it has a delicate, sub-acid flavour, not easily equalled. Perhaps it might be introduced into the South of France; let me recommend the Société d'Acclimatisation to elect a few honorary members, and not—as they now do—to expect that travellers will pay for the pleasure of serving them. The principal vegetables were watercress, onions, and various bulbs, calavances or beans, okras, bengans or egg-plants, yams, kokos, and sweet potatoes. The edibles are fufu, balls of finely-levigated cassava flour, sweet ágádi, boiled rice or maize wrapped up in leaves, and ginger-cake; whilst toddy was the principal drink.

Between the market and the sea is the butchers' yard, a ragged and uncleanly strip of ground. The cattle are small, humpless, and long-horned, brindled, or dun, like the Alderney cow; when small, they cost 3*l*. They are driven in from the Fúlá country and the interior, and their beef tastes not unlike what one imagines the produce of a knacker's yard to be. It is peculiar, yet true, that nearly all the meat thus supplied to an emancipated colony and to anti-slave cruisers, has been bought with slaves. Buffaloes once existed here and on the Bananas;

---

boil the unripe fruit of this tree : it is almost as good as vegetable marrow. Also, if cleaned out, filled with forcemeat, and baked, it much resembles the "badinján mahshi," or stuffed egg-plants of Egypt.

they are not found now. Milk is dear, and not plentiful; Englishmen raw in the tropics object to goat, but frequently put up with milch-pig—they are said to be kept for the purpose here—or with a something worse. Butter is oily and rancid. Hogs, as might be expected, are common as in Ireland; there are also long, lean, hairy, black and white sheep, which do not supply an excellent mutton. Goats are plentiful, and their flesh would be good if it had any taste. The poultry list comprises fowls and partridges, ducks and geese, the Muscovy or Manilla duck, and the spur-winged goose from Sherbro.

Behind the meat market is a double row of houses with shops upon the ground-floor, not unlike a Banyan's street in India, but infinitely smaller, meaner, dirtier. Here the stranger can buy dry goods and a few curiosities of Mandenga manufacture—grigris, spears, bows, and saddles and bridles, like those of the Somal, both perfectly useless. The leather, however, is excellent, second only to that of Morocco. A dirty hovel, inscribed "Lunch-house" on a sign-board, flanked by a Union Jack and a Yankee gridiron, represents the American hotel, a hole kept by a Liberian negro; it is the only hostelry in the place.

Having exhausted the bazaars, and the mystic hour of twelve having struck, we again repaired to the Post-office, where, by displaying that humility and respectfulness that became us in the presence of a superior race, Don Jack-in-office graciously permitted us to post our letters. We then passed under the triumphal arch of African architecture—it felt somewhat like being sent classically *sub jugum*—and struck up the road leading to Government House. At the porter's lodge—it was shaded by a fine bamboo, here an exotic brought from the East or West Indies—a constable carried arms, and showed us into a shrubbery of great beauty. I can understand how, with the immense variety of bud, flower, and fruit suddenly presented to his eyes, the gentleman fresh from England took six months to recover the full and free use of all his senses.

At the entrance-portico stood a Zouave sentinel. The residence is large and rambling, built, like many of our English country houses, piecemeal; there is nothing to recommend it but the inmates and the fine view of the sea below. We spent a pleasant day at Government House, in the "Red Grave," as this portion of the great cemetery of the Anglo-Saxon race is called.

Anxious to obtain information touching the palm-nut and kernel trade, we called upon the principal commercial authority, and one of the Legislative or Executive Council (styled Hon.). When the nut was shown to him, the consul at once recognised a species different from that which he had found at Zanzibar and in Central Africa. There the fruit was in berries, like a highly-magnified grape-bunch; here it is as a spike; this, moreover, it is much smaller and less fleshy than on the other side of the Continent. The oil-trade of the West African coast barely dates from the beginning of this century. In 1808, 200 tons, or 8000*l.* worth (assuming the ton = 40*l.*), were exported. In 1856, under the influence of demand and steam navigation, not to mention the suppression of slave-export, which drove the natives into the hard and narrow path of legitimate trade, the export had risen to 40,000 tons, representing two millions of pounds sterling,* now reduced to one

* The value of the palm oil imported into the United Kingdom annually exceeds one and a-half million sterling; the quantity in 1861 amounted to 740,332 cwts. Compared with the imports of this article in 1860, this shows a falling-off to the extent of 63,994 cwts. With the exception of about 27,000 cwts. brought from Portugal, the United States, British India, West India Islands, and other countries not specified in the official returns, the entire supplies are obtained from the various settlements on the Western Coast of Africa.

The quantities and places of shipment for the years 1860 and 1861, together with the values and prices for the latter year, are subjoined :—

	Imported in		Value.	Aver. pr.		
	1860	1861.	1861.	1861.		
	Cwts.	Cwts.	£	£	s.	d.
Portugal . . .	6,250	4,250	9,173	2	3	2
Fernando Po . . .	4,347	6,842	14,615	2	2	9
Portuguese Possessions on Western Africa . .	—	6,077	13,227	2	3	6
Western Africa (not designated)	754,087	657,765	1,403,541	2	2	8
United States, Northern Atlantic Ports . .	—	7,616	16,150	2	2	5
Sierra Leone . . .	9,288	15,637	33,543	2	2	11
British Possessions on the Gold Coast . .	16,866	27,057	58,551	2	3	3
India, Singapore & Ceylon	—	10,724	21,716	2	0	6
British West India Islands	9,571	3,060	6,630	2	3	4
Other Countries . .	3,917	1,304	2,807	2	3	1
Totals . .	804,326	740,332	1,579,953			
	740,332					

Decrease in 1861 .   63,994

With the exception of 52,515 cwts., the whole of the above was brought into this country in British vessels.

and a-half. It increases, however, and though the earth oils of the Far West and Russian tallow will presently cause great changes in the trade, it is capable of an almost unlimited development.

Before 1850 the kernels were thrown away, after the native fashion, despite their valuable yield of oil—30 per cent.—their cake, useful for fattening animals, and their refuse to be converted into compost. In that year 4096 bushels of husked kernels found their way to England. In 1856 the total shipped from S'a Leone and the adjacent coast was 150,000 bushels of charred kernels, which, at a minimum of 35*l.* per ton of oil and 3*l.* per ton of cake, would represent 48,000*l.** There is evidently much to be done in this way. The want of population and industry must be supplied by effectual machinery, which has not yet been invented. At present, in the oil rivers, the kernels are either thrown away or used as fuel; at Badagry shiploads are lying about, but no one takes the trouble to collect them. Moreover, the English manufacturer must learn from the Marseillais the best and most economical methods of purifying and preparing the oil. The natives toast the nuts over a wood fire, pound them in large wooden pestles, and boil the mass in country pots. The scum is then skimmed off, and is known as black or nut-oils. Other tribes burn the nut, and collect the fatty matter that drips from it. Mr. Macgregor Laird's fellow-explorer

---

* The figures are taken from the Hon. Mr. Heddle's letter of May 8, 1857, published in Dr. Baikie's " Report upon the Development of the Trade of Central Africa."

of the Niger, Mr. Oldfield, who died at S'a Leone in
1859, used to extract from the neglected kernels a
beautiful clear oil, ˉequal to the newly-discovered
paraffin.

The mercantile world in England is too apt to imagine
that, because the West Africans have opened the palm-
oil trade, they will succeed in cotton-growing. The
deduction is not fair. The former is easy, the latter difficult, to cultivate; this wants regular labour at epochs
verging upon the excessive, that is the lightest form of
work. As yet, cotton has never been grown to perfection
except by slave races—those of the Southern States
of America. Egypt ranks, or rather ranked, next during
the days of Mohammed Ali Pasha, who confiscated all
the acres not devoted to his favourite growth; and India
—a free country, but a starving—brings up the rear.

We were shown some specimens of the gum copal,
from Mallicorie, a district about thirty miles north of the
river, and from the lowlands about Sherbro Island. It
was lumpy, and of a dead, dull white colour, like the
best gum Arabic; the absence of the goose skin proved
it to be what is called in Zanzibar chakazi, jackass, or
raw copal. We tasted some coffee, growing wild—
nearly in the parallel of Mocha, between the rivers
Pongo and Nuñez, which, according to accounts, the
French have lately annexed. The territory comprises
about fifty miles of coast, with an unknown interior
depth along the latter river, possibly extending to Kara-
gwah, where the shrub grows spontaneously, and to that
Kafa, which may have suggested to the Arabs a name

for the new beverage.* The French traders prefer the small, bright, brown-yellow beans to the Mocha, and are rapidly monopolising the supply. Another native product which will become valuable is the "tallow-nut," locally called "mút." It is taken from a pod, and resembles in size and shape the Brazil nut; the tree, though rendered rare by destructive bush-burning, still lingers on the hills behind Freetown, and may be found growing wild all along the coast. These productions of West Africa are of many different kinds, and few of them are as yet known. The West African trade, which in these parts is now four centuries old, will soon develope itself in good earnest. Formerly ships were contented to anchor off the mouths of rivers, and to sail away with a little gold-dust, ivory, and pepper, and a few slaves. Now, agents and masters will push their way into the more salubrious interior, and open up new and unexploited sources of wealth. When Sanitaria shall be erected, and the white population settled at an altitude above sea level, where it can retain its energy and resolution, when greater facilities of locomotion and intercourse are afforded, and, lastly, when the Africans are compelled by circumstances to become a working people, the "Black Coast" will become a valuable possession.

---

* Coffee, it is well known, was introduced into Arabia by the Shaykh el Shazeli, who had visited Harar and possibly southern Abyssinia ; "Káfá," the name of the place that supplied the plant, would account for the reason why the Arabs chose for it the old word "Kahwah," which means old wine. If coffee be indigenous to West Africa, it is another instance of Abyssinian vegetation extending to the opposite coast.

On the morning of the next day appeared alongside of us the gunboats, bringing a different class of objects —servants and beasts.   Ships in these latitudes become small menageries, especially when homeward bound: every one is anxious to carry something back—a grey parrot, or a pair of palm-birds, a monkey, a mongoose, or a ground-pig.   Darkey has heard of certain small sums having been cleared thus in England; he therefore asks from twice to ten times the value of his live goods. An otter, from the rivulets behind Freetown, was bought for three half-crowns; sundry snakes were offered for sale—the Mandenga snake, three to four feet long, black upon a yellow ground,* and a venomous-looking cobra with flat cordiate head, broad like all the more ferocious animals.   Whilst the owners are "making trade," the "pull-a-boys" amuse themselves with hauling in flat fish, which, on account of its bonyness, no one but themselves will eat.   Servants in shoals presented themselves begging "mas'er" to take them down coast.   In vain; the S'a Leone man is handier than his Southern brother, he can mend a wheel, make a coffin or cut your hair, operations which in other places must remain wanted. Yet no one—at least if not a perfect greenhorn on the coast—will engage him in any capacity.   In civility and respectfulness, he is far below the Brazilian or the Cuban emancipado.   He has learned a "trick or two:" even a black who has once visited Sierra Leone is considered spoiled for life, as if he spent a year in England.

---

* It is described to be a small boa, but I did not see it.

Ship masters prefer the "blue nose"—the Kruman—from Cape Palmas, despite the taunt of being a "bush boy " thrown at him by his more civilised companions of S'a Leone. The S'a Leone man is an inveterate thief; he drinks, he gambles, he intrigues, he over-dresses himself, and when he has exhausted his means, he makes master pay for all. With a terrible partiality for summonsing and enjoying himself thoroughly in a court of law, he enters into the spirit of the thing like an attorney's clerk ; he soon wearies of the less exciting life in the wilder settlements, where debauchery has not yet developed itself,—home sickness then seizes him, and he deserts, after probably robbing the house. He is the horror of Europeans; the merchants of the Gaboon River prefer forfeiting the benefits of the A. S. S. to seeing themselves invaded by this locust tribe, whose most beautiful view is apparently that which leads out of S'a Leone. At Lagos and Abeokuta S'a Leone has returned to his natural paganism, and has become an inveterate slave-dealer, impudently placing himself under native protection and renegading the flag that saved him from life-long servitude. Even during the Blackland's short stay, the unruly, disorderly character of the man often enough showed itself by fisticuffing, pulling hair, and cursing, with a mixture of English and African ideas, that presented a really portentous *tout ensemble*.

Landing at the slippery Government wharves—it must be a black joke on a rough night, when you know that a few feet below you there may be a shark with six rows of teeth, and jaws that will decapitate a horse—we proceeded to spend our second day at S'a Leone. The sensation was of a hot and sickly heat, not as it is generally described, of a "furnace presenting its parched mouth." Mr. Jumbo had promised to procure me a carriage, and had failed; he therefore received what is popularly called "the sack." The swells keep vehicles, and there are a few for hire; but when the carriage is forthcoming, the horse is down, and when the horse is up, the carriage is nowhere. Horses live at S'a Leone a maximum of four years, and generally die of staggers, caused by the worm, or of loin disease—paralysis of the hind-quarters. They come from the Fula, Susu and Mandenga countries; they are mere tattoos, with mouths like old boots; and they are generally very vicious, from ill-treatment. The best fodder is the ground-nut leaf, and the precaution is to keep them out of draughts by day and protect them from cold at night. Despite which they soon lose strength and pluck, becoming misplaced as an Arab in Malabar. Even English dogs, if they are to be kept in this world, must be tended as carefully as babies at home, rigorously limited to soup and farinaceous diet once a day, with sulphur and water to drink, and be washed, combed and dressed morning and evening. Asses, as usual, in Africa live where horses die, and perhaps mules from Tenerife or Cape Verde Islands might survive their nobler dams.

Failing to secure a carriage or a hammock—there are some pretty networks, red, black and yellow—we proceeded on foot, under the guidance of a commissariat

officer, to call upon the Rev. Mr. Jones, a West Indian,
one of the oldest inhabitants in the place, and the best
preacher. He formerly edited the "African Herald," a
"coloured," perhaps I might say a buff, organ. Since
that time it has or has not passed out of his hands, and
become the "African Weekly Times." The "Sierra
Leone Gazette" was given up when the Wesleyan
Methodist Society established in July, 1842, the "Sierra
Leone Watchman." A second journal has been started,
the "Free Press;" a radical paper, representing Young
S'a Leone, and the editor is always quoted as the
"funny man," the "serio-comic party," and in reply he
has used up all his adjectives. A third is about to issue,
the "Intelligencer," a white or "blue" paper, intruded
to prove, if possible, the truth of what has sometimes
been asserted at negro indignation meetings, namely,
that a white man, if he "behaves himself," is as good
as a black man. Journalism * at S'a Leone is still, as
might be expected, in the lowest stage of Eatenswillism
—a melancholy contrast to its brother of Liberia. Mr.
Jones, who is a walking register of local events, was at
the time of our visit proceeding to perform a very grand
marriage ceremony at the cathedral—for the less civilised
the people, the more importance they attach to the

---

* The following is a list of journals now published on the west coast
of Africa, from Cape Spartel to the Cape of Good Hope :—

S'a Leone—1. African Weekly Times ; 2. Free Press.

Liberia—1. Cavala Messenger, Cape Palmas ; 2. Liberia Herald ;
3. Monrovia Messenger.

Gold Coast—West African Herald.

Abeokuta—Iwe Irohin.

display which I, for one, begging pardon of all Belgraviã, consider a most barbarous and indelicate exhibition. He kindly turned back, invited us into his house and gave us the required information. He spoke highly of Dr. Winterbottom's book on S'a Leone, published in 1804. The author was a surgeon in the service of the old West India Company, which has produced so many eminent men, amongst whom Dr. Copland, the celebrated compiler of the "Dictionary of Practical Medicine," may be cited. He lived long enough to see his writings well "shroffled," without acknowledgment, by all subsequent travellers, and three years ago he died at Shields. Mr. Jones also commended the "White Man's Grave," by Mr. Rankin, colonial chaplain at Gambia, and "Missions in Western Africa," published by the Tract Society. As regards "A Residence in Sierra Leone, by a Lady," the opinions of the colony ran high against this "Bird's Eye View," because of its truthfulness. The lady was the wife of a pensioned judge of the Mixed Customs Court, lived seven years secluded at Carnes' Farm, and is said to have painted life at S'a Leone in exceptionally sombre colours. Her sketch of a sojourn upon the Lion's Range is certainly not tempting. Young gentlemen about to marry in England hide the work from the fair intendeds. I cannot, however, but admire the elaborate sketches of scenery, and the fidelity of those descriptions concerning which I have a right to form an opinion.

After taking leave of Mr. Jones, who concluded some excellent advice about retaining life in the tropics, with the valuable motto "Take it easy," I proceeded to inspect the only antiquity which S'a Leone knows. It is an outscarp of primitive rock, below King Jimmy's bridge and alongside the waterworks. According to some, Sir Francis Drake, the discoverer of California and its gold, and the brave knight of whom the Virgin Queen said, that "his actions did him more honour than his title," here left his name with the date of his first visit; others have correctly attributed it to Sir John Hawkins, the great slaver. In 1562,* this captain landed at S'a Leone, freighted three ships with 300 negroes, and carried them to St. Domingo: he returned to England, after making a goodly sum of money, in September, 1563. In the next year he sailed with the Solomon, the Swallow, the Brazen Tyger, and the Jesus of Lübeck;— what a name for such an errand! In one place he could purchase only 10 negroes; "obtained with the loss of seven of his best men, among whom was the captain of the Solomon, besides seven-and-twenty men wounded." On the 27th January, 1565, he went to the West Indies, and "brought the Spaniards to reason;" in other words, forced them to take his live cargo at Burboroata. He was assisted by the merchant princes of London, and he

---

* The first cargo was run by Gilianez, in 1442. Missionaries and lecturers are exceedingly fond of charging the miseries of Africa upon Europeans, especially the English. This is partly true, as far as intertropical West Africa goes. The north, however, must have sent many millions of slaves, in olden times, to the shores of the Mediterranean, and the "Periplus of the Red Sea" speaks of the trade on the eastern coast as if it had long been established. However, such clap-trap looses the purse-strings—as it is intended to do—and is a safe hit where not one in 1000 hearers knows anything of the subject.

obtained a patent for his crest, "a demi-moor in his proper colour." But two centuries afterwards he would probably have been hung, so rapid is our progress in morality. In 1567 he attacked Cape Verde, where many of his men were wounded with poisoned arrows, which brought on what appeared to be tetanus. He was a fellow-combatant with Drake against the Armada, and died in 1595. The memory of this old naval worthy blossoms in the dust at S'a Leone as the "first slaver."

The tramp of negro feet and the waters of the rivulet have totally effaced the inscription, which was, they say, legible 20 years ago. The rock is covered with griffon-ages, and some well-cut square letters extending to the ground : it is easy to read,

M. A. RVITER

VICE—AMIRALL—

VAN—HOLLANT.

Near this rock is King James's well, a spring of great purity, which supplies the shipping. On the other side of the ravine is the town gaol, at the south-west end, near what is called "Kru-town brook," a mountain drain. This prison is conducted on philanthropic prin-ciples; the daily allowance is a quart of rice, and a quarter gill of salt, and the prisoners lie on their backs and sing comic songs like sepoys.

As no carriage was forthcoming, we hired a boat, and proceeded westwards along the shore, wishing to see the "fashionable" drive to Kissy, where local honeymoons are spent, the racecourse, which, as in India, forms the favourite riding-ground, and the site of Granville Town.

The day cleared up, the sun shone warm and bright;
the white sand beach and eternal verdure of the low
Bullom shores were invested with a halo of beauty, which
it derived from on high ; and the colours were those of
Heligoland in the song,—gold sand, green strand, red
land, all set in lapis lazuli above, and sapphire framework
below. The scenery of the lovely charnel-house thus
seen is charming, *mais c'est la mort*—it is the terrible
beauty of death. Mrs. M—— well describes this sensation : "I felt amidst all the glory of tropic sunlight
and everlasting verdure, a sort of ineffable dread connected with the climate." Even when leaving the
"pestilent shore," she was "haunted by its shadowy
presence." This is womanly, but a little reflection must
suggest it to man. Passing north of Battery Point,
alias Fort Falconbridge, and other high-sounding
names, we debouched upon a deep little bight or cove,
Susan or Sawpit Bay, which much resembled those
described during our steaming in. It is also called
Destruction Bay—a gloomy name,—where ships convicted of carrying " Bales," " Dry goods," or " Black-
birds," were broken up ; some traces still remain. The
washerwomen were at their craft, the sawpits were idle,
and the more juvenile, dressed *secundum naturam*, were
bathing. The Susu and other African tribes used to
punish by slavery a man who looked upon the fair sex
" cleaning" itself, and a few years ago an English
traveller thus committing himself was severely flogged.
From behind Susan Bay the huts of the lower town
stretch upwards, rounding Barrack Hill, and looking

not unlike the architecture of white ants. Another shoally projection introduced us to Fourah Bay, of which "Susan" is a section. In the high background is a fine brook, cold, clear, and pure, affording a delicious bath; it is almost dry in the hot season, and it swells to a fiumara during the rains. Its extent was then a diminutive rivulet, tumbling some 2000 feet down a shelving bed; it falls into Granville Bay, that adjoins Fourah. The neighbourhood used to be dangerous at night—many murders were committed there. On the way we passed boats manned by the Timni—Timmani, Timaneh, Timnay, Temneh, or "Timne," as M. Koelle's "Polyglotta Africana" prefers to call them. Of old the lords of S'a Leone, they still come down for trade from Porto Logo, Waterloo, and other places up the river, with rice and cocoa-nuts, and not unfrequently console themselves for their losses by a little hard fighting; witness their defence of the Modúka stockade in December 1861.* The boats are heavy row barges,

* The following is a brief account by one of the Government officers :—

"Head-quarters, Dec. 19, 1861.

"My dear Sir,—You will like to hear the news—40 Timanehs have been killed ; only five dead bodies were found in the stockade. The slaughter was by our allies, the Kossos, living in the country, who took advantage of the flight from the stockade, followed them through the night, and burnt six of their towns. The 40 killed are well-authenticated and their names known ; probably many more whom we have not yet heard of. They must have carried the wounded out of the stockade when they fled. The attack commenced about 4 P.M. on the 18th. All the troops, with the exception of the gunners and officers, were ordered to lie down and wait the assault. It was while at the

with a framework of sticks for an awning over the stern; an old Mandenga with white beard sits at each helm. They row *simplex munditiis*—at S'a Leone a man is punished for not wearing breeches, and thus the place becomes a rag-fair. The Timni men are dark negroids, with the slightest infusion of semitic blood; some had their eyelids and part of their faces coated with chalk for ophthalmia. They appeared to be merry fellows enough, and were certainly the only men in the colony who pretended ever to work. From afar, melting into hazy indistinctness, appeared the bluish sails of little boats which carry a proportionally immense amount of muslin; of these fishing-boats some ply by day, others by night. Arriving at a rocky point below the missionary establishment, now partly converted into a bishop's palace, we disembarked and visited the place. It nestles comfortably near the Hippodrome of S'a Leone and Granville Bay, where " satisfactions " are given. A satirical doctor declares that during 40 years of *rencontres* there has not been a single casualty; he is more witty than wise: I heard of one gentleman who had been winged. Old Granville Town has completely

---

gun that Sergeant Knight was killed, being shot through the head. Finding that the gun was doing little execution, the commander of the troops, Major Hill, turned to Captain Jones to ask him about assaulting, when he received a shot between the chest and shoulder-blade. Captain Jones advanced immediately, and the place was taken in 11 minutes.

"Return of Casualties.—Major Hill, wounded dangerously: Captain Jones, wounded slightly; Captain Williams, wounded slightly; Sergeant C. Evans, wounded slightly; three privates, wounded dangerously; irregular troops, 20, some dangerously wounded, and others slightly."

disappeared, the ruins of the last house are gone from
the broad grassy plain on which the first colonists pitched
their tents.   North-eastward stretches the mysterious
river, which for 400 years has, like the Nile and the
Niger, concealed its head from the white man's gaze.
Nothing would be easier than the exploration.   With
a little Arabic literature and Mandenga vernacular, a
traveller, properly attired and accoutred, would, I believe,
find this an excellent point *de départ.*

We returned by the "Kissy Road," the pet promenade
and show walk of the place.   The vegetation was magnificent, running up to the feet of the hills that rise
suddenly from the plain.   The approach to S'a Leone
was heralded by a row of shops, much smaller and more
miserable than those near the market-place.   There are
whole streets of these rabbit-hutches, the contents of
which, "mammy," when day is done, carries home in
a bly upon her head, possibly leaving " titty " to look
after the remnant till she returns.   The stock in trade
may represent a capital of 4*l.*, the profits 1*s.* per diem.
Yet " daddy" calls himself merchant, gets credit, and
passes his evening in smoking cabbage-leaf cigars—as a
gentleman should—with his friends.

That evening was to witness an important event.   The
bachelors of Tower Hill Barracks had invited various
guests, of whom I had the honour to be one, *à diner,*
at 7 P.M.   Dr. Morphew kindly sent me a nag, and at
6 P.M. I found myself jogging up the steep ascent.
The difference of temperature explained the superior
salubrity of the place.   The officers are not paler nor

more emaciated than those of an East Indian corps, and
of the men—no economy, they fall off as rapidly as
Europeans in these lands—only four had died in the
eight months after their arrival. During the terrible
yellow fever of 1858-59,* when the lower town was
almost depopulated, and all who could manage to retreat,
retreated, the only fatal cases in the barracks were those
brought up from the low land, and the disease did not
spread there. Tower Hill derives its name from a ruined
martello, supposed to have been built by the Dutch, and
now used for stores. The barracks are composed of six
large bungalows, built on the hill crest, and the area or
yard is girt with a low, dark, loop-holed wall, and easily
accommodates the garrison,† two companies of the second
West India regiment, with two captains and two sub-
alterns—all the rest being on the staff or on detached
duty. They contain cool and lofty rooms twenty
feet high,— including a billiard - room with a table
curiously levelled,—and are surrounded by shady and
airy piazzas, where the wind, when there is any, must find
its way. For many years they had jalousies and half-
windows only, instead of glass, which forced the inmates

---

* During this year, of 120 whites, 30 left the place, 30 died, and
of the remainder few escaped without sickness. The epidemics of
1839-1840, and of 1847-1848, were nearly as bad. In the former,
Warburg's drops were, it is said, tried, and, succeeding with fever, they
failed to cure yellow fever. Government has very properly ordered
another trial. There is a popular superstition that every tenth year is
a "clearer off" at S'a Leone. The elements fight against it, but
unfortunately man will not trouble himself to fight against the elements.

† I could learn nothing concerning the S'a Leone militia, except
that the company's officers and the adjutant are supplied by the line.

to sit in darkness during rain. I sat there to enjoy the
view. Though the season of the smokes has not set
in, the sun, with rays of lilac red, set over a splendid
panorama of land, sea, and town, whose homeliness
had now disappeared. Mingling afar with the indistinctness of the horizon, the nearer waters set off by
their golden and silvery sheen the capes and far projecting tongues which stretched in long perspective
below; while the Sugarloaf, father of mountains, rose
in solitary dignity high above the subject hills. It
was truly a beautiful prospect. On the near slope of
Station Point I saw the first of the bush burnings;
they are like prairie fires in these lands, and sometimes
they encircle Freetown with a wall of flame.

Night comes on quickly in equinoctical regions;*
it was announced by the grating of crickets, the buzzing
of beetles and cockroaches, and a frog concert, where
the orchestra was in superior strength. We dined in the
mess-room, which was hung round with palm-leaves. The
servants were orderlies in white cotton clothes, including
gloves and chokers; the style of waiting seemed to
consist chiefly of staring wildly at you, or indulging in
a broad grin when you call for any article, and then,
as if by sudden inspiration, rushing off to fetch the
wrong thing. It seems impossible to persuade the
negro mind that fish and beef are not eaten together,
and that the same plate is not intended to hold, at one

---

* In this latitude the English day is 12 hrs. 29 sec. 45 min. ; the
shortest, 11 hrs. 30 sec. 14 min. ; and the maximum of difference,
49 min. 31 sec.

time, pork and mutton. And as they prefer that
your coat should suffer rather than their own, a champagne bottle is rarely opened without a mishap, perhaps
a cork in the eyes of some very testy elderly official.
The style of a regiment may be known by its mess.
When strangers are welcomed, introduced to the
"women," and placed near them in good seats; when
all the officers take wine—'tis an obsolete custom, but
a kindly—with them, and do not await an introduction before addressing them ; when the bottle circulates freely, after the cloth, the chaplain, and the
crinolines have been removed, and when introductions
to pretty partners follow,—then we, the stranger-world,
cannot but enjoy ourselves. After the feed, the room
was cleared, and dancing was done to the sounds of fife
and drum, which were excellent. How much better are
these simple instruments than the terrible medley which
so offends the ear of taste in military bands,—and from
the brass bands may Phœbus Apollo deliver me ! The
African climate, however, has a mood too melting to
render dancing pleasant or even pleasing to look at.
And no Englishman seems to think that the inexorable
day comes, the day of stoutness in the waist, of face
scarlet as the coat, and—how shall I say it ? of
perspiratory excess (will that do ?)—when he should
abandon the seducing enjoyment. But no ! he dances,
and he dances on like an upright turtle revolving upon
its own pivot, topped with perchance bald scalp or grey
bristles, which, seen under such influences, are not
honourable. Let us, O my middle-aged friends ! leave

these graceful exercises to graceful youth—especially in the tropics.

Individually disliking to stand in a doorway, and witness a style of saltation which European fastidiousness has deprived of all its charms, I retreated to an officer's quarters, where with a pleasant companion who could speak of the "absent but not forgotten," and alternate silence sweetened by the herb which Thevet invented and Nicot named and sang,

> " O Tabac ! O Tabac ! mes plus chères amours !"

—of course there was nothing more material upon the table—I spent an agreeable evening. The Freetown day usually concludes, as in Indian out-stations, with a mild game of whist; it may be a pleasant amusement, but, in my humble opinion, cards with small stakes are somewhat like writing a book gratis. We took leave, about the merrier hours, of our hospitable hosts, and descended the hill *en masse*, with a lantern to preserve our shins from boulders, and our total selves from ditches and ravines. The town of course was dead asleep, but my companion's gig was waiting at the shipping stairs, despite which and the sharks, I found myself, at 2 A.M., once more on board the African steam-ship "Blackland."

Our departure from S'a Leone was advertised for the next morning, Friday. It was regretted by none, despite the hospitalities of the place, except by our Frenchman, who, having found at the Spanish vice-consul's *une cuisine Française*, appeared willing to pitch his tent in the lion's den. The morning broke dull and grey, heavy lowering clouds banking up from the Home of Fevers, the long, low Bullom shore, and the air was rather warm than cool, as heavy rains entitled us to expect. In the tropics it is still a tenet, doubtlessly inherited, that rising with the lark—to use a home phrase where no two-legged thing of this name exists— strengthens the white constitution for the heat and burden of the day. The contrary is the opinion of the wise of Freetown : they declare sunrise to be dangerous as sunset, that a morning mist is miasmatic as evening dew, and that those who want fever, have only to expose themselves at a time when the stomach is not strong. I believe them. Even in England no man of sense— old Indians not alluded to—rises, except in midsummer, before the world is brushed and broomed, aired and sunned. Early from bed is enjoyment in the dry and healthy regions of Arabia, it is not wholly unadvisable in sub-humid Egypt, and it becomes an abomination in the bleak and sombre North, as well as in the rank and fetid bush of Western Africa.

We rose betimes that day, because we expected a treat; our gallant captain had been subpœnaed as a witness in a police case between Messrs. Elliot and Johnson, the rival black pilots, who had joined issue upon the subject of dues. After breakfasting and preparing ourselves for the climate of the Court House, we landed, but not at the Government wharf. As the surf ran high, and we had no wish to break our legs, we chose another *débarcadour* by the side of the commissairat, where a rude little breakwater protects

from positive risk. We walked for a mile or two to
St. George's Pool, another pleasant bathing-place under
the hills. A tope of bamboos surrounds the little "eye"
of water, and a neighbouring cottage supplies mats, and
lights for the subsequent cigar. Entering the "palace
of Justice" at 10 A.M., the specified hour, we found it
wholly untenanted. The beak would not, we were
informed by a surly clerk coloured *café au lait,* put in
an appearance for another hour. We strolled about,
and thus lost what *habitués* of Marylebone call a "nice
case." A Mandenga, accused of insulting a girl, was
placed in the dock, duly convicted, and summarily fined
40*s.*, or condemned in default to fourteen days' prison,
by the police magistrate, a captain in the "2nd West,"
who, "standing no nonsense," gives general satisfaction
to the Europeans of S'a Leone. He fines them 5*s.*,
whereas not a few of his predecessors made the proportion 5*l.* to a white, 1*s.* to a black man; and he is called
"Captain Ten Pounds," because in the case of negro
misdemeanor he prefers that sum to the "fiver."
Several of the culprit's fellow-tribesmen were standing
at the court-door. It was impossible not to be struck
by the superiority of their deportment and appearance.
Their loose and ample robes, even when of poor stuff,
gave them breadth as well as height, and the picturesque folds contrasted wonderfully well with the grimy
slops of the poorer Christian, and the caricatured imitation
of our dress—itself a caricature—affected, at much loss
of comfort and aspect, by "Gentlemen," the richer
negro classes. There is a manliness and honesty in

the Mandenga's look, wholly wanting amongst the
"liberated." The dignity of El Islam everywhere displays itself; it is the majesty of the monotheist who ignores the degrading doctrines of original sin, the sublime
indifference to life which Kazi wa Kadar—we must
meagrely translate it fatalism—confers upon the votaries
of "The Faith." As regards education, I believe the
Mandengas to be, despite the want of governmental
instruction, as well advanced in the three Rvs. as any
other tribe in Freetown. I found them able to recite
their prayers, to repeat the shorter chapters in the
Kalam Ullah, and to read the religious sentences which
I wrote for them. In the space below the gate stood a
Fakih—our learned travellers in, and writers on, Western
Africa call him "fetish man"—a venerable elder with
almost Arab features, tall fez, loose white burnous,
and shalwars gathered in at the ankle, like those of the
Bombay "Bohra." I could not resist the temptation of
an *as' salamu alaykum*, and enjoyed the widening of
eye and nostril with which he made the *de rigueur* reply
to so auspicious a salutation proceeding from a source
apparently so unseemly.

There are who may consider these remarks pre-
judiced, and attribute to mere antipathy my small
appreciation of the Christianised African, and my claims
for the Moslem of a palpable superiority over the
missionary converts and the emancipated populace of
S'a Leone. They may, however, rest assured, that
not only I, but every one with me,—from those who saw
Africa and a Moslem for the first time, to the veteran

Meccan pilgrim, one and all,—made the same remark.
The fact is " *Azhar min el Shams*."

The police court at S'a Leone is managed much like
that of Westminster. The beak sits upon a tall desk, the
clerk at a lower one before him. In the right corner is a
dock, the usual loose box. The large whitewashed room
is bisected by a railing. The rough and ragged are in
the outer half; their betters, who have boots or *bottines*
and whole breeches, occupy a bench in the interior,
where also the " distinguished visitor " is, or rather may
be, accommodated with a chair. The other officials are
constables, men of all tints, from *café noir* to *café au
lait*, and habited in police uniform, a blue coat with red
facings and metal buttons. The witnesses are allowed
to hear and to converse with one another, a contrivance
which must considerably facilitate matters to them.

The knotty question was, did or did not Mr. Elliot,
the plaintiff, first put off from the shore, first make for
the mail steamer, and consequently has he or has he not
first claim to pilotage? I had no doubt of the legality of
his pretensions, nor, if there be any truth in " Saunders'
Physiognomie," had Mr. Johnson. The plaintiff, examined his witnesses like a heaven-born lawyer—if such
epithet can be applied to the "devil's own"—and cross-
questioned them with an expertness engendered evidently
by hard practice. He puckered up his vicious forehead,
rubbed for ideas his beardless chin, and appeared to revel
in the usual trickery and chicanery of a negro court. The
witnesses stood for examination upon the steps leading
to the magistrate's desk, took the Bible in hand, and

parrot-like repeated the usual form of imprecation, shirk-
ing, if possible, the kissing process. When will civilised nations abolish this fetish-like process of swearing,
and substitute for it an affirmation with an equal penalty
if violated? What want of sense it shows if judge and
jury are compelled to elicit truth by a mere superstition. What power it places in the hands of an
unscrupulous man who knows that Jove both laughs at
lovers' broken vows, and is slow to punish the perjury
of witnesses,—even of one who holds, as many pious
souls do, to the doctrine of mental reservation. After
the swearing ensued a bout of forswearing that would
make any one with the slightest respect for the sacred
volume shudder. The object of each witness was so to
stand that he could catch the eye of his "daddy" or boss;
the cross-questioner then took him by the shoulders and
forced him to front the other way. When the witness
had the weakness to balk at his perjuries, the plaintiff
raised his index toward the ceiling, declaring that "dis
he be God-palaver." Thus adjured, the witness took his
leaps like a man. The police magistrate made notes of
the long tissue of shameless falsehoods with exemplary
patience, a scrupulousness which reminded the consul of
that pious Madras major on the Neilgherry hills, who, in
years gone by, caused a certain Portuguese "buttrel"
to suborn a prodigious amount of false witness. And
pleasant to relate, whilst those of elder generation were
thus enjoying the excitement of perjury, the junior on the
other side of the building, separated by the thinness
of party-walls, was refreshing itself with psalms and

spiritual songs. This nuisance cannot be abated. The police magistrate may object that the vile symphony gives him the megrims, distracts his attention from his duties. The only consequence is, that he will be politely invited by the director of the school to "make tracks." I must mention the conclusion of the case. Mr. Elliot, who was non-suited, sprung up, and blatantly declaring his resolution to appeal, ran off to some lawyer for the purpose of laying a caveat against the money being paid to Mr. Johnson. All was fearfully technical.

When weary of the monotonous course of lying, we thought it as well to hear the psalmody. Ascending the staircase in the gable opposite the court-house, we passed down the hall, and saw through the open door the young idea at its mental drill in the hands of a pedagogue, apparently one of the αναιμοσαρκα, who, ghastly white, with Paganini hair, sat at the head of the room, the ruling spirit of this unruly rout. Down the long length, whose whitewashed walls were garnished with inscriptions, moral, legal, and religious, all sublime as far as size went, stood parallel rows of negrillons, in the vast costumal variety of a ragged-school. They were bolt upright, square to the fore, in the position of " 'tention," their naked toes turned out to an angle of 60°, little fingers close to the seams of their breeches—when they had any—heads up and eyes front. The body and features generally were motionless, as if cut in ebony ; nothing moved but the saucer-like white eyes and the ivory-lined mouths, from whose ample aperture issued a prodigious volume of sound. Native assistants

in black faces and yellowish - white chokers, carrying
music scores, and armed with what is commonly called
a cane, sloped along the rows, standing occasionally to
frown down some delinquent whose body was not perfectly motionless, and whose mind was not wholly fixed
upon the development of sacred Time and Tune. I have
no doubt that they sung

> "The sun, the moon, and all the stars," &c.

precisely in the same spirit as if they had been singing

> "Peter Hill ! poor soul !
> Flog him wife, oh no ! oh no ! "

Or that equally imposing Jamaican hymn

> "God 'um lub 'um nigger well,
> God 'um twig 'um by 'um smell ;
> When 'um nigger to 'um cry,
> God 'um gib 'um punkin pie-ie-ie."

Which shares the honours of negro popularity with

> " O open the door, Maggie Dudah (three times).
> Beauty, I want to come in ! "

It is a pity that time and work are thus wasted. The
negro child, like the East Indian, is much "sharper"
than the European—at six years of age he will become
a good writer; in fact, he promises more than he can
perform. At the age of puberty this precocity — for
certain reasons—disappears, and the 'cute lad becomes a
dummer jünger. Of course it is a mistake to overstrain
his faculties at school, to make him learn aught that
is useless, to teach him algebra, as it were, before arith-

metic. Mrs. M. thus describes her small girl-servant from one of these schools :—" She looks about nine years old, and, as far as reading goes, she knows nothing more than her alphabet, can yet repeat the Prayer-book catechism by rote, and one or two hymns, utterly ignorant all the while of the import of a single word." Even in Europe education exercises the judgment too little, the memory too much; consequently, there are more learned men than wise men. This system is on the change, and the Gymnasium is gradually taking the place of the Athenæum ; the *corpus sanum* being the first requisite for the *mens sana.* Amongst missionaries the English language seems to be held a second revelation. Instead of two to three hours of reading, writing, and arithmetic, and six of the work-yard or shop, the boys are kept nine hours in school, and no inconsiderable part of the time is devoted to learning verse by heart, and to practise a vocalisation which it is hard to hear without pain.

Thus concluded my experiences at S'a Leone. Before going on board, however, I have something to say about the present state of the colony, and that my remarks may be intelligible it will be necessary to look back into the past.

Fifteen years after Lord Mansfield had established the sublime but unphysiological principle that a slave cannot live on English ground, our people turned towards Western Africa, sorrowing for their newly-found sin. The first English attempt at colonising her deserted slave preserves was in 1787, during the days of the African Company, when certain benevolent individuals, headed by Messrs. Smeathman and Granville Sharpe, originated a scheme for restoring several hundreds of destitute runaways to their native land. The rocky peninsula of S'a Leone, from the Rokel to the Ketu river, twenty square miles, was at once purchased from the Timni chief, Naimbamma, "king" of the country, and the emigrants were forwarded in the "Nautilus" to their destination, which they reached in May. Many died of disease, some drank themselves to death, others ran away, and but few of the 400 remained when the second batch of settlers came upon the stage.

In 1790, three years after the first attempt, the colony of S'a Leone was re-established under the company of that name. The negroes who had remained loyal to England during the American Revolution, had fled to and settled in Nova Scotia. Finding that bleak land wholly unsuitable, they sent a delegate to England proposing themselves as candidates for the new West African settlement. The directors of the S'a Leone Company applied to, and obtained from Government a free passage for the Nova Scotians, and embarked them at once. A hundred Europeans and 1136 negro settlers, led by Mr. Clarkson, landed upon the Lion's Range, after losing on the passage sixty of their number, in March, 1792.

Accustomed from their youth to rice and maize, to bread and meat, the new-comers sickened on cassava and ground-nuts. They went out without frame-houses, and the rains set in early—about the middle of May—

before they found shelter. It was the history of the Bulama expedition once more. The whites were attacked with climate-fever, which did not respect the doctors, and the settlers, after many quarrels and great insubordination, saw 800 of their little band carried to the grave. Then a famine broke out; a ship from England, freighted with provisions, stores, and frame-houses was driven back by a storm, and did not arrive till nearly the end of the rains. Forty-five acres had been promised to each settler—viz., twenty to the husband, ten to the wife, and five to each child. It was found necessary to reduce the forty-five to four, and the denseness of the bush rendered those four unmanageable. Disgusted with Granville, the first negro settlement, whose site is now, as I have said, a grassy plain, they persuaded King Tom, chief of the country, by presents from the company, to allow them the use of his land and water-springs, and presently they built the fort and the present Freetown.

But war had broken out between France and England, causing the frequent detention of vessels, and a store-ship in the harbour happening to take fire, a worse misfortune awaited them. On a Sunday morning in April, 1794, as the unfortunates were looking out for the company's ship "Harpy," a French squadron sailed into the roadstead, drove the negroes into the bush, and landing in force, pillaged "the church and the apothecary's shop," and burnt the boats and town. The enemy then laid waste Granville, sailed up to Bunce's Island, and finally captured two vessels, besides the expected

" Harpy." Having thus left their mark, they disappeared after granting, at the governor's urgent request, two or three weeks' provisions for the whites. Famine followed, with sickness in its train, and the slave-dealers in the neighbourhood added all they could to the sufferings of the settlement. This is the independent history of the Nova Scotian settlers, as they are still called by their descendants now living at S'a Leone.

In 1800 and 1801 the settlers, roused by a small ground-rent imposed by the company upon their farms, rose in rebellion. The movement was put down by 550 Maroons,—*les nègres Marrons,*—principally descendants of Coromanti negroes, who were sent from Jamaica to S'a Leone. Hence arose the ill-feeling which in the earlier part of this century prevented the two rival sections even from intermarrying. Many of the disaffected settlers left the colony; some fled to the wild and the wild ones of the interior, and some few remained loyal. Rumours of invasion by the natives began to prevail. The governor was unwilling to believe that King Tom should thus sacrifice his own interests, until one morning, when forty war-canoes, carrying armed Timnis, were descried paddling towards the point. Nova Scotians and Jamaicans fled to the fort, and next morning the Timni drum sounded the attack. The governor, who attempted to parley, was wounded; but the settlers and colonists, who, well armed, were fighting for existence, beat off the assailants, and the Maroons of Granville Town completed the rout. After this warning a wall, with three gates, which were closed from 7 P.M. to

7 A.M., and strong watch-towers, were built round Freetown.

Notwithstanding all precautions, another "Timni rising" took place in 1803. The assailants paddled down from Porto Logo, landed at Kissy in large numbers, and assaulted Freetown, headed by a "Gri gri," or witch-woman, dancing, jumping, and drumming. Dividing into three storming parties, they attacked the gates with courage; but at last they were beaten back without having killed one man. The dead savages were so numerous, that the governor, fearing pestilence, ordered them to be cast into the sea.

After these troubles the colony remained at peace for some years, under the auspices of the S'a Leone Company. In 1807, the year that witnessed the abolition of the slave trade, possession was transferred to the British Government. Then commenced the system of installing at S'a Leone the Liberated Africans captured by British cruisers. In 1819, when a West Indian regiment was disbanded at Jamaica, 1222 soldiers and their families were added to the population. But this measure, making the place a black Botany Bay, soon ruined the chances and the hopes of the colony. Had it been carried out with due precautions, it would have worked abundant good by supplying hands. As it is, it has produced nothing but evil. I will attempt to explain why.

The black population of Freetown is assumed at 17,000. Of these there are still descendants of the older races: firstly, the Nova Scotians, or settlers;

secondly, Maroons, Sherbro Bulloms, the latter speaking Bullom, and mostly Methodists of the Lady Hunting-donian sub-sect, and Jamaicans, or colonists; thirdly, come the "'Cruits," emancipated, or liberated African slave-criminals. The old feud has now waxed faint, but it has by no means given place to combination between the two former races.* Thus both have fallen far behind the "'Cruits," who, naturally more energetic, have usually been petted and patronised by the Colonial Government. These barbarians, many of whom I have said are atrocious criminals, have been made English-men by wholesale, with eligibility to hold any manner of office, and all the other precious rights of English-men. Instead of being apprenticed† or bound to labour, as in similar cases a white man would certainly have been, they are allowed to loaf through a life equally harmful to themselves and others.

I need hardly quote the copybook to prove that idleness is the worst of all evils.

There is hardly a peasant in the place. With good management the colony might have become a flourishing portion of the empire, extending deep into Africa, and opening up to our commerce lands teeming with varied

---

* Mrs. M—— reports this very improper speech on the part of an elderly "settler woman." "Well! it is only my wonder that we settlers do not rise up in one body, and *kill* and *slay*, *kill* and *slay!* Dem Spanish and Portuguese sailors are quite right in making slaves; I would do de same myself, suppose I were in dere place!" "He is only a Liberated," is a favourite sneer against the new-comers.

† There have of course been governors—I will not mention names—who have attempted to enforce the regulations touching apprenticeship, but death, recal or disgust has always shortened their term of rule.

wealth.   Now it is the mere ruin of an emporium, and
the people, born and bred to do nothing, of course cannot prevail upon themselves to work.   But agriculture
is always despised by the "improved African," and he
will not labour at it uncompelled.   He is good only at
destruction—the excellent coffee and the tallow-nuts
have been cleared away for fuel.   Indigo and cotton,
coffee and arrowroot, squills and jalap, oil-palms and
cocoas,* ginger and ground-nuts, are to be grown; but
the people are satisfied with Indian corn and vegetables,
especially the cassava, which to Africa is a curse as
great as the potato, according to Cobbett, has been to
Ireland.   Petty peddling is the " civilised African's "
forte.   He willingly condemns himself to pass life between his wretched little shop and the chapel of Jehovah
Shallum; to do nothing on week-days, but scrupulously
to rest during the Sabbath.†   His beau-ideal of life is
to lie in the piazza, removing what the Rev. Mr. Wolff
was requested to remove, to chat, grin, guffaw, and
intone hymns, snuff, chew, and smoke, and at times drink
"kerring-kerry," a rum which costs one shilling per
bottle.   Such is the life of ignoble idleness to which we
condemn these sable tickets-of-leave by not rendering
industry compulsory.

The Christian tenderness of the British Government,
again, has tended to demoralise them.   In the Bights

* At S'a Leone there is a "freit," that if a white man plants a
cocoa-nut tree, he dies shortly afterwards.

† All missionaries praise the African for his strict observance of the
Sabbath.   He would have 365 Sabbaths in the year if possible, and
he would as scrupulously observe them all.

of Benin and Biafra, where the chief walks about with fetishman and executioner, there is still some manliness amongst men, some honour amongst women—the outward and visible form, at least, if not the "inward spiritual grace." There the offending wife fears "saucy water" and decapitation; here she leaves the husband—the latter more rarely abandons the better half—with impunity. The women have become vicious as those of Egypt, the basest of kingdoms—worse than the men, bad as they are. What the state of morality at Sa' Leone is they who are connected with the hospitals best know. Theft is carried to such an extent that no improvement is possible at Freetown, which, as regards property, is the most communistic of communities. One instance—a medical officer lately brought from Tenerife some superior poultry for breeding purposes. The birds were carefully watched, but though put under lock and key, they were heard, and were forthwith all stolen.* The robbers are expert to a degree; they work at night, nude, and well-greased; and like the Komanche, they choose the hour when the tornado is most violent and the footfall cannot be heard. The men fight by butting with the head, biting, and squeezing. The women have a truly horrible way of putting the obnoxious out of the world. Ask an Aku if an Ibo is capable of poisoning you, he will emphatically say "Yes." Make the same demand of an Ibo touching an Aku, and he will not reply "No."

---

* It is the fashion to attribute in slave communities every evil, robbery included, to slavery. S'a Leone is a notable instance that want of work is a far more efficient cause than servitude.

Nor has the influence of S'a Leone upon the West African coast been in any way for good. All know that this colony, intended for a "model of policy," and founded with the main object of promoting the progress of the country generally, has been perhaps the greatest obstacle to improvement. She would retain to herself every advantage, and allow none to others. She became an incubus in 1820, when the African Company was abolished, and when all British possessions from 20° north to 20° south latitude were made her dependencies. Her ill-will was scotched in 1844, when the Gold Coast, despite all her struggles, became independent. And her evil influence will cease when Admiralty Courts shall be established in the Bights, and when Africans recaptured shall be carried wherever they are most wanted.

With respect to the relative position of Japhet and Ham—perhaps I had better say Ham and Japhet—at S'a Leone, I may remark that English ultra-philanthropy has granted at times almost all the wishes of the Ethiopian melodist—

> " I wish de legislatur would set dis darkie free,
>   Oh what a happy place den de darkie world would be !
>   We'd have a darkie parliament,
>   An' darkie code of law,
>   An *darkie judges on de bench,*
>   Darkie barristers and aw' ! "

I own that Darkie must be defended, and well defended, too, from the injustice and cruelty of the class whom he calls " poor white trash." But protection

should be within the limits of reason. If the white
man is not to be protected against the black man, why
should the Jamaica negro be protected against the
coolie? Because he requires it? I think not. Though
physically and mentally weaker than his rival, he can
hold quite enough of his own,—as S'a Leone proves—
by combination, which enables cattle to resist lions.
Albus is naturally aggressive; if not, he would not now
be dwelling in the tents of Shem and the huts of Ham.
He feels towards Contrarius Albo as the game cock
regards the dunghill cock.* Displays of this sentiment
on the part of · the whites must of course be repressed.
Do so freely, but not unfairly. England, however, is still
in the throes of her first repentance. Like a veteran
devotee, she is atoning for the coquetries of her hot
youth. But a few years ago she contracted to supply
the Spanish colonies for thirty years with 4800 slaves
per annum, and she waged wars and destroyed cities for
a traffic which Cardinal Cibo, at the end of the seven-
teenth century, on the part of the Sacred College, to the

---

* Of late it has become the fashion for the missionary and the lec-
turer to deny, in the presence of Exeter Hall, the African's recognition
of the European's superiority. "The white man," writes Mr. Robert
Campbell, a mulatto, "who supposes himself respected in Africa because he is white, is grievously mistaken." I distinctly assert the
reverse, and every one who has studied the natural history of man,
must have the same opinion. The same egregious nonsense was once
propounded before the Ethnological Society—where with some ethnology there is no anthropology—by another "African." And yet
the propounder, the late Mr. Consular Agent Hansen, whose death
by the bye was an honour, and the only honour, to his life, had
shaved his wool, and at the time was wearing a wig of coal-black hair
like a Cherokee's. Is imitation no sign of deference ?

Kongoese missionaries denounced as " a pernicious and abominable abuse." For this, and for the 2,130,000 negroes imported into the West Indian estates between A.D. 1680 and A.D. 1786, Britannia yet mourns, and Rachel-like, will not be comforted, because those niggers are not. What the inevitable reaction shall be, *quien sabe ?*

I do not for a moment regret our philanthropy, even with its terrible waste of life and gold. But England can do her duty to Africa and to the world without cant and without humbug.* She can contend with a world in arms, if necessary, against the injurious traffic, but she might abstain from violently denouncing all who do not share her opinions upon the subject. Antislavery men have hitherto acted rather from sentiment than from reason ; and Mr. Buckle—alas ! that we should hear from him no more—may be right in determining that morality must not rule but be ruled by intellect. Let us open our eyes to the truth, and eschewing "zeal without knowledge," secure to ourselves the highest

---

* Such cant I hold to be in their mouths who talk of the "sin and crime" of slavery. As the author of "Six Years in the West Indies," (a brave book, considering the date of its publication, 1825,) truly says, that the spirit of Christianity tends to abolish servitude is clear, that it *admits* of servitude is even still clearer. The authorised version of the Bible, like the Constitution of the United States, very prudently shirks the word "slave," and translates by "servants" the δοῦλοι or bondsmen, whom St. Paul enjoins to be subject to their κυρίοι or masters, and elsewhere δοῦλος, a chattel, is opposed to ᾿ελεύθερος, a freeman. How astonished St. Athanasius and St. Augustine would have been, had the idea of an "underground railway" been presented to them ! What fulminations they would have showered upon the inventor of the idea !

merit—perseverance in a good cause when thoroughly disenchanted with it. We have one point in our favour. The *dies atra* between 1810-1820, when a man could not speak or write what he thought upon the subject of slavery, is drawing to a close. Increased tolerance now permits us to express our opinions, which, if in error, will wither like the grass in an African day; if right, will derive fresh increase from time.

There are several classes interested in pitting black man against white man, and in winning the day for him, *coram publico.* An unscrupulous missionary— it is the general policy of the English propagandist to take violent parts in foreign politics *—will for his own ends preach resistance to time-honoured customs and privileges which the negro himself has conceded. An unworthy lawyer will urge a law-suit, with a view to filling his pockets; a dishonourable judge or police-magistrate will make a name for philanthropy at the expense of equity and honour; a weak-minded man will fear the official complaints, the false-memorialisings which attend an unpopular decision, and the tomahawking that awaits him from the little army of negrophiles at home. But the worst class of all is the mulatto—under which I include quadroon and octaroon. He is everywhere, like wealth, *irritamenta malorum.* The "bar-sinister," and

---

* And not only the missionary, but also the sex which—I am told— has a mission. I was at Florence in 1850, when our fair countrywomen added not a little to its troubles by dividing into two factions, the Italian and the Austrian. Some wore national colours, others went so far as to refuse waltzes proposed to them by partisans of the hostile nation.

the uneasy idea that he is despised, naturally fill him with ineffable bile and bitterness.   Inferior in point of *morale* to Europeans, as far as regards *physique* to Africans, he seeks strength in making the families of his progenitors fall out.   Many such men visiting England are received by virtue of their woolly hair and yellow skin into a class that would reject a fellow-countryman of similar, nay, of far higher, position; and there are amongst them infamous characters, who are not found out till too late.   London is fast learning to distinguish between the Asiatic Mir and the Munshi.   The real African, however—so enduring are the sentimentalisms of Wilberforce[*] and Buxton—is still to be understood.[†]

It is hardly fair to pull down one system without having another ready in its stead.   I therefore venture to suggest certain steps toward regenerating—diffidently, though, on account of the amount of change to be made

[*] In the West Indies "Willyforce nigger" is a vile term of abuse addressed to a Kongo or Guinean recaptive, by the liberated of an older date.   What a use of an honoured name !

[†] Can I give a better proof of my assertion than the following extract from the English press :—

"There was a grand field-day in the fashionable world of Brighton on Thursday week.   A coloured lady—Miss Ina Sarah Forbes Bonetta —of royal descent, and who had had the good fortune to be adopted by an English Captain of the Navy, and to be educated at the expense of her Majesty, was led to the altar by a coloured gentleman, Mr. James Davis, a Sierra Leone merchant.   She was escorted by a bevy of dark beauties, and he was honoured by the attendance of coloured grooms. They were married by the Bishop of Sierra Leone, assisted by an African clergyman."

Miss I. S. Forbes Bonetta, the African princess, was a little slave girl, "dashed" by the late king Gezo of Dahomey to the late Lieut. Forbes, R.N., of H.M.S. "Bonetta," hence the names.   A similar present

in—our unhappy colony, which for years has been steadily declining.

As an author of the last century says: "Ideas of perfect liberty have too soon been given to these people, considering their utter ignorance. If one of them were asked why he does not repair his house, clear his farm, mend his fence, or put on better clothes, he replies that 'King no giv him work dis time,' and that he can do no more than 'burn bush and plant little cassader for yam.'" I doubt if this ingrained idleness could now be extirpated from the "colony-born" or elder generation; but it might be obviated in the "Kingyard men," the fresh importations of recaptives, and in the creoles, as children of liberated Africans are called here. They should be apprenticed for seven years, with superintendents to see that they clear the soil, plant and build; otherwise the apprenticeship would be merely nominal. For the encouragement of agriculture, I would take a heavy tax from small shopkeepers and hucksters, who, by virtue of sitting upon a shady board, before a few yards of calico and strings of beads, call themselves merchants. Another very heavy tax—at least 100*l.* per annum—upon all grog-shop licences, very few of which should be issued in the colony. Police magistrates are perfectly capable

---

was made to Mr. Consul Beecroft; that "princess," however, died at Fernando Po, and the *malheureuse* never commanded a grand field-day in the fashionable world of Brighton. Lieut. Forbes took his *protégée* to England, published a portrait of the little negro girl in the first volume of his "Dahomey and the Dahomians," and nearly lost his commission for presenting her as a "princess." Of Mr. Davis I know little beyond having narrowly missed seeing him in irons at Lagos.

of settling disputes amongst these people, and of dealing out punishment to the offenders; moreover, in all cases the fines should go to the Crown, not to the complainant; in civil cases, however, there might be an appeal home, for the benefit of the litigious. This measure would wipe off at one sweep inducement to engage in actions which the presence of a judicial establishment suggests, and which causes such heart-burning between Europeans and Africans. I would not allow a black jury to " sit upon " a white man, or *vice versâ ;* and, in the exception of a really deserving mu-latto, I would rather see him appointed Lord-Lieute-nant or Secretary of Ireland than acting Governor or Secretary at S'a Leone.*

I am convinced that something of the kind will be done, when the real state of affairs in this unfortunate colony is ventilated in England. There are men who are always ready to let bad alone, and to hold that

> " What has answer'd so long may answer still ;"

but the extension of steam navigation, and the increased number of travellers and visitors, will not allow progress for want of a little energy, even at S'a Leone, to be arrested.

* The following extract from the " Free-press," S'a Leone, Aug. 15, 1862, may be quoted as a proof that all Africans do not consider themselves fit for English citizenship. "Not long ago our contemporary, 'African Weekly Times,' remarked that the 'African race are not fit to exercise the privileges of citizenship,' the very fact of which assertion unfolds to us the spleen by which the editor is actuated." And it is to be observed that the contemporary alluded to is the most respectable member of the West African press.

Concerning the climate of S'a Leone there is a diversity of opinion. Let me quote Dr. Madden's report. Two witnesses are being examined; and the dialogue proceeds thus:—

"*Q.* Do you think the health of the settlement has improved of late years?

"*Dr. F.* I think it has improved.

"*Dr. A.* I do not conceive it has improved of late, particularly since 1837.

"*Q.* Are the natives subject to many or few diseases?

"*Dr. F.* Comparatively few.

"*Dr. A.* Yes, to many.

"*Q.* Are diseases of the lungs common?

"*Dr. F.* Not common.

"*Dr. A.* Very common."

Captain Chamier remarks, "It is needless to say one word about the climate of the coast of Africa. We have been taught to regard it as the worst under the sun; and certainly I, for one, am not going to gainsay it" ("Life of a Sailor").

Mr. Judge Rankin observed that the unhealthy reputation of S'a Leone was maintained by policy on the one hand and ignorance of the truth on the other; and he contrasted the improved healthiness of the colony with the West India Islands; but Mr. Judge died a few days after. So it is with Dr. Macpherson, of the African Colonial Corps. It appears ill-omened to praise the place; and after seeing it, I no longer wonder at the "Medical Gazette" (April 14, 1838) affirming that "on statistical writer has yet tried to give the minutest frac-tion representing the chance of (even) a surgeon's return from S'a Leone." And of late years the settlement has declined, and of course the climate has deteriorated.

It is only just to own that during my three days in the Red Grave I had little to complain of negro insolence. I paid every one employed about double. All asked treble; but the annoyance went no further. Still it was impossible to mistake the character of these spoiled children, their puerile inept ways, their exceedingly bad language, their constant intoxication, and their disposition to quarrel on all occasions. A subsequent comparison between Cape Palmas and S'a Leone gave me the exact ratio of difference between the civilised American negro and the semi—or, rather, semi-demi-reclaimed English *protégé*.

At 4 P.M., on the 13th of August, we left this unfortunate mistaken colony. The last circumstance in it was the late arrival of a negro servant whom I had promised to forward for his master, an officer at Loando. He had no ticket, and no permit, consequently, under pain of losing £250, our captain could not allow him to embark. This practice, now obselete in the East Indies, the object of which is to prevent the escape of debtors and of men flying from justice, is still enforced at S'a Leone. May its shadow never be less! May it increase a thousand-fold, at least while S'a Leone remains a scourge to the coast.

Bidding adieu to the green shores of the Red Grave, and giving the redoubted "Capenter" a wide berth,

we steered to the south-west, avoiding the shoals of St.
Anne, which hem in the coast. During the night we passed
Sherbro Island, where, according to general opinion,
Hanno, the Carthaginian, concluded his periplus, and
anticipated M. Du Chaillu, by carrying away the spoils of
the gorilla. Nothing can be more precise than the
estimate of days in this earliest of log-books. At the
same time, nothing is less applicable to this part of the
coast. If Sherbro be the terminal island, where is the
Fiery Mountain, which is distinctly described as a
volcano? South of Fogo or Fuego, in the Cape Verde
Islands, there is no such feature,* nor could there have
been, even 3400 years ago, except the Camaroons.
What, again, in this part of the coast, can be the "Horn
of the South"? I quit the subject for the present,
afterwards to return to it.

The weather was rough and squally, the southerly
wind still endured, and the aspect and temperature were
those of St. George's Channel in the month of June.
On Sunday the wind veered round to the north. Old
Boreas changed his robe from green to blue, and the
empyrean was clear as if we had been in an English
August. Presently we passed Cape Mount, the last
residence of the Franco-Italian slaver, Captain Canot,
whose memoirs have been published at a shilling, by
Messrs. Milner and Sowerby. The book wants but one
thing: it was written not by the adventurer himself,
but by some German "cooker-up." It is right well

* Moreover, Hanno was coasting along the main land, from which
Fogo cannot be seen ; its distance from Cape Verde is about 300 miles.

worth reading, upon the honest old principle, *Audi alteram partem.* Those who, like the greatest part of the untravelled public, look upon a slave-ship as a scene of horrors, and the skipper as the presiding demon of the Pandemonium, will be surprised to read M. Canot's conscientious endeavours to comfort and preserve his man warehouse. The details of a slave captain's hard day are most interesting, and they bear upon their front the stamp of truth. His figures show that his efforts were successful. Out of cargoes of 188 and 220 shipped on board the "Arentatico" and the "Fortuna," a total of only six was lost, or one and a half per cent. : far less than the average of our emigrant vessels. Bosman observes,—it may astonish the reader,—that "the English slave-ships are always foul and stinking; on the contrary, ours (the Dutch) are for the most part neat and clean." The Mount lies some ninety miles from Sherbro, and 170 from the extremity of St. Anne's shoals. It is a noble landmark, rising like a huge stud from the smooth front of the water before us. By way of contrast to the old slaver's home, Liberia, formerly the Grain Coast, was behind it upon our port bow. It claims for its limits the whole country from the Sherbro River, the southern boundary of Sherbro Island (12° 35′ west longitude) and the San Pedro River (6° 40′ west longitude), a length of about 4500 miles from north to south, with an average breadth of sixty miles, and a jurisdiction extending to one league (three nautical miles) off the shore at high-water mark. This, it will be seen from the chart,* includes the sovereignty of the Gallinhas River, which the Liberians declare to have been purchased from King Mannah, with money contributed mainly by the late Mr. Gurney. The chart shows no less than twenty-six parallelograms extending at right angles from the shore, and stated to have been acquired by "conquest and purchase," between the years 1822 and 1857. The central are the most ancient, the southern and the northern are the newest, acquisitions.

On the other hand, the natives, especially the Krumen, complain that, after permitting the foreigners to dwell amongst them, they have found themselves continually despoiled of their possessions; that once the lords of the soil they have sunk into Liberian citizens. Every African traveller knows the meaning of land purchase in these regions. There are two ideas innate in the African mind, but apparently incomprehensible by the European. The first is the non-alienation of land. The negro never parts with his ground in perpetuity. He has always the reservation, in the case of a stranger, that the land and its improvements revert by right to him after the death or departure of the original settler, who thus becomes a mere tenant. Should the settler's heirs desire to remain *in loco,* he expects a fresh qualification, which he will attempt to raise as high as possible. Public opinion, however, will compel him to be satisfied with an equivalent of the "dash" paid *ab initio.* The second idea is

---

* Republic of Liberia. Capt. Vidal and Lieut. Bedford, 1836—8, with additions from a MS. dated July 4, 1861.

even more repugnant to the English mind. In Africa, once a slave, always a slave. There is no such thing as absolute manumission; the *libertus*, or freeman, himself would not claim it. The Cape Coast Artillery, for instance, is composed of Fantis redeemed from servitude. After completing their service they must enjoy their pensions under the fort guns, otherwise their owners would claim them and their property. The African phrase is " 'Pose man come up slave, he be slave all time."

The idea of Liberia dates from the days of President Jefferson, who proposed to deport free " contrabands " from the United States to some part of Africa. The Colonization Society, organized by Mr. Finlay, sent in 1818 a deputation to Freetown, and several negroes were settled at Sherbro Island. Disliking the place, and dying in great numbers, they purchased land of King Peter, at Mesurado, and hoisted the American flag. This original "grant of land"—again a Europeanism!—made by the king and native chiefs in April, 1822, to the American Society for Colonizing the Free People of Colour of the United States (a private association, including Messrs. Clay and Webster, which began at Washington in 1816), extended, after a deadly failure at Sherbro, from a little north of Half Cape Mount, to a little north of Piccaniny Sesters (Sestos), about 300 miles. Here 6000 liberated negroes were established amongst 80,000 natives. As by the laws of the *then* United States the Federal Government could not hold colonies beyond the sea; the new settlement was placed under an agent, governor, or superintendent, and two magistrates, appointed by the society. Presently Bassa Cove was added. In 1827 the colony was contented with gaining a constitution. In August, 1847, dissolving connection with the Society, her home Government, she declared herself an independent Republic, and excluded whites from citizen life: the name of "Liberia" was suggested by the Rev. Mr. Gurley. In the northern third was built Monroe—so called from President Monroe—the capital, badly situated near the malarious mouth of the shallow and useless Mesurado River, probably the Montserrado.* The new Republic, Mrs. Stowe's most frouzy paradise, was placed under the united protection of England, France, and America, who assisted her with gifts of arms, schooners, and colonists' necessaries. Now she has, after forty years, grown to nearly fifteen times her original size. But in these days even Eden would be compelled to "annex."

About 4 P.M., we were off the Cape, River, and Town of Sinou, the land of the Krumen Their limits are insignificant, but their enterprise entitles them to honourable mention.

---

* The Gula, well known as the "Gollah niggers" of the Southern States, inhabit the lands in the interior of this country.

CHAPTER VI.

SIX HOURS AT THE CAPE OF COCOA PALMS.

"Cape de las Palmas, a fair high land; but having on the eastern
side some low places by the shore which look like red cliffs, with white
streaks resembling highways, reach the length of a cable."
Capt. JOHN LAKE, *the first English visitor to this coast in* 1554.

16TH SEPT., 186—.

I HAD heard of Cape Palmas, that it is a headland
discovered by the Portuguese about 1450; that it is so
called from the cocoa groves in its vicinity; that it
became a territory of Liberia when that "young and
flourishing republic," as she loves to call herself, started
up, like California, in Lucian's Minerva, in 1847; and
that in days now historic, times of the slaving rage,
ships usually made this point for rice and water, and
bent to the south-east. I had also heard the dictum
of an American skipper as regards Uncle Tom's Refuge
for the Destitute, namely, that in years to come the
baboons would be putting off to trade with Liberians'
skins. Such was the modicum of my knowledge before
landing at Cape Palmas; and perhaps the reader may be
in the same position which I then occupied.

Early on the morning of the 26th August, after a
run of 500 miles, we were expecting to see the Cape of
Palmas; but, steaming easily along, we had been

carried by the current past the sunken Athole Rock,* where, about eight months before, the "Roderick Dhu" had come to grief. It is a dangerous place, about one mile and a half from the shore, and surrounded by twelve fathoms of water; the rock however can be distinctly seen. The merchant ship was surrounded in a few minutes by a score of canoes, which quadrupled their number in a short time: when in force they look like Cornish wreckers, and have been known to murder the unresisting crews. Presently we found ourselves with head turned northwards, engaged in *retrousser chemin.* The Great Gulf Stream, which bifurcates about the Azores or Western Islands, here trends to the south, with a considerable amount of easting. The land is low, and it is by no means easy to make Cape Palmas without feeling for it. The principal marks, as in the Nigerian Delta, are conspicuous clumps: umbrella trees, lone trees, two trees, stump trees—in fact, every variety of trees, including the old naval surveyor's "Remarkable Tree with Three Crows upon it." These signposts often suffer from lightning and other causes, and a ship finds herself ashore in consequence. The nomenclature of the settlements is as peculiar as the landmarks. We now enter the regions of Great and Little, Grand and Piccaniny, Whole and Half, *e.g.,* Great Bassa, Little Bassa, Grand Sestos, Piccaniny Lahou, Whole Cavally and Half Cavally. Some of the names are palpable corruptions from the French; for

---

* So called from H.M.S. "Athole," which struck there on the 16th Dec., 1830.

instance, the great and little Bootou of our pilot-books.
M. de Bouet-Willaumez distinctly traces them back to
the old remembrances of France, in spite of the half-
English half-Spanish dialect which has been found
on the West Coast of Africa.   He explains the word as
"*butteau,*" from "*butte,*" the well-known old Norman,
and still used in the great Western Prairies; and this
would render it significant and descriptive of the place.
We have seen that, at the end of the twelfth century,
when other European nations were asleep, the Normans invaded and conquered a portion of the Canary
Islands.   In a future page I shall touch upon their
claims to have discovered the Gold Coast.

At 7 A.M. we saw the bars and breakers that garnish
the mouth of the Cavalla River, fourteen miles east of
Cape Palmas.   It is pronounced Cavally, and by very
John Bull skippers, Cawally; it is properly Cavalla, so
called by the Portuguese, because within one horse
distance of Palmas.   The river, whose course is nearly
direct north and south, extends unobstructed seventy-
five miles into the interior,* but the bar is always troublesome and often dangerous.   It has been proposed to
lay down rails of hard wood from the Cape to the River,
and thus to reduce the five hours' march to two.   Some
few miles from the mouth lies the Grand Devil, the
Delphi, Mecca, or Jerusalem of Kruland.   The people
describe it as a large rock, too extensive to walk easily
round, with an aperture opening into an interior cavern.

---

* In the Hydrographic Chart, the river Cavalla is made about 14
miles long, decidedly an error.

The votary makes his offering of white beads, animals, leaf tobacco, and rum, which are placed in the cavern, and are miraculously removed. The mysterious "suffing" —something, as my informant Tom Bes'man, Kru head-man of the African steam ship "Blackland," called it— answers any questions in any language, even in English. It is no doubt some sturdy fellow, who laughs in his sleeve, like the priest sitting in the breast of the Sphinx — Africa's most appropriate emblem—or in the lap of Memnon. The Kru, however, are made to believe in the preternatural disappearance of the gifts. You might as well argue with an alchemist against transmutation, with a Hindu against metempsy-chosis, with a Frère Ignorantin against transubstantia-tion. A tree standing near the river is pointed out as the local Lot's Pillar; some philosophic and Voltairian black was thus suddenly punished for his impious curiosity. There is no difficulty in visiting the place unprofessionally; several masters of ships 'have, it is said, gone through the various ceremonies. The fetish-man—"demon doctor" the missionaries call him— would probably do his best to prevent any inquiry; but, like all his tribe, he doubtless would not resist a douceur. At the same time prudence would be advisable.

A more interesting place upon the Cavalla River, is Cavalla Town, a few yards from the stream whose bar breaks and foams before us. We can distinguish an islet of black rock whose name is derived from the river, a church embosomed in tall trees, and along the coast a beehive-like scatter of small villages. At Cavalla the

Right Rev. John Payne, " Missionary Bishop, Protestant
Episcopal Church, United States of America, at Palmas
and parts adjacent," resides.   He edits a newspaper, the
"Cavalla Messenger, or Good News from a Far
Country," with that well-worn motto, "Ethiopia shall
soon stretch out her hands unto God," * which has, I
believe, been and ever shall be quoted by every man who
ever has written or who ever shall write a missionary
book into which the name of Africa enters.   Published
by the Protestant Episcopal Mission, it had reached, in
September, 1861, No. 3 of vol. ix.; and, considering its
difficulties, it is very creditable to American energy.

Passing Half Cavalla, a missionary station so called
because lying half way to the river, we saw at a distance the Cape of Palms: first a dotted line of tall
cocoa trees, scattered and conspicuous ; afterwards a long
spit of dark ground, apparently cut off by sand or water
from the river.   Presently black points in the water
grew to Kru canoes.   They are pointed at both ends,
crescent-shaped, and so curved that both cusps are high
out of water, which form acts in fact as weather-boards.
Except those of Batanga, they are the crankest things
on the coast ; a caique on the Bosphorus is like a ship's
barge in comparison.   At a little distance they are in-
visible ; the paddler, who sits on his shins, is apparently
treading water ; and when near, every undulation of the

* Psalm lxviii. 31. As this was written about 1050 years B.C., and
comparatively nothing has been done during 2912 years, the "soon"
in question probably means that she may have to wait till A.D. 4700,
or so.

"marmor" seems to bury them in its bosom. Dr. Vogel, the botanist, who on 17th December, 1841, died at Fernando Po, the day before he was to ascend the Peak, compares them to the Berlin "seelen verkanfer." I never sent an Englishman off in them but once, and he was nearly drowned. Without practising balance it is impossible to sit them. They are composed of a single branch of cotton wood, poplar, or African teak, charred internally with fire, and then easily hollowed out with an adze; there are half a dozen cross bars to prevent a collapse, and the woodwork is so massive that when waterlogged they do not sink. The single paddler, an amphibious animal quite at home on the sea, sits in the centre or the stern,—it is curious that he has never dreamed of a canvas or mat cover,—baling occasionally, as is always necessary with a scoop, or by kicking the water out of the boat, screaming "Bateo! Bateo! Gi'way, Gi'way!" and making his little craft skim the waves round and round our ship in a style that surprised us. This visitation of canoes, unusual at this distance, was caused by their mistaking us for the leeward mail; and they were flocking to plunder *à l'aimable*, as is their fashion, friends home returning from "down coast," where beads and cloth, arms and ammunition, grow. A little lower there are robbers, who delude the Kruboy into their canoes and strip him of all he has. There is something touching in the way in which they confide themselves to an English ship. When a sail draws in sight, they put out with songs, choruses—*levant et carmina curas*—and loud screams of "Bagri! bagri!" and they race each other,—they never can work except with some excitement—till they reach her. Then they lie upon their paddles, and long and anxiously scrutinize her, to distinguish if she be a Frenchman or a Spaniard; when they ascertain her to be an Englishman, they are over her sides in a moment. Steaming past Russwurm,* or Deadman's Island, so called because it was the common burial-ground, we remarked its tilted-up strata in the amorphous trap formation, and the many dangerous washes and diabolitos that outlie it. After passing the only ship in port, a Monrovian schooner, full of black and yellow jacktars, we went on easy, and anchored about half a mile off the town. The "Blackland" was at once boarded by Krumen, who swung themselves up by the chains, grinned at us with teeth like those of a garden rake, shook hands—who has taught this horrible practice to the universal West African Coast?—and proposed to take service. The toilette was in African style, *sans gêne*, sometimes only a pocket handkerchief about the lumbar region. Their appearance struck me as grotesque. Conceive the head of a Socrates or a Silenus upon the body of the Antinous or Apollo Belvidere. A more magnificent development of muscle, such perfect symmetry in the balance of grace and strength, my eyes had never yet looked upon. But the faces! except when lighted up by smiles and good humour—expression to an African face is all in all—nothing could be more unprepossessing. The flat nose, the high cheek-bones,

---

* Mr. Russwurm, coloured, was founder of the "Liberian Herald" in 1837, and afterwards Governor of Maryland, Liberia.

the yellow eyes, the chalky-white teeth pointed like the shark's, the muzzle projecting as that of a dog-monkey, combine to form an unusual amount of ugliness. To this somewhat adds the tribe mark, a blue line of cuts half-an-inch broad, from the forehead-scalp to the nose-tip; in some cases it extends over both lips to the chin; —whence they are called Blue-noses, like our North American friends, not however because inactivity precludes circulation,—whilst a broad arrow or wedge pointed to the fore, and also blue, occupies each temple, just above the zygomata. The marks are made with a knife, little cuts into which the oily smoke of a gum is rubbed. Their bodies are similarly ornamented with stars, European emblems, as anchors, &c., especially with broad double lines down the breast and other parts. But of this remarkable tribe more at the end of the chapter.

The aspect of the little settlement at Palmas is not unpicturesque, and it suggests a pure and healthy climate, which is not far from being the case. It is a bold headland of red argillaceous earth, based upon a black micaceous granite, tufted with cocoas and tapestried with verdure everywhere beyond the breaking of the waves. A flagstaff, with cleats nailed on instead of ladder and rungs, bore above the steamer signal the arms of Liberia, stripes and a Lone Star, stolen from Texas and not paid for. It stands in front of the Mission-house, a large building with ample piazzas and shady verandahs. Behind this is the square tower forming the lighthouse—a poor affair, a stable lantern stuck upon a pole. The ridge crest is thinly lined with tall houses of timber or stone, and they extend in scatters to near the water. The headland or promontory, 100 feet high and half a mile long by a quarter broad, is apparently cut off by a low sand spit; the country behind is grandly wooded, and from an eminence the blue heads of little hills rise above the alluvial plain. The Cape is a kind of out-post, and the turning point from the Windward to the Leeward or eastern coast. The body of the settlement, yclept Harper, after a "remarkable negro,"—it contains about 1500 souls,—lies further east. On the other end of the cliff, where in charts Fort Hall occupies the ground, there is a single gun placed upon an elevated bulge. The little river of Cape Palmas discharges itself north of the headland.

Availing ourselves of the captain's gig, the Consul and I went on shore, after crossing the mimic bar formed by the confluence of the river and the stream. The rollers were so small that they had hardly power to wet us; they succeeded, however, in occasionally capsizing a Kru canoe. The paddler, nothing afflicted by the accident, puts her on her back again, bales her out, and reseats himself with a dexterity the result of a life's practice. At the landing-place we found sundry large stone buildings, Mr. Macgill's and Mr. Potter's stores, and, wonderful to relate, black carpenters at their benches and black coopers—I saw nothing of the kind at S'a Leone—hard at work, refitting old casks for new palm oil. Two native huts standing by, were of the most approved Central African style, circles of twenty to thirty feet in diameter, with peaky conical roofs, whose eaves extended almost to the ground, a single low door, in entering which chin must touch knee, leading to the one room inside, where raised floors of tamped clay supported in the centre the chimneyless fireplace—all this might have been on the Tanganika Lake.*

The women were mostly in the "small countries," as plantations are called in "blackman's English," or gathering palm-nuts, which are exported in considerable quantities from this part of the coast. Amidst a crowd of men and boys, each carrying his little paddle and baling-scoop for fear of "'tief man," we ascended a few rough steps cut in the steep red-clay bank, and found ourselves in a lumber tenement, at once post-office and custom-house, which looks much like a large hen-coop perched upon a ladder. The letters were now distributed with the usual hurry and excitement. The African Steamship Company found it necessary to give up Goree, Monrovia, and Badagry, because they caused a mere waste of coal; so the correspondence of the capital—about 240 miles to the north-west or up the coast—is carried from Cape Palmas in the "Seth Grosvenor." The "Liberia" mail ship was described to me as a Yankee steamer, a house

---

* I propose at some future time, if the subject falls not into worthier hands, to show by the similarity of houses and utensils, manners and customs, arts and arms, religious rites, &c., that at some early epoch, there must have been an intimate intercourse between Eastern and Western Africa, in fact, throughout all Africa south of the equator. We observe essential differences between Great Britain and Little Russia; between the two shores of the Dark continent there is abso-lutely none.

of sundry stories built upon a broad shallow flat.   In October, 1860, the British Consulate was removed from Liberia in consequence of the bad treatment of a British subject, a sailor on board the " Quail," a ship of war that had been presented by England to the young Republic.   Mr. Roberts, ex-President, and acting as Her Majesty's Consul, gave medical attendance to the sick seaman, and sent in his account to the authorities, who thought proper to ignore it.   Consequently this pauper settlement lost the expenditure of 500*l.* a year, and the Consulate will, *on dit,* be transferred to Cape Palmas, where an English agent is really required to settle disputes between Krumen and their employers.   The weak point of a knowing African, even in the Land of Freedom, is that he is perpetually outwitting himself.

After leaving the mails, we ascended the rest of the steps, and on the way met two American gentlemen— whites ; to them we related, not without an irrepressible chuckle, the story of Bull's Run,—perhaps the most remarkable style of "taking ground to the rear" that history has ever had to chronicle.   The account was received with a curious mixture of incredulity and consternation. What ! the North whipped ! What would follow next ? *Après ça, le Déluge !*   The war in the once United States, however, is causing great injury to the missionary establishments, which are supported by voluntary contributions.   These alms now go to arms and ammunition, so that the missionaries must suspend the building of churches and reduce the number of their beneficiaries, to say nothing of personal inconvenience and privations, with which, in these climates, they can ill afford to put up.

We presently found ourselves at Marshall's Hotel, a lumber building on the cliff, commanding a pretty view. The inner rooms are furnished with tables, sofas, and easy chairs; the mats and rugs are neat and clean, and cocoas, white-washed after the fashion of Philadelphia and Baltimore, shade the front. There is an ordinary as in the United States—the *table d'hôte* is preferred to the "domestic circle," or solitary feeding. In fact all is America blackened. At Monrovia the Army and Navy Hotel, kept by a Jamaica woman, is said to be the best on the West African coast. The honourable owner of Marshall's Hotel, a man of colour, who is agent of the African Steamship Company, and also one of the county senators, bade us kindly welcome, and offered his services in showing us about the settlement. Our Consul was anxious to engage a gig's crew and two Krumen as personal servants. Although the destination was Fernando Po, the verandah was soon crowded with aspirants from ten to thirty years old; they behaved, however, decently; they did not crowd upon us, and when told to go away, they went. At S'a Leone there would have been an action—at least a summons. There was something natural and consistent in the appearance of these semi-savages, who, clothed in dirty coats and ragged pantaloons, would appear like the half civilized negro, simply disgusting.* Their

---

* "I can't tell you," said a lady missionary at Abeokuta to me, " what a pleasure it is for us to see our converts decently dressed like

black skins, their pink loin-clothes, and their bead neck-laces, are their proper attire. And however scanty the dress, it rarely appears immodest amongst the uncivilized. Whatever little is worn is manifestly intended for con-cealment. *Au contraire,* amongst the civilized, however much is worn, is too often intended to make half revela-tions. They lay in this quarter-naked state under the trees and squatted in circles, and at times a wild gusty song, in which all joined antiphonally, with an accompaniment of nature's castanettes—palms clapped upon thigh and calf—arose long and loud, transporting one mentally from the Cape of Palms to the Lake Regions of Central Africa. Whenever an old negress, attached to the mission and dressed in broad-brimmed straw and calico gown, brushed by them rather rudely, they would exclaim, "Eh! you no care? you all same white man?" suggesting that only the white man has a prescriptive right to kick them. The sole ridiculous figure in the party is one Tom Pepper, "headman for shore," who wears in these dogdays an English black tile, and a pea-jacket over his breech-cloth. Tom, how-ever, is an invincible sloven, and cares less for dress than any noble member of the House of Lords.

From the Hotel we walked to the Mission House—the large building near the lighthouse—and were pleased with the contrast between this little place and S'a

---

Europeans, and not like the heathen." It is easy to understand the feeling, but I find it impossible to share it. Why should pagandom have all the handsome dressing, as the devil is said to have all the good music, and not a little of all the good poetry?

Leone. The houses are mostly two-storied, of stone or lumber, the latter, however, generally raised upon a strong foundation : servants' rooms and offices are in the lower part; in the upper are the bed-rooms and parlour, surrounded by a shady piazza—an excellent sanatory arrangement. They are roomy and comfortable, the exteriors are unstained, and the gudewife keeps the inside neat and clean : a great difference from the tumble-down, soiled, and sullied aspect of a homestead further North, where women do nothing but sit before their "blies" in the market. Around the tenements are little gardens of okras and cabbages, rose-apples, guavas, oranges, limes, and prickly pears, plantains, breadfruits, the Patanga cherry, with fruit and flavour resembling both the peach, and the chirimoya, a vine from Cape Coast Castle, and an Indian bamboo from the Gaboon River. The hoe is large, and has a long handle—an invariable sign of industry. There are pigeon-houses and poultry yards, the latter well stocked with fowls, ducks, and turkeys; the infidel pigs are round and fat; the small humpless black cattle are well filled out, and even the prick-eared curs—some one has said that they and the women are in these lands the test of prosperity—wear a look of comparative comfort. In the east I saw a long strip of bright sand masking a long lagoon from the sea. At Palmas begins that system of natural canalization which runs parallel with the coast in places many hundred miles, and with a considerable depth into the interior. These lakes are of two kinds : those caused by infiltration of salt water through the porous sand are briny, half-bitter, like the Dead Sea, and even the heavy rains fail to sweeten them. The others receive one or more rivers; they are, therefore, brackish, rather than briny, and during the wet season they often burst their way through the sandy embankment. Both are equally fetid and miasmatic, and almost impossible to drain on account of the lowness of the bed; both also have hitherto been used for the worst of purposes. Slave barracoons were built within spy-glass sight of the cruizers, who directed all their energies, naturally enough, to those points : the lagoons enabled the exporter to boat his cargo up or down the coast, and to ship it out of the enemy's sight. Let us hope that as these days go by, the network of lagoons, acting as a counterpoise to the bars and breakers that impede navigation, will do its work in the Herculean task of reclaiming Africa.

After 100 yards or so, we arrived at the Mission House, where, as the Rev. C. E. Hoffman was still busy with the Post, we introduced ourselves to Madame. The place had that neatness and order which at once told me it was no Bachelors' Hall; there were knicknacks, portraits, and similar *gentilezze*, which follow in the wake of women only. There is no place where a wife is so much wanted as in the Tropics ; but then comes the rub—how to keep the wife alive. A gruff Scotch merchant-captain on this coast once told me, that rather than bring out his "missus," he would "heave her into the river." Cape Palmas is hardly an exception to the general rule of African insalubrity, and the time of our visit was at the end of the latter rains,—one of the worst seasons. Yet we were shown a little Africo-Anglo-American, who looked far less pallid and pasty than European children in the lowlands of India. The year, hereabouts, has four divisions, the others being the dries, the early rains, and the middle dries. The climate thus resembles that of the Gaboon and its adjacent coast; in the Bights of Benin and Biafra there are no middle dries—the wet time sets in heavily at the end of May, and in places lasts till early November.

We had a long chat with Mr. Hoffman, of New York. With that energy which characterises "our Transatlantic cousins," he had set his shoulder to the wheel; scrupulously avoiding, and invariably rebuking in his subordinates political interference, the rock upon which English missionaries split.* He had turned his endeavours towards improving the settlement, directly and indirectly —the latter, of course, by means of the Press. He had lately returned from Nti Lu, *alias* Bolan's, a small and new station near the Cavalla River, where Mr. and Mrs. Messenger—also whites—had made their home. He had, on July 9, also travelled and boated 85 miles inland to the head of the Cavalla River, over a land hitherto unexplored, and had found it exceedingly pleasant and fertile. Though stopped by the inhabitants of the high Webo or Diebo country, which were then fighting with their neigh-

---

* Except the Wesleyan, who have the strictest orders not to meddle with politics. Dr. Livingstone has given his own version—and everybody has read it—of the squabbles between the English missionaries and the Dutch yeomanry at the Cape of Good Hope. The public would be rather surprised to hear the counter-statement.

bours, his kindness to a native chief on a previous occasion, now enabled him to pass through safely. There were hills which, however, could not aspire to be called mountains: in the low lands rice was growing five feet high, and in the uplands there was a cotton with shortish staple, but a large and heavy boll. He learned the names of twelve tribes before him, all under charge of one man, and he returned, not compulsorily, but because required at home.* Mr. Hoffman had heard from many of the people that the upper tribes bring down cloth, arms, and ammunition, from a river, at whose mouth European ships anchor. He says they called it Niga; he concluded, naturally enough, that this must be the upper stream of Kwara, Joliba, or Great River, whose head waters, in our latest maps, are called the "Ahmar," and still lie a line of dots.† The country, of

---

* Proceedings of the Royal Geographical Society, London, Vol. VI., No. II., pp. 66-67. It is to be noted, that after a couple of days journey, the traveller found the country hilly, the weather cool and pleasant, and a good fire necessary to make himself comfortable. Moreover, he distinctly asserts "he met with no hindrances from the natives." I extract his last passages which are geographically interesting. "Near the source of the Cavalha River, another river flows from the hills, by which the natives receive English goods, cloths, salt, guns, &c., from vessels at its mouth. This river they call 'Nigá.' I have very little doubt but that one of the sources of the Niger will be found a few weeks' travel east of Cape Palmas, and that this is the river to which the natives referred."

† "Africa," by Keith Johnston, F.R.S.E. : Messrs. Blackwood, Edinburgh and London. I wish that maps would follow the vulgar practice of other printed things, and use dates; now they are mysterious as "ladies of a certain age." In "Palm Land, or West Africa, Cincinnati, 1856," a book written quite in the "Ercles vein," by a Mr. Thompson, unmistakeably one of the "Zouaves of Christianity,"

course, will be trying and difficult to traverse; perhaps, however, asses might be used to advantage. The animals could be brought from Liverpool by steamer, at a cost of 8*l.*; I should prefer them from Tenerife.

Mr. Hoffman is of that spare figure and nervous diathesis which best enable a man to endure tropical hardships and fatigues. He had been encouraged by his explorations to take daily walking exercise, and he intends to carry on his discoveries still further. I

and to whom especially the remarks which follow in the text apply, we read that the sources of the Niger, coy as those of her sister Nile, have been discovered by "Brother Brooks" of the Mendi mission. Unfortunately the direction assigned to them is entirely wrong. The following is a condensation of the story :—

It appears that the brother once travelled about 200 miles north-east of Sherbro Island, over a country where all the streams ran to the west and south-west, the direction of the rivers Big Boom and the Gallinhas, or St. Paul's. Having reached the "Kong Mountains," and ascended them for two or three days, in which he made some fifty miles, he came to an extensive table-land, so full of bog, swamp, and mud, that he was compelled to trot over sticks. Out of this morass flowed two streams, one to the south, the other to the north or the north-east—the first that he had seen taking this direction. It was a dashing little brook : the natives called it "Quarra" (Kwara), and a village near it was named "Quarroo." Mr. Thompson assumes this to be the Niger. But, setting aside the difficulty of the morass sending forth two streams in different directions, it is evident that, unless all our charts are erroneous, 250 miles north-east of Sherbro Island would place the traveller on the western crescent of the Kong Mountains.

The latter are almost as mysterious as the sources of the Niger. The name is derived from Park. In Mr. Macbriar's Mandingo Vocabulary we find that Konko means a hill : hence, doubtless, our garbled name. Mr. Thompson remarks, that the highlands explored by "Brother Brooks" were called by the natives "Kahm," and one of the villages "Kahm-boa-mat," or mountain road. He opines that Kahm might have been corrupted to Kong, which is not likely.

exhorted him to communicate with the Royal Geographical Society of Great Britain, and wish him every success. For African exploration the Anglo-American is probably the best of men, physically and morally : his energy and sobriety are far superior to that of the older family, and he has had from his youth sufficient experience of Africans to—despite overwrought English sensibilities regarding the black men—appreciate their merits and demerits, and to treat them as they should be treated. He is a favourite wherever he goes, by reason of a certain freedom of manner which is liked everywhere save in England. ·The only pity is that he should ever appear in print. Then he is compelled by Public Opinion— that tyrant which renders the Free Republic the worst of despotisms—to introduce some fustian "bunkum," and *ad captandum* sneers touching kings and queens, lords and landlords, the decadence of England, and the oppressively brilliant prospects of the United States, the blessings of a democracy, and the curses of limited monarchy, till every New World reader thinks himself, very vainly, a shining light to those who dwell in the outer darkness of European civilization.

After seeing the Mission House, we walked with Mr. Hoffman to the adjacent building, St. Mark's Hospital, Cape Palmas. Three lots of ground were secured for a society, of which Bishop Payne became *ex officio* president; officers and managers were elected, and the laying of the corner-stone on the 24th April, 1859, was commemorated with prayers, addresses, and speeches, which *more mericano* did not fail to see themselves in print. The

worthy missionaries found some difficulty in collecting
even a portion of the 500*l.*, at which the cost was estimated. The site chosen was excellent—healthy, if there
be any place so on this coast—facing to the S.S.W. on the
Cape summit, with a clear slope to the channel, which,
three fathoms deep, separates the land from Russwurn's
Island; and with a beautiful prospect of the blue beyond.
The institution, supported by voluntary contributions, is
intended for the benefit of colonists, natives, and European seamen, and it is proposed to place it under the
charge of some " Christian Lady." The building, when
I visited Cape Palmas, was approaching completion,
and would be partially opened next year. It is a solid,
substantial edifice, with thick walls of cut stone, forty
feet by twenty-two. An upper ward will accommodate
in-door patients, and the officers' quarters, and the dis-
pensary are on the ground floor. The beams, rafters, and
scantlings are mostly cedar or African mahogany, both
fine close-grained woods, which the Admiralty may find
useful. The planking is of brimstone-wood, so called
from its colour; the close-grained texture tries tools
severely, but it takes a polish equal to satin-wood, and
will be a favourite with European cabinet-makers; its
hardness gives it immunity from the attacks of those
small destructionists, the termites, here called bug-a-bug.*
I have no hesitation in strongly recommending this hos-

* The fine African timbers, for ship building purposes, fetch in
England from 2*s.* 6*d.* to 3*s.* 6*d.* per foot, or 6*l.* 5*s.* to 8*l.* 15*s.* per load
of fifty feet. Others realise much more, especially when suitable for
masts. At Fernando Po a cedar was measured, and found to be a total of

pital to the merchants of Liverpool and Bristol; in fact, to all who are connected with the West African coast.* Cape Palmas is at present the only establishment of the kind between Tenerife and Ascension. We shall at some time have one of our own upon the Camaroons Mountains.

240 English feet high—of which ninety were clear of branches —seven feet in diameter, and, calculating from the specific gravity of European cedar, thirty-nine tons of timber. The minimum value of the 120 scantlings, into which it could be cut, would be in Spain 120 doubloons.

* The following appeal tells its own story :—

St. Mark's Hospital, Cape Palmas.—The work has commenced, and now we respectfully appeal to all :

To Christians.—That we may glorify God in this work, by healing the sick, and administering to the wants of the suffering.

To the Friends of Colonization.—Many of the emigrants sent here suffer from sickness, after the period of six months has passed, during which they receive aid from the Colonization Society. They have no houses provided for them ; cases occur where death follows from the want of care for a little longer season. In some cases of older residents, death has followed from ulcers and other diseases, which, had they been judiciously treated, valuable lives would have been saved.

To Captains and Seamen.—We seek to build a house where you may find sympathy and care, and receive such medical treatment as you may need on that sickly coast.

To Merchants and Shippers.—Give us of your abundance, that we may take care of those who command your vessels and gather your wealth.

To the Friends of the Heathen.—Make us the almoners of your gifts, that we may minister temporal relief to those whom we also would seek to win to the religion of Christ.

To all whose eyes meet these lines.—We ask your aid, for although we have but briefly written, the object will commend itself to you more and more on reflection ; the Institution is greatly needed, and the end in view is noble and blessed.

Donations and communications may be sent to the care of Rev. S. D. Denison, Secretary Foreign Committee, No. 19, Bible House, New York ; Dr. James Hall, Secretary Maryland Col. Society, Baltimore ; Rev. A. Crummel, Cor. Secretary, St. Mark's Hospital, Cape Palmas,

But—Britannia is middle-aged and averse to hurry—a few years will probably elapse before it can be made available.

W. A. ; and C. C. Hoffman, Rector St. Mark's Hospital, Cape Palmas, W. A.

Boxes and packages to be addressed, St, Mark's Hospital, care of Hon. J. T. Gibson, Cape Palmas, W. A.

Donations of furniture, wearing apparel, bedding, provisions, medicines, &c., are solicited.

Signed in behalf of the Officers and Managers,—Rev. C. C. Hoffman, Rector ; Rev. A. Crummel, Cor. Secretary ; Joseph T. Gibson, Superintendent of Co. of Cape Palmas.

It gives me great pleasure to state that the object set forth in the above appeal has my most cordial approbation.

Jno. Payne, Bishop Prot. Epis. Ch. U.S.A. at
C. Palmas, and parts adjacent.

Extract from the Report of the Rt. Rev. J. Payne, Bishop Prot. Epis. Ch. U. S. A. at C. Palmas, and parts adjacent, to the Board of Foreign Missions, New York, U. S. A. :—

"The earnest Rector of St. Mark's and of the Orphan Asylum, whom God continually gives grace to devise good and liberal things, has commenced, during the year, a Hospital for the accommodation of invalid colonists, natives, and foreigners of all nations visiting the Port of Cape Palmas.

"This Institution is no further connected with the Mission than by its constitution to secure the pastoral care of one of its Missionaries. It is, however, so important—being the only cne of the kind on the coast—that it will receive a generous support from the benevolent of this and all other countries interested in the commerce of Africa, and the welfare of its inhabitants."

END OF VOL. I.

LONDON: BRADBURY AND EVANS, PRINTERS, WHITEFRIARS.

VOLUME II

CONTENTS OF VOLUME II

WANDERINGS IN WEST AFRICA.

CHAPTER VI. (*continued*.)

SIX HOURS AT THE CAPE OF COCOA PALMS.

" Cape de las Palmas, a fair high land ; but having on the eastern
side some low places by the shore which look like red cliffs, with white
streaks resembling highways, reaching the length of a cable."

Capt. JOHN LAKE, *the first English visitor at this place in 1554.*

16TH SEPTEMBER, 186—.

AFTER subscribing to the Cavalla Messenger,* and
taking leave of Mr. Hoffman, with gratitude for his
kindness, indeed highly pleased with the civility of all
after our short but sharp experience at S'a Leone, we
walked back to the Hotel, where we found a luncheon
provided for us by Mr. John Marshall. Our leave of
absence was soon ended ; we unfolded umbrellas—a pre-

* It is published monthly at Cavalla, the head-quarters of Bishop
Payne. The printing, which is tolerable, is "done" by two native
youths. The subscription, payable in advance, is fifty cents (two
shillings) per annum ; or, including postage per steamer, seventy-five
cents.

caution never to be disregarded in these latitudes, where
the more you know of the sun the more you respect him
—and took our way to the boats. On the steps a document was handed to me: it bore the novel direction:

> For Nanpopo (Fernando Po),
> Mr. Friday,
> In the care of one* Crewman (Kruman).

The Consul had failed in recruiting men. "Nanny
Po," was a word of fear to the Krumen; they had been
made to work in gardens and on the roads, and they
complained—most falsely, I afterwards found—of "*puoco
comer, mucho trabajo.*" Some of them had been engaged
for one year, not two, and had been kept for three—the
usual time—to the great sorrow of their mammies and
to the abiding resentment of themselves. Hearing the
Consul speak a few words of Spanish, they decided him
to be "a 'Panyer," and resolutely refused, with characteristic independence, to accompany him. One man
came down to the wharf and expressed willingness to
engage; he asked, besides passage to and from his country,
and food, clothes, and lodging, $4 and 2 pezetas *per
mensem*—$2 being the usual wages. His terms were
agreed to, but he forgot to come on board. We also
failed in buying Kru canoes, which are useful for fishing
and for sending notes to ships in harbour. They are
usually plentiful, and sell for 1*l.* each; the people,
however, in actual sight of "siller," declared that they

* The African language has no indefinite article: hence *one* is always
used for our *a*.

wanted all their craft, and I know the African too well to
waste time when he urges that plea and takes that stand.
Cape Palmas, called Bàmnepo by the natives, is in
the county of Maryland, the easternmost of the five into
which the Liberian Republic is divided, beginning from
the east Sinoe, Bassa, Mesurado, in which the capital
stands, and Kassa, the northernmost which contains the
much-vexed Gallinhas River. It was begun in 1834 by
the Maryland State Colonization Society, which granted
to it an annual sum of 2000*l.* from the treasury. The
Governor, or, as he is here called, the Superintendent
of Public Affairs at Cape Palmas Station, is Hon.
J. C. Gibson, who is under the present President of
Liberia, Hon. S. A. Benson,—who succeeded ex-President Roberts,—a good working man, but as arbitrary as
democrats when in power are apt to be. There are two
senators—Hon. J. Marshall, and Hon. J. Moulton.
Whenever a dispute arises between the colonists and the
natives, a council, composed of the Superintendent and
the Senators, together with the African Headman, holds
"palaver" upon the subject. The Krumen have as
yet shown a rooted aversion to all taxation; they prefer
to be plundered wholesale, at uncertain periods, by their
own people, than pay a certain and invariable, though
trifling assessment, for law, order, and protection. Consequently Harper is rather depressed for want of means.
The principal income is from ships entering the harbour;
they are charged 3*l.* 1*s.* for anchorage and lighthouse
dues. Another tax might be put upon water, of

which there are good, but not abundant, springs at the
Cape. The number of Krumen who flock to this station
for employment seldom falls below 1500, and of course
it is made a source of profit to individual colonists. The
Republic desires that trade be restricted to six ports of
entry, of which Harper is one.*

The Methodists who, about eight years ago, established
themselves in these lands, number the largest body of
Christians in Liberia—their annals, however, are a necro-
logy. The reader may see below the state of the Protestant Episcopal Mission at the time of my visit.†   In the

* Of these 'six, three are in one county, and one in each of the
others, viz. :—

Roberts Port, ⎞
Monrovia,   ⎬ Mesurad County.
Marshall,   ⎠
Buchanan, Bassa County.
Greenhill, Sinoe County.
Harper, Maryland County.

† "*The Mission Field about Cape Palmas.*

"It was a wise and merciful Providence which first directed the
Protestant Episcopal Mission, and others, to Cape Palmas and parts adjacent. It was the healthiest of the settlements then made on the
coast. Unlike some other portions of the Liberian coast, the tribes
around had not been thinned or broken up by the slave trade and
domestic wars which it ever excites. While the Cavalla River, alive
with an active trade, opened a highway eighty miles into the interior.

"These favourable circumstances, made known by Dr. James Hall,
then Governor at Cape Palmas, and Rev. Dr. Wilson, who accompanied
him on his expedition to purchase land for the colony, determined the
Foreign Committee of the Protestant Episcopal Church to commence
their missionary work at Cape Palmas.

"In the autumn of 1836, Rev. Dr. Savage arrived at Cape Palmas,
Mr. James M. Thomson, a Liberian, had been employed by the Foreign
Committee to make preliminary arrangements, and had so well

several settlements of Rocktown, Fishtown, and Springhill there are about 130 catechumens, who are instructed by

occupied his time that when Dr. Savage arrived, the lot at Mount Vaughan was partially cleared, and Mr. Thomson had gathered a small native school in a thatched house on the premises.

"On July 4th, 1837, Rev. Messrs. Minor and Payne joined Dr. Savage. By this time the first Mission House at Mount Vaughan was so far completed that, by putting up curtains, we managed to make out three rooms for the Mission family.

"In the Mission field they found Rev. Dr. Wilson and associates of the American Board occupying Cape Palmas, Rocktown, Fishtown, and Half Cavalla ; and Rev. F. Burns, of the Methodist Mission, regularly in the colony.

"The field immediately about the Cape being so well occupied, the Protestant Episcopal Mission at once directed its efforts towards the interior. Accordingly, while Mr. Payne officiated for a small colonist congregation, and occasionally at 'Joe War's Town' (not Hoffman station), Grahway and Perebo, Mr. Minor was sent to make arrangements to open a station at Dihně (Dinnah), on the Cavalla, thirty miles from its mouth.

"The lot had been selected for the building and the plan of the house decided upon when the people of Bărěkě, a larger town midway between Mount Vaughan and Dihně, insisted upon our having a Mission station at their place before going beyond them.

" As they commanded the road, we could do no better than fall back on Bărěkě. Here, again, Mr. Minor had gone and selected a Mission lot ; and King Tedi Bliâ had visited Mount Vaughan to complete arrangements for building, when suddenly war broke out between Bărěkě and the colony, and our progress was again arrested. Soon after this, Dr. Wilson, of the American Board, and associates determined to remove their Mission to the Gaboon River, and their stations about Cape Palmas were gradually transferred to the Protestant Episcopal Mission."

" General Statistics of the Protestant Episcopal Mission at Capes Palmas and Parts adjacent.

"We give this month the general statistics of our Mission. We shall be most happy to receive from our brethren the coast statistics of their Mission, and any items of intelligence connected therewith.

three Anglo-Americans and their families. With excellent sense the missionaries employ their pupils for a short time in reading and writing, ciphering, and psalmody, and for a long time in learning trades and handicraft. Education is cheap; the poor pay but 2 cents, the rich $5, a year. They thus form a Civilization Society; whilst others, neglecting all things save the cure of souls, are successful in producing, as the phrase is, more convicts than converts. They possess however a great advantage in the collaboration of a coloured population, not from Jamaica, or from what

"Stations.—Colonists, 6 ; natives, 15. Total, 21.

" These Stations extend 270 miles along the coast, from Monrovia to Taboo ; and seventy-five miles interior, from Cavalla to Bohlen.

"Missionaries.—Foreign, 4 ; colonists, 4. Total, 8.

"Catechists, Teachers, and Assistants.—Foreign, 5 ; colonial, 8 ; and native, 18. Total, 31.

"Baptisms (past year returns imperfect).—Infant, 13 ; adult, 21. Total, 34.

" Confirmations (past year), 37.

" Communicants.—Foreign and colonists, 211 ; native, 158. Total, 369.

"Boarding Scholars.—Colonists, 37 ; natives, 104. Total, 140.

"Day Scholars.—Colonists, 133 ; natives, 250. Total, 383.

"Sunday Scholars.—Colonists, 334 ; natives, 150. Total, 484.

"Candidates for Orders.—Foreign, 1 ; colonists, 4 ; natives, 2. Total, 7.

" Field of labour of Liberia.—Three counties, eight native tribes— aggregate population, 16,000.

"The Grebo language reduced to writing : Genesis, four Gospels, Acts, Common Prayer Book (in part), Bible History, Life of Christ, Hymn Book, Primer, Grebo History and Dictionary—published in the language. Also, printing press ; paper—the 'Cavalla Messenger '— published monthly."

may perhaps be worse, Barbadoes, but from the United States. Civilized and perfectly capable of managing and utilizing their wild congeners, the colonists appear in a most favourable light after the semi-reclaimed Akus and Ibos, their northern neighbours. They have even proposed to take charge of S'a Leone; and I doubt not that, if permitted, they would soon effect important changes. Liberia is a Republic, that is to say, she is pretty far gone in the ways of despotism—the only fit government for "Africa and the Africans." "*Morte alla constituzione !*" (in these lands) I exclaim with the unhappy Florentines, when they marched in arms through their streets and put a forcible end to a system which imposed upon them by an ambitious and unscrupulous *medio ceto*, a dynasty of doctors, lawyers, professors, and professional politic-mongers, enslaved them to 1000 rogues *in esse*, instead of to—possibly—one.

Liberia is at present in trouble; we heard many rumours of wars, and saw martial preparations when on shore. The Spanish vice-consul of Accra, who was on board, did not disembark at Cape Palmas. At S'a Leone our Frenchman—there is always one on board in these steamers—had blurted out something which might not have pleased H.I.M.S.S. La Ceres. According to him this gun-boat had sailed from Fernando Po to settle a dispute touching the Gallinhas River. She had entered the harbour and had attacked the "Quail," generally known as the "Lively Quail," in the harbour of Monrovia, and had sunk her and her crew, receiving but a single shot through her cabin door. The "Quail" is an old schooner, now carrying three guns—one 32-pounder and two 12-pounder carronades. She was presented by the British Government to assist in the suppression of the slave trade. She is one of the two that compose the "Liberian Navy;" the other vessel, a gift from the United States, never puts out to sea.

Now all this was a *canard*. The facts proved to be as follows. Of course there are two versions of the affair: that of the Spaniards, and that of the Liberians. I will give precedence to the former.

The Spaniards assert that a small vessel named the "Buenaventura Cubano," touched, on her way from Tenerife to Fernando Po, at the Gallinhas River, and was cast upon rocks inside the bar. That the master, seeing an opportunity, began to trade for palm-oil, when the "Quail" of Liberia attacked her, hauled down the Spanish flag, plundered the cargo, and compelled the master and men to fly from assassination. That the goëlêtte "La Ceres" was sent for the purpose of demanding satisfaction at Liberia, where, finding batteries and ships prepared to attack her, she fired into the "Quail" and retired. They deny the right of Liberia to the Gallinhas waters, and they assert that were the contrary the case, as they have neither treaties nor established usages with Liberia, that the latter cannot be allowed to molest their subjects. Finally, they demand suitable reparation for the offence, and indemnification for the loss of the cause of dispute.

The Liberians, on the other hand, declare that Prince

Mannah, the Chief of Gallinhas, reported to head-quarters that a Spanish ship was in the river with slave gear on board, and collecting her live cargo. That the "Quail," having ascertained these facts, captured her on the 30th May, 1861, and was about to tow her to Monrovia for judgment at the Admiralty Court, when the officer commanding Her Majesty's ship "Torch" sent the prize crew away, and hauled down the (single) star-spangled banner of the Republic, and on the 13th June, 1861, burned the Liberian prize. That, so far from injuring the Spanish subjects, they had been permitted to go to S'a Leone, where there is a Spanish consul-general, and to take with them all necessary supplies; moreover, that Prince Mannah had provided them with a large canoe. That the "Ceres," having reconnoitered the harbour of Monrovia, returned about fourteen days afterwards, and steamed in under pretext of visiting the President. That without any warning she began firing, on the 11th September, 1861, into the "Quail," when the batteries gave her such a dose that she was glad to make her escape.* That the Gallinhas is within the Republic's jurisdiction, and she is bound by treaties with Great Britain to suppress slavery within her dominions. Finally, that her weakness is her strength quoad the great Powers of Europe; that one of them has weakened her authority with the aborigines, and that she is entitled

---

* The "Cavalla Messenger" confirms this:—"The ' Ceres' received so spirited a response from the ' Quail,' which was anchored under the fort's guns, that she withdrew, having suffered, it is said, considerably."

to reparation for the attack of the "Ceres" and remuneration for the legal prize burned by the British officer.

This great question evidently turns upon the ownership of the Gallinhas waters. In 1842, block-houses were recommended to the British Government for the suppression of slave trade—evidently showing that in those days it was not Liberian territory. In 1848 took place the after-dinner conversation between Lord Ashley and Mr. Gurney with Mr. President Roberts, and the wily negro persuaded them that by paying 2000*l.*, slavery would be eradicated from the Gallinhas River and,— 700 miles annexed to the Republic. In 1849, H.M.S. "Albert," Commander Dunlop, broke up the slave factories—they had been previously injured by Captain Denham, R.N.—and carried off European traders and 1200 slaves to S'a Leone. The Republicans, however, insist that the land and the several points known as the Gallinhas were bought on the 13th April, 1850, from Prince Mannah and the other chiefs. On the other hand, it is believed that the Prince totally denies the transaction. As has already been said, Africans have no idea of permanently alienating land which is common property, not that of the king or chiefs; even a written contract implies, according to their ideas, only that the stranger has the rights of citizenship and of personal occupancy.* A joint commission is, I believe, in orders

* Of course our popular writers in "Chambers" and so forth assert that the native chiefs transferred the sovereignty of their country to the Liberian Government, and general readers believe them. It is thus that history is written. Evidently the natives should be consulted,

to settle the north-western limits of Liberia. Should the Gallinhas fall to them, they purpose to establish another port of entry either on that river or on the Shebar, and where it would not be too near Roberts Port, and to name it Gurney, after their late benefactor.

It would hardly be fair to leave Cape Palmas without saying something touching its peculiar population. The theme has been treated by every writer upon the subject of this coast, Owen, Boteler, Smith, Wilson, Hutchinson, and Durrant, not to mention dozens of others. Yet there is more to say than has been said.*

The word Kru—written Croo, Kroo, Krou, and, by other writers, Carow and Crew, upon the principle that Sipahi became Sepoy, or Seapie—is a corruption of the name by which the people call themselves "Kráo." It is a small tribe, living about half-way between Cape Mesurado and Cape Palmas, about seventy-five miles above or to the north-west of the latter. The district extends from twenty to thirty miles along the coast, and

---

and if the sale be *bonâ fide* it should be confirmed to Liberia, and *vice versâ*. At present, uncertainty causes much irritation, and the merchants of Sierra Leone are preparing to assert their joint rights to the Gallinhas by force if necessary.

* The following remarks concerning the origin of the Kru are derived from information received from Bishop Payne, and from the Introduction to his Dictionary of the Grebo Language. New York : Jenkins, Frankfort Street, 1860.

The little volume contains about 2500 words, or nearly half the language. It is to be hoped that this excellent Minister of the Gospel will soon publish his expected Grammar of the Grebo tongue.

perhaps, as much into the interior. They had originally
five chief settlements, which, beginning from the north-
west, are Little Kru; Settra Kru the chief town, Krubah,
Nanna Kru, or Kru Settra, and King Will's Town. They
were the first to go to sea, and, as some twenty other
tribes, numbering, perhaps, 150,000 souls, followed their
example, all are now known by the common name
Krumen. As Mr. M'Queen says, they never enslave one
another; yet they were the life and soul of the Spanish and
Portuguese slavers, and they proved themselves probably
the greatest kidnappers on the coast. They first began the
peculiar tattoo, which the adjoining tribes soon imitated,
and now they are in the habit of buying bushmen and
boy-slaves, and marking them like themselves, thus
transforming them to " Krumen," that they may be
engaged as seamen. When the slave-trade began to
decline, they preferred the service of ships of war and
merchantmen, they visited S'a Leone in considerable
numbers, and they became the Coolies and Lascars
of West Africa. They seem to be created purposely
for the oil trade.

The chief tribes that followed their example were the
people of Niffu, or Piccaninny Sess; the Bwidabe, or
Fishmen; the Menawe of Grand Sess, the Wiábo of
Garoway, the Babo below Cavalla River, the Plabo,* and

---

* On this part of the coast, all the places and tribes have double
names.   The Cavalla River is called Dokrinyun ; Cape Monrovia,
Trubo ; Cape Mount, Chepe ; Drewin, Wayra ; St. Andrew's, Nisonti ;
and Settra Kru, Wete. Of individual names, more hereafter.

others, extending to Cape St. Andrew's, and about forty
miles into the interior. Of these tribes, who are all
cognate, as their language and physique prove, the most
influential are the Grebos of Cape Palmas : the total
number, however, probably does not exceed 40,000.
Like the peoples generally upon the African coast, they
have lately come from the interior. Their own tradition
is, that a Kobo Kui, or foreign house—no doubt some
European slave factory—was found by them on arrival
at Cape Palmas. Their earliest settlements near the sea
were behind Berebi, sixty miles to the eastward. After
becoming too numerous for their narrow limits, a portion
of them determined, Irish-like, upon a kind of exodus
to the west. The movement was secretly managed,
because it was opposed to the wishes of the majority.
Whilst embarking, a number of canoes were capsized,
and those in them were left behind. They were called
Woríbo, or the Capsized, from the verb Wore. The
others, who succeeded in bounding over the waves, took
the name of Grebo, from the jumping grey monkey,
Gré or Grí.

Proceeding up the coast, the Grebos landed detached
parties in the country now inhabited by the Bubos, at
Cavalla and at Cape Palmas, where they built small
temporary settlements. They continued their migration
as far as Grand Sesters, forty miles above Cape Palmas :
at length, directed by an oracle, they all gathered together
and built on the Cape of Cocoas a large town, called
Bwini, or Bwimli. These wanderings account for the

close analogy of the Grebo tongue and that of Sino (written Sinori, or Sinoe), in N. lat. 5° 1′, or about ninety miles to the north-west of Harper. At Grand Sesters there are still large branches of the Grebo family, and many merchant-ships prefer them as being the best-conducted men. After them are the people of Niffu, or Piccaninny Sesters. For fishing, the Fish-men are the best servants.

Strictly speaking, it is incorrect to call the Grebo "Krumen." As, however, the people of this coast readily converse together, hold constant intercourse, and are remarkably like one another in physique, as in *morale,* they may be described as one, and the best name for them is that which custom sanctions— Krumen.

The peculiar contrast of feature and figure which distinguishes this people has already been described. The features are distinctly African, without an admixture of Arab; the conjunctiva is brown, yellow, or tarnished, a Hamitic peculiarity; and some paint white goggle-like ovals round the orbits, producing the effect of a "loup." This is sometimes done for sickness, and invalids are rubbed over with various light and dark coloured powders. The skin is very dark, often lamp-black; others are of a deep rich brown or bronze tint, but a light-complexioned man is generally called Tom Coffee; and people put waggish questions touching his paternity. They wear the hair, which is short and kinky, in crops, which look like Buddha's skull-cap :

and they shave when mourning for their relations : a favourite "fash." is to scrape off a parallelogram behind the head, from the poll to the cerebellum ; and others are decorated in that landscape or parterre style which wilder Africa and Germany love. The back of the cranium is often remarkably flat, and I have seen many heads of the pyramidal shape, rising narrow and pointed high to the apex. The beard is seldom thick, and never long ; the moustachio is removed, and the pile, like the hair, often grows in tufts. The tattoo has been described : there seems to be something attractive in this process— the English sailor can seldom resist the temptation. They also chip, sharpen, and extract the teeth. Most men cut out an inverted V between the two middle incisors of the upper jaw ; others draw one or two of the central and lower incisors ; others, especially the St. Andrew's men, tip or sharpen the incisors, like the Wahiao, and several Central African tribes. Odontology has its mysteries. Dentists seem, or rather seemed to hold as a theory, that destruction of enamel involves the loss of the tooth ; the Krumen hack their masticators with a knife, or a rough piece of hoop iron, and find that the sharpening, instead of producing caries, acts as a preservative, by facilitating the laniatory process. Similarly there are physiologists who attribute the preservation of the negro's teeth to his not drinking anything hotter than blood heat. This is mere empiricism. The Arabs swallow their coffee nearly boiling, and the East African will devour his agali, or porridge, when the temperature would scald the hand. Yet both these races have pearls of teeth, except when they chew lime or tobacco.* The Krumen, like most other wild people, always wash the teeth after eating. A cleanly race, and never passing a day—unless it be very cold—without bathing, the African fetor is not always perceptible, but it exists.† The hands and feet are large and coarse, but not such outrages to proportion as the races further south.

The Krumen show all that propensity to ape Europeans which characterizes the African generally. A noble savage enough in his semi-nudity, when a single shukkeh covers his middle—the women wear even less—with a bead necklace, and coarse iron, ivory, or brass rings round his wrists and ankles; he is fond of making himself grotesque, as an old-clo' man. The hat is borrowed from the sailor; it is of every form—chimney-pot, Kossuth, skull-cap, naval casquette, red nightcap, straw or broad-brimmed wide-awake; not unfrequently it surmounts a bandanna, or some gaudy kerchief. A tooth-stick is in every mouth, and not a few snuff or chew. The neck is variously decorated, from the band of hairy skin to the Popo, or Aggri bead,‡ which, on the Gold Coast,

---

* On the other hand, it is said of the Guanches at Tenerife that "they drank nothing but water, and that only at a certain period after eating anything heated, for fear of destroying their teeth."

† The Persians find a similar fetor in the Jewish race, and call it by a peculiar name—"bui shimit." This, however, arises probably not so much from the conformation of the skin, as from the extreme impurity of the race.

‡ Much has been written touching these beads, which are dug from

is more valuable than gold. The favourite ornaments
are strings of leopards' teeth, small chains of brass and
iron, and beads of every form and substance—glass and
porcelain, white and black, blue, green, and yellow ; the
necklace is used to hold the clay dudheen, of European
make. The wrists bear from one to half a dozen ivory
bracelets, rings painfully cut out with a knife, and turned
with a wet cord rubbed to and fro ; the most pretentious
of these decorations have the wearer's name engraved
upon the ivory in coloured letters, or upon a brass-plate,
or expressed in metal tacks forming the words; they are
at once passports and characters for future service. On
the arm, also, is the Gri, or Fetish, leopards' teeth, or
the smallest deer-horns, with cowries and other " medicine " bound on by a bit of string. Ligatures round the
ankles are similarly fetished, and some are drawn so
tight that the cord leaves a deep mark upon the skin.
I presume that, like the tribes of the Arab Bedouins,
these are intended for ligatures in case of snake bites;
they are certainly the only alleviation when suffering from
cramp, a painful nervous disease in these lands, ever
liable to be induced by cold, wet, or confined positions.
They are fond of finger-rings, but care little whether
they are gold, silver, or brass. The pagne, or loin cloth,
is generally a cheque of white and pink or blue; it is
tied round the waist, or tucked into a cord : and only
great swells have cricket, military, or elastic belts. Some

the ground. Many are found upon the Liberian coast, and cannot be
imitated in Europe. Some travellers have derived them from Egypt.

carry sticks of peculiar shape, edged and notched like
certain Hindostani swordblades. The few women whom
we saw were shaven-pated and nude to their loins, which
were covered with the scantiest cloth : they showed a
decided steatopyga and the pulpy African development.
Their principal ornaments were massive brass anklets; and
all were at work, carrying upon their heads rice-bags in
wicker cradles, and freshly-caught fish in the bark band-
boxes described by Central African travellers. The children are attired *secundum naturam,* except the mission
boys, who are decently clad in loose jackets and pantaloons : they have all two "given names," *è. g.,* A. B.
Smith ; and the negrillons about the house are also
promoted to shirt and loin-cloth.

The Rev. Mr. Wilson, late of the Gaboon Mission,
who, some thirty years ago, took so active a part in
purchasing land for the colony, has well and accurately
described in a book to which the reader is referred,* the
curious polity of this people. Like the Guanches of
Tenerife, and indeed most primitive people from Etruria
to India, the Kru Republic is divided into four classes,
which can hardly, however, be called castes. These are
the elders, the middle-aged men who form the soldiery; the youth who aspire to become warriors; and
the demon doctors, priests, and physicians. As amongst

---

* Western Africa ; its History, Condition, and Prospects. New
York : Harper and Brothers, 1856. Chap. 6 is the best treatise on the
Kru Republic that I know. Generally the work abounds in flaws, but
if properly edited it would form a good handbook of Western Africa.

the Wanyika of the Eastern Coast, there appears to be a regular initiation to each step in rank.* The two first classes meet in deliberative assembly when any measure touching the public interests is proposed; the juveniles, however, are expected to be seen and not heard, except when the subject discussed has special reference to their own body. Oratory, as amongst all African tribes, is greatly cultivated, and to judge from its effects upon the audience, with success. A highly aristocratic form is secured by the preponderance of the first class in the commonwealth. The youths are hardly permitted to hold property; if they return wealthy from beyond the sea their gains are systematically appropriated. Nay, more: even an elder who presumes to excel his fellows in riches or importance is at once reduced, for " too much sass," to the general level. The " sauce-wood," or red wood of the giddu tree, ordeal is fearfully prevalent amongst them, killing its thousands; the only check is, that if the defendant survives the poisonous draught, the plaintiff must drink it in his turn. Capital punishment is rare, except in cases of murder or witchcraft, where the criminal is beaten to death or drowned. As usual amongst uncivilized people, even the Chinese, little difference is made between wilful murder and justifiable homicide : the object seems to teach the value of human life. Adultery and theft are punished by fine,

---

* "Among the Wanyika the orders are three in number : Nyene, the young ; Khánbi, the middle-aged; and Nfaya, the old."—Zanzibar, and Two Months in East Africa. Blackwood's Magazine, Feb., 1858.

and the informer is regarded with general contempt. Another check upon crime is the system of headmen. The eldest male member of the several families into which the tribes are divided, is at once their representative in palavers, and their security for good behaviour. Property is held as a kind of joint-stock, and from it fines and other penalties for misdemeanors must be paid.

The *morale* of this people appears to the European exceedingly contradictory, not to say unintelligible. The same, however, may be affirmed of all barbarous tribes, where viewed with purely civilized eyes. For instance, the Krumen have, for the last two centuries, been a race of sailors; they have chosen what is by no means an undangerous profession, and they are accustomed to cross the perilous bars, and to trust themselves to the mercy of the sharks and the breakers. Yet they are arrant cowards. When real firing begins on board ship, they will run and hide themselves in the coal bunkers. During the descent of the Niger, in 1859, when the hostile villages below Abo shot at the Government Contract Steamer " Rainbow," Captain Creen, it was necessary to drive the Krumen from their retreat behind the paddle-boxes. They will desert their master upon the least appearance of danger. It is impossible to mistake their state of panic: if a roller strikes a boat unexpectedly, they will lay oars by, gaze with a blank face, and if the stick be not used, rise to spring overboard. The least corporal punishment makes them scream like women, and, unlike most Africans, they are exceedingly sensitive to pain. Sickness afflicts them mentally as well as bodily; and if one of a boat's crew be lost off a bar, or devoured by sharks, it is found advisable to send the others home. The canoe men or Guinea men on the other hand, if supplied with a gallon of rum, will forget the mishaps by the next day. Kru poltroonery is open and unaffected; other African tribes appear ashamed to show it; the Kruman, however, boasts of it. If you ask him to fight, he replies unblushingly that he has but one life, and wishes again to see " we country." I have no doubt that excessive affection for their own land and for their parents—especially for the mother—partly causes this loathing to face danger. But though there are exceptions amongst them, and some few are brave, even to ferocity, as a rule there is no mistaking their timidity. During the Indian mutiny, it was proposed to levy a Kru battalion, and officers were selected for that purpose. The project suddenly fell to the ground, owing, it is said, to the contradictory statements of the best authorities; some recommending the Krus as excellent food for powder, others reporting them as far readier to run away than to do battle. I made many inquiries upon the subject, and after seeing much of the Krumen, and learning something of their language, I satisfied myself that they would be quite useless as soldiers; they would not fight, they prefer ship-work to shore-work, and as their women never travel, they would not willingly engage themselves for any length of time. "*Un des plus grands malheurs des honnêtes gens,*" says a French author, with great truth, "*c'est qu'ils sont des lâches;*" this, however, cannot be applied to Krumen. Besides cowardice, their principal fault is thieving, a disposition which they never fail to evince; and nothing comes amiss to them, from wholesale robbery to petty prigging. Like the true coward, too, they are bullies when they meet those more timid than themselves. Some years ago they seized the north-west part of Fernando Po, from the feeble Bubes, plundered the people, carried off the women, and were defeated only by the combined action of the natives by land, and Governor Beecroft who attacked them from the sea. When the Niger expedition was encamped at Jeba, in 1857-58, the Kru seamen stole from them about 140*l.* worth of cloth, cowries, mirrors, and small ware. The robbery was discovered by the natives firing the grass, and the whole was consumed. Fanaticism ruined the unfortunate Niger expedition of 1841—Philanthropy and disputes that of 1857-62: these rascally Krumen were actually allowed to remain unflogged. Their favourite style of thieving, however, is on the smallest scale: knives, penknives, and scissors, will be taken out of the master's room, turnscrews and brass-tipped ramrods will disappear most inexplicably. They have no hesitation in robbing from one another's boxes, arms, and ammunition, wire, padlocks, and similar articles. When a crew is dismissed, the master usually insists upon the large chests in which they have stowed away

their goods, being examined, and finds nothing: the
cunning villains have either trusted their spoils to a
comrade, or they have sent them on by another ship.
They never, except when soundly flogged, "peach" upon
one another; and if one of a gang commits a robbery,
all expect to benefit by it. Similarly, if rations be given
to one out of twenty, he will share it with the other
score. Provisions are never safe from them. Goats
hungrily browsing will be brought in dead by them an
hour or two afterwards, strangled secretly, and made to
appear as if bitten by snakes. When this is done, the
only way is to throw the body into the sea; if buried
they will exhume and devour it. My plan was to dig a
hole, and after heaping the earth up, write upon it in
large letters, " Thou shalt not steal!" Poultry cannot be preserved from them. They are fond of drink,
and will suffer even bodily pain to obtain it. In various
journeys I have never drunk my own last bottle of cognac:
that operation has been performed by some Kruboy of
·the party. The greatest robbers are the St. Andrew's
men; they are hard-working fellows; honesty, however, never seems to suggest itself to them. I have
no belief in punishment as regards the individual
punished, not a shade of faith in its ever doing him
good. As an intimidation to others, if properly
managed, it may possibly have its uses. Its real
objects, however, should be to repay society for the loss
that it has sustained, and to defend the body social from
further attacks by the same hand. But to manage it

properly, it must everywhere be modified. In England we still practise the barbarous and useless system of capital punishment in case of murder, and we make the penalty lighter for theft. In most parts of Africa I would treat the robber much more severely than the assassin.

As regards morality, in its limited sense, the Krumen are not bright in the scale of creation. Adultery is punished, it is true, by a fine, and in the case of a wealthy or powerful man, there may be a "great palaver." The European stranger, however, travelling in their country is expected to patronise their wives and daughters, and these unconscious followers of Lycurgus and Cato feel hurt, as if dishonoured, by his refusing to gratify them. The custom is very prevalent along this coast. At Gaboon, perhaps it reaches the acme; there a man will in one breath offer the choice between his wife, sister, and daughter. The women of course do as they are bid by the men, and they consider all familiarity with a white man a high honour.*

The Kruman believes in the "education of travel." He leaves home early, learns a little waiting, and perhaps makes a voyage to England; he never, however, returns there, dreading the cold. At the age of puberty he ships under some headman, who began life in the same

* Dr. Livingstone, chap. 25, asserts, "I have heard women speaking in admiration of a white man, because he was pure and never was guilty of any secret immorality." This is amongst the Makololos : he would have heard them speak in anything but an admiring way about continence in these regions.

way, and who having learned a little English, and the handling of a rope, engages a gang of youngsters. A good headman takes as much from his dependents as possible, stopping their pay on all occasions; he is expected to defend the master's property from them—which often he does not do—and to punish them severely with his own hand. It is this comparative energy and willingness to do work, which together with their independent bearing, has given the Krumen such a name on the coast;—bad as they are, all the rest are worse. We are rapidly, however, spoiling these men. About ten years ago they were happy to receive 5*s.* per month, in goods, which reduced it to 3*s.* As in India, however, so here, servants' wages are increasing, till they threaten to become exorbitant. Now, on board H.M.'s ships they are paid the wages of ordinary able seamen, 1*l.* 10*s.* per month, or 18*l.* per annum. Besides which, they are entitled to the rations of a white man, and their compensation money will probably run up to another 12*l.* per annum. The pay might be reduced to $5 per month, and rice rations, with beef every two days; thus the cruisers would not injure the trade. There is for them an inexplicable charm on board a man-of-war. They are very proud of their uniform; which, however, renders them effeminate and more subject to disease, than those who are less clothed; they would, I think, look much better with shaven heads, red caps, and short blue drawers. They treat with a certain contempt the "river boys." Yet, African like, they must desert at times, especially after a good flogging from the headman, for not keeping a bright look out. On the other hand, a vessel of war wanting Krumen, has only to give a hint to those of the nearest merchantman, and they will be smuggled on board presently; this has been done by fellows, who wrapped up in navy shirts, and with caps pulled over their faces, have passed out unrecognised, even by captains of the mail steamers. But a Kruman who has once served on board a ship of war, is like a foreign domestic in an English family, useless for all other purposes. When shipped at S'a Leone for merchant service, their wages are more than those who embark at Cape Palmas; nominally the former now receive 30s., the latter $2 per month in goods, which reduce it to $1. Some picked gig-crews in the Oil Rivers, receive $5, besides additional clothes and caps; the average pay, however, is from $3 to $4. A crew, well picked out of a number of men, is wonderful to look at; their muscles stand out almost like those of that caricature, the Farnese Hercules; they row at a stretch 40 miles, pulling as if for dear life, and at the end they seem as little fatigued as white ants. Generally the headman's pay is double that of his boys, and coin is never given. Their rations are 1½ lb. of rice or yams a day, with salt meat or fresh steak once or twice a week; they usually eat three times, breakfast at 9, dine at 2, and sup at 7 P.M.; when working hard, they are allowed a liberal allowance of rum. Tobacco depends greatly on the master; it is, however, a favour, not a

right; they expect to receive a clean cloth worth,
say 18*d.*, every Sunday; it is more general, however,
to give them the Sunday cloth, as they call it, every
three weeks. They will ship for long voyages, but
scarcely ever engage themselves for more than three
years. On the other hand they dislike all shore work,
and will not act as servants for more than two years.
Their favourite period of engagement—here, as in India,
steam navigation shortens service and prolongs furloughs
—is "one time yam come up, twel' moon." If kept
beyond their limits, they begin by waxing surly, they
proceed to refuse work, and they end, African like, by
taking the law into their own hands. I have known
cases where they have threatened to fire a factory, and
many in which they have plundered the store, launched
a boat, and gone off no one knows where.

The object of the Kruman's expatriation is to make
money, with which he can return home—the thing has
been done in England—enact the gentleman, and marry
a wife; when his purse is empty he sets out once more ;
not willingly, for to use his own phrase, he is "nigger
for ship, king for country." After four or five voyages,
he has learned English enough to become a headman,
and by peculating in his turn, he lays the foundation
of a large family. Until then, he has ever been received,
as he returns, with noisy festivity, but his gains have
been appropriated by the family council, and applied to
the common stock. Now he spends his own money,
chiefly in purchasing wives. The whole superstructure of

Kru society is built upon polygamy, which is much after the Mormon principle, a division of labour.* Servants do not exist, the language has no name for them, and domestic slavery is very limited; moreover, as no gentleman in Africa can demean himself by work, which he considers in the light of convict labour, the institution winds itself round every heart. He is a "small boy" when yet unmarried; he begins life with one wife, and he hopes to end it with a dozen or two, when he retires

---

* The Rev. Mr. Wilson remarks : " It is not a little singular, however, that the females, upon whom the burden of this degrading institution (polygamy) mainly rests, are quite as much interested in its continuance as the men themselves. A woman would infinitely prefer to be one of a dozen wives of a respectable man than to be the sole representative of a man who had not force of character to raise himself above the one-woman level."—Western Africa, chap. 1-4.

There is nothing singular in this : the polygamy of the Latter Day Saints derives all its force from the preference of the women. Were they to oppose it, nothing could preserve the institution.

Moreover, it appears that in the various branches of the human family, the relative development of the female to the male greatly varies. In some, the Africans for instance, the woman's inferiority is constant and salient. In others, as the Anglo-Saxon, there is a far greater amount of equality between the sexes. We see the same thing in the lower animals : whilst in the Gallinæ the male has a marked superiority over his mate ; in the Falconidæ the female is superior in strength, size, and courage ; and in others—the Canidæ and Solidungulæ—the powers are as equally balanced as possible.

It is, doubtless, this superior physical and mental development which has placed the women of the Indo-Germanic family in their present exalted position. Yet they willingly abdicate it. There are no more submissive polygamists than the Englishwomen at Great Salt Lake City, except, perhaps, the Americans, who—I speak only of those whose fathers were born and bred in the New World—are somewhat highly coloured copies of their English cousins.

from business, a consummation most devoutly wished for. This seldom happens before he has reached the age of fifty. There is nothing peculiar in Kru nuptials. The girl-wife's mother is first propitiated with small presents; then the dowry is settled with her father and his family, who are the real owners of the property. The senior wife is the first in rank, and respectable men always keep a separate establishment for each spouse. On the husband's death, the wives become the property of the brothers, who can transfer them if they please. When a woman is ill-treated, she runs away to her father's family, but a "big palaver" is sure to follow this elopement. The children of course love the mother better than the other parent, but they must follow their father should a split take place between the tribes.

The religion of the Kruman is a fanaticism so vague and undeveloped that no writer has, I believe, ventured to treat upon it. It has been already mentioned that they have Diyabo*—*sing*. Diyá—or "Devil Doctors," as Europeans call them, whose preparation for the ministry and position in the community is precisely that of the North-American Indian's medicine-man. Their oracle at the Grand Devil has also been alluded to. The commonalty however appear to have few, if any, exercises which can properly be called religious. During the whole of the Niger expedition, from 1857 to 1862, only one case was observed; on the night of the "Dayspring's" wreck, Grando, the second headman, stood near the bank, quite

* The syllable -bo means, I believe, a class.

upright, with his face to the West, and howled till dawn, occasionally waving the right arm. Two or three sat around him, but no one joined with him. They will not eat blood nor the heart of cattle; they swear, by dipping the forefinger in salt, pointing to earth and heaven, and then tasting the condiment. This custom reminds one of the Salt Eaters, *i.e.*, Rice Christians of the Kongo River, and the various salt-incantations of Asia.

When a man dies a fire is kindled every evening before his house to warm his Ku,* *i.e.*, his ghost or himself, and food is placed at his grave. He may appear in one or in several children. Or leading the goat or the bullock slain at his funeral, he may wend his way to Menu of the Kwi—Ghostland, which some place at Gedeye, in the remote interior—where, after confessing his misdeeds, he will take rank according to the sacrifice made and his means. But if a wizard, he must wander about the gloomy swamp and fetid marsh for ever. These ideas show a dawning of the " continuation theory;" but the West African, unlike the Egyptian, who probably invented the idea, has no conception of a corporeal resurrection.

The Rev. Mr. Bowen ("Central Africa '), asserts that a Kruman who attempted to learn reading would be

---

* In Bishop Payne's Grebo Vocabulary, Ku, *plur.* Kwi, is explained —devil, dream, departed spirit. Menu, or menuke, is the intermediate place through which persons are said to pass to their final destiny, and where they review all their past deeds, before going into Kwiya Orán, the City of the Manes.

killed; this is far from being the fact now, if it was then. Of all the Pagans on the coast, the Kru have been found the most difficult to convert on account of the dishonour and expulsion from the tribe which such conduct entails. Of late years there have been a few cases, and in a future page the reader will see a fine specimen of superior rascality on the part of the " divert." In the neighbourhood of the mission stations, near Cape Palmas, the more civilized Grebos do nothing on Sundays; but, as I have said before, an African will ever be most happy to practise as much idleness as you choose to preach.

Like the negro race generally, the organs of language, as well as of time and tune, are well developed in the Krumen. They find no difficulty in picking up a few words of English, though they speak it with a savage accent; of course, correctness or extent of vocabulary is beyond their powers, yet they can distinguish a brogue or a provincial accent, and they call Scotchmen " bush Englishmen"—a definition that would come home to Dr. Johnson's own heart. They have no poetry, and few legends; whilst their music is monotonous to a degree. Yet they delight in it, and often after a long and fatiguing day's march they will ask permission to " make play," and dance and sing till midnight. When hoeing the ground they must do it at the sound of music; in fact, everything is cheered with a song. The traveller should never forget to carry a tom-tom, or some similar instrument, which will shorten his journey by a fair quarter.

They are good mimics, and I have seen some laughable caricatures of various European nations. "Chaff" is with them as favourite an exercise as in civilised London, and they can say the most biting and sarcastic things imaginable. I have met fellows whose remarks, conveyed in broken English, were as humorous as those of any Irishman. They are great at pantomime, and with some twenty English words can tell a long story, as well as a Sioux of the Prairies. There are no noisier people on the coast; in our stations they are relegated to outhouses, placed well out of hearing.

The Kru.language, as has been seen, possesses about 5000 vocables. The grammatical forms are simple, and by no means numerous. Most writers declare the tongue to be exceedingly difficult of acquisition. I found it quite the contrary; and the Liberian colonists, if they cannot speak it, are generally able to understand it. Mr. Smith,* in a most amusing little work, asserts that every Kru word is made to end in O; he has misconceived the sign of the vocative to be an integral part of the word. He also opines that the "Kroo language seems to be composed of vowels only," whereas in few tongues are there more explosive consonants, harsher gutturals, or a stronger nasalization that half masters the articulation. We find in it also the duplicated initial consonants, as *nn* and *mm*, which an Englishman would pronounce with a semi-elision of a prefixed indefinite vowel. Its

* Chap. 10, Trade and Travels in the Gulf of Guinea. By J. Smith. London : Simpkin, Marshall, and Co., 1851.

chief merit seems to be the facility with which a Kruman can make himself heard at a distance, when a
European would require a speaking-trumpet. The
Rev. Mr. Wilson, who discovers a similarity between
one-fifth of the words in the Mpongwe of the Gaboon
and the Kisawahili of Zanzibar and of the eastern
shores of the continent, detects none between the
Mpongwe and the Kru dialects.* Yet I cannot but
find most distinct resemblance, not so much in vocabulary, however, as in the grammar and the spirit of
the language.

"Blackman's English," opposed to "high English,"
or " deep English," in this part of the world is a literature whose professor has hitherto been the British
sailor. I leave to the reader's imagination the style
of expression which it has engrafted upon the African
mind. Queer tales are told of words starting up in the
presence of ladies—words which, falling amongst an
English assembly, would act like a 10-inch shell. Every
traveller has made merry with the ridiculous names
which the Kru boys have borrowed for themselves from
the English, *e.g.*, Nix, Black Trouble, Salt water, Bottle
o' beer, and Six-finger Jack.† Yet their own names are
by no means unpleasant or difficult to learn, nor can I
see the force of calling Nábwe, Kofá, Tiyá, and

---

* Western Africa, chap. 4.

† On the Gold Coast, children born with six fingers are strangled :
amongst the Kru and other tribes of Lower Guinea they are not
injured.

Nákú, Black Will, Two Glass, Seabreeze, and Tom Brass.*

Remains to consider the Kruman in the light of a domestic servant. In this phase he does not shine—a more clumsy-handed, pig-headed clown could not be found even in Europe. He steals anything he can lay his hands upon; he becomes idle to the last degree, and though personally clean enough, his ideas touching that virtue in respect to plate and porcelain are still embryotic. He either breaks or he mislays everything entrusted to him, and he never works except when the master stands over him; he never attends to an order, and he would see all " master's " property eaten by white ants rather than take the trouble to remove it. There are worse servants on this coast even than the Kruman, I own; for instance, the Camaroons and the Calabar men; yet even with him, your house is as uncomfortable as fancy could conceive.

About noon on the 16th August we set out once more, and steamed down the coast, which was bright with the delightful air of the fine season. We had shipped at Cape Palmas about 5000*l.* worth of Krumen, who were proceeding to the Oil Rivers; they, or rather their employers, pay for their diet and passage $10 per head. Their supper on board was a study of savagery. Their favourite food is ever rice, and they prefer it to the best bread, and pine for it at times when they cannot

* At the end of this chapter the reader will find a specimen of Kru vocabulary, kindly supplied to a friend by Bishop Payne.

obtain it. It must be far more nutritious than that of India, for they eat it dry and get through an immense amount of labour without other sustenance. A large cauldron, containing a pint per man, was brought on deck and portioned into five messes, around which, after a furious chatting and gesticulating like excited baboons, all squatted. They ball'd the rice by squeezing it with either hand, left as well as right, thrust it into their mouths, looking like chickens being crammed, and swallowed it almost whole with a powerful action of the œsophagus. They did not drink till after the meal, as is the custom of Asia; when full they satisfied their thirst at the tank. If meat appears, it is a signal for a scuffle; the strongest manage to snatch a few mouthfuls each, and the weaker get none.

Though fresh from home they are in good spirits; they love a change, and the world is all before them. Returning after two years or so, they will be in the state described as being "strung upon wires." They have boxes to protect and their property will not be safe from thieves and the ocean till it is lodged in their huts. They have pitiably suffered in health, and are allowed no medical luxuries on board; even a change of diet is unattainable, and the attendance of a doctor is a matter of personal humanity. Some of them by touching the railings have given to the passengers craw-craw, and other horrid skin-diseases, which have found their way into English homes. It is a touching sight to see some poor fellow, with the death rattle in his throat, lying

unheeded upon the deck, whilst all others are craning
their necks over the bulwarks, and stepping over his
almost unconscious body to get the first glimpse of "we
country." Should he die, the corpse must be taken
on shore, or there will be what the African dreads, a
"palaver." And when "Jack Kruman" reaches his hut
and greets the wives of his bosom, he cannot love them
till he has perfectly satisfied himself with the strictness
of their conduct during his absence.

Beyond Cape Palmas, the coast line is a beach of
bright white sand, from which the slave barracoons have
now disappeared; in the foreground an occasional rock
or ledge rises awash from the level, and the background
is a deep strip of black forest, here and there broken by
tall trees. We are soon fairly beyond Liberia, formerly
called the Grain Coast. This ambiguous name has
caused many a mistake, but the grain in question is
not a cereal but a condiment—rejecting, at least that
etymology, which supposes it to have been derived
from cochineal, which in those days was considered
not an animal but a vegetable. It is a real cardamom
(*A. Grana Paradisi*), of which many varieties grow
along the whole length of the western coast of intertropical Africa. The flower is of great beauty on account of the glowing pink bracts; the shrub is cane-
like, and the fruit, which appears close to the ground, is
a pyriform pod with crimson skin enclosing black brown
seeds, surrounded by a juicy placenta. Nothing is more
pleasant or reviving on a long, thirsty march, than a

handful of these cardamoms; the acidity of the pulp contrasts most pleasantly with the pungency of the spice. By the Dutch they were called Guinea Grains; by the trade, Malaguetta pepper; and the demand in Europe in the sixteenth century led to the discovery of many ports on "the coast." It was then principally used for giving fire and flavour in spirituous liquors, and especially for adulterating beer. At last its importation into England was forbidden, cases of poisoning being attributed to it; and Europeans in these regions still believe that some species are injurious, and that they were mixed with the true grains. The natives use this cardamom extensively as a condiment and a medicine : it is a stomachic, a carminative, and an external irritant. The people of the Gold Coast, when suffering from headache, rub over the forehead a paste of Malaguetta pepper. The powder is applied during the hot fit of fever, as ginger is in India for rheumatism and for fugitive pains. It is spirted out of the mouth over the part affected, or a paste made with water is rubbed on like a poultice, or applied in streaks. The dead also are perfumed with this pepper and sweet scented plants. Inasmuch as when bruised and soaked in sherry, it makes excellent bitters, it will, once more, I believe, find its way into the European markets.

Note.—For the following specimen of the real Kráo language, I am indebted to the kindness of Bishop Payne :—

KRU AND ENGLISH.

N.B.—The vowels are written after the system of Sir W. Jones, modified as used in Lane, Richardson's Persian Dictionary, &c. : *g* is always hard, as in get ; the letters *c*, *q*, *x*, and *y* are supplied by *k*, *ks*, and *i*.

Ni-o-ju	Man	Bla-bi	Sheep
Ni-o-no	Woman	Bok-er-o	Goat
Di-u-be	Child		
Mi	Father	Na-ji-o	I see
Ni	Mother	Na-uo-i	I hear
Mi-e-ju	Brother	Na-u-ru	I speak
No-ru	Sister	Mu	Go
Nī	Water	Gi	Come
Nā	Fire	Di-e	Eat
Ser-a	House	Na-ni	Drink
Bun-go	Door	Na-mu	Sleep
Bu-ōm-bī	Window	Na-dub-i	Wash
Nam-bu-rī	Seat	Ma-na	Walk
Kri	Farm	Na-pīn-de	Cook
Ku-ō	Rice	Mu-ne	Carry
Kin-a	Oil	Na-nu-de	Make
To	Salt	Na-ni-em	Give
Po-pa	Bowl	Na-uk-be	Take
Ja-bi	Jar	Na-ti-e	Buy
Ja-bi	Boiler	Pu-ri-em-bu	Sell
Gi-u-ro	Sun	Bi-si-um	Thank
Tsho	Moon	Gī-rum	Love
Na-pi	Star	O-ro-de	Well
Ni-ba	River	Na-po-pa	I am sick
Ku-ra	Field		
Tu	Tree	Iī	Yes
Bu-ru-a	Grass	Ie	No
Nne	Wood	So-na-to	To-day
So-ba	Stone	Po-pla-ka	To-morrow
Du-bo	Head	So-ra-ma	Yesterday
Nu-me	Bird	Kre-kre	Quickly
Ni	Fish	Da-ka	Long since
Sōng	Fowl	Gi	Above
Bi-li	Cow	Bre	Below

CHAPTER VII.

TWENTY-FOUR HOURS AT CAPE COAST CASTLE.

18TH SEPTEMBER, 186—

> "—— If you cannot swim,
> Beware of Providence."
>
> *Shelley.*

To the east of the Grain Coast—in maps—lies the Ivory Coast, now a misnomer. Hardly a tusk has been exported from it for the last score of years; the animals having been driven away by the "hot mouthed weapon." The present Ivory Coast is the region south of the Camaroons Mountains, extending to the Gaboon River and Cape Lopez. The old Ivory Coast had but four settlements—Fresco, Cape Lahou or Nifá, Jack-a-Jack, Grand Bassam and Assini, the two latter French. After passing these we enter the Gold Coast; it was once a celebrated region, which produced the GUINEA for England; now, all known about it by the public at home is, that it is somewhere about Africa.* How little

---

* That popular book, Haydn's Dictionary of Dates, is the best proof. The ninth edition, published in 1860 by Mr. Moxon, informs us, under the word "African Company," that "the rights vested in the *present company* are by 23 George II., 1749," whereas that company expired about forty years ago. Another well-known book—Brookes' "Gazetteer," revised by Mr. Findlay, and published 1861—omits the

it deserves this neglect, and how much may be made of it, will be shown in a following page.

There is a question of great interest touching the discovery of this coast. The Portuguese have claimed and secured the whole honour: in our encyclopedias and school-books, which are copied one from the other, no other nation is even mentioned. Their own account of it* is that Fernâo Gomes, a worthy and honest citizen of Lisbon, obtained from the Portuguese Government, in 1471, permission to trade on these coasts for five years, with this proviso: that he should pay to the Portuguese Government the annual sum of 44*l*. 9*s*. Also that he should make annual voyages of discovery from Sierra Leone along the coast to the distance of 300 miles; so that, at the expiration of the stipulated period of five years, 1500 miles should have been explored. In consequence of this agreement, El-Mina

date (Appendix, 926) at which the Gold Coast becâme an independent, government. When shall we have in England a good set of popular, and especially educational works, in which our youth will not learn that of which they must unlearn half ? Not long ago I found some young friends painfully impressing their brains with the fact that the United States "contained nearly thirteen millions of souls."

* This is quoted from "Six Years of a Traveller's Life in Western Africa." By Francisco Travassos Valdez. Two vols. Hurst and Blackett, London, 1861.

The book should have been called "Voyager's Life." It is nothing but a coasting from Lisbon to Loando and its dependencies, with an occasional *relâche* at the islands on the way. The frontispiece of the first volume is copied from M. Gamitto's "O Muata Cazembe ;" the frontispiece of the second is taken from the same. It is about a parallel to Mr. Macbriar's "Africa and the Africans."

was discovered, and also Cape Catherina, in 1° 50′
south latitude and 9° 2′ west longitude.

On the other hand it has been seen that Norman
Knight conquered part of the Canary Islands in 1400,
and that M. Bouet-Willaumez has successfully inter-
preted the corrupted name, Boutou, on the Kru coast,
by referring it to the old Norman establishments which
were founded at " all the Bassas, great and little." The
Père Labat, the Sailor Villaud de Belfons, and many
writers, of whom Barbot is the most known, claim for
the French, exclusively, the honour of being the first
explorers of this coast. According to them a company
of Dieppe merchants, in the reign of Charles the Fifth,
between 1364 and 1413—nearly a century before the
Portuguese entered upon their grander career of discovery
—sent an expedition to the Gold Coast, which founded
commercial colonies at Goree and Cape Verde, at Sestro
Paris, now Grand Cestros, at Petit Dieppe, near Basa or
Bassa, on the mouth of the St. John's River, and at " the
Bay of France," now Rio Fresco. This is repeated in the
" *Mémoire sur le Commerce Maritime de Rouen, par Ernest
de Fréville*," who states the date to be November, 1364,
and the number of vessels to have been two of one hundred tons each. In 1382 the merchants of Dieppe and
Rouen combined sent three exploring ships, of which one,
the " Virgin," reached Commenda and Mina, so called
from its " gold mines," from which the blacks brought
large supplies of the precious metal. In 1583—others say
1386—they built a strong factory, and left a garrison of

ten or twelve men, and in 1387 the settlement, which had further been enlarged, was provided with a chapel. Large imports of gold, ivory, and pepper, found their way from these places to France, and an active trade continued till the European war in 1413 caused them all, after a career of fifty years, to be abandoned. Even in Barbot's time (1700), one of the El-Mina castles was called Bastion de France, and there was an old inscription beginning with M.C.C.C.—the rest defaced. At Goree there were, it is said, similar remains. These wars continued to agitate France till 1490, nearly eighty years after the abandonment of their West African colonies. Meanwhile the Portuguese, who had learned the way, had taken the place of the explorers, and have ever since claimed the honour of discovery.

The Portuguese are naturally wroth at this attempt to pluck a leaf from their laurels. Let me quote M. Valdez: "Respecting the early settlers, ridiculous follies were propagated by Père Labat, and the seaman Villautbelle-fond (*sic*), but these were invented 270 years after the Portuguese historian, Gomes Ennes d'Azurara,* who was contemporary with the discovery of Canagá, or Senegal, and who was honoured with the confidence of the celebrated Infante D. Henrique; and therefore we

* Chronica de Descobrimento e Conquista de Guiné, escrita por Mandado de El Rei D. Affonso V., pelo Chronista G. E. de Azurara, precedida de una introducção e illustrada com algumas notas pelo Visconde de Santarem, 8vo., Paris, 1841. Also, Memoria sobre a prioridade dos Descobrimentos Portugueses n' a costa d'Africa Occidental, pelo Visconde Santarem, Paris, 1841.

must believe (*"Je n'en vois pas la nécessité"*) the assertion made by this writer in his ' Chronicle of the Discovery and Conquest of Guinea,' that the Portuguese were the first who discovered the entrance of the Senegal. The claim of the Norman pirates of the fourteenth century (N.B., this is hardly fair) to the discovery is supported by an allegation that Norman words may be traced in the language of the natives, and that an inscription has been discovered as follows—' M.C.C.C.' ! ! ! Now I defy the quickest ear to discover anything resembling the Norman in the language of the Mandingoes, Jaloffes, Cassangas, Bauhans, or Feloupes ; but he whose eye is so clear as satisfactorily to decipher the inscription above mentioned, may possess an ear capable of defining sounds such as those referred to. So much for national enthusiasm and fanaticism ! " Such verbiage is by no means satisfactory in face of M. Bouet-Willaumez. Nor is the Rev. Mr. Wilson's remark at all more conclusive :— " This account of French discovery in Africa is not sustained by any contemporaneous writers, either French or Portuguese. The natives of Africa have no traditionary knowledge of any such visitors to their country ; and what discredits the picture still more is, that Azembuja, the man sent out by the Portuguese government to build the castle at Elmina, found no traces whatever of any fort or castle at that place." As if Africans in 1856 had any tradition extending back for centuries, or as if a Portuguese or any other official of those days, when ordered to erect a fort for his sovereign in the Land of

Gold Mines would confess priority of claim on the part
of another and a rival nation!

It is to be hoped that a question of such historical
importance will not be dropped. *A priori,* the claims of
the French are strong, but they have been suffered to
rest in obscurity. Their weak point at present is the
absence of contemporary evidence. But the Bayeux
tapestry, a chronicle of far older date, has been found,
and perhaps some fortunate discoverer may alight upon
a document which shall set the question at rest.

The history of English transactions on the Gold Coast
is equally interesting. The first commercial voyage made
by our countrymen was in 1551, when Captain Thomas
Wyndham, who afterwards died of fever in the Benin
River, after loading his ships with Malaguetta pepper
at the Cestos River, reached the Golden Land and returned to England with 150 lbs. of dust. On the 10th
January, 1662, the Royal Company, or Company of Royal
Adventurers of England trading to Africa, was incorporated under patronage of the Duke of York, afterwards
Charles II., and in the same year James Fort was built at
Accra. Its object was nearly entirely the carrying on of
the slave trade, and the attacks of the Dutch under the
great De Ruyter compelled it, in 1667, to surrender
its charter to government. The second, or Royal
African Company, was incorporated on the 27th September, 1672, with powers and privileges to maintain and
extend the African trade. It entered upon its functions
with vigour, and soon possessed fifteen forts and factories

on the coast, of which, however, Bosman* gives a poor account. Despite the Assiento contract the company became indebted, and followed in the way of its predecessor. In 1752-4 the "African Company" was established with free trade on the Gold Coast to all His Majesty's subjects: this bound them not to interfere as before with private adventurers, or what was then called "interlopers." This was the first blow to the prosperity of the coast. The American Revolution ensued; the Abolition movement followed, and the establishment of Sierra Leone struck the final blow. In 1821 the African Company, being bankrupt, was abolished: the British forts, settlements, and possessions on the Western coast of Africa from 20° N. to 20° S. lat. were made dependencies on the colony of Sierra Leone; and the bill passed through Parliament in 1821. In 1827, owing to the expenses of Sir Charles Macarthy's Ashantee war, the home government gave up the forts to the merchants as factories on various conditions, especially that Cape Coast Castle and James Fort, Accra, should remain dependencies of Sierra Leone, and that affairs should be managed by an African committee of three merchants, and a paid secretary, resident in London and appointed by government. A parliamentary grant

---

* William Bosman was chief factor for the Dutch at Elmina, in the days of the Royal African Company, and he seems not a little to have despised his neighbours. He was an active and most efficient man, and his " Description of the Coast of Guinea," is equally valuable for its observation, and amusing by its dry humour.

of 4000*l.* per annum was allowed for the repair of forts, the maintenance of schools, and presents to the various Fanti chiefs. The local establishments were a lieutenant-governor and president of the council, a council, justices of the peace, civil commandants at Annamaboo, British Accra and Dixcove, and the officers of the guard—100 men— with surgeon, schoolmasters, and interpreters. Pending these arrangements, Mr. John Jackson was made president, but as it was considered desirable to choose an officer wholly unconnected with trade, Mr. George Maclean, who had served in the African corps, and had accompanied, in 1826, Colonel Lumley as military secretary to the Gold Coast,—of him more anon,—was made lieut.-governor and president in 1830. The crown resumed possession of the Gold Coast in 1844, and the first governor was Commander Hill, R.N.

The East Indies and Western Africa both began to attract the attention of England in the days of the Virgin Queen. Her Majesty granted, in 1585, a patent to Lords Leicester and Warwick, allowing them to treat with the Barbary States for twelve years, and in 1600, two hundred persons petitioned their sovereign to establish the Governor and Company of Merchants of London trading with the East Indies. But West Africa is distant 3000, India 10,000 miles from England, and the difference enabled the company that ruled the land from the Himalaya to Cape Comorin, though younger by 15 years, to outlive for 37 years the company that ruled 40° of intertropical Africa.

The annals of the two great rivals are instructive: British Africa being near home has been greatly neglected, because mostly under home orders; it is, and long has been, a string of ruinous forts and settlements. British India, on the other hand, being beyond the range of interference from head-quarters, soon became the most splendid possession ever held by a European nation.

India, I may observe, has been conquered despite of England. Had het steamers and the electric wires of the present day been in operation a century ago, we should still have had a comptoir at Calcutta, Madras, and Bombay, with perhaps a strip of protected territory; our possessions, in fact, would have been like Bathurst, Sierra Leone, and Cape Coast Castle. But happily for England, a letter in those good old times took a year before its answer came. Every new governor or governor-general was tempted to war by some native king or chief; perhaps he was not unwilling to distinguish himself, and—rich men rarely ran the risks of climate— he might sometimes have had an eye to profitable results. Thus, hostilities were declared and duly reported to the Court of Directors. At the end of a year arrived a loud objurgation from those elderly ladies, rating at all aggressive measures, repudiating a policy of territorial aggrandizement, and much " bunkum " of the same manner. But it reached too late. A province, in which probably you could wrap up Great Britain, had been in turn fought down, well looted, and annexed with the tax-gatherer in full activity. Nothing more of course was to be said about the matter. The Court of Directors saw before them new patronage for sons and nephews, and the *Imperium in Imperio* became great *malgré lui.*

I am now firm astride upon India, an old hobby which will take the lead; in truth—may the reader pardon me! India was once the "gorgeous East;" a bit of the "Arabian Nights," which home people delighted in, and highly overvalued. This was followed by a reaction. The Indian uncle died out: the old Nabob was found to look at every sixpence. The Pagoda-tree, when struck, yielded no rupees. Presently the Public—shrewdly suspecting that their Eastern Empire, far from being worth untold sums, was actually in arrears, (despite all its gold bed-steads and jewelled saddles,) some 2,000,000*l.* per an-num—waxed wroth, rose up, laid hands upon it, and, after discussing the idea of giving it up, began to treat it by administering to it homœopathic doses of scientific political economy.

Were Russia or France blessed with such a field for labour, they would soon make it pay five or six millions of pounds sterling, by some such "unconstitutional" means as these :—

> They would at once clear off two governors, who are mere head-clerks—two commanders-in-chief, mere major-generals—and two councils, viz., those of Madras and Bombay: in both these places business could be transacted quite as effec-tually by a secretary to the Supreme Govern-

ment and a major-general in command of sundry
brigadiers.

They would abolish the civilian system and its high
salaries, recruiting the ranks from military officers,
who could be eligible after suitable examinations.
They might retain Suddur and Supreme Courts, and
organise Cassations, and even Chancery Courts, at
the several Presidencies, for the benefit of wealthy
natives who wish to ruin themselves by law; but
these luxuries should not extend beyond a radius
of fifty miles.

They would cherish the Panchayat, or native jury,
merely superintending it to obviate unjust decisions.

They would not inflict upon the natives their own
taxes,—income-tax, licence-tax, stamp duties, heavy
import dues, and other hateful foreign appliances.
They would prefer the indigenous system of a capi-
tation or poll-tax, the house-tax, the Nazaranah or
succession duties, and benefices levied from each
Pergunnah, according to popular settlement, and in
due proportion, as did the English of the old day
when burghers were first returned to Parliament.

They would transform all their regular black army
into irregulars, and never allow an East Indian to
learn the scientific branches of the service—artillery
and engineering.

They would systematically disarm the population, by
transporting all those who fabricated, and by impri-
soning all who possessed, weapons of war.

Finally, they would cleave to hereditary offices—
which would create a conservative party in the
country, and confirm all tenures of "hak" or
vested rights.

But a constitutional people would not attempt even
the first of these measures. Its idea of economy and its
policy must be to cut down the pay and allowances of
the ensign and the assistant-surgeon, and to spend some
30,000*l.* a year upon local governors, commanders-in-
chief, and members of council.

I now return to the Gold Coast.

During the night of the 18th August we steamed past
the mouth of that queer formation, called picturesquely,
and not unaptly, the Bottomless Pit. Here the great
bank of gradually shelving sand is split by a submarine
valley, funnel-shaped, and opening seaward. At the
head of this gully, close to the beach, there are twenty
fathoms of soundings, with a soft bottom of bluish mud.
At one mile off shore the breadth between the two sides
of the ravine is less than a quarter of a mile, with 100
fathoms of depth; at three miles' distance it is about
one mile by 200 fathoms. As the lead brings up pieces
of coralline, and a madrepore formation is observable in
most places east of Accra to the river bottom, this valley
may be a depression, like the submerged Coral Islands
once known to exist near Zanzibar.

The next point of interest was Grand Bassam, a clump
of villages at the mouth of the Costa River, where the
French, in 1843, built Fort Nemours. According to

some, the experiment was a failure ; others declare that a good business in gold is still done there. The same may be said of Assini, or Fort Joinville, another Gallic possession about twenty-seven miles east of the Costa River. Three miles to the west of the latter is the Gold River, which Bosman makes the western boundary of the Gold Coast. Beyond Assini lie the Four Hills, or Hummocks, of Apollonia, called by seamen Cape Apollonia ; the name reminds one of the Apollo Bunder, which should be named Palawa, at Bombay—ridiculously classical. Here the English had a fort, which is now crumbling to ruins. In 1848, Captain Winniett, who succeeded Captain Hill as governor, attacked "Quawe Accah," King of Apollonia, who had killed the French Commandant of Assini, and took him prisoner, and became Sir William Winniett.

We are now off the Windward, which is here the western division of the Gold Coast.*   It extends from Cape Apollonia (2° 35′ W. long.) to the mouth of the Secoom River (0° 3′2″ W. long.), about eight miles west of Fort James, Accra, about 170 nautical miles. The leeward, or eastern districts, begin at the Secoom River, and stretch to the mouth of the Volta, in 0° 41′ 2″ of east longitude, or 44·4 miles of direct distance. Thus, in modern times, the Gold Coast, bounded by Cape Apollonia, and the Volta River, has a sea front of 225 miles. In Bosman's

---

* It is regrettable that geographers encourage this most ambiguous style of nomenclature. Thus the Windward Islands in the West Indies are the western ; in Eastern Africa, windward means eastern.

day it had narrow limits; "the Gold Coast, being a part of Guinea, is extended about sixty miles, beginning with the Gold River, twelve miles above Axim, and ending with the village Ponni, seven or eight miles east of Accra."

The gold export, and afterwards the slave-trade, studded this coast with forts and factories; twenty-five are mentioned—about one to each eight miles; of these, three were Danish, two Brandenburghers, and the rest belonged to the English and Dutch. At present seven English and four Dutch establishments are kept up;*

---

* In the windward coast the English possessed, going from the West, Apollonia, Dixcove, British Secundee and Commendah, Cape Coast Castle, Annamboo, Fort Coromantine, Tamtamquerry, Gúmwah, Mumford, and Winnebah. The latter place was destroyed in 1812, when the frigate "Amelia," Capt. Irby, revenged the murder of the commandant Mr. Meredith, who had been tortured to death by being compelled to walk over burning grass and shrubs. The fort was blown up, and "for many years afterwards, English vessels passing Winnebah were in the habit of pouring a broadside into the town, to inspire the natives with the idea of the severe vengeance which would be exacted for the spilling of European blood " (Mr. Brodie Cruikshank's "Eighteen Years on the Gold Coast," London, 1853). To which may be added, that they fired into the wrong place, the real culprits being the people of a neighbouring village, who remained unhurt.

On the windward coast the Dutch had Axim, Brandenburg, Hollandia, Accoda, Bootry, Tacorady or Tacorary, Dutch Commendah, Chuma, Mouree, Dutch Coromantine, Apam near the Devil's Hill, and Barracoe.

On the leeward coast the British had only Fort James, Accra; the Dutch, Dutch Accra, Labaddi, Pona, Temma, and Prampram or Kbuprán, or Kpukprán; whilst five belonged to the Danes, viz., Christiansborg with its out-station Fredericksborg, Augustenborg near Tesha or Tassy, Fredensborg at Great Ningo, Kongenstein at

the other fourteen issues for the life-blood of Africa which these leeches sucked to some effect, have been abandoned with the traffic which called them into being. These deserted forts and ruined castles affect the voyager with melancholy as he passes these sunny shores. And even the posts, which are still maintained, appear ruinous and squalid; really, for appearance' sake, Britannia ought to look after this out-of-the-way corner of her estate, or give it up altogether. Half of the sum now wilfully wasted upon the Dover harbour, a work pronounced practicable by those engineers who maintained the Suez Canal to be impossible, would prevent our being ashamed of out-stations, than which

Adda on the Volta, and Prindsenstein at Quittah. Slavery being abolished throughout their colonies by the Danes in 1803, these places became useless. On the 17th August, 1850, the king of Denmark sold his forts on the Gold Coast to the British Government for 10,000*l.* England thus obtained exclusive possession of all the seaboard from Accra to the Volta, a rich country, of which, hitherto, no use has been made.

The real site for a settlement would be at Addah, near the mouth of the Volta, and on its right bank, where the Danish fort is fast falling to ruins. The river called by the Accras Shilau, by the Akwimbas Ainzá, by the Addas Joh or Firao, and by the Portuguese, on account of its windings, Rio Volta, is a good highway into the interior. On 28th October, 1861, Lieut. Dolben, R.N., ascended it in boats for 120 miles, until near the Kpong Rapids, where he turned back. He reported the country on the banks to be fertile and well cultivated, and the people, though a slave trade was still established amongst them, in the main, friendly. Lieut. Dolben was of opinion that the rapids could be passed by a short portage, and that the upper course of the river is of considerable length. Now that Accra has been ruined by the earthquakes of 1862, the head-quarters might be more easily transferred to Addah.

at present even Portuguese India shows nothing more wretched.

At sunrise we were off Cape Trespuntos, or Three Points, an excellent land-mark, the three headlands of which—the central is the proper Cape—lie, respectively, fifty, forty-five, and forty miles from Cape Coast Castle; the two more distant from the stream are densely wooded; the third, or nearest, is a bare "neat's tongue," backed by a growth of forest. A little to the west lies Axim Bay, where the Portuguese built Fort St. Anthony, which soon fell into the hands of the Dutch, who also became finally possessed of Fort Brandenburg, originally belonging to the Elector of that name. In 1700 it was a large depôt of gold trade; now it is a crumbling ruin, perched on an eminence, and backed by black bush and tree, which stand out from the glistening white sea-sands on both sides. East of the Cape is another Dutch ruin—Acquidah, or Accoda. The seas about Trespuntos were animated with shoals of fish pursued by gulls, and fishermen with huge straw hats were casting large seines from small canoes.

After doubling the third point, we sighted Dixcove, originally Dick's Cove. At this point begins the Ahanta, or Anta Country, once rich in gold, which may still be procured there, and ever gifted with a rich and fertile soil. It extends to near Seconda, with about forty miles of seaboard, and thirty of depth, being backed by the equally rich, but turbulent, " Wassaw "

Country, which the English have named after "Thaddeus of Warsaw." Behind that, again, lies the land of Dinkira, whose early battles with the Ashantee kings were famous in their day. Dixcove dates from 1681 ; it was finished in 1688, and became the strongest outpost on the coast ; it has a territory totally independent of Ahanta, about five miles of sea-shore, and twenty miles inland. From the sea we could distinguish the large whitewashed building some ninety feet above the water, and about the dwarf bay were some apparently fine houses. The place contains an officer and four men, together with an assistant-surgeon—all supplied by the Gold Coast Artillery, and the little garrison ever feels suicidal. It is well backed with wood, which, however, the people are unwilling to see felled ; and upon the glassy roadstead floated a single French brig. The coast now becomes a succession of settlements. Within sight of Dixcove, and separated by a black islet and reefs, called Sanco Stone, lays Boutry, upon whose ruins Fort Bartenstein, an *enceinte* apparently half way up a hill, still flies at times the Dutch flag. Five miles, going westward placed us opposite Pompendi, a native town guarded by a treacherous formidable reef, upon which the waves dashed with a long swell. About six miles from Pompendi was Takorady Point, a long, low tongue, dark at this distance, but when nearer, red : a native town appeared from the sea in the shape of a few huts ; a single schooner composed the shipping, and the Dutch fort, once a place of importance, could hardly be distinguished. It was the scene of severe troubles in 1837, when, on 23rd October, the Dutch military commandant of Boutry and his assistant were treacherously slain by one Bonsoo, chief of the Ahantas. The latter followed up their success by attacking the Dutch troops at the pass of Takorady, and killing many men and four or five officers. In July, 1838, Governor Verveir revenged the outrage by capturing Bonsoo, and dispersing his men. Within the seaboard is the "Adoom country" of old geographies. Another four miles placed us off Point Secondee, where the whitewashed remains of Fort Orange occupy a bold rocky cliff, some fifty feet above sea level.

The next point of interest was Chama, also written Chumah and Essama, and by the people pronounced Ishámá. Its fort, St. Sebastian, built by the Portuguese, fell as usual into the hands of the stout Hollanders. We could plainly distinguish from our deck a large and solid European building, overlooking a native town. About a mile eastward of the fort, a sudden depression in the long wavy curtain of cliff from seventy to 300 feet high, denotes the position of the two lagoons, between which the Chumah, or St. John's River, finds its way into the sea. The Chumah people call it Prah, and prefix to it the word Bossum, meaning fetish, or sacred. Little is known of this, the largest stream on the Gold Coast, except that the bar at the mouth, being barely two feet deep, renders it useless. Col. Stahrenberg, as reported by Bowdich, ascended it for three days in a canoe, till stopped by a large cataract, near which his men would not venture; and it is reported as flowing through fertile plains, between banks clothed with magnificent timber. The outfall discoloured with bubbly green the pure blue waters off the mouth, and the bottom was the soft mud, which navigators prefer to the hard sand. They can plough a way through the former; the latter, aided by the surf, soon breaks, by bumping, the ship's back.

The Bossumpra River is the western boundary of the Fanti people,* and separates them from their powerful neighbours, the Santi or Ashantees. The former country is now, like the Ionian Islands, under British protectorate, the general nature of our tenure being a ground-rent paid to Caboceers and headmen ; the former mediatorial influence, rendered necessary by the slave trade, has of course ceased. Crossing the Prah, on the part of the Ashantees, is considered equivalent to a declaration of war, as passing the Border was in the olden time, when England and Scotland amused themselves by invading each other. It is the general opinion in the colony that the Volta is an arm of the Prah ; if this be the case, our maps require considerable alteration. Strange that during two centuries of residence in these regions we should not have taken the trouble to lay down so crucial

---

* The "Ethiopic Directory" (p. 390), asserts that "the Fanti country, after a dreadful war of extermination, may be now considered as incorporated with the kingdom of Ashantee," and that "in 1824 the Fantis were nearly annihilated." They are still, however, a powerful tribe, wholly independent of the Ashantees.

a point.   Should the Prah and the Volta prove to be
one, anastomosing at some place to the north-east of
Kumasi, the capital of Ashantee, and south of the Sarem
country, we have a gold country in equilateral-triangular
shape whose base is a sea-line of 150 miles, and whose
sides may conjecturally be laid down at 220 miles, or an
area of more than 15,000 square miles, of which the
greater portion is rich in hitherto partially exploited
gold.

The history of Ashantee wars, which began in 1807,
is that of the African coast generally.   In these lands
there are two great axioms of native policy.   The first
is never to admit strangers into the interior for trade,
which it is the interest of the maritime tribes to monopolise, and they live in idleness at the expense of the
"Bushmen," or people of the interior.   For this point,
which is first in life to them, they will fight to the last,
and hence the main difficulty of opening up the "Dark
Continent."   The second is the ambition of the inner
peoples to obtain a point *d'appui* upon the coast, where
they can sell their goods at their own price.   This explains the frequent wars and irruptions of Ashantee and
Dahomey against the maritime people, and the want of
permanency in the latter.   They become demoralised
by indolent living, intercourse with white men, the
disuse of arms, and the deleterious climate of the lowlands, and thus they are less fitted to resist the hardier
and more warlike tribes that pour down upon them.
Dr. Livingstone (chap. 21) asserts "no African tribe

has ever been destroyed." Nothing but the profoundest ignorance could have dictated such a declaration. I affirm, on the contrary, that from the Kru country to the Gaboon, there is not an ancient people now settled on the seaboard, including even Dahomey; that they supplanted the races who formerly possessed those civilized seats; and that many, the Mpongwe and the old Calabar people, are likely to become extinct before the close of another century. The margin of Africa, in fact, like that of other solid bodies, is continually wearing off.

The Ashantees fought hard for their primal African desideratum. Their first southerly movement, in 1807, was headed, according to Bowdich, by Sai Tootoo Quamina. Mr. Meredith ("Account of the Gold Coast") has accurately described the siege of Annamaboo, in which, though our countrymen showed the greatest possible gallantry, the Ashantees had the upper hand, and Col. Torrane's concessions encouraged them to repeat the attempt. In 1811 they again defeated the Fantis at Apam, and carried to Kumasi the bell of the Danish Fort at Addah. In 1816 the Fantis were obliged to own their supremacy, and to pay an annual tribute. The mission of Messrs. James, Bowdich, and Hutchinson, in 1817, kept the peace by means of a treaty for six years. On the 11th March, 1822, Brigadier-General Sir Charles Macarthy, who had long served upon the coast, returned to it as Governor of Sierra Leone and its dependencies, and proceeded on board H.M.S. "Iphigenia," Commodore Sir Robert Mends, to take possession of the forts on the Gold Coast. He encouraged the Fantis to resist the annual subsidy paid to the King of Ashantee, and when that monarch marched down with 15,000 warriors in January, 1824, he proceeded to meet him with about 1000 white soldiers and a mob of native auxiliaries. The Governor seems to have fallen into the mistake of despising his enemy. A fight took place at Assamacow, near the Bossumpra River, on the 21st January, and Sir Charles Macarthy was killed, together with eight officers of the 2nd West India regiment and the Cape Coast militia.* According to Major Ricketts ("Narrative of the Ashantee War"), " his heart was eaten by the principal chiefs, that they might *imbibe* his bravery; his dried flesh and bones were divided amongst the Caboceers, who always carried them about as fetishes for courage, and there is a local tradition that his head, with his spectacles on, was exposed upon a pole." The Ashantees ravaged the coast, and through the year fought with British native forces now successfully then with loss; but failing to take the castle, they were compelled by sickness and want of provisions to retire. In 1826 they again advanced upon the seaboard, but on the 7th August they were utterly routed—though they attacked on Monday, their lucky day—at the fatal field of Dodowah, so called from a village on a bushy plain, about twenty-four miles northeast of British Accra. According to Major Ricketts,

---

* As has appeared in a previous chapter; the people of the Gold Coast assign to their beloved Macarthy the fate of Cato.

" among the sad trophies of the day was supposed to be
the head of Sir Charles Macarthy, which was sent to
England by Lieutenant-Colonel Purdon; it was taken
by the Aquapim chief.   The king carried it always
with him as a powerful charm, and on the morning of
the battle he poured rum upon it, and invoked it to
cause all the heads of the whites on the field to lie
beside it. The skull was enveloped in a paper covered
with Arabic characters and a silk handkerchief, over all
was a tiger skin, the emblem of royalty." The skull,
however, was subsequently suspected to be that of the
King Tootoo Quamina, who perished in the action. The
people of Cape Coast Castle still swear by Karte
Ukuda, or Macarthy's Wednesday, a strong oath with
high penalties for perjury.*   Finally, peace was concluded with the Ashantees, and trade with the interior
was reopened on the 27th April, 1831.

Since that time, though there have been many rumours
of wars, the Ashantees have remained at peace with us;
but, as in the case of Russia and Turkey, such a state of
affairs can hardly be expected to continue.†

East of Ishama lay a line of reddish cliffs, here

---

* All the tribes upon this coast have a different oath.   The Ashantees swear by Meminda Kormanti (Coromanti Saturday), when their
great king Osai Tootoo was slain by the Akims.   The Fanti chief of
Abra, by the "rock in the sea," near Annamaboo, where he took refuge
from the Ashantees in 1807.   The Annamaboo chief, by Igwah, or Cape
Coast Castle, which protected him when he fled from the Ashantees.

† This was written more than one year ago; 1863 proves the pre-
diction to be correct.

patched with wood, there bare of forests, springing from a straight sea beach, in which baylets with dwarf arms and shallow chords succeeded one another. About noon we passed Commenda Point, which before 1820 was an important post to English and Hollanders; the former chose the eastern, the latter the western bank of the little River Soosn. Native huts cluster around them both, and a background of lagoon poisons the air. Viewed from the westward, Commendah, or, as the natives call it, Ekky-Tikky,—some write Akataykin—is backed by a high arm, an insulated formation known by the promising name of Gold Hill. One feels once more in " Californy."

At 1 P.M. we were abreast of the castle of St. George del Mina, popularly known as Elmina, the first European establishment upon the Gold Coast.* All the landing-places upon these shores are infamously bad, causing great loss of life, except at Elmina and Apam, both belonging to the Dutch. Here the little river Beyah (Byham?) allows light vessels to unload in safety under the castle walls, and supplies good water; the want of which, causing dysentery and various diseases, has given to Guinea what Bosman calls its " dreadful mortal name." The lower fort, called St. George, stands obliquely fronting the sea, on a black rock a little above water level; it has double walls and long batteries, with rectangular towers instead of bastions, and a tall

---

* Built by the French in 1383, rebuilt by the Portuguese in 1481, captured by the Dutch in 1637, and finally ceded to them with its dependencies in 1641.

dungeon-looking work in the rear. Above it, on a hill about 100 feet high, and commanding both fortress and tower, stands Fort St. Jago (St. James), a parallelogrammic whitewashed pile, with a single central tower, and somewhat resembling a hospital with its chapel; it is, however, strongly laid out. The large native town, with its red-brown mud walls and bistre thatching, is divided into two parts : one on the peninsula formed by the *embouchure* of the little river, and under the guns; the other extends along the beach to the westward of the stream. These defences have repeatedly resisted the whole force of Ashantee. A single schooner, the "Ionian," of Salem, lay off the port, which in the early part of the eighteenth century exported 3,000,000*l.* of gold. The settlement contains a governor, secretary, and a commandant of troops, about seventeen white officers, and sixty men, who are clad in blue dungaree. They are by no means healthy; the high walls exclude the air, "sopies" induce liver-complaint, and "personal economy" is neglected. According to Dr. Robert Clarke, late of H.M.'s Colonial Medical Service,* no less than twelve officers died in the eight years between 1851 and 1860. They are on the best of terms with their neighbours of Cape Coast Castle, but intercourse is necessarily rare. Animals being wanted—wholly

---

* "Remarks on the Topography and Diseases of the Gold Coast :" an excellent paper read before the Epidemiological Society, Monday, 7th May, 1860, and partly published in No. II. of the Parliamentary Reports of Her Majesty's Colonial Possessions, issued February, 1861.

unable to live on this part of the coast—they must call upon one another in hammocks ; the distance along the beach, only eight miles, thus takes three hours, and the expense is about ten times that of a London Hansom. Dr. Clarke calculates the expense of locomotion by "dawk," that a journey of some ten miles on the Gold Coast costs nearly as much as to travel by third-class train from Aberdeen to London.

Beyond Elmina we passed a small bay, with its country residences and farms, where the governor and the principal merchants live, and the Sweet River and its village that divides the English protectorate from the Dutch. The country behind was a line of downs, a broken surface of little wooded hills and intervening basins, which tells distinctly its tale of gold, and which morning fogs prove to be swampy. The mysterious malaria we know is there, and men die off as if in a scurvied ship, yet it shows no sign. The German traveller Monrad, asserts that he never saw on this Costa Rica a European past fifty. In such places all officials ought to be in couples, one present, the other on leave in England; nor ought residence ever to be prolonged beyond three years. This is the system which is gradually growing up in the Oil Rivers further south, and until lands are drained and water is distilled, it would be advisable to try it here.

Presently the profile of Cape Coast Castle became

> "Distinct in the light clear air, with
> A flood of such rich dyes
> As makes earth near as heavenly as heaven."

It charmed our senses after the foul, gloomy reek of the S'a Leone coast. At a distance it was a long green-grown tongue of reddish land, broken with dwarf cliffs and scaurs, and lined below with clean sand. Upon the outline appeared three projections : a fort at the root, a second about the centre, and a castle with a mass of native huts at the tip. The first, which lies north-west of the settlement, is Phipps' Tower, alias Fort Victoria ; a martello thing, abandoned, but kept in repair, and so placed in defiance of Vauban, that in the hands of an enemy it would command castle and town. The second, or central post, is Smith's Tower, now Fort William, built by Mr. President Maclean, another artless martello, pretty, but circular below, and, in defiance of all archi-tecture, square above, mounting twelve guns, commanded by No. 1, and commanding No. 3. It has a lighthouse, 192 feet above sea level, but skippers declare that the light never fails to disappear at two A.M., and that a harbour master being, like York, "wanted," the reflec-tors will not reflect ; whereas those at S'a Leone, under opposite conditions, have lost all their silver by over-burnishing. Also a ball used to be dropped from the castle's flagstaff at the instant of Greenwich mean solar noon ; but since the death of the patron-saint of the place, Mr. Maclean, few of the governors of Cape Coast Castle have been addicted to astronomy. The principal castle is upon the tip of the tongue and the native town clusters behind it.

At two P.M. we anchored one mile off the landing-place; the water was low, no bad condition, and the day was that of the dry season. A local superstition, however, declares that the surf is always worst between the new and full moon. Presently we were surrounded by canoes, wall-sided rudderless troughs, from twenty to forty feet long, with gunwales rather bending inwards from the right angle. All had weatherboards in the bow, planks raised two or more feet out to keep out the seas,— such as the forec'sle of the British navy in the days of Henry VIII. Others are provided with a funnel of woodwork at the fore, in the shape of a huge thimble. The only danger of this craft is of their "turning turtle." The paddles are small trefoils, short and stoutly made, to lift the vessel over shallow water. In the smooth, deep rivers of the South we shall find them with long and broad lanceolate blades, the better to hold water. The crew are Fantis, once a currish race, thoroughly cowed by the more warlike Ashantees; under our peaceful rule, however, they have waxed rather insolent. They catch us dexterously from the dangerous ladder, and, as they make for the shore, all sing " Whi' man cum agen," —White men come again,—with remarks, in their vernacular, doubtless highly personal. The great art of landing without a sea is to watch when the wave breaks, backing water, if necessary; a calm interval is found, all " clap on steam," and riding over the crest of a billow, run upon the sand before the rise of the next breaker. They all then tumble out, land the passengers upon their shoulders, and haul up the canoe.

On this occasion, however, we did not escape well, there were too many in the boat to be carried off pick-a-back at one trip, and we were received upon the beach by a host of starers.

The rollers are feared at Cape Coast Castle. The landing-place is a small bay under the north-east bastion, protected by a reef jutting out from a ledge of rocks. The Harmattan season, December, January, and February, shows the smoothest seas; from May to August there is generally a terrific surf, the full violence of the Atlantic rolling in from the south and west, and for days together canoes cannot put out. An excellent landing-place and a wet dock might be made behind the main outcrop : it has often been proposed—the excuse is that there would be difficulties. The fact is, that, after the sand has been removed, the rock would require a little blasting, which would be too much for Cape Coast energy.* What can be expected, when a colonial engineer passes some twenty years at a place, and leaves, as the only memory, a temple of Cloacina, already hastening to decay ? Again, at the disembarking place, about twenty yards from the castle and sea-gate, lies a lot of thirty-two pounders. They were landed here some fifteen years ago, and have been left to rust away because no one had industry enough to remove them. Throughout the castle indeed I would rather fire with blank cartridge than with ball;

---

* I am happy to say that many of these remarks are obsolete in 1863.

paint fills up honeycombs, but is a poor protection against gunpowder.

Ascending the few feet of ramp, we entered the long gateway of the Cruizing Cape Castle.* The foundation is called Tabara, *alias* Tahbil, *alias* Tabirri Rock, and a similar solitary outcrop to the westward is known as Tabara's Wife. The former is the supposed residence of a great fetish, who comes forth at night white and giant-like, to drive away malicious ghosts. During the yam season, sacrifices of goats, fowls, and vegetables are made to it, and they attract a multitude of "turkey-buzzards.". The material is a dark gneiss, through which granite and quartz have protruded. It rises eighteen to twenty feet above sea level, yet in violent storms, the rollers, dashing clean over the rock, which echoes to their thundering roar, sweeps heavy spray over the outlying batteries of the southern front up to the mess-room windows, forty feet high. The castle is a most irregular building, of quadrangular shape, if any, with bastions at each angle, and batteries originally intended for 100, but now mounting some sixty to seventy useless old iron guns. It is comfortable enough as quarters,

---

* The Portuguese called it Cabo Côrso, the latter a sea-term, meaning a cruizing ; Bosman uses the word Cabocors, and the English ridiculously perverted it into Cape Coast Castle. (S. Lopez de Lima, Ensaios sobre a Statistica das Possessaõs Portuguezas, Libr. II. part i. p. 7.) He also corrects the following English inaccuracies : Biafra, St. Thomas, Annobona, Escardos, Chama, Axim and Cabo Lopez into Rio das Maffras, San Thomè, Annobom, Escravos, Sama, Axem and Cabo de Lopo Gonçalves.

but useless for modern warfare; it has all the vastness of
Europeo-Oriental architecture in the olden time. Such
erections in these days are impossible. Probably built
piecemeal, it covers several acres of ground; in parts it
is four stories high. The gateway leads into a large
triangular space, occupying the east of the *enceinte*, used
for drill, and adorned with two thirteen-inch mortars,
and five fine old Danish brass guns, lately brought from
Quittah. To the north of this *terre pleine* are double-
storied buildings, used as barracks and for other purposes; on the south is a sea wall, twenty feet high
with the Tabara bastion mounting two mortars and
nine guns; which fortification unmistakeably wants
casemates. The west is flanked by a long transverse line
of double-storied buildings, that divide the castle into
two unequal parts: they contain the council chamber, or
the *palaver* hall, and the civil quarters. A double flight
of steps leads to this north and south range of buildings,
which are high, solid, and roomy, and are not destitute
of a certain magnificence. The western gallery is paved
with squares of black and white marble, like the Sayyid's
Palace at Zanzibar, and His Excellency still occupies the
office where President Maclean used to transact business, at the head of a small staircase separating it from
the old observatory, a kind of cockloft, afterwards the
dressing-room in which Mrs. Maclean was found by her
servant lying dead across the door. Passing through
this central building by an arched gateway, guarded
by two cohorns, you enter a smaller triangular space

called the spur battery; casemates in its northern side
are used for stores, and in those opposite some of the
troops are lodged; the centre is occupied by a guard-
room, built over one of the best tanks in the place, and
there is a gateway opening upon the town.

Before mess, which was at the unnatural hour of four
P.M., we went forth to attend a *cause célèbre* in the
Court-house. Walking along the main portion of the
building, which, fronting the sea, forms the conspicuous
curtain between the two bastions at the flanks, we
walked into the barracks, and found the men in a state
more merry than wise. This is the Yam Feast, or Black
Christmas; a ceremonial intended, it is said, to impress
upon the native mind the risk of using the unripe, or
even the young vegetable whilst it continues soft and
waxy. It may not be gathered under severe pains and
penalties before the day appointed by the chief. On
such festivals the Kings of Ashantee and Dahomey put to
death a certain number of their subjects, the better to
teach Hygiene to the rest. The harvest-home is in September, at which time all who can afford it enter the
state known as "half-seas over." Armed companies, commanded by their captains, carrying their flags like regiments in New York, promenade the streets, and faction
fights are disagreeably common. It has not been found
possible to abolish this system of "companies," which
causes great disorders on the Gold Coast. The barracks
are decidedly overcrowded, and than overcrowding no
fault can be more fatal in these lands. We saw, also, a

reading and billiard-room, the table of which was, at any rate, superior to that of S'a Leone; a better one, however, has been proposed. The officers' quarters are in the northern line of buildings fronting the sea; in the basement of the same is the hospital, tolerably light and well ventilated. The old slave dungeons are visited by those only who enjoy such mild morbidities as slave markets and old barracoons. Dr. Clarke describes these black holes as being under the south or sea battery, and " access to them is obtained through a winding archway, which opens into crypts formed by the divisional supporting walls of the battery, being feebly lighted and ventilated through grated apertures in the sea wall, which reeks with dankness from the percolation of water."

The Court-house, or rather room, is at the eastern extremity of the tall curtain fronting the sea; it is a dirty little hole, thronged almost to suffocation with a rough crowd busy as wasps. A certain captain of marines, lately appointed postmaster and receiver-general of revenue at Cape Coast Castle, had fallen out with an " African," formerly a tax-gatherer, then a civil commandant, and now ——. The European called the African an embezzler of customs revenue. The African instituted a counter-charge against the European of neglecting his duty, and began a civil action for defamation of character; the result of which was, that the Englishman was fined 25*l.* Of course the place was split in two. Some declared that Japhet was rightly served for saying anent Ham things that could not be proved. Others declared that a noted truth had been twisted into a libel by men jealous, because a local appointment had been given out of the colony. Touching juries at this place, the editor of the " West African Mail," then published at Cape Coast Castle, thus confirms the assertion of his S'a Leone brother, and being, as he says himself, " an African from scalp to s*****m," he is entitled to belief and deference on the part of a British public :—

" JURIES.—We must say a word about juries in Cape Coast. We consider juries here a mistake ; the *respectable* people don't like to sit. If they can avoid it, they *won't* sit. Often persons are summoned to sit as jurors who are in fact mere ragamuffins. *These* never refuse. Their verdict can be bought for a glass of beer or three-penny worth of tobacco. We think it would be well for the court to order a list of *householders* to be made out and kept in the court, and when a jury is required, the clerk of the court should be directed to summon some dozen of these householders, whose names should be written on slips of paper, and put into a hat or a box, and then the names of six (the legal number of a jury on the Gold Coast) drawn out. In a very important case that was heard a few days ago, a man was put into the jury box who was a notorious swindler and rogue. On one occasion the defendant nominated all the jurymen, and the court permitted this. It seems to us, that in all this there is much that calls for reform ; but, unfortunately, what is everybody's business is nobody's business. There are now so many judges, and each judge is so wretchedly paid, that we cannot be astonished if their Honours decline to be bothered with more court work than they can help."

There is no part of the world, I may assert, where there is a worse feeling between black and white than upon the Gold Coast. The arrogance *de part et d'autre* is most comical to a stranger. There are about 100 Europeans in the land : amongst these there are many excellent fellows, but—it is an unpleasant confession to make—the others appear to me inferior to the Africans, native as well as mulatto. The possibility of such a thing had never yet reached my brain : at last, in colloquy with an old friend upon the Coast, the idea started up, and after due discussion we adopted it. I speak of *morale ;* in intellect the black race is palpably superior, and it is fast advancing in the path of civilisation. It cries for " regular lawyers," and is now beginning, even at the out-stations to file schedules of bankruptcy.

We dined at the mess of the Gold Coast Artillery. Hereabouts begins the compulsory semi-starvation which afflicts West Africa as far south as Loando. Food is scarce, and what there is affords but little nutriment. Moreover, cooks are detestable, and there is a terrible sameness of diet. As a rule, it is all fowl, till the lean poultry—about the size of an English pigeon—ends by giving one the scurvy. Beef is not to be had, and the tasteless goat's flesh must take the place of mutton.

Turkeys are sometimes brought from the neighbourhood of Quittah; and even fruit is rare. Fish, however, is plentiful, and the older residents upon the coast adhere mainly to this lenten diet. The country-made dishes are good and wholesome, but somewhat too finely pounded and too much worked to suit the English palate. But, if rations were scarce, hospitality, Steinwein, and Moselle were not; and upon these we contrived to rough it. The mess reminded the consul of the old camping days at Kurrachee, in Scinde, or the Unhappy Valley.

The G. C. A., which initials, by-the-by, the facetious grumbler interprets Great Curse of the Army, because promotion is so easily obtained in it, dates from 1851; in that year it succeeded the Royal African corps of three companies, each 100 men, stationed at S'a Leone, the Gambia, and Fernando Po. This artillery corps began with 300 men, commanded by seventeen European officers, and it was further increased by a band of fifty supernumeraries. About 120 are stationed at head-quarters; the same number at and about Accra; whilst the rest are scattered over the out-stations, and are supposed to co-operate with the Pynims—petty head men, who act as police. The main object of the levy was to act as a preventive to slavery and human sacrifice, which is effected by breaking through the influence of the chiefs; and so far have we been successful, that even the Okros, or Fetish boys, are no longer put to death. The cost, however, cannot be less than 20,000*l.*

per annum, and I suspect that Irregulars would cost much less, and be equally efficient. The men are chiefly runaway serviles, for whom a compensation of $40 is paid to the owners—another proof, if aught were needed, how difficult it is to avoid slave-dealing,—and the soldier's price is deducted by instalments from his pay. The men have a standing grievance touching salary; they receive 7 *d.*, whereas the West Indian private's pay is 1*s.* a day; moreover, they are liable to " cuttings," and their uniform is a useless expense to them. They are armed with an efficient Enfield carbine and sword-bayonet, and they wear the Zouave uniform. Though often ragged and incomplete, wanting stockings, for instance—it looks gorgeous near the blue tuft and yellow facings of the Dutch. It is, however, cumbrous, comfortless, and unhealthy, admirably adapted for Tripoli, equally ill-suited to the Tropics. Sad tales are told of their state of discipline, and few expect to see the corps live long.*

---

* Since this was written, an open mutiny broke out. On the 3rd October, 186—, the troops, after vainly attempting to murder certain of the officers, fled to Napoleon, an out-station distant about four miles. Two days afterwards, the place was visited by H.M.S. " Wye," and on the 7th, Major De Ruvignes, civil commandant at Accra, whose energy probably saved the Coast, sent up some 50 suspected men in H.M.S.S. "Brisk" and "Mullet." The Europeans, 15 in all, not to mention six or seven mulatto gentlemen, were in the fort, and the mutineers had entrenched themselves in their new quarters. The serjeant-major was sent to them, but they refused all terms. Being hated like poison by the natives, and aware that the chiefs and people generally would unite to destroy them, they gave up their arms on the 9th, and on the next day they were persuaded by Mr. Usher of the commissariat, to

It would scarcely be fair to judge of the *morale* of men who are almost in open mutiny ; these Fantis, however, are said at times to have fought pretty well—at least not worse than their neighbours. With very few exceptions, such as the Bijugas, the Ashantees, and the Dahomans, there is no more timid race than the maritime tribes of Western Intertropical Africa; even the three above mentioned are not more remarkable for valour than the Hindu, who, "meak and mild," as we called him, could prove himself a tiger at a pinch. It is otherwise on the Eastern Coast, and I attribute the difference to the intermixture of Arab blood.

The officers of the Cape Coast army expect a company after a period of three years' service from the date of lieutenant's commission, and after six years of actual service they are entitled to a majority; moreover, a captain may retire upon 150*l.* a year. This is being liberal of promotion with a witness : the least precaution

embark for trial at S'a Leone. Capt. Luce of H.M.S. "Brisk," carried between 80 and 90 to their destination ; of these one was shot at S'a Leone, and another was landed for the same purpose on the day when I left Cape Coast Castle (13th Nov. 186—). For protection against further outrage, Capt. Luce left in the castle a party of 21 marines, with Lieut. Ogle, Royal Marine Artillery. They had rations for five weeks, and were confined to barracks between 9 A.M. and 4 P.M. Great care was taken of them, and the only loss was one man, by an accidental fall from a window. No subsequent outbreak occurred. The only danger, in these cases, is the first "flare-up." Thus ended the great Gold Coast mutiny, which, though almost bloodless, should methinks be a standing warning against employing men in their own country. We know it in England and Ireland ; in Africa they have still to learn this simple wisdom.

that should be taken would be to make all colonial officers of the scientific branches pass examinations before entering the home establishments. The Dutch have made six years their minimum term of service on the Gold Coast : after twelve years an officer retires on full pay. Their system is in some points superior to ours. A man will not interest himself in the progress of a place where he pitches tent for a short time ; he retires before learning a sentence of the language, or becoming at all acquainted with the people, much less with the capabilities of the country. To these short periods of service I ascribe the undeveloped, or rather the wholly neglected, state of the Gold Coast, whose resources are a matter of mystery ; and such will be the probable effects of frequent furloughs to the future Anglo-Indian. On the other hand, there is the climate, against which Englishmen, apparently by reason of their habits, are unfitted to contend. Whilst Americans, Germans, and Hamburghers have passed safely through years of residence in the Island of Zanzibar, it has not a single English house, the difficulty being, to speak plainly, that of finding a man who will not drink. In these days of monthly steamers and circulating libraries, breaking the monotony of existence, when the semi-starvation of which men whose vital powers are lowered by a tropical climate, die, can now be replaced by generous living ; when it is known that quinine, liberty, and constant occupation rob the most dangerous climate of half its risk ; the climate of the Gold Coast has lost nothing of its sting or of its victory. Bosman's remark still, I fear, applies to the English: "Their forts are very meanly garrisoned, as if it were sufficient to build forts, furnish them with cannon and necessary provisions, without men, in which the English are everywhere deficient." Besides which, he adds, that in those days our people took six years to build a fort.

No one lands at Cape Coast Castle without pilgrimaging to the "last resting-place of the poetess 'L. E. L.,'" and, of course, without inquiring into her "sad, eventful history," which has, however, nothing of

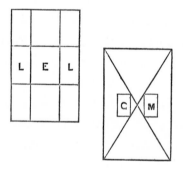

romance. For "L. E. L." is known where Miss Landon is not, and her fate has been the subject of curiosity to many that have never read the "Improvisatrice," or, "Romance and Reality." The graves of Mrs. Maclean and her deeply-injured husband are on the large triangular drill-ground of the Castle. It is a local practice to bury the dead in dwelling-houses, and the custom is not confined to Pagans; the floor of the surgery, the kitchen, and the medical store-rooms of the colonial hospital have all been used for interment. The tramping of soldiery upon the pavement had well nigh defaced all the traces of the tombs,* when the pious hand of Governor O'Connor restored them. The graves now lie parallel to each other as in p. 78 : the St. Andrew's Cross denotes the nationality of the deceased.

On the wall of the north and south buildings a Latin inscription, on a neat tablet of white marble, records the death and the survivor's grief. I had always believed that upon the groundwork of a statue intended for Washington the Great, and representing a more than half-nude figure, extending its arm towards the Capitol, as if the latter had been a barber-surgeon intent upon phlebotomy, I had discovered the very worst Latin inscription in the world. My natural exultation at the success was justified by a sentence beginning with "monumentum *istud*"—ending with *faciebat*. But great is the use of travel. Cape Coast Castle supplied me with a further bathos of Latinity in the neat tablet above alluded to.

---

* The Rev. Mr. Wilson, in "Western Africa," curiously says, "that Governor Maclean and his distinguished partner lie side by side under the cold sod of this African fort." This reminds one of Sir William C. Harris's description of Eve's grave at Jeddah, being a green sod, where there is not a patch of grass. I much wonder what these gentlemen understood by sod ?

" Hic jacet sepultum
Omne quod mortale fuit
Letitiæ Elizabethæ Maclean,
Quam egregiâ *ornatum* indole," &c., &c.

There was a sister tablet a few yards off, placed,
I believe, in honour of Mr. Swanzy, here a well known
colonial name. It was shivered by the shock of the
huge mortar fired in front of it.

The true history of Mrs. Maclean's death is known
to many, but who, in writing the life of "L. E. L.,"
would dare to tell it ? Owning that *de mortuis nil
nisi verum* should be our motto, how would it be possible
to publish facts whilst actors in the tragedy are still
upon the stage of life ? And after their death it will
be forgotten. The author of a certain report on the
Gold Coast, during his short and feverish residence as
Commissioner, a guest of President Maclean, succeeded
in casting upon his host's public efficiency a serious slur,
which was afterwards satisfactorily removed by a select
committee of the House of Commons. On the other hand,
the author of "Eighteen Years on the Gold Coast,"
showed himself an injudicious friend, far worse than any
foe, by asserting that, after a certain *esclandre*, the house-
hold was very successful. But enough of these private
matters. Mr. Forster, M.P. for Berwick, the warmest
of President Maclean's well-wishers, openly asserted
that the flood of calumny poured upon him arose from
the enmity of an individual in the Colonial Office, who
was pettily jealous because affairs at the Gold Coast,

with a miserable pittance of 4000*l.*, were managed
far more effectually than at the pet S'a Leone, where
economy has never been the order of the day. Hence
the "President of the Council of Government," than
whom a better servant of Government was never known
on this coast, was charged with having encouraged
slavery under the local name "pawning"—a fatal accusation in those days—and with neglecting official duty for
private correspondence.

Standing over the graves we heard the story of Mrs.
Maclean's death, and nothing could be less probable
than the popular version. A homeward-bound vessel
was preparing to sail. At 7 A.M. she left her husband's room, and proceeded to write letters before
dressing in the little room opposite, once used as an
observatory. A Mrs. Bailey, her servant, had been
sent to the store-room to fetch some article; she returned after a few minutes, and found against the door
a weight, which proved to be the corpse of her mistress.
The servant distinctly asserted what has been since
denied, that a phial was still in the dead woman's hand,
and that the phial contained a preparation of prussic
acid. But here comes the rub. The authoress's
spirits had been weakened, she had ceased to play at
ball, and she was suffering from a heart disease which
produced fits or spasms. The local account, however, is,
that she was in the habit of taking prussic acid to stimu-
late her energies, a use probably unknown to Scheele.
At any rate, calumny found its way home, and the

President was reduced to the secondary position of Judicial Assessor at Cape Coast Castle. There he died in May, 1847, to the deep and lasting regret of the whole population, black and white.

The "balance," as Yankee Doodle says, of the twenty-four hours, was pleasantly spent at the quarters of Mr. Usher, a commissariat officer, who was serving out his two years *de rigueur* upon the coast of Western Africa. The profound quiet of a tropical night, derived a stillness deeper still from the contrast with the noisy rattle of the tiller-chains, whose perpetual jiggerty-jig made one long for a mild anæsthetic of turpentine.

Betimes in the next morning we sallied out to see the town. After 10 A.M. a European becomes a prisoner at home for the day, until his jailor, the sun, has disappeared. As there are no riding animals, and hammocks conceal the view, we used what I have heard called "Shanks his mare." We issued from the gateway at the north of the western, or spur battery, and slowly sauntered into the open. Opposite the gate is the esplanade, a cleared space for parading; from this a broad street, lined with ragged umbrella-trees, a kind of ficus, runs towards the north, dividing the town into two parts. Immediately on our left was the unfinished Protestant church, of which 600*l.* were granted by the Colonial Office and the War Department. This Africo-Gothic aspires to the honour of consecration by the Right Reverend the Bishop of Sierra Leone, and meanwhile much resembles the porter's lodge in the new style of cemetery. A large room in the upper part of the castle's northern range, or sea front, was formerly used as a chapel; it was, however, secularized into officers' quarters by the recommendation of a sanitary report published by the Commissioners 30th June, 1857. At the upper end of the main street, which rises gently, is the substantial and sober looking meeting-house of the Wesleyans, a body that is owned to have done some good in this part of Africa by abstaining from politics, and by teaching, not only Christianity, but trade. The sides of the highly irregular street are incongruous mixtures of whitewashed houses and red-brown clay huts, some double storied, and of superior dimensions, after the fashion of the olden times, but most of them palpably native; those of Europeans may show green jalousies, but the earth walls and dingy roofs of dull grey thatch, are like the Africans. The right, or east side of main street, is a straggling line of habitations that slope down into a rugged rocky hollow, and thence upwards to the side of a corresponding eminence. The shape of the native house is a hollow square; here, however, the form is undeveloped, compared with what we shall see at Abeokuta and Benin. As in all tropical countries, there are attached compounds where women do domestic work and where children gambol under the umbrella-tree. On the Gold Coast intermural sepulture has reached its climax. The pernicious practice of burying in the basement of the dwelling places, renders any improvement of the town a matter of the greatest difficulty. The custom appears

to have arisen from a barbarous vain-glory; the corpse
is placed in the handsome abode which it built for itself,
and survivors point to the last home of a wealthy man.
With the dead body, which is sprinkled with gold dust,
are interred pearls, precious metals, and ornaments,
Aggri, or Popo beads, and clothes of the greatest value;
thus, Lombard Street being in the future, whilst the
material exists everywhere, these tombs become banks
of deposit, as it were, and the family, especially the
eldest son, draws from them when required. The idea
of burying treasures with the dead dates from the
earliest days of history, and the Jews, whose rites and
ceremonies show distinct traces of African fetissism,
long preserved the custom. The wise king placed
treasures in his father David's grave, and when Asa
died, he was " laid in the bed which was filled with sweet
odours and divers kinds of spices, prepared by the
apothecaries' art." On the Gold Coast, even when the
family vault is exhausted, they are as unwilling to part
with the tomb-home, as a wild Irishman with his wretched
shanty on the hill-side. The material of the walls is
sun-dried brick, or more often swish, clay puddled with
water; this red mixture is built in courses which are
allowed to harden before others are added, and they
easily dry during the hot season. They require, however, a substantial thatch and overhanging eaves, otherwise they are cut and channelled by the rain, and in
damp places the foot of the walls should be protected by
stone work, or by cactus, from burrowing animals. As

timber is not used, it is no wonder that the habitations, after a heavy downfall, subside like the puddle palaces of Scinde.

The floors are of mud, daubed over strong lathing, the equivalent of our English "post and plaster;" the rooms are dark, damp, rarely washed, and ill-ventilated; foul linen lies upon the bed or hangs against the wall; offals, and bits of putrid fish strew the ground and encumber the corners; whilst outside, dirty green pools, and all manner of refuse taint the air. The houses are over-crowded, there are 6000 to 7000 souls in the place, and they are not sufficiently scattered. The usual number inhabiting a small two-storied tenement will be twenty; and as lodging is scarce, respectable people must live separated by a thin party-wall, if any, from some disreputable fellow, drunk all day and half the night with cheap spirits from the United States or the Brazils. Cloacinæ, public and private, are unknown; and the Galinazo and the Pariah dog are hardly numerous enough to remove the garbage about the huts. There are municipal corporations both at Cape Coast Castle and at Accra; there are also detailed police regulations for the removal of such impurities. They are, however, a dead letter, and the nuisance cannot be abated without the direct interference of the authorities, who stop their noses and say no more about it. A walk through the north-east of the town at once shows the cause of its high death rate. Those who are curious to see what an hotel may be, have only to visit Dick's or

Sam's—the *locanda* of the Apennines is a palace compared with them.

The men—I do not speak of the "native gentlemen"—are dressed after the African fashion, in a loin cloth and a larger sheet, both of cotton. The latter is removed from the shoulders on meeting or addressing a superior, and its picturesque folds assume the shape of the Roman toga. They are a tall and not ill-formed race, when they have no skin diseases, with chocolate coloured skins, noses rather high at the bridge, and a fair development of the facial angle which escapes the quasi-gorillahood of the real "nigger." The women would not shine in Mr. Barnum's beauty show; when young, however, they have the usual *beauté du diable,* and if their features are not Grecian, their limbs are. I wish "figures" might be added; unfortunately their bosoms are unsupported, and as they wear the same dress as the men, defects become painfully prominent. The Fantis are perhaps the most civilized people on this coast; unfortunately El Islam has not yet taught womankind the propriety of veiling their bosoms. Under the loose cloth all wear the "Shim"—smallest of "languti" or T-bandages, secured round the waist by a string of large gold beads when the wearer is wealthy, of glass or clay when the contrary is the case. These articles are hung in numbers about the houses, and often puzzle strangers. When due attention is paid to this article it must be beneficial to health. They have the feminine ornaments usual in semi-civilized and half-clad lands, ear-rings, necklaces, bracelets, armlets, finger and toe rings of brass, if not of gold, and metal anklets, oval shaped, and drooping over instep and heel. There are, however, in their toilettes, two very decided novelties to an English eye—whether to be recommended or not to the Hebes at home, the reader may judge. The head-dress in married women is that described by Park among the "ladies of Karta and Ludamar." The hair, which, though curly, grows eight to eleven inches long, is shaved or cleared away round the head to remove straggling pile, and to define the line of departure. The rest of the locks, well combed and greased, are drawn tightly up to a tall ridge, either wholly natural or blown out with padding. There is a back comb of gold or jewellery, if possible, and some coiffures have a terminal top-knot, whilst others end abruptly like a pillow turned upon its edge.* Women of rank would be ashamed if this monstrous *Chinoise* were not exaggerated to the utmost. In the fifteenth century, however, our ancestresses must have been as much troubled. The other *nouveauté* is a "nice thing" in "bussles." The "cankey," as it is called, is a huge pincushion, a stuffed oblong of calico, provided with two tapes, and so fastened round the waist that the two loose corners and the edge between them stand shelving upwards from the owner's back. It thus forms a continuation to the person suggesting that the caudal region has been very lately suppressed. This racing-like pad

---

* At S'a Leone, when people suffer from scurvy and relaxed uvula, they tie a bunch of hair, *en toupet,* tightly on the top of the head.

is supposed to act as a saddle for the baby to ride upon;
unfortunately for the explanation, it is worn by little
misses hardly in their teens.   I therefore attribute it
not purely to fashion, but to that natural and instinctive
admiration of Steatopyga from which the Authoress of
Crinoline does not appear to be free.

We passed one of the two graveyards lying to the
windward of the castle.   These enclosures are, as usual,
foul places of wet sepulture, dank with fetid vegetation,
and poisoning the air of the houses and huts around
them.   The other, I am told, is equally badly situated, and
also surrounded by a dense population.   Besides these
cemeteries, which are appropriated to Christians, graves
for Pagans are dug about the beach, and the slaves,
when not thrown into the sea, are buried " promiscuously " along the lanes or pathways of the *faubourgs*.
Dr. Clarke recommended " that the Christian burial-
ground should be closed up, and that cemeteries should
be opened to the leeward of the town, where there is
abundance of land lying waste suitable for the purpose,
and where a piece of ground might also be set apart
wherein to bury the dead of the Pagan and slave population."

Leaving this burial-ground stained and dreary, we
passed out of the town into the bush, where gamboge
trees, with flowers like hollyhocks, were conspicuous, and
we breasted the rough ascent leading to Fort Victoria.
The soil was a reddish-brown argile, thinly clothed with
quartz nodules, mica flakes, and feldspar; in places

thin rivulets had furrowed the surface, and bands of quartzose rock crossing the course, would have conveyed an intelligible hint to a Californian or Australian prospector. Ascending the eminence, which is about a mile from the castle, we found an extensive prospect, bounded southwards by the sea, and northwards, or inland, the horizon was a wavy mass of little hills, paps, and hummocks, all bushy, and prolonged in crescent-shape towards the Atlantic. A few were rounded at the summits, others had table-tops; none, however, showed signs of cultivation, being shaggy and with trees between; and the only road in sight was the narrow ribbon winding through the valleys, and taking the direction of Kumasi. It is now easy to follow in the path of Bowdich, Dupuis, and Hutchinson. The King of Ashantee, however, can hardly be visited without a dash of at least 100*l.*, for which he will probably return 40*l.* in gold dust, and, as has been said, hammock travelling, especially over mountains and on long journeys, is very expensive. Besides which, an unknown visitor is compelled to await at the frontier permission to visit the capital, and etiquette will not allow this to arrive for some days,—when in Kumasi, various pretexts will prevent you seeing the king till a second delay ceremonious has taken place. And, lastly, it is said that his Majesty has invariably refused a transit northward to all travellers, fearing lest they should make some arrangements for trade with the " people on horses," probably Moors or Africo-Arabs,

who, the tradition is, are impatiently expecting the
arrival of white men. It was the same at Dahomey,
and the reader will readily remember the difficulty with
which Mr. Duncan* penetrated into the interior from
Abomey. A large lake, and other geographical curiosities, are reported to exist between Ashantee and the
" Kong Mountains." The country is described as consisting of rich grassy plains and savannahs, contrasting
with the thick bush-forest of Ashantee, and the people
are said to furrow the land with ploughs. Perhaps, in
these days, by proper management and by liberal presents, the interdict might partially be removed, and the
explorer permitted to advance under an escort of the
king's guards.

On our left, or northward of the castle, Fort Macarthy
occupies the crest of a detached little hill. Below us,
and about one mile north-west of the city, lies a lagoon,
like those which deform the environs of James Fort and
Christiansborg, a " silver liquor " to the bird's-eye view,
but nearer a pond prevalent with foulness and fever,
and full of crabs more than suspected of anthropophagy.
This intensely salt " marigot," which in the dry season
is about one mile in length by half that breadth, is sepa-

---

* Mr. Duncan was sent as Vice-Consul to Abomey in the days of
Gezo, father of the present sovereign. He was an adventurous traveller,
but by no means an educated man or a man of the world, and the
Dahoman used to say of the Englishman that he wished the King of
England would "send him a man with a head." Gezo was, although we
consider him a barbarian, a very remarkable man, dignified, and gifted
with uncommon penetration : as my informant, who was on friendly

rated from the Atlantic by a narrow strip of sand.
During the rainy season, when freshened and swollen
by the drainage of the hills, and the streams that flow
from the spongy and reedy morass at its landward
extremity, it partially discharges itself into the ocean.
Warping will be difficult, and drainage impossible here;
the sole's level is below the sea. Kurrachee has its
" Clifton," and similarly this lagoon has been provided
with a " Mount Edgcumbe," a pigmy scaur overhanging
the impure lake. Another bad formation calling
loudly for reform is impartially placed at the east end of
the town and intersecting part of the suburbs—a deep
fiumara cribbled with water-holes and gold-diggers'
pits, strewed with animal and vegetable refuse, and
dammed by a sand-bar across the mouth. Whilst these
things continue in *loco,* Cape Coast Castle must expect to
retain as evidence maladies which, like dracunculus and
dysentery, are sporadic at deadly Bathurst and S'a
Leone. It can hardly wonder that scrofula, ulcers, krakra,* herpes, *noli-me-tangere,* leprosy, and foul defœ-

---

terms with him, said, he could tell a visitor's calibre in half an hour.
His son, Badahong, the present ruler, gave promise of superior civilisation, but he has followed in the ways of his ancestors. How little the
general public at home know of this class of people may be gathered
from this fact : An enthusiastic lady—I will spare her name—wrote,
strongly urging me to take her with me to the City of the Amazons.
She intended, by a magic lantern, and by pronouncing some words in
the vernacular (the list desired was duly specified), to terrify the king
into abolishing human sacrifices—to become a Christian and a Roman
Catholic ! It is incredible, but it is true.

* A bad kind of scabies, commonly written Craw Craw. It is not

dations, are rather the rule than the exception. For the unusual frequency of ophthalmia, deafness, land-scurvy, and elephantiasis, the people have mainly to thank their own indolence. Medical men find the atmosphere surcharged, they say, with that specific poison which breeds "Yellow John" at S'a Leone and the Gambia. I should be astonished if it were otherwise. Yet even here Nature, as is her wont, has planted a remedy where she has placed the poison. "Connor Hill," or "One-tree Hill," on the north-east of the town, is said to be a sanitarium; there, and there only, Europeans should be stationed. There is a dwarf platform on the summit which is capable of accommodating all the Europeans in the station, and if the castle is ever to be defended, this is the position for a strong battery of Armstrongs. Were I governor of Cape Coast Castle, my hut should be built there during the first month.

Returning homewards, we passed, on another emi-nence to the west of the town, a house and school belonging to the Wesleyan establishment; both appeared neat and clean. Standing upon the balcony was his Reverence Prince John, *alias* Usu Ansah, who, with his cousin Kwántibisá, son of the King of Ashantee, were given as hostages to Mr. Maclean in 1830. The youths were forwarded to England for education. When they returned to Africa in the Niger expedition, they settled

---

confined to mankind; goats, and other animals, often die of it a few days after arrival at Fernando Po; it is most easily communicated, and on board ship it has run through the whole crew.

at Cape Coast Castle, where Prince John remained as "interpreter, class-teacher, and local preacher." He appeared in the shape of a very black man with a white necktie, *more Africano;* as Mr. Paul says of the Maori,* he looked "snobbish, so to speak, when clad in European costume." I could not but admire the vastness and the barbarous splendour of the houses, built by residents in the days before steamers, when men expended hundreds, whereas they now grudge a "flimsy." They reminded me of Richard Lander's description of Mr. Hutchinson's style of living at Annamaboo,—"His silken banners, his turreted castle, and his devoted vassals recalling, the manners and way of life of an old English baron." One stone pile, "Gothic Hall," built by Mr. Hutton, would be considered a handsome residence even near London. The two stags on the columns flanking the gate, and wearing crowns around their necks, are in the style of a certain tall house near Rotten Row, in the palmy days of those honoured animals.

Under the western walls of the castle women were panning the sand of the shore for gold; as in Ashantee, this washing is the peculiar office of the weaker sex. They shovelled up with their hands the finer "stuff"— the metal sinks through the coarse material—and filled, with three parts of it to one of sea water, a calabash, a wooden bowl, or a metal pan. The implement was then whirled, as in California, Australia, and all gold-washing

* New Zealand, as it was and as it is. By R. B. Paul, M.A., late Archdeacon of Nelson. London : Stanford, 1861.

countries, to and fro, with and against the sun. The lighter contents were thrown out by dexterously canting up the vessel, and after repeated washings, the precious metal appeared in flakes and dots, with an occasional grain shining out of the black emery that remained at the bottom. At Cape Coast Castle the scarlet beans of the *Abrus precatorius*, used from Senegal to Calcutta by goldsmiths—Ca da Mosto observed them in 1454,— are the customary weight. Bosman calls them Dambas.* In Ashantee they still employ for the purpose little figures of labourers and mechanics, the "Fetishes" of the old Dutch·writers. At the end of five minutes one of the women produced a small pinch of gold, which she sold to us for sixpence.

After that I lost all patience with Cape Coast Castle. Will our grandsons believe that in these days a colony which cannot afford £150 per annum for a stipendiary magistrate, that men who live in a state of poverty, nay, of semi-starvation, are so deficient in energy as to be content with sitting down hopelessly whilst gold is among their sands, on their roads, in their fields, in their very walls? That this Ophir—that this California, where every river is a Tmolus and a Pactolus, every hillock is a gold hill—does not contain a cradle, a puddling-

---

* He makes 1 damba = 2 stivers,
   24   ,,   = 1 angel,
   16 or 20 angels = 1 ounce.

There is also mention made of black and white beans heavier than the above, and called Tacoes.

machine, a quartz-crusher, a pound of mercury? That
half the washings are wasted because quicksilver is
unknown, and that pure gold, selling in England for
3*l.* 17*s.* to 4*l.*, is here purchasable for 3*l.* 12*s.*? That
whilst convict labour is attainable, not a company has
been formed, not a surveyor has been sent for? I
exclaim with Dominie Sampson, " Pro-di-gious ! "

The population of the Gold Coast is rudely estimated
at 400,000 souls, scattered over a surface of 8000
square miles; its scantiness and its slow increase are
attributable to the destructive slavery of the last, and
the bloody wars during the first decennia of the present
century, with other minor causes, uncleanliness, drunk-
enness, neglect of hygienic precautions, and the mismanagement of children. Their occupations are agriculture, mechanics, and fishing, and the wealthier
classes are acute traders. The principal manufactures
are cloth weaving, mat and basket making, and working
in metals; their goldsmith craft, however, is not to be
compared with the rudest East Indian work. Native
rings and watch-chains are bought by Europeans as
curiosities; their only value, however, is in the weight
of metal. They can pan salt, mould bricks, and many
have learned the arts of masonry, carpentering, and
cabinet work. In these trades they are far superior
to the Krumen and other wilder races, but they yield
to the S'a Leone men, because the latter have
more European tuition. The fishermen use hand-
seines and deep-sea lines, and as canoe-men they are

valued at Lagos and other places on the southern coast.

There is sufficient civilisation to produce a very marked distinction of classes. Bosman divides the people into five orders, viz. :—

1. Kings or captains, synonymous words : under our protectorate, however, this class naturally languishes. Krensil, for instance, is the reigning chief of Cape Coast Castle, but the people describe him as a poor devil.

2. The Headmen, or civil fathers, called Caboceros, or Caboceers, from the Portuguese Caboceiros, with the Pynims, or sub-chiefs, policemen, who promulgate edicts and who act as criers. The former are the hereditary official representatives of towns, who keep order, appease tumults, direct the operations of their subordinates, and lead in the superstitious rites which each season brings round with it. They issue summonses by peons, who carry message-canes—long staves, with gold or silver heads, and corresponding with the chob of Hindostan—or by way of token they bear their master's gold-handled sword. These men have large households, consisting of three classes—blood relations, dependants and slaves, or pawns—*ouvriers libres.*

3. Those enriched by inheritance or trade : though slaves, they are treated by the better class as a rich Pariah by a Brahman, who risks pollution for profit. Bosman thus quaintly derides the authors who call this class noblemen : "It will not a little redound to my honour, that I have for several years successively been

waited on by these noblemen in the capacity of a footman, without having the least respect to his nobility."

4. Peasants and mechanics.

5. Slaves, either sold by their relatives or taken in
war, or come so by poverty. As Sir Benjamin Pine,*
then Governor of the Gold Coast, justly defined it, the
whole social fabric, "woof and warp," is slavery. The
mutual relation of master and servant, especially in case
of the home-born, is much the same as in the days
of Abraham; the slave may accumulate wealth, and
theoretically what is his is his master's. Popular custom
draws a broad line, and desertion in case of cruel usage
is a never-failing remedy. The bush slaves, called
Donkos, are brought mostly from the country north of
Ashantee; they are brave and hardy, and their services
in the "Krobo campaign" of 1858, and the troubles
in Abrah (1859), proved them to be superior to the
Fantis, their proprietors. Some wealthy men have great
numbers of these chattels, and cases have been known
in which claims wholly without foundation have been
set up by individuals to whole families. As has been
said, the okra is no longer slain; and the custom of
Panyarring,† seizing one man for the fault of another—
once common along the whole western coast—is systematically discouraged.

The Fanti of Cape Coast Castle, or, as purists write

---

* It is no small satisfaction to the Gold Coast that the brother of
this excellent officer now holds the same position.

† The word is said to be Portuguese, but I have been unable to
trace it.

the word, Fante, are a cognate race to the Ashantee.* The tradition of their separation is as follows. When at war with the Akim country, a great famine occurred in the land. The Fanti lived on fáñ, herbs or cabbage, hence they were called, from *didi*, to eat, Fanti. The others were eaters of sañ, barn stores, Indian corn, yam, &c., hence Sandidi, Santi, Ashanti. The connection between the races now separated by such fierce feuds is proved by community of language—the Oji, or, as others write it Otyi. The Fanti dialect, however, is, less soft and agreeable than the Ashantee. It has all the characteristic features of the Ga of Accra tongue, the Ewe of Dahomey and the Yoruban families, and it belongs to the Hamitic class, which extends, with many varieties, from south of the Sahara to the Cape of Good Hope. The other countries in which the Oji is spoken are Akim, Akwapim, and Akwam, called by the English Akwambu. As usual in these African languages which delight in individualising general ideas, their proverbs form an extensive and curious literature.†

The habits of the people have been greatly modified by the century and a-half which elapsed since Bosman

---

* I have not thought it advisable to change such words as Ashantee, Accra, and others, which have been naturalised amongst us by long residence, utterly incorrect as they are. Bosman and the other travellers write, with comparative accuracy, Asianti. The proper form is Asante, in which we first converted the difficult palatal aspiration into Ashante, and then added another error, Ashäntée, accenting —like absentee—the ultimate instead of the penultimate vowel.

† " Grammatical Outline of the Oji Language." By Rev. H. N. Riis of the Basle Mission. Basle: C. Ditloff, 1854. Pp 111-136.

described the " Fantynean negroes," who "so horridly plagued the English," though to meet *perfide Albion* was like "going to the devil to be confessed." Many of the old Hollander's descriptions, however, are still to be recognised. The mass of the people are pestilent pagans, and, considering their intercourse with us, few of them speak English. The sexes eat separately, and both are equally fond of tobacco. All who can afford the luxury are polygamists, and the first wife rules the roast; but all are equally the absolute property of the husband. The men are jealous of one another, and fatal quarrels often arise. The boys are circumcised before puberty.* This rite, however, is confined to certain families, and is performed with peculiar ceremonies. At Accra, for instance, a rock rising from the sea is the proper spot. The sister's son inherits to the prejudice of direct descendants, telling with a fatal significance that it is a wise child indeed that knows its own father. There are various ceremonies for girls arriving at a marriageable age, and for women about to become mothers for the first time. During gestation there is a complete separation of the sexes, not only here, but almost everywhere up the West African coast. When a woman dies in childbed, the body is cast out into the bush. The funeral customs resemble the wakes of the Jews and the Irish; there are hired præficæ, and the men shave the head in token of mourning. For some time the shoulder

* For curious information upon this subject, see Dr. Clarke's "Sierra Leone," p. 49.

bone of a sheep, slaughtered to make the funeral feast, is placed upon the new grave. If a man die insolvent, his body is kept above ground till his debts are paid, and this often happens in a country where the legal interest is fifty per cent. per annum, or per diem. Travellers on the Gold Coast have often remarked corpses placed on platforms, and covered with a cloth, till reclaimed by the debtor-heirs. No one would bury a chance corpse, because, though such Samaritan inherits the property of the deceased, he also becomes liable for all the liabilities. Nothing would be easier than to do away with so barbarous a practice—"East Lynne" informs us that England is not wholly free from it—by a promise of indemnity on the part of Government to the debtor. Witchcraft is exceedingly common, especially the form called "putting into Fetish," which is rendered penal by Government. To these spells they attribute death and all manner of diseases, including the much dreaded "broke back," for which that part of the body must be treated by aphrodisiacs. The charge of sorcery must be purged by ordeals, of which there are many; amongst them the corsned, or consecrated cake, of our Anglo-Saxon progenitors. An infusion of the mellay tree, or a decoction of the Edum bark, are swallowed by the accused, who if they escape are pronounced guiltless.

The religious ideas of the Fanti are, as usual in Africa, vague and instinctive. Each person has his Samán— literally a skeleton or goblin—a private Fetish, an idol, rag, fowl, feathers, bunch of grass, bit of glass, and so forth : to this he pays the greatest reverence, because it is nearest to him. The Bosoms are imaginary beings, probably of ghostly origin, called "spirits" by the missionaries. Abonsám is a malevolent being, that lives in the upper regions ; Sasabonsám is the friend of witch and wizard, hates priests and missionaries, and inhabits huge silk-cotton trees in the gloomiest forests ; he is a monstrous being of human shape, of red colour, and with long hair.* Nyankupon,† or Nyame, is the supreme deity, but the word also means the visible firmament or sky, showing that there has been no attempt to separate the ideal from the material. This being, who dwells in Nyankuponfi, or Nyankuponkru,‡ is too far from earth to trouble himself with human affairs, which are committed to the Bosoms ; this, however, is the belief of the educated, who doubtless have derived something from European systems,—the vulgar confound him with sky, rain, and thunder. Kra, which the vocabularies translate "Lord," is the Anglicised okro, or ocroe, 'meaning a

* The reader will not fail to remark the similarity of Sasabonsam to the East Indian Rákshasa, the malevolent ghost of a Brahman, brown in colour, and inhabiting the Pipal tree.

† Mr. Beecham ("Ashantee and the Gold Coast," pp. 171-2) explains this word to mean greatest friend, a poetical and phonetical misapprehension. Mr. Riis derives it from Poñ (pong), a common termination in Oji words, and signifying high, great ; and from Nyáñ, to rise, raise ; the whole meaning the very great, or the most high.

‡ The vocabulary explains these words to mean Heaven, the house, or habitation, of God, and of the departed spirits of good men ; opposed to Abonsámkru, hell, where the devil Abonsám rules over the wicked. I suspect these to be purely European imported ideas.

favourite male slave, destined to be sacrificed with his
dead master, and " sunsum," " spirit," means a shadow,
the man's umbra. The Fantis have regular days of rest—
Tuesday for fishermen, Friday for bushmen, peasants,
and so on.

The first missionaries to the Gold Coast were the
Portuguese; about a century ago they were followed by
the Moravians, but of these ancient establishments there
is now not a trace. The first English missionary in
these diggings was the Rev. Thomas Thompson (1751).
After cultivating the field for four years he returned to
England, taking home with him several natives for
education at Oxford. Of these, Philip Quako occupied
for fifty years the chaplaincy of Cape Coast Castle, and
died in the savour of Fetishhood. In the autumn of
1834, the committee of the Wesleyan Missionary Society
sent the Rev. Joseph Dunwell, a man spoken of as highly
as Brainerd and Martyn, to the Gold Coast. He died
there in 1835, and was followed by Mr. Thos. Freeman
in 1838; but this is entering upon modern times, when
the men who "make history" still survive. The Wesleyans have extended themselves on the sea coast of the
Gold Region, and they monopolise the field as do the
Church Missionaries at Sierra Leone and Abeokuta;
the American Episcopals at Liberia and Cape Palmas,
and the Baptists at Fernando Po and the Camaroons.
Besides Wesleyans there are Basle Missionaries about
Accra and Akim, and Bremen men to the east and
north of the River Volta. Mr. East ("Western Africa,"

p. 289), speaking of his own sect, says, "The beneficial effects of this mission are very conspicuous." It requires a perspicacious and microscopic eye to discern them.

On the evening of the 19th August, after taking kindly leave of our good hosts, we soon passed over, under a full head of steam, the seventy miles between Cape Coast Castle and Accra. I could think of nothing but gold, and perhaps the reader may not be unwilling to receive a few details concerning the precious metal, in a continent which, when opened up, will supply us with half-a-dozen Californias.

CHAPTER VIII.

GOLD IN AFRICA.

" Slave of the dark and dirty mine :
  What vanity has brought thee here ?"
                                    Leyden.

"Gold ! gold ! gold ! gold !
  Bright and yellow, hard and cold ;
  Molten, graven, hammer'd, and roll'd ;
  Heavy to get and light to hold."
                                    Hood.

BARON HUMBOLDT first announced the theory, that
gold is constant in meridional ranges of the paleozoic
and metamorphic formation. In this he was followed
by Sir R. Murchison, and he was *not* followed by
Professor Sedgwick. The latter "has no faith whatever in the above hypothesis, though it led to a happy
anticipation," which followed erroneous premises. He
continues, "what we seem to know is, that gold is
chiefly found among paleozoic rocks of a quartzose
type," and, moreover, that, "some of the great physical
agencies of the earth are meridional, and these agencies
may probably—and in a way we do not comprehend—
have influenced the deposit of metals on certain lines of
bearing." He thinks, however, it would be a "hypo-
thetical misdirection" to say that a quartzose paleozoic
rock cannot be auriferous, because its strata is not north

and south," and that "experience must settle this point."
The supporters of the meridional theory may quote as
instances East African Ghauts, the Oural Mountains,
the Sierra Nevada of California—which includes the
diggings in British Columbia—the Australian Cordillera,
the New Zealand ranges, and the Western Ghauts of
India. On the other hand, there are two notable exceptions—the Central Indian region, in which Sir R.
Martin and others, as long as thirty years ago, were
convinced that the natives washed for gold; and, still
more remarkable, the highly productive African chain,
which, for want of a better name, we still call the Kong
Mountains.*

The fact is, that gold is a superficial formation, and
has been almost universally distributed over the surface
of earth's declivities. This want of depth, Sir R.
Murchison is fond of illustrating by the hand with the
fingers turned downwards; these represent the golden
veins, whilst the palm denotes the main deposit. It is

---

* A similar imperfect generalisation is the old theory, that gold per-
tains not to islands. Malachi wore a collar of Irish gold, probably
from Wicklow. It has been found in Cornwall and other parts of
England, and in Scotland ; and there are few Californians who do not
believe that Queen Charlotte's Island will form rich diggings.

Another remark has lately been made, which pretends to no more
than to discover a curious coincidence. The Oural chain lies 90° west
of the Australian diggings, and the Californian Sierra Nevada 90° west
of the Oural. But, on the other hand, the fourth quadrantal division
falls into the Atlantic between Western Africa and the Brazils ; and
Eastern Africa, a highly prolific metallic region, is 20° west of the
Oural, and 120° east of California.

the contrary with other metals. Gold mines, therefore, are now rare—except in newly explored or exploited lands of primitive formation, where it is common, nay almost universal; the article, whose utility was early recognised, soon disappeared from the older workings. The Californian digger, provided with pick, pan, and shovel, made $10 per diem in 1852; in 1862 he still makes $2·50 and in 1872 he probably will make $0. The anciently auriferous countries, especially Arabia, have been stripped of their treasures, perhaps before the dawn of what is called true history; * and if they linger in Sofala, it is by reason of the people's ignorance; † they never traced the metal to its matrix.

* I allude to the Hammæum littus of Pliny, which appears to coincide with the modern Hazramant.   Perhaps, however, the gold of Arabia is not wholly exhausted : it is difficult to believe that the rude appliances of savages and barbarians can extract anything but the coarsest particles from the dirt.

Some years ago, an English traveller, who had seen gold dust brought to Cairo from the coast of Western Arabia, north of Yaṁbu, applied to Dr. Walne, then Her Majesty's consul, for facilities of exploring the place. The sage reply of that official was, that gold appeared to be becoming too common.   Other officials, equally sage, have since made the same remark.   I refer them to the end of this chapter for my reply.

† In Eastern, as in parts of Western Africa, the natives have a curious superstition, or, rather, a distorted idea of a physical fact. They always return to the earth whatever nuggets are found, under the idea that they are the seed or mother of gold, and that if removed the washing would be unprofitable.   They refuse to dig deeper than the chin, for fear of the earth "caving in;" and quartz-crushing and the use of quicksilver being unknown, they will not wash unless the gold appears to the naked eye.   As late as Mohammed Ali Pasha's day an Egyptian expedition was sent up through Fayzoghlu in search of the precious metal, brought down by the eastern tributaries of the Nile : it

Setting aside the vexed question of the identity of Ophir and Sofala, and the fact that in early times gold was brought down from the eastern regions of the upper Nilitic basin, Western Africa was the first field that supplied the precious metal to Europe. The French claim to have imported it from El Mina as early as A.D. 1382. In 1442, Gonçales Baldeza returned from his second voyage to the regions about Bojador, bringing with him the first gold. Presently a company was formed for the purpose of carrying on the gold trade between Portugal and Africa; its leading men were the navigators Lanzarote and Gilianez, and the great Prince Henry did not disdain to become a member. In 1471, João de Santarem and Pedro Escobar reached a place on the Gold Coast to which, from the abundance of gold found there, they gave the name of Oro de la Mina, the present El Mina. After this a flood of gold poured into the lap of Europe, and at last, cupidity having mastered terror of the Papal Bull, which assigned to Portugal the exclusive right to the Eastern hemisphere, English, French, and Dutch adventurers hastened to share the spoils.

The Portuguese, probably foreseeing competition in the Atlantic waters, but sure of their power in the

---

failed, because the ignorant Turks expected to pick up ounces where they found only grains. There are many traditions still extant in Egypt, of mysterious travellers floating down the Nile in craft of antique build, accompanied by women of blackest colour, but with Grecian or Abyssinian features, and adorned with rings, collars, and bracelets of pure gold, in shape resembling those found in the tombs of ancient Egypt.

Indian seas, determined, about the middle of the 16th century, to seek gold, of which those who preceded them had heard, in Eastern Africa. The Rev. Father João dos Santos, of the order of San Domingo, has left us, in his " History of Eastern Ethiopia," a detailed account of the first disastrous expedition. According to him, Dom Sebastian was scarcely seated on the throne of Portugal* before he sent to Sofala an expedition under command of Francis Baretto, who, " penetrating into ' Macoronga '† and 'Maniça,' discovered mines of gold in these kingdoms, of which, by his prudence and valour he made himself master." Baretto, having successfully passed through, despite a harassing warfare, the territories of the Qui-teva or sovereign of Sofala, who fled from his capital, Zimboo, and having contracted with the Moorish or Arab sultan‡ of Manica a treaty of amity, which included

---

* Don Sebastian, grandson of Don João III., was born July 20th, 1554, and at three years of age ascended the throne of Portugal. His subsequent romantic history is well known.

† Mr. Cooley (" Geography of N'yassi," p. 16) has confounded the "Mucaranga" with the "Monomoezi." Captain Burton (" Lake Regions of Central Equatorial Africa," pp. 228-9) found the Wakaranga, a people wholly distinct from the Wanyamwezi : the former being a small tribe living near the Tanganyike Lake, south of the Wajiji. Mr. Cooley still, I believe, keeps his own opinion, and persists in writing these tribal names with an initial, M or Mu, which, being an abbreviation of Mtu, a man, signifies only the individual.

‡ In the " Periplus" attributed to Arrian (A. D. 64-210), chap. 16, we are told that Rhapta, probably Kilwa (Quiloa), and the adjacent regions were held by colonists from Muza, *i.e.*, Bundar Musa, near Aden. Gold is not mentioned amongst the exports, which are confined to ivory, rhinoceros' horns, and tortoiseshell.

the article that the King of Chicanga should admit the strangers to trade throughout his territories for gold dust and other merchandise, reached at length the goal of his ambition. His proceedings are told as follows : *

"The Portuguese were enchanted at having in so short a time concluded a treaty of such advantage to their sovereign, and so beneficial to the realm ; they, moreover, flattered themselves with the hope of acquiring store of gold, with which to return enriched to their country ; but when they saw what toil was requisite for extracting this precious metal from the bowels of the earth, and the danger incurred by those who worked in the mines, they were speedily undeceived, and no longer regarded their fortunes as instantaneously made. At the same time they were induced to reflect that the labour and risk of digging the gold from the abysses whence it is drawn, are such as to stamp that value on it which it bears from its consequent rarity.

"These people have divers methods of extracting the gold, and separating it from the earth with which it is blended ; but the most common is to open the ground, and proceed towards the spot where, from certain indications, ore is supposed to abound. For this purpose they excavate vaults, sustained at intervals by pillars, and notwithstanding they make use of every possible precaution, it often happens that the vaults give way, and bury the subterranean sappers beneath their ruins

---

* Dos Santos, "History of the Ethiopians," Book II, chap. 1-3.

When they reach the vein in which the gold is found, mixed with the earth, they take the ore as it is, and put it into vessels full of water, and by dint of stirring about the water the earth is dissolved, and the gold remains at bottom. *

" They likewise take advantage of heavy rains, which, occasioning torrents, carry before them whatever loose earth they meet in their way, and thus lay open the spots where gold is embedded in the ravines. This the Caffres collect, and wash with care to purify from the grosser parts of its earthy admixture.

" Those people, also, however unpolished they may seem, yet possess a secret peculiar to themselves for discovering the gold concealed in certain stones, which they likewise have the ingenuity of extracting, constantly observing the same practice of washing it well to separate all earthy particles from the metal, and thus rendering it equally lustrous with that obtained from the earth. This gold is, however, much cheaper than the other, either owing to its being more common, or to its being obtained with more facility and at less expense than that exfodiated from the bowels of the earth.

" It is a matter of fact, that this country is rich in gold and silver mines, but these metals are not so easily obtained as is imagined; for the Caffres are prohibited, under penalty of death and the confiscation of their

---

* The reader will remark that at all times, and in all places, gold has been washed or procured in the same way—a fair instance of the instinctive faculty in mankind.

property, from discovering the site of the mines, either to their neighbours, or to those who pass through their country. When a mine is discovered, the persons finding it make wild outcries, to collect witnesses round them, and cover the spot, above which they place some object to denote the site; and far from being susceptible to be prevailed upon by strangers to point out these spots, they avoid encountering them as much as possible, for fear they should even be suspected of such a deed.

"The motive of the sovereign for enacting these prohibitory laws, and for exacting a declaration to be made to the Court of all mines discovered, is that he may take possession of them,* and by preventing the Portuguese from becoming masters of one portion, give no room for succeeding warfare on their part to seize on the remainder."

---

* The same was the practice of the Indian Rajahs. Whenever a ryot discovered either treasure or gold in situ, he was most cruelly treated, to compel him to confess and to give up what he had secreted. As, of course, he had secreted a part of his *trouvaille*, it was a hard struggle between his cupidity and the ruler's bastinado. About 1840, some peasants near Baroda, in Guzerat, found lumps of gold, which they carried before His Highness the Gaikwar, and received in return a terrible flogging. The Hindu, with that secretiveness which has ever been his shield against the tyranny of rulers and conquerors, resolved for the future to keep his good fortune to himself. The quantity of gold which from time to time has appeared amongst these people, made the shrewder sort of European suspect. But the inertness, or, rather, the terror of new things, that possessed the then rulers of the land, "threw cold water" upon all attempts to trace the diggings, which, accordingly, were worked by the people till the present year. This is the simple history of " gold mining in the Deccan."

The melancholy fate of this expedition deserves mentioning   After passing through Zimboe,* where the Quiteva received him with open arms, Baretto returned to Sofala.   Being now on good terms with the sovereign of that place, and Chicanga, he resolved to open a road into the kingdom of Mongas, the dominions of the Monomotapa, who opposed him with a large army.

* De Barros, describing the ruins of Zimboe, mentions an inscription over the gateway of a fort built with well-cut stones and no lime, whose surface was twenty-five palms long and a little less in height.   Around this building, which, like the Kaabah, might have been a pagan Arab temple, are bastions—also of uncemented lime—and the remains of a tower, seventy feet high.   The inscription was probably in the Himyaritic character, as "Moors well versed in Arabic" could not decipher it. This was repeated to Mr. Lyons M'Leod ("Travels in Eastern Africa," Vol. I., chap. 10) at Mozambique.   Dr. Livingstone ("Travels in South Africa," chap. 29) discovered Zumbo in lat. 15° 37′ 22″ S., long. 30° 32′ E., about 8° W.N.W. of Kilimani.   At the confluence of the Loangwe and Zambezi, he found the remains of a church, a cross, and a bell, but no date and no inscription.   The people of Senì also state that there are remains of large edifices in the interior ; unfortunately they place them at a distance of 500 leagues, which would lead them nearly to the equator north, and to the Cape of Good Hope south.

† Dr. Livingstone ("Travels in South Africa," chap. 30) explains the word Monomotapa successfully, I think, to mean the "Lord (mone, muene, mona, mana, or morena; are all dialectic varieties, synonymous with the Kisarahili muinyi, which means master, sir, kyrios, &c.), and Motapa," the proper name of the chief.   The ancient Portuguese assigned to the Monomotapa the extensive regions between the Zambezi and the Limpopo rivers, 7° from north to south.   The African traveller, however, is not so successful in explaining the corrupted term, Monomoizes, Monemuiges, and Monomuizes—for which, see Journal of Royal Geographical Society (Vol. XXIX., pp. 166 et seq.)

Dr. Beke ("On the Mountains forming the Eastern side of the Basin of the Nile," p. 14) defends, against Mr. Cooley and Captain Burton, M. Malte Brun's "Mono-emugi, ou selons un orthographie plus

Baretto signally defeated the "Caffres," and reached Chicona, where he found no gold mines. An artful native, however, buried two or three lumps of silver, which when discovered brought large presents to the cheat and dreams of Potosi to the cheated.* Baretto, in nowise disheartened by discovering the fraud, left two hundred men in a fort at Chicona, whilst he and the remainder of his forces retired upon Senã, on the Zambezi. The Caffres then blockaded the fort, and having reduced the gallant defenders to a famine, compelled them to make a sortie, in which every man was slain.

The ruins of Maniça, north-west of Sofala, and west of and inland from the East African ghauts, are described as being situated in a valley enclosed by an amphitheatre of hills, having a circuit of about two miles. According to Mr. Macleod, the district is called Ma-

---

authentique *Mou-mimigi*." The defence is operated by enclosing after the latter, in italics, another version in parenthesis, and with an interrogation, thus [Nimougi ?] ; and the French geographer's orthography " being fortunately based on the theoretic root," is pronounced " more authentic than any hitherto proposed in its stead." How often will it be necessary to repeat, that Mono-emugi and Mou-nimigi are merely corruptions of M'nyamwezi, a man or individual of the Land Unyamwezi ?

  * A French adventurer tried a similar trick upon the Imam Sayyid Said, father of the present Prince of Zanzibar. He melted a few dollars and ran the fluid upon bits of stone, which were duly shown to His Highness. But the old Imam, whose cupidity was equalled only by his cunning, took them to his friend, Colonel Hamerton, Her Majesty's consul, who, finding the matrix to be coralline, had no difficulty in detecting the fraud.

touca (the Matuka of Dr. Livingstone's map), and the gold washing tribes Botongos.* The spots containing the metal are known by the bare and barren surface. The natives dig in any small crevice made by the rains of the preceding winter, and there find gold dust. These pot-holes are rarely deeper than two or three feet, at five or six they strike the ground-rock. In the still portions of the rivers, when they are low, the natives dive for nuggets that have been washed down from the hills. Sometimes joining together in hundreds, they deflect the stream, and find extensive deposits. Mr. M'Leod heard of mines 400 to 500 miles from Sofala, where the gold is found in solid lumps, or as veins in the rocks and stones.

The result of Dr. Livingstone's travels is, that whilst he found no gold in the African interior, frequent washings were met with in the Mashinga mountains† and on the Zambezi river; no silver, however, was met with, nor could the people distinguish it from tin, which, however, does not establish its non-existence; he heard from a Mashinga man, for the first time, a native name for gold, " Dalama."‡ The limits of the auriferous

---

* Dr. Livingstone places the Batonga people west of Zumbo, and 4° to 5° N.W. of Matuka, or Maniça.

† These elevations are on the western frontier of the great Marave people.

‡ In Kisawahili they have but one word for gold, Zahábú, which is palpably derived from the Arabic ذهب. None of the people living in the interior, or even the tribes beyond the coast line of Zanzibar, are acquainted with the precious metal : they would prefer to it brass or copper. The appreciation of gold on the part of the so called "Kafir"

region are thus laid down : " If we place one leg of the compasses at Tete, and extend the other 3° 30′, bringing it round from the north-east of Tete by west, and then to the south-east, we nearly touch or include all the known gold-producing country." This beginning from the north-east would include the Marave country,* the now "unknown" kingdom of Abutua, † placed, however, south of the Zambezi, and coming round by the south-west, Mashona, or Bazizulu, Maniça, and Sofala. Gold from about Maniça, is as large as wheat grains, whilst that found in the rivers is in minute scales. The process of washing the latter is laborious. " A quantity of sand is put into a wooden bowl with water, a half rotatory motion is given to the dish, which causes the coarser particles of sand to collect on one side of the bottom. These are carefully removed with the hand, and the process of rotation is renewed until the whole

races points to an extensive intercourse with Arabia, if not to a considerable admixture of Arab and Asiatic blood.

* Dr. Livingstone gives six well-known washing-places, east and north-east of Tete, viz. : Mashinga, Sbindúndo, Missála, Kapéta, Máno, and Jáwa.

† Mr. Cooley ("Geography of N'yassi") questions whether there be such a kingdom as Abutua, or Butwa. He derives it from Batúa plur. of Motúa (in Kisawahili wátu plur. of M'tu), signifying men. The Amazulu, when they attacked Delagoa Bay, were called by the same name ; but the Portuguese throwing back the accent changed that word to Vátua, of which Captain Owen made Fetwah. So, in 1822, the tribe that fell upon the Bachwáná (Bechuana) were, we are told, called Batúa, but the missionaries recognised the meaning of the word. Though it is " now unknown," Dr. Livingstone has inserted it into his map.

of the sand is taken away, and the gold alone remains.* Mercury is as usual unknown. Formerly 130 lbs. of gold were submitted to the authorities at Tete for taxation, but when the slave trade began, the Portuguese killed the goose with the golden eggs, and the annual amount obtained is now only eight to ten pounds.

It is evident that gold is by no means half worked in Eastern Africa. As in California, it appears to be found in clay shale, which for large profits requires "hydraulicking." The South African traveller heard that at the range Mashinga, the women pounded the soft rock in wooden mortars, previous to washing; it is probably rotten quartz, and the yield would be trebled by quicksilver and crushers.

It is highly probable that the gold formations in those East African ghauts, which Dr. Beke is compelling to become the "Lunar Mountains," are by no means limited to the vicinity of the Zambezi. In gold prospecting, as every geologist knows, the likeliest places often afford little yield and sometimes none. The author of "The Lake Regions of Central Africa," describes a cordillera which he struck, about 100 miles from the Eastern coast, as primitive, quartzose, and shaly; unfortunately time and health hindered him from exploring it. The same writer, in "First Footsteps in East Africa" (p. 395), indicates such formation in the small ghauts, and on the western side of that range he

---

* This is absolutely the present practice on the Gold Coast, and perfectly agrees with Mungo Park's descriptions.

is reported to have found gold. What steps he took
do not appear; he was probably disheartened by the
reflection that all his efforts would be opposed with
might and main in official circles. Possibly he feared the
fate of Mr. Hargreaves, of Australia, who obtained a
reward of 10,000*l.*, when 1 per cent. of export would
have made him master of eight millions. Local jealousies
at Aden also certainly would have defeated his plans, if
permitted to be carried out; and the Court of Directors
had already regarded with a holy horror his proposal
to build a little fort, by way of base upon the seaboard near Berberah. Leaving, however, these considerations, we are justified by analogy of formation and
bearing in believing that at some future time gold
may be one of the exports from Eastern Intertropical
Africa.*

Returning to Western Africa, we find in Leo Afri-
canus, who is supposed to have died about 1526, that
the King of Ghana had in his palace " an entire lump of
gold "—a monster nugget it would now be called—not
cast nor wrought by instruments, but perfectly formed
by the Divine Providence only, of thirty pounds weight,

---

* I cannot, however, understand the final flourish of Dr. Beke's
paper above alluded to. He declares that the discovery of gold in his
"Mountains of the Moon" will occasion a complete and rapid revolution, and ends thus : " We shall then, too, doubtless see in Eastern
Africa, as in California and in Australia, the formation of another new
race of mankind." We have seen nothing of the kind in Western
Africa, where for four centuries the richest diggings have been known.
In fact, they have rather tended to drive away Europeans. Why then
expect this marvel from Eastern Africa ?

which had been bored through and fitted for a seat to the royal throne.* The author most diffused upon the subject of gold, is Bosman, who treats, however, solely of the Gold Coast.

The first region which he mentions is Dinkira, under which were included the conquered provinces of Wásá (our Wassaw, or Warsaw), Encasse and Juffer, each bordering upon one another, and the last upon Commany, (Commenda). There the gold is fine, but much alloyed with "fetishes," oddly shaped figures used for ornaments, and composed sometimes of pure mountain gold, but more often mixed with one-third, or even half, of silver and copper, and filled inside with half weight of the heavy black earth used for moulding them. The second was Acanny, the people of which brought the produce of their own diggings and of their neighbours of Ashantee and Akim: it was so pure and fine, that the negroes called all the best gold "Acanny Sika," or Acanny gold. The third was Akim,† which "furnishes as large quantities of gold as any land that I know, and that also the most valuable and pure of any that is carried away from this coast; it is easily distinguished by its deep colour." The fourth and fifth are Ashantee and Ananse, a small province between the former empire and Dinkira. The sixth and last is Awine, our Aowin,‡ which formerly used

---

* Similarly, the king of "Buncatoo" had a solid gold stool, which caused his destruction at the hands of his neighbours of Ashantee.

† It still supplies gold, and will be alluded to in a future page.

‡ The old traveller, however, is wrong, when he says, "I take it

to export large quantities of fine and pure gold, and
they " being the civilest and the fairest dealers of all the
negroes," the Dutch "traded with them with a great deal
of pleasure." They were, however, finally subdued by
the Dinkiras.

According to Bosman (Letter vi.) "the illustrious
metal " was found in three sites. The first and best was
" in or between particular hills :" the negroes sank pits
there and separated the soil adhering to it. The second
" is in, at, and about some rivers and waterfalls, whose
violence washeth down great quantities of earth, which
carry the gold with it. The third is on the sea shore,
near the mouths of rivulets, and the favourite time for
washing is after violent night rains.* The negro women
are furnished with large and small troughs or trays,
which they first fill full of earth and sand, which they
wash with repeated fresh water till they have cleansed it
from all its earth; and if there be any gold its pon-

(Awine) to be the first on the Gold Coast, and to be far above Axim."
Aowin is the region to the west of the Assini river, whereas Axim is
to the east of the Ancobra river ; thus the two are separated by the
territory of Apollonia. He apologises, however, in the same page for
any possible errors. " I cannot inform you better, because the negroes
cannot give any certain account of them (the various diggings), nor do
any of our people go so far ; wherefore I must beg of you, my good
friend, to be contented." Despite which, however, he may yet be
right, and his critic wrong.

  * So, "in Coquimbo of Chili," says Sir Richard Hawkins, " it
raineth seldom, but every shower of rain is a shower of gold unto
them, for with the violence of the water falling from the mountains, it
bringeth from them the gold."

derosity forces it to the bottom of the trough, which, if they find it, is thrown into the small tray, and so they go on washing it again, which operation generally holds them till noon ; some of them not getting above the value of sixpence ; some of them pieces of six or seven shillings, though not frequently ; and often they entirely lose their labour."

The gold thus dug is of two kinds, dust gold and mountain gold. The former is " fine as flour," and the more esteemed because there is no loss in melting. The latter, corresponding with our modern " nugget," varies in weight from a farthing to 200 guineas ; it touches better than gold dust, but it is a loss from the stones adhering to the stone.

The natives, in Bosman's day—and to the present time—were " very subtle artists in the sophisticating of gold." The first sort was the Fetish before alluded to.* They also cast pieces so artificially, that whilst outside there was pure gold thick as a knife, the interior was copper, and perhaps iron—then a new trick—and the most dangerous, because difficult to detect. The common " false mountain gold " was a mixture of the precious metal with silver and copper, extremely high coloured, and unless each piece was touched, the fraud passed undetected. Another kind was an artificially cast and

---

* We are also informed that the same Fetishes were cut by the negroes into small bits, worth one, two, or three farthings, and the people could tell their value at sight. These Kakeraa, as they were called, formed the small change of the country, as our 3*d.* and 4*d.* bits do now.

tinged powder of coral mixed with copper filings : it became tarnished, however, in a month or two.

The official tests of gold were as follows :—If offered at night or in the evening large pieces were cut through with a knife, and the smaller nuggets were beaten with a stone, and then tried as above. Gold dust was cast into a copper brazier, winnowed with the fingers, and blown upon with the breath, which caused the false gold to fly away. These are not highly artificial tests. Bosman, however, strongly recommends them to raw, inexpert people (especially seafaring men), whom he bids to remember the common proverb, that "there is no gold without dross." These greenhorns, it seems, tested the metal by pouring aquafortis upon it, when ebullition or the appearance of green proved it to be false or mixed. "A miserable test, indeed!" exclaims old trunk-hose, justly remarking that an eighth or tenth part of alloy would produce those appearances, and that such useless niceness, entailing the trouble of drying, and causing the negroes to suffer, is prejudicial to trade.

With respect to the annual export from the Gold Coast, Bosman reckons it in peaceful times, when trade

---

They were current all over the coast, and seemed to pass backwards and forwards without any diminution. The reason for this was, that they sold in Europe for only 40s. the ounce : the natives mixing them with better gold tried to palm them upon the purchasers, but the clerks were ordered to pick them out. A similar custom down the coast, was to cut dollars into halves and quarters, which thus easily became florins and shillings.

is prosperous, to be "23 tun." The 7000 marks are disposed of as below.* Mr. M'Queen estimates this exportation at £3,406,275. The English trade has now fallen to £360,000 to £400,000 per annum.†

The conclusion of Bosman's sixth letter may be quoted as highly applicable to the present day. " I would refer to any intelligent metallist, whether a vast deal of ore must not of necessity be lost here, from which a great deal of gold might be separated, from want of skill in the metallic art ; and not only so, but I firmly believe that large quantities of pure gold are left behind, for the negroes only ignorantly dig at random, without the least knowledge of the veins of the mines.   And I doubt not but if this country belonged to the Europeans, they would soon find it to produce much richer treasures than the negroes obtain from it ;

---

* The Dutch West India Company yearly exported, Marks 1500
The English African Company   .   .   .   ,,   1200
The Zealand interlopers as much as the Dutch, viz.   ,,   1500
The English interlopers about 1000, usually, which
    they have doubled .   .   .   .   .   .   ,,   1000
The Brandenburghers and Danes together, in times
    of peace .   .   .   .   ,,   1000
The Portuguese and French, together .   .   .   ,,   800

Which makes   7000

For several years before Bosman's time, the Dutch export had been reduced by one-half (750 marks). Mr. Wilson, however ("Western Africa," chap. IV.), is evidently in error, when he makes Bosman to estimate the "amount of gold exported from the Gold Coast at 800 marks per annum."

† Dr. Clarke ("Remarks," &c.), gives 100,000 ounces. This was the

but it is not probable that we shall ever possess that liberty here, wherefore we must be content with being so far masters of it as we are at present, which, if well and prudently managed, would turn to a very great account."

In several countries, as Dinkira, Tueful, Wásá,* and especially Akim, the hill region lying due north of Accra, the people are still active in digging gold. The pits, varying from two to three feet in diameter, and from twelve to fifty feet deep, are often so near the roads that loss of life has been the result. "Shoring-up" being little known, the miners are not unfrequently buried alive. The stuff is drawn up by ropes in clay pots, or calabashes, and thus a workman at the bottom widens the pit to a pyriform shape: tunnelling, however, is unknown. The excavated earth is carried down to be washed. Besides sinking these holes, they pan in the beds of rivers, and in places collect quartz, which is roughly pounded. The yield is very uncertain,

---

calculation of Mr. Swanzy before a parliamentary committee in 1816. Of course it is impossible to arrive at any clear estimate. Allowing the African Steam Ship Company a maximum of 4000 ounces per month, we obtain from that source 48,000 ounces. But considerable quantities are exported in merchant ships, more especially for the American market. Whilst, therefore, some reduce the total to 60,000 ounces, others raise it to half a million of money.

* Wásá (Wassaw, Warsaw, Wossa, Wasau, &c., &c.) has been worked both by Dutch and English; they chose, however, sickly situations, brought out useless implements, and died. The province is divided into eastern and western, and is said to be governed by female chiefs—Amazons?

and the chief of the district is entitled to one-third of the proceeds. During the busy season, when water is abundant, the scene must resemble that described by Dr. Livingstone near the gold-diggings of Tete; as in California and Australia, prices rise high, and gunpowder, rum, and cotton goods soon carry off the golddust. During the repeated earthquakes of July, 1862, which laid waste Accra, the strata of the Akim hills were so much shaken and broken up, that, according to report, all the people flocked to the diggings and dispensed with the shafts generally sunk. There are several parts of the Gold Coast where the precious metal is Fetish, and where the people will not dig themselves, though perhaps they would not object to strangers risking their lives. One of the most remarkable is the Devil's Hill, called by Bosman, Monte de Diablo, near Winnibah, in the Aguna (Agouna) country. In his day, a Mr. Baggs, English agent, was commissioned by the African Company to prospect it. He died at Cape Coast Castle before undertaking a work which, in those days, would have been highly dangerous. Some authorities fix the Seecom river as the easternmost boundary where gold is found. This is so far incorrect that I have panned it from the sands under James Fort. Besides which it is notorious that on the banks of the upper Volta, about the latitude of the Krobo (Croboe) country, there are extensive deposits, regarded by the people as sacred.

The Slave Coast is a low alluvial tract, and appears to

be wholly destitute of gold.* According to the Rev.
Mr. Bowen, however, a small quantity has been found
in the quartz of Yoruba, north of Abeokuta; but, as in
the Brazils, it is probably too much dispersed to be worth
working. And the Niger, which flows, as will presently
be seen, from the true auriferous centre, has at times
been found to roll down stream-gold.†

The soil of Fanti and the seaboard is, as has been
seen, but slightly auriferous.

As we advance northwards from the Gold Coast the
yield becomes richer. In Ashantee the red and loamy
soil, scattered with gravel and grey granite, is everywhere
impregnated with gold, which the slaves extract by
washing and digging. It is said that in the market-
place of Kumasi there are 1600 ounces' worth of gold—
a treasure reserved for State purposes. The bracelets
of rock-gold, which the caboceers wear on state
occasions, are four pounds in weight, and often so
heavy that they must rest their arms upon the heads of
their slave boys.

In Gaman, the region to the north-west of the
capital, the ore is found in large nuggets, sometimes
weighing four pounds. The pits are sunk nine
feet in the red granite and grey granite, and

---

* Some years ago the late Consul Campbell, of Lagos, forwarded to
Her Majesty's Foreign Office bits of broken pottery, in which he detected
gold. When submitted to the School of Mines, the glittering particles proved to be mica.

† Silver is also said to be found near the Niger, but of this I have
no reliable notices.

the gold is highly coloured. From 8000 to 10,000 slaves work for two months every year in the bed of the Barra river. There, however, as on the Gold Coast, the work is very imperfect, and in some places where the metal is sacred to the Fetish, it is not worked at all. Judging from analogy, we might expect to find the precious metal in the declivities inland and northwards from Cape Palmas, and in that sister formation of the East African ghauts, the "Sierra del Crystal." The late Captain Lawlin, an American trader, settled on an island at the mouth of the Fernan Vaz, carried to his own country, about the year 1843-44, a quantity of granular gold, which had been brought to him by some country people. He brought back all the necessary tools and implements to the Gaboon River, but the natives became alarmed, and he failed to find the spot. Finally, according to the tradition of native travellers, the unexplored region called Rúmá,* and conjecturally placed south of the inhospitable Waday, is a land of goldsmiths, the ore being found in mountainous and well-watered districts. It is becoming evident that Africa will some day equal half-a-dozen Californias.

Mungo Park supplies the amplest notices of gold in the regions visited by him north of the Kong Mountains. The principal places are the head of the Senegal

---

* This may be the "Runga," of our maps, with whose position Rúmá corresponds. My informant wrote down the name from the mouth of a Waday man at Lagos.

river, and its various influents; Dindiko, where the
shafts are most deep, and notched, like a ladder;
Shronda, which gives two grains from every pound of
alluvial matter;* Bambuk and Bambarra. In Kong-
kadu, the "mountain land," where the hills are of
coarse ruddy granite, composed of red feldspar, white
quartz, and black shale, containing orbicular concretions,
granular gold is found in the quartz, which is broken
with hammers ; the grains, however, are flat. The diggings at present best known are those of Manding.
The gold, we are told, is found not in mines or veins,
but scattered in sand and clay. They vary from a pin's
head to the size of a pea, and are remarkably pure.
This is called Sana Manko, or gold-powder, in contradis-
tinction to Sana birro, or gold stones, nuggets occasionally
weighing five drachms. In December, after the harvest-
home, when the gold-bearing Fiumaras from the hills have
shrunk, the Mansa or Shaykh appoints a day to begin
Sana Ku—gold-washing. Each woman arms herself with
a hoe, two or three calabashes, and a few quills. On
the morning before departure a bullock is slaughtered
for a feast, and prayers and charms are not forgotten.
The error made by these people is digging and washing
for years in the same spot, which proves comparatively unfruitful unless the torrent shifts its course.

---

* This would be $\frac{1}{3500}$ (avoirdupois), whereas the cascalhão, or alluvium,
of Brazil is $\frac{1}{13000}$, and remarkably rich and pyritical ores in Europe
give $\frac{1}{200000}$. Yet M. D'Aubrie estimates the gold in the bed of Father
Rhine at six or seven millions of pounds sterling.

They never follow the lead to the hills, but content
themselves with exploring the heads of the water-courses,
which the rapid stream denudes of sand and clay, leaving
a strew of small pebbles that wear the skin off the finger-
tips. The richest yield is from pits sunk in the height
of the dry season, near some hill in which gold has
been found. As the workers dig through the several
strata of sand and clay, they send up a few calabashes
by way of experiment for the women, whose peculiar
duty it is to wash the stuff, and thus they continue till
they strike the floor-rock. The most hopeful formation
is held to be a bed of reddish sand, with small dark
specks, described as "black matter, resembling gunpowder," and called by the people Sana Mira, or gold-
rust : it is possibly emery. In Mr. Murray's edition of
1816, there are illustrations of the various positions, and
a long description (Vol. I. p. 450, and Vol. II. p. 75) of
the style of panning. I will not trouble the reader
with it, as it in no way differs from that now practised
on the Gold Coast and Kaffir lands. There is art in
this apparently simple process. Some women find gold
when others cannot discover a particle; and as quicksilver is not used, at least one-third must be wasted,
or rather, I may say, it is preserved for a better
day.

The gold dust is stored in quills, stopped with cotton,
and the washers are fond of wearing a number of these
trophies in their hair. The average of an industrious
individual's annual collection may be two slaves. The

price of these varies from nine to twelve minkali,* each of 12*s*. 6*d.*, or its equivalent in goods, viz., eighteen gun-flints, forty-eight leaves of tobacco, twenty charges of gunpowder, a cutlass, and a musket. Part of the gold is converted into massive and cumbrous ornaments, necklaces, and ear-rings, and when a lady of consequence is in full dress, she bears from £50 to £80. A proportion is put by to defray expenses of travelling to and from the coast, and the greater part is then invested in goods, or exchanged with the Moors for salt and merchandise.

The gold is weighed in small balances, which the people always carry about with them, and they make, like the Hindus, but little difference between gold dust and wrought gold. The purchaser always uses his own "tilikissi," beans, probably, of the Abrus, which are sometimes soaked in Shea butter, to increase their weight, or are imitated with ground-down pebbles. In smelting gold, the smith uses an alkaline salt, obtained from a ley of burnt corn stalks. He is capable, as even the wildest African tribes are, of drawing fine wire. When rings—the favourite form in which the precious metal is carried coastward—are to be made, the gold is run without any flux in a crucible of sun-dried red clay, which is covered over with charcoal or braize. The smith pours the fluid into a furrow traced in the ground, by way of mould. When it has cooled, he reheats it,

* May not this word be an old corruption of the well-known Arabic weight, miskál ?

and hammers it into a little square ingot or bar of the size required. After a third exposure to fire, he twists with his pincers the bar into a screw shape, lengthens out the ends, and turns them up to form the circle.

It must now be abundantly evident to the reader that the great centre of West African gold, the source which supplies Manding to the North, and Ashantee to the South, is the equitorial range called the Kong. What the miueral wealth must be there, it is impossible to estimate, when nearly three millions and a half of pounds sterling have annually been drawn from a small parallelogram between its southern slopes and the ocean, whilst the other three quarters of the land—without alluding to the equally rich declivities of the northern versant—have remained as yet unexplored. Even in northern Liberia colonists have occasionally come upon a pocket of $50, and the natives bring gold in from the banks of streams.

Mr. Wilson* remarks upon this subject, " It is best for whites and blacks that these mines should be worked just as they are. The world is not suffering for the want of gold, and the comparative small quantities that are brought to the sea-coast keep the people in continual intercourse with civilised men, and ultimately, no doubt, will be the means of introducing civilisation and Christianity among them."

I differ from the reverend author, *toto cœlo.* For such vain hope as that of improving Africans by Euro-

---

* "Western Africa," Chap. X.

pean intercourse, and for all considerations of an "ultimately "vaguer than the sweet singer of Israel's "soon,"
it is regrettable that active measures for exploration and
exploitation are not substituted. And if the world—
including the reverend gentleman—is not suffering for
the want of gold, there are those, myself for instance,
and many a better man, who would be happy at times to
see and to feel a little more of that " vile yellow clay."

CHAPTER IX.

20TH SEPT., 186—.

VERY early in the morning of Friday we arose, and walked the quarter-deck, wihsing to see as much as possible of the coast of gold. The land about Winnibah, "the Forest Country," as it is called, extending as far west as Cape Apollonia, is a curtain of undulating rocky hills, none apparently above 200 or 300 · feet in height, with deep grassy valleys, swampy, and discharging little rills. The vegetation, which clothes almost every foot of soil, is of that dense oily kind most fit to sustain life under alternations of excessive humidity and of extreme drought. We could easily distinguish from the quarter-deck acacias and mimosas, wild dates, adansonias, and guinea palms. Most conspicuous in the morning grey was the Devil's Hill, a tall cone between Apam and Winnibah, a celebrated mining locality, dignified by many a local legend. Then came the woody hill, on whose seaward flank is the

---

* I cannot swear that Accra means the Land of Ants, nor that Mnyamwezi signifies the Land of the Moon, still there is a certain significance about them both which justify me in using them,—at least, when not writing a report to the Royal Geographical Society.

ancient Dutch port of Barraco. Lastly, Cook's Loaf, much in the shape of a *petit pain*, introduced us to the shallow bay of Accra, where we cast anchor at nine A.M. The scenery was a yellow shore, dotted with green, and backed with pale blue hills. For landing on this coast, there are no worse months than July, August, and September. Fortunately for us it was a dull day, and the wind had not power to raise the dreaded surf. Eyes were cast anxiously towards the edge of the beach at times, as thin white froth appeared above the smooth but undulating sea, with its livid leaden tints, but a glance was sufficient to satisfy us that in landing we risked nothing but wet jackets.

Seen from the offing, Accra is imposing, in its own way. A jotting of azure blue hill, the threshold of the Aquapim highlands, distant from sixteen to twenty miles, rising 1500 to 2000 feet above the sea, and forming an amphitheatre for the plain below, appears upon the far horizon. The old capital of the leeward districts stands upon a red beach, which pronounces itself, not condescending to a slope, and its base is lined with black rocks and ledges that chafe by opposing the in-vading tides. The centre of attraction is James Fort, a picturesque old building, which must have been re-garded with awe in the days of falconets and culverins. The "negro quarters," which spread out to the north-east and north-west of the fort, do not show from this offing, which confines our view to the large square and parallelogramic houses that take open distance along the sea frontage. There are two which attract every eye westward—the castle-like pile called the Commodore, and nearer to the fort, the Big House. Here and there a wind-wrung cocoa, forming a natural vane, whilst bent away tremblingly from the bullying south-west wind, broke the somewhat bald and monotonous scatter of habitations. On the eastward, or to the right of James Fort, lies the Dutch Crevecœur—why it should so be called I have not yet discovered, as an order to capture it ought not to break a man's heart—sedulously white-washed, and more protentous in appearance than its English neighbour; and further still, after a long narrow strip of yellow sward, surmounted by a stratum of equally bright green verdure, appears upon a jutting rock the once magnificent castle of Christianborg. It rises boldly from a black rock, at whose feet the tides ceaselessly surge, and beyond it is a ledge upon which the waves incessantly break in the calmest weather.

Landing in a canoe, with high weatherboards—the surf here is a litle worse than at Cape Coast Castle—we made for a dark reef to the westward of the fort, and we passed behind it through a little channel which might easily be improved; there is, however, a better place nearer the fort. The sea-horses reared and shook their foamy manes outside the rocks, inside we had nothing more than a high tide at Dover or Weymouth. We were seated in chairs in the fore part of the canoe—the usual place in these landings—and as she touched the sands, our "pull-a-boys" springing into the water, carried

us all out high and dry. A dollar is well laid out
on such occasions ; a moment's delay may often see the
stern of the canoe half swamped by a breaker. Ascending the unclean bank by a stiff rampart or *tranchée* of red
clay, banded with strata of what is about to be sandstone,
we entered upon the Parade-Ground, or Esplanade,
an open space between James Fort and the whitewashed stone-box called the hotel. The "Grande
Place" did not look well : a rough square, with a few
gutters for drains, strewed with bits of brick and bottles,
and backed by negro quarters and shabby huts facing
the sea. Like Stamboul, the capital of the Leeward
Districts of the Gold Coast, loses all its picturesqueness
by closer inspection, and the place has the quiet, hopeless, cast-down look of a veteran bankrupt.

Mr. Addoe, the African proprietor of the British
Hotel, was civil and obliging : the interior of his establishment was in Anglo-Indian style, combining mena-
gerie with old curiosity-shop, and not without a touch of
Booksellers' Row, as I believe Putea-Sancta Street is now
called. In the unswept yard was sunk a large tank of
solid masonry, with mildewed walls, and a surface overgrown with a broad-leaved duck-weed, which is supposed
to keep water sweet. Dysentery, according to Dr.
Clarke, is "by far the most fatal disease on the Gold
Coast, both to the European and native," and the
people consider it highly contagious.* I ceased to

---

* It is dangerous in the tropics to despise popular opinions touching
the contagiousness of a disease, which is notably not so in colder

wonder at this being the case; after tasting the water, and a month or two subsequently spent in the country climates, such as phthisis in Italy, and "morbus gallicum "—without actual contact—in Persia. Central African travellers have also remarked that in those old homes and birth-places of small-pox, it falls upon a village or a caravan like a plague, and the Portuguese of Goa will not pass to leeward of a house where a confluent case is known to be.

It may be presumptuous in a non-medical man to offer an opinion upon such a point. I cannot, however, but concur in all the advice which Dr. Clarke offers upon the treatment of the West African scourge, dysentery. He informs us, p. 37 : "That whereas European medical officers almost always prescribe soups, slops, and farinaceous substances ; the natives diet the patient with dry and nutritive aliments, in fact, animal food. And this," says Dr. Clarke, "is the secret of the great success attained by the people of the country." In my experience, I always found the same thing. The vital powers of the sufferer being greatly lowered, he requires as much support as possible : good meat, beef tea, but no slops, essence of meat, fresh fruit, and mild stimulants, port or champagne. These will not create acidity, the invariable effect upon a deranged stomach of vegetable food ; moreover the latter does not support the patient sufficiently. In all dysenteric cases, however, the first point for consideration is the existence or non-existence of hepatic complications. If these be absent, and the disorder be entirely local, opium may be used ; it is a fatal treatment when an organic derangement of the liver has given rise to the disease. Above all things, relapse is to be guarded against.

In dysenteric cases the natives have another adjunct to their multifarious simples and tisanes. The patient is directed to rise at daybreak, and to sit wholly undressed in the cool and pleasant morning breeze until 6 A.M. He is then washed in a cold unstrained infusion of macerated plantain-roots, lime-tree leaves, cassava plant, and roots of the water-lily ; the skin is anointed with Shea butter ; "pampa," a gruel of Indian corn, is given to drink ; and the process is generally followed by a sound and refreshing sleep. This cold "air-bath" is a form of cleanliness which has yet to be adopted in England ; it will doubtless follow in the wake of the Turkish bath. Its merits have long since been discovered in India, where, after the sensation of living in a poultice—the effect of European clothing—the exposure of the skin is greatly enjoyed.

convinced me that the fatality of the climate might be greatly diminished by a distilling machine. Mr. Addoe does a little business in stock. Accra is better provided than most part of the coast with supplies: small but good turkeys are brought from the breeding-places at the mouth of the Volta,—Jellakofi, usually called "Jelly-coffee," and Quittah, with its now deserted fort. They are bought here for 6s., and a little down the coast are worth at least $2: at Fernando Po one of them has cost a pound sterling. Pigs and poultry are bred at head-quarters. The interior supplies excellent farm land, and a man might soon make a small fortune by breeding sheep and goats, and by selling milk and vegetables to mail-steamers and cruisers. But "sun he be too hot, mas'er!" There are also curios at the British Hotel—monkey-skins for dames' muffs—there are inland some pretty specimens, jetty black, with pure white beard and whiskers; they are worth $1 per dozen. A fierce dog-faced baboon or two, with a strong propensity for a bite at your tendon-Achilles,* amuses himself in captivity with perambulating a rail; and dozens of Guinea parrots—little valued because they cannot speak, though they want the voicelessness for which the Greeks envied the wives of the Cicadas—twist and turn upon their perches on the

---

* It is this tendency in the monkey that induced the learned and Rev. Dr. Adam Clarke, in his "Commentary on the Bible," to propose that the ape should take the place of the old serpent in the Book of Genesis,—that most curious of cosmologies.

ground-floor piazza ; whilst an eagle is chained to a post in the yard corner.

Not much prepossessed by the appearance of the establishment, where precocious urchins, hardly in their teens, were chewing sápo,* and laying the cloth for breakfast, the consul and I prepared for a walk round the town. We were accompanied by poor Hollingworth, of H.M.'s ship " Prometheus," one of the best and kindliest fellows that ever wore a blue jacket. Six months afterwards he fell a victim to the deadly climate of Lagos. Before setting out we had a palaver with a " cook-boy," as Anglo-Indian ladies persist in calling him, who was willing to engage himself for " Nanny Po." The cook-boy, however, owning to a proclivity for " sucking the monkey," and demanding as wages £5 per mensem, we did not subject him to expatriation. In most parts of India a stranger, if wise, would have hesitated to expose himself to the sun at 10 A.M. On this coast, however, even Europeans enjoy immunity from sun-stroke :† the natives, as the black-skin everywhere seems to do, enjoy themselves in the living "lowe."

* A bunch of fibres of the plantain and other trees, which, like the lïf of Egypt, is used as a sponge ; a mouthful is chewed to clean the inner part of the teeth, and is then applied outside like a tooth brush. Some of these fibres are bitter astringents, and doubtless beneficial.

† Dr. Clarke attributes this immunity to the relaxation of the system, by which profuse perspiration follows the least exertion, thereby equalising the circulation and preventing local congestions. This is true : it is dangerous to sit, though not to walk, in the sun. But I would also suggest that the humidity of the atmosphere, forming at all seasons a veil for the sun's rays, greatly mitigates the absolute heat.

Our first walk was to the British Salt Lake, as the Accra Lagoon, lying west of the town, is called. These formations are of two kinds, which I may term longitudinal and latitudinal. The former is disposed at an angle, more or less rectangular, to the coast; it is usually in a sink between two waves or tongues of high land, the lower bed of some watercourse, which flows only during the rains, and which, being below sea-level, is fed by percolations through the raised sand strip which acts as its embankment. The latitudinal is generally the formation of a permanent river, which spreads out over the depressions on either side of its bendings : the Volta river offers the perfection of this feature. Nothing can be worse than British Salt Lake, which runs far into the interior; it is historic ground, the fatal field of Dodowah lying near its head. Though fetid with decomposed mud, and haunted by sand-flies and mosquitoes, it is the favourite walk and ride with the Europeans of Accra. Between it and the sea are a number of pits, where the natives—fair and not fair —bathe in a touching approach to the pure Adamical costume. Turning inwards past "the Commodore"— as the large and well-built pile belonging to the Bannerman family—its tank contains the purest water in the place—is called, we walked towards the north, and had a fine view of the Aquapim and other hills, of which two cones, named Mount Bannerman to the west-north-west, and to the north-east, Kwabenyang, called on our charts Mount Zahrtman, are the most conspicuous.

The nearer country was adorned with the Palmyra, the
French Ronnier, and it is everywhere a tree of good
omen. The roads were bordered with datura—fortunately the people ignore its poisonous narcotism—and
with thick hedges of prickly pear, whose only fault is a
proclivity to extend itself unduly : the fruit is eaten by
children, but the whites have not yet learned to appreciate the Maltese favourite.* The people whom we met
on the road were mostly she-"pawns," sauntering towards
the plantations; they did not, however, neglect to address
us with the normal Heni odse — where thou comest
from ? To which we were taught to reply Ble-e-e-o—
meaning softly—*tout doucement*—it is peaceful here.
At some distance from the town, stood Garden House,
once a shooting-box, whence sportsmen issued to slay
leopards and moose-deer — probably the Koodoo. It
was a fine old building, but, like the rest, dark, deserted,
and sadly ruinous, whilst the grounds around it were
a mere waste of bush. We strolled into the cemetery,
whose hingeless, rusted gate offered no obstruction, and
found it on a par with the habitations of the living.
Returning by the north-east of the town, we passed by
the Big House, another stately pile, that belongs to the
Hansen family ; it is even more broken down than " the

---

* On the Mediterranean shores it is considered cooling and wholesome, especially in summer. Englishmen at first dislike its insipidity,
but they soon accustom themselves to it. The only difficulty about it
is removing the thorny peel, which cannot be done without much
practice.

Commodore." Mr. Addoe has married one of the daughters of the house, which, as usual, has a burial-ground on the lowest or ground-floor. Query, how is it that these houses are never haunted? What can become of the ghosts? It is said to have cost £12,000, in a place where money is worth double what it is in England, and the original proprietor died before he had carried out his plans of purchasing and clearing the frontage. A little beyond it was the French factory, and the Wesleyan Mission-house, bought from old Mr. Bannerman. In the town the women had their legs stocking'd and striped, like a clown's face, with some whitish, clayey substance; they were "making custom." The men as we passed bared themselves to the waist, which is equivalent to a cavalry-man dropping his right arm. All appeared civil and respectful: they are said to enjoy English rule, and to wish that we were sole possessors of the land—a great contrast to the East Indian. The pot-bellied children never appeared without a lump of native bread in their hands, a circumstance which accounts for the inordinate mortality of these juveniles— about one in three arriving at the years conventionally termed "of discretion." The alleys—streets they could not be called—were dirty and slovenly; sweeping seemed to be unknown; and the lank, sharp-snouted, long-legged pigs that haunted the heaps, were engaged in anything but rooting up truffles. This nuisance can hardly be abated: at times private orders are issued to cut short the days of Paddy's friend, as Pariah dogs are slaughtered in India; but the people attributing it to a porcine pestilence, send their pets into the country for change of air. The houses were of the hollow square form, more preserved than those of Cape Coast Castle, but less so than the Yoruba habitations. In most court-yards a female slave was bending, with pendent bosom and perspiring skin, over a stone roller, which, working along a concave slab, reduced the maize and obdurate holcus to a fine flour. Nothing can be more gloomy than these mud huts; their never whitewashed walls and seedy brown thatches are sad to behold. A few yards placed us once more upon the parade-ground.

Re-entering the hotel, we refreshed ourselves with brandy-pawnee, the pawnee being Patent Quinined Water, which has a high local reputation. After a discon-solate glance at the interior, and a gloomy anticipation of breakfast, a bright thought suggested itself. We walked over to the fort, passed inside despite the lowering glances of a shoeless Zouave, whose chestnut-coloured stockings, not unmatched with toes protruding through the tips, gave his legs the appearance that the English-woman in Paris seems to love—of two large chocolate sticks, and introduced ourselves to the Civil-Com-mandant, Major De Ruvignes, who, whilst finishing off business for the forenoon, welcomed us most kindly. He had brought to Africa a goodly stock of East Indian campaigning experiences, and we found ourselves in for pleasant day, when we had no right to expect any such thing.

I must break the thread of my tangled discourse to moralise "some," as Jonathan, or rather the two Jonathans, have it. In extensive travel there is catholicity of experience, especially in the cuisine. Few races, except the Esquimaux, the Hottentots, and the Australians, possess not a dish or two that might profitably be naturalised at home; whilst we in England have too many, which might, equally advantageously, be changed for others. Nor is the subject one of light import. *L'homme d'esprit seul sait manger.* Only fools and young ladies care nothing for the *carte.* Who but the idiot would affront his polarity (as Mr. Emerson, if I rightly understand him, terms man's individuality) by adhibiting to powers exhausted in a tropical climate, a refreshment of boiled mutton (*proh pudor!*) and caper sauce,* or a stuff invented, when meat was dear, to choke off appetite, and for which the speech of Europe hath no name—" pudding?" "Religion," says the sage Soyer, " feeds the soul, Education the mind, Food 'the body." *La destinée des nations dépend de la manière dont elles se nourrissent* is the wisdom of another wise man. This age of high progress is beginning to suspect a fact of which it never doubted in its days of barbarism— namely, that the babe at the breast imbibes certain peculiarities according to its nutrition.

---

* Well do I remember, in days of youth, our "elegant" and chival‧ rous French chef at Tours, in fair Touraine, who at once retired from the service because he was ordered to boil a gigot—"*Comment, madame, un—gigot!—cuit à l'eau, Jamais! Neverre!*"

These reflections, philosophical as good gastronomy is the truest philosophy, emanate from the memories of that day's breakfast. The people of Accra are notoriously good cooks; but, as amongst unpolished races, the men, who in civilisation attain heights of excellence to which the humbler sex may not aspire, are here notably inferior to their partners. The best of *cuisinières* are, of course, those of birth and breeding, and in their places Madame can direct the actions of her slave girls without compromising herself, as would be the case in an English kitchen, where we find Mrs. A——, with arms akimbo, ruling the roast, and brooking no rival luminary in her firmament. I can name and describe the qualities of the dishes to which we paid more particular attention, but their composition is complicated and tasteful enough to puzzle the brains of the lady who writes the cookery book. "Kankie" is native bread : the flour, at first not unlike the "yaller male" of the Land of Potatoes, must be manipulated till it becomes snowy white : after various complicated operations—soaking the grain, pounding, husking, triturating, and keeping till the right moment, it is boiled or roasted and packed in plantain leaves. It is as superior to the sour, brown, sodden mass tasting of butter-milk—like palm-wine and mildew, used by Europeans on this coast and called bread, as a Parisian roll to the London quartern loaf. "Fufu" is composed of yam, plantain, or casava; it is peeled, boiled, pounded, and made into balls, which act the part of European potatoes, only it is far more savoury than the vile tuber,

which has potatofied at least one nation, and at which no man of taste ever looks, except in some such deep disguise as a *maître d'hôtel.* There were also cakes, seasoned with the fresh oil of the palm kernel, but they had a fault,—over richness. *En revanche,* the fish and stews were admirable ; the former is the staple supply of the coast, and old residents live upon it.*
"Kinnau" is fish opened, cleaned, stuffed with mashed green pepper, and fried in palm oil. The oil used for these purposes must be freshly made, thoroughly purified by repeated boilings, till free from water and fibre ; the sign of readiness is a slight transparent yellow tint, supplanting the usual chrome colour. "Palaver sauce" is a mess of vegetables, the hibiscus, egg-plant, tomato, and pepper, boiled together, with or without fowl or fish. "Palm-oil chop" is the curry of the Western coast, but it lacks the delicate flavour which turmeric gives, and suggests coarseness of taste. After some time Europeans begin to like it, and there are many who take home the materials to Europe. Besides palm-oil, it is composed of meat or fowl, boiled yam,† pepper,

* The fish is mostly a kind of herring, of which large quantities are cured and sent to the interior, even as far as Ashantee. Turtle is turned in the Hamattan season, beginning with December : after March they breed, and are unfit for food.

† The West African yam is of two kinds—white and yellow : the former is sweet, the latter bitter, and consequently preferred by the natives and by old hands amongst the whites. It never has the internal light purple tinge, nor the drug-like flavour which renders this vegetable anything but a favourite in India. The best yams in this part of the world are grown by the Bubes of Fernando Po.

and other minor ingredients. I always prefer it with rice; pepper, however, is the general fashion. The best and only sensible drink with this "chop," is palm wine, but the article is seldom to be procured sweet, and it mixes very badly for the digestion with all other fermented liquors. Next to it claret, but by no means Burgundy, which would recall a flavour, perhaps already too strong. And I advise the young beginner to conclude his "palm-oil chop," especially when eaten at a native house, with a "*petit verre.*" The last dish which shall be mentioned—it affects the palate of reminiscence with a pleasant humidity—is "kickie," a most intricate affair of finely minced and strongly flavoured fish or fowl; it is served up in Accra-made pots of black porous clay, into which the pepper sinks so thoroughly that after a few months it heats its contents. It has the one great advantage, like the West Indian "pepper-pot," of always coming up to table fresh from the fire.

After the *déjeûner dînatoire*, not without *aliquo mero*, we walked round poor old James Fort, which dates from the days of Charles the Martyr. It is an irregular square, flanked by bastions, and provided with two stories; the eastern side contains, or rather contained, a large saloon used for business purposes, and on the ground floor are the dungeons in which prisoners were immured. The sides of the fort proper are about 145 feet long; outside the gateway, however, there are the courts, surrounded by loopholed walls, and separated by a tumble-down building called a court-house. It is

built upon the outer extremity of Accra Point, on a
rocky foundation, about 36 feet above sea level. A low
ledge of reef projects far into the sea, and at an expense
of 5000*l.*—20,000*l.* being annually wasted upon a local
corps — a breakwater of rough stone might easily be
made there. It has been repeatedly recommended, and
it was even expected to be undertaken : but who cares
for Accra on the Gold Coast? This place, once the
great ambition of Europe, has now fallen—fallen—
fallen—even from the memory of the Gazetteer. In
Brookes and Findlay (MDCCCLI.) we read, for all information—

* "ACRA, or ACCARA,"—neither spelling admissible—"a territory
of Guinea on the Gold Coast, where some European States have forts,
and each fort its village. N. lat. 5° 25′, W. long. 0° 10′."

A fine-looking massive building it must have seemed to
the eyes of its own generation. It was the furthermost
of their works upon this Coast, which will never look
upon its like again. When I first saw it, however, the
gateway was bending humbly forwards, the walls were
lézardés, by rain dripping through the mortarless inter-
stices, the ramparts were in holes, the rooms ruinous, the
old iron guns, of some dozen various calibres, were scaly
as the armadillo, and the whole place wore the tristest
aspect of desolation. Some 1000*l.* per annum would
have kept all these places—Cape Coast Castle, Accra
Dixcove, and Christiansborg—in proper order; no great
addition to an expenditure of £24,000 or £30,000 per
annum. Now all is ruin. Books tell us that the coast,

from El-Mina to Benin is still rising, and that rocks and ledges, before below, are now flush with the water. The earthquake of 1858 tended to hasten the growth.*

No one visits Accra without inspecting its neighbour, Christiansborg. Our coach and six presently appeared at the door; a quaint contrivance,—a four-in-hand of negroes to the fore, holding little cross-bars, and two pushing in the rear. The late Lieutenant Forbes, of Dahomian celebrity, used to wax extremely wroth at this degradation of men to cattle. I regret to own that it felt very refreshing after the banalities of hammocks, palanquins, and sedans. Horses, which die at Cape Coast Castle after a few months, here live for years: their owners, however, are careful not to take them into the bush. The reason generally given there is, that they catch complaints which are fatal. I cannot, however, but think that it is the tzetze, or some kindred fly, which destroys them. Wherever the bush and the tall grass are cleared away, these noxious animals, whose poison seems to be derived from the rank vegetation surrounding them, disappear. They are no longer upon the actual seaboard, which, perhaps, has been too much denuded of trees,—Nature's screen-work against the malaria of

---

* About April, 1862, seventeen distinct shocks, extending through six weeks, added increment to it, and on the 10th of June, 1862, when the rolling of the ground split every stone house in Accra, I distinctly saw that the level of the rock ledge had been upraised from the sea. The same day, however, was fatal to the three forts; and the clerk of the works, sent from England to report upon the state of those belonging to us, declared that it was useless to attempt repairs.

the inner marshes. Within five miles north of Accra, I was severely stung by a large brown gadfly, of which specimens were secured. They were unfortunately lost; but though without books of reference and preserved specimens it is impossible for me to identify the animal, my impression is that it is the true tzetze, which Dr. Livingstone has limited to the southern branch of the Zambezi. The author of the " West Regions of Central Africa," brought home with him a fine large glossina, which was pronounced at the British Museum to be the true G. morsitans. Mules and asses might succeed even where horses fail. The only trouble in keeping these animals is the difficulty of finding proper attendants. Nothing can be more inhuman or neglectful than the West African stable-boy; he mounts his charge when unobserved, and rides him like a beggar, wears the cloths by night, and unless the master is present robs the grain and kankie with which his charge is fed. Besides which the fellows seem constitutionally unable to keep a horse clean, and to ride an animal out of condition and one quarter groomed is to drink *Romané glacé* out of a tin pannikin—both lose all their pleasure.

Our novel go-cart dashed through the streets at full speed. We passed through the Salt Bazaar, a kind of market, where women were sitting, before them were stores of fish and vegetables, ground-nuts, and palm-oil, and large flat baskets filled with the infinity of small cheap articles chiefly required in barbarous life. This led us to another square. On its seaward side stands the Dutch

fort Crève-cœur, which M. Bouet-Willaumez described as
an "abandoned ruin." It is a large pile of building,
at the edge of the cliff, with a tall turret and a large
courtyard. Being freshly whitewashed it wore an
aspect somewhat superior to our ruin, but during the
earthquakes it fared much worse, which was bad indeed.
A Dutch negro soldier or two sat at the door, but never
ventured upon the least sign of salute, eyeing us with all
the repose which marks the caste of Canaan bin Ham.
We also found a Wesleyan chapel, standing solitary at
the landward side of a square, not unlike the parade-
ground. Its style of architecture was that of the olden
meeting-house, generally copied from that useful but
not ornamental tenement, a barn. It disdained steeple,
and being a week-day the doors were of course shut.
Under its shade a small party of young negresses were
enjoying their favourite relaxation of a dance. Nothing
is more grotesque than their style of saltation. A
couple stands up *vis-à-vis*, and raising the foot alternately
both stamp upon the ground as bears are taught to do.
This presently becomes a leap in the air, during which
the hands are thrown out, palms forwards, and are met
by the partner opposite. If there is any failure the
couple breaks off with loud shouts of laughter, and
another set stands up in their stead. On great occasions
at Accra there are, I believe, dances which are as ceremonious as the East Indian Nautch; we had not, however,
time to see them.

Presently we emerged from the town upon a level high

road of no despicable construction. Originally the work
of the merchants at Accra, it is now kept in order by
the civil commandant. The hard red clay, often the
débris of ant masonry, dispenses with the necessity of
metalling, though not with that of repairing at the end
of the rainy season. The avenue of umbrellas and
tamarinds which, bending to the N. E., acted as natural
waves, gave it almost a south-European look. The
country around, although in the heart of the dry season,
afforded me an unexpected pleasure. Not a trace of
bush, jungle, or mangrove swamp around: in the
yellow daylight. the rolling surface, here gently swelling,
there sinking with a graceful curve, was clothed with
golden grass; and here and there a tall tree, a " motte "
of underwood, a solitary cactus, or a clump of evergreen
woo'd the traveller to its green shade. Herds of cattle
browsing in the distance gave it a pastoral appearance,
and beyond the prairie formation of the lowlands rose
forest,—not primeval, as Dr. Daniell calls it, but rather
land that has lain fallow for some scores of years. The
people call this Ko, as opposed to Ná, the grassy
savannah. The consul had never seen so many ant-
pyramids since leaving the Somali country : they studded
the land; tall broken cones of red ferruginous earth, the
favourite building material of the white termes belli-
cosus, the bug-a-bug of S'a Leone, which gives to the
region a mistaken name.* There is game to be found
in the land—" horse-deer," 13 to 14 hands high, ante-

* Accra is derived, through the Portuguese, from Inkran, or

lopes, the noble African partridge, and the "bush-turkey," which I believe to be a floriken : the animals, however, take to cover at once, and cannot be dislodged without curs. There is a kind of wild cattle, called on the Gaboon river, Nyára : it seems to exist everywhere in the maritime region—I found the same animal on the Gold Coast. Mr. Thompson ("Palm Land, or West Africa," p. 168) mentions it in the grass plains near Sherbro, and Mr. Valdez calls it Empacasso in Portuguese Africa,—Empacasseiros are the huntsmen who make a profession to kill it. Leopards are only too numerous. Hippopotami and crocodiles are plentiful in the Volta river. Spur-fowl exist in the bushes. I prefer, small as they are, the delicious curlews that pace the sands. Wild geese appear at certain seasons ; the meat is fat, rich, and juicy. Elephants must exist in the interior, as the people are plentifully supplied with scrivellos and tusks of moderate dimensions. The only drawback to a gallop over this fine open country is the number and size of the crab holes, which rival the biscacheros of the South American pampas. During the rains, when verdure invests these charming slopes, and a thicker herbage clothes the woodland, the view must be a repose to the eye.* The horizon in the north showed a distant line of fading blue hill, the

---

"drivers," not white ants. Others say it was so called on account of the ant-like swarming of its numerous population.

* Compared with S'a Leone the rains in Accra are light, averaging a little above 80 inches. They are sufficient, however, to flood the

threshold of Ajumanti, Akim, and Ajuapim. In the latter, Akropong, the king's residence, and Abude, are now stations of the Basle mission : the distance is laid down at 20 to 30 miles from Accra, the height is 2000 to 2500 feet above sea level, and the climate is described to be delightful. The Ajumanti range is a day's hammock march from James Town, and being drier, is preferred by many to Akropong or Abude : the air is delicious, the water pure, and abundant stone and timber everywhere, whilst mechanics and supplies, at slightly advanced prices, are readily procurable from Accra. On the seaward slopes there is still a Danish ruin, bearing the inscription—

Frederiksgave

VI.

1832.

and intended as a sanitarium for the officers of Christiansborg. The fine estate around it, called the Queen's Plantations, has been granted to Major De Ruvignes, the civil commandant, on consideration of his paying annually a pine-apple quit-rent. Anything—from coffee to cotton—would grow here, and will grow well, whilst the air is pure and cool, and the mosquito plague of Accra is unknown. At the foot of the range is Abokobi, another station of German missionaries, and in the hills various farms and plantations belonging to the merchants of Accra. Coffee has been grown there, but all has now run wild. Mr. Freeman has been much more successful

lowlands, and as the soil is clayey, to stop travelling. The best season for excursions into the interior is the Harmattan.

near the Secoom river: at this time he has, I suppose, 10,000 plants. The German missionaries in Ajuapim also attempted it, but want of gardening skill made their efforts vain. Cotton was tried, and succeeded admirably. Mr. Swanzy, an eminent merchant, laid out large sums, and produced an excellent staple; since his day, however, the trees have been entirely neglected. The Accra copal is of poor quality, and fetches in the market far lower prices than that of Angola, Benguela, Kongo, or S'a Leone. Guinea grains are procured spontaneously everywhere in the hills, but this once celebrated spice, like the Balm of Meccah, has now become a weed. The mountain land of Akim lies about a week's easy travel to the north, with a little westing from Accra; it is divided into two districts, the eastern, of which Ojadan is the capital, and the western, whose capital is Chebi. The people, who know, though they cannot avail themselves of, their country's resources, are desirous of seeing it colonised by Europeans. Two very rich diggings have lately been discovered in Akim. There is no doubt that by paying a certain per-centage to the king and his Pynims, Europeans would be allowed to work them. It is described as a beautiful region, abounding in fruits and flowers: its botany would doubtless instruct Europe, but where are the botanist, the geologist, and the student of natural history on the Gold Coast? The great industry throughout Akim is gold. According to travellers the local fetish is called Kataguri; it appears in the shape of a large brass pan, which dropped down from heaven; in token of its high descent it is secured with all mystery in a fetish house, and is surrounded by drawn swords and axes overlaid with gold.*

After a two miles' drive through a country which it was a pleasure to look at, we reached the outposts of Christiansborg. The first sign was a cemetery, where the missionaries lie apart from " *dee hayden*," with whom they have associated during life. Ensue some quasi-European houses in which the " consort,"—such is the ambiguous term which the native " housekeeper " enjoys in these lands,—is located by the absent " householder." A martello tower, once considered a strong defence, stands sentinel on this approach to the main work. Around it, and to the northwards, clusters a native town, rising phœnix-like from it ruins. It was bombarded to correct a mutinous tendency, in 1854, by H. M. S. Scourge, followed by a squadron of six English vessels, and a large native force, which had collected, was easily dispersed. Unfortunately the lines of streets have been carelessly laid down, and, as has been explained, it is more difficult to remove a Gold Coast town than a West Africo-English

---

* At Accra the commandant showed me some of these swords, which had been sent in token of submission by one of the chiefs of Krobo, a highland about 60 miles north-east of James Town. They were short, broad, and heavy falchions, apparently of rusty hoop iron, in shape somewhat like the dreaded Turkish scimitar of the olden time—now known only in pictures—but adorned with open work near the end, like fish-slicers or Highland dirks, the handles and pommels being thinly plated with worked gold sewn together, and hammered close to the wood.

settlement. The holes from which the earthen material
of the houses was excavated are allowed to remain, and,
filled by every rainy season they must be small hotbeds
of malaria. The native town showed us a peculiar sight.
"Can the Ethiopian change his skin?" is a question
which has been asked some time ago, in distinct expec-
tation of a negative reply. My day at Accra enables
me modestly, but decidedly, to reply that he *can*. Outside
a hut sat a strange-looking being, a spotted man, such as
we read of in books that treat of ethnology and of skin-
diseases. The ground-colour of his superficies was an
unwholesome pink white, and the rest was a series of
deep black splotches. He was well-known to all in the
place; a few years before he had been a negro; he
gradually changed to a white man, and when we saw him
he was again recovering his *rete mucosum*. I saw
another anthropological curiosity at Accra. The Albino
in Africa has been noticed by every traveller, the semi-
Albino has not. My specimen was a man with features
and cranium distinctly belonging to the " poor black
brother." His complexion, however, was *café au lait*,
his hair a dull dead yellow, short and kinky as that of
all his tribe, and his eye-pupils were of a light and lively
brown. I afterwards saw many of the same temperament
at Benin, and one—the chief Sandy—at Batanga : my
little "Travellers' Library," however, does not allude to
this *lusus naturæ*.

Near the entrance of the old Danish castle there are
some large whitewashed quarters, occupied by the Basle

Mission's Gesellschâft, and a number of white-haired children broke the monotonous prospect of little waddling niggers and long-legged trotting pigs. This Mission holds the hill-country, and by combining commerce with Christianisation, has succeeded in establishing half a dozen stations. The members arrive in Africa like timid sheep, very humble; they wax bolder in time, as the fox in that fable where he met the lion, and they end by being as offensive to the community as were the frogs to King Log. An abominable charge was brought by their superior against a highly respectable English merchant at Accra: an action for libel of course ensued, the cause came into court, and the defendant altogether failed to substantiate his calumny. Yet the jury—partly negroes and partly whites, lower in the scale of creation than black men—brought in the peculiar verdict that the accusation was a libel, but that it had been made without malicious intent. These Germans carry matters with a high hand. An English brother happening to come under their displeasure, they took from him his wife and children—by a process of divorce which they had no right to pronounce—and actually married her to one of their own number. I will not mention names unless the truth of this assertion be disputed by the culprits, in which case I will.

Christiansborg Castle, like its brethren Crève-cœur and James Fort, is founded upon a rock, and bears upon its walls the date of erection, A.D. 1694. This strong point, flanked on both sides by sandy bays, stands some thirty-five feet above sea-level; it is fronted by scattered ledges and outliers, upon which at most seasons, a heavy surf breaks, consequently the landing is fit only for canoes. Built by degrees, it has grown into a large but irregular building, a square of 190 feet on each side, with a variety of party-walls, ramparts, bastions, and outworks, all of solid stone masonry, which must have cost a "pretty penny." The first room is a fine *salon*, called the council-chamber, enlivened with bright blue bands of paint; under it, however, are noisome dungeons. Besides this there is a chapel, now closed, a hospital, sundry store-rooms, and officers' quarters. It is garrisoned by a detachment from Accra, and so scanty are supplies, that the Europeans never miss mail-day, and generally dine away from home; no skipper can pass the place without being mulcted in a bit of fresh beef, or, that failing, salt pork. The air is damp and unwholesome; articles hung against the walls generally mildew, and the human animal fares even worse. The fort was built originally by the Portuguese, but after repeatedly changing masters, it was confirmed to the Danish crown in the year inscribed upon its walls. In 1850, the King of Denmark, as has been said, sold all his northern provinces for the sum of 10,000*l.*, to the English. I should have preferred paying these moneys for the archives; they were, however, removed with the establishment. The Danish trace is still met with in the interior, although the names of the towns do not end in —by. You meet, however in out-

of-the-way villages, with Miss Hesse, Miss Engmann,
and other unmistakeable signs of the Danes.

The view from the ramparts is extensive and picturesque. Under the north-eastern walls of the Fort is
a clump of cocoa-nut trees, where the "wa 'ful waddie"
is erected when required. A little beyond it is a lagoon,
or rather a hole of stagnant water, fit only for crocodiles, and well accounting for the unsanity of the
place. Looking eastward, about two and a-half miles
along the sandy tract which runs uninterrupted as far
as Sandy Bluff, the western point of the Volta's embouchure, we see a clump of trees on rising ground, denoting
the site of a well-known village, Labaddi, by the natives
called Lá, and the seat of the Great Fetish Lá-Kpá.
The people are fierce and fanatic, and show a disposition to be troublesome. The commandant had
pointed out to me, within the *enceinte* of St. James
Fort, the grave of a Labaddi fetishman, who had been
lately hung for a barbarous murder. The operation,
owing to the struggles of the patient, had been long and
severe, and the corpse had been buried and kept under
surveillance in James Fort, lest the people should believe in a local Resurrection. The fellow had declared
under the death-tree that he would return and haunt
the man who caused his destruction, and there are those
who believe that he has returned—once at least. Three
miles beyond Labaddi is a country whose prettiness is
difficult to describe; in a charming stretch of park land,
tapestried with grass, and relieved by clumps and scat-

tered trees, lies Tesha, or Tassy, properly Tesi, once guarded by Augustenborg, a Danish fort. But no more shall European eyes view these charming scenes from that *point de vue ;* the inexorable earthquake came, shook Christiansborg down to the rock, and breaking the head of an assistant-surgeon, compelled the garrison to camp out upon the plain.

Bidding adieu to this "Castle o' Balwearie," we walked to the north and entered a large building, not unworthy of comparison with the Commodore and the Big House. The owner was not at home, so we ascended the stairs, and sitting in the saloon, made ourselves comfortable with cocoa-nut water, "laced" with cognac. The house, which had all the qualifications for a Governor's palace, belonged to a Mr. Richter, a Danish merchant, one of the wealthiest. His portrait still hangs upon the wall, a kitcat, showing a mild and gentlemanly unmoustachioed face, supported by a swathe of muslin, around which was a high horse-collar, that formed part of a blue cloth coat, and brass buttons; as the intelligent reader will have anticipated, a bunch of seals hung from the fob. And yet this quiet old gentleman must have been a terrible Turk—skeletons have been found in his under-ground dungeons, and his name is like that of "Draque" in the New World.

After this we walked still further north for about half a mile, to the old Fredericksborg. On the road we passed a most forbidding-looking German missionary, who was driving before him a herd of little negroes, habited in

striped calico. Not a hand was raised to the hat: in a
country "croom" not a soul would have passed us without
a kindly greeting. It is one of the worst points in these
Christianisers that they are ever endeavouring to raise
man against man; their theory is "love one another,"
their practice is jealousy and hate. After a quarter of an
hour we came upon the outskirts of the place, where our
men began to tread cautiously. Serpents in exceptional
numbers come forth to bask in the burning sun, and
some are so full of fight, that, instead of running away,
they will, it is said, rise and fly at an intruder. The land
also is covered· with a tall growth of spear-grass, which
at once works its way through serge, and hooks its barbed
points into the flesh ; *crede experto,* and never travel in
the inner Gold Coast without antigropelos (is that rightly
spelt?) or top-boots. Frederiksborg contained only two
stone houses, but they were handsome and well built of
cut slabs. They are now uninhabitable; the material
has been filched by the garrison at Christiansborg, and a
wall half-pulled down in these regions is soon level with
the ground. It was not safe to enter the *débris;* we
therefore contented ourselves with an outside view. The
Gold Coast has already more remnants of antiquity than
the American Republic, where the Nauvoo Temple is the
only ruin between the Atlantic and the Pacific Oceans.

We then remounted our coach and six, and proceeded
at a spanking pace, which spoke well for the wind and
bottom of our cattle, towards James Town. The beauty
of the view, the contrast of ruin and perennial growth,

the terrible sereneness of Nature, unchanged, inexorable, so utterly beyond the emmets, black and white, that burrow and nest upon earth's surface, filled my mind with a sudden and profound sadness. Like the builders of these deserted homesteads, I have sought this coast, determined to show what can be effected by energy not undirected by intellect. And now, under that glowing sun, and with that ever-smiling prospect before me, a voice seems to say that all my efforts shall be vain, perhaps even vainer than theirs. I felt relieved when we had plunged into the alleys of James Town.

A succulent dinner prepared us for the ever-increasing *disette* of the A. S. S. We are now lapsing into tropical diet,—beef that looks like dead horse, fowls barely the size of pigeons, and turkeys whose breast-bones pierce through their skins. The gallant captain of the " Blackland " began to bang his pop-guns before the ground-nut soup was off the table—the only object of which proceeding was to double-shot a 24-pounder, in case he might be disposed, contrary to contract, to give us the slip. Nothing so unpleasant, however, occurred. We dined in peace ; and I bade adieu to my excellent host with a regret, lightened only by his promise to accompany me, at the first opportunity, to Kumasi, capital of Ashantee. A rush through the breakers, and a frantic paddling ;—in half an hour more we were on board.

The tribes of the eastern Gold Coast, Accras, Krobos, Krepis, Agotims, Awunahs, and Addahs, differ greatly

from the Akan, or western races, in *morale* and *physique*.
There the people are larger and finer men than on
the windward coast; I have never seen such tall, mus-
cular, and powerful negroes as at Addah. The women
are equally well-grown, and withal remarkably hairy.
Their complexion is rather a dark red than black.
Placed between the two great despotisms of Ashantee
and Dahomey, they are free even to anarchy, and though
fierce as *coqs de combat* they are disunited, or rather
hostile. According to Bowdich, the people of Accra,
like those of Mombas, rose up against the Portuguese,—
they had settled here in 1492, and were guilty of great
cruelties,—executed the governor and the garrison on
the spot where they still take the earth to rub on a
new-born child, in memory of the event. They show
considerable improvability. The children on the Gold
Coast are named after the days on which they are
born. Kwashi, or Sunday, our well-known Quashie;
Kajjo (Cudjoe), Kwábino, Kwáko (Quacco), Kwaw, Kofi,
and Kwamina, or Saturday. The same is the case in
Ashantee, where the king's last name is the birthday,
which necessarily returns once a week, and the first is
the title Sai or Osai, borne also by the principal nobles.
Here the first-born son is Tete, the corresponding
daughter Dede; the second pair are T*ete* masculine, and
Koko feminine; the third, Mesa and Mansa; fourth,
Anan and Tsotso; fifth, Anum and Manum; sixth,
Nsia and Sasa; seventh, Ason, masculine and feminine;
eighth, Botfe; ninth, Akron; tenth, Badu. The three

latter are common to both sexes.   With few exceptions,
they are taken from Oji numerals, as amongst the
Romans, Quintus, Decimus, &c.   European officials get
a native prenomen from the day on which they land;
the real *nomen* is some nickname, which the witty
knaves choose with peculiar felicity.   Thus an esteemed
friend of mine rejoices in the style and title of Kajjo
(Cudjoe) Frafra—"Monday Flatface."   They respect
Europeans beyond their fellows; there is no personal
risk in travelling through the wildest parts of the
country, and the people would willingly see our power
extended. ·In the smallest crooms, or country villages,
a house is cleared for the traveller, and in the larger
settlements there is always a guests' room set apart for
strangers.   Where the chief resides he will prepare an excellent breakfast of pepper-soup, kankie, and native stews,
and the table will be loaded with champagne and claret,
gin and cognac.   If they find any fault with our policy,
it is the lax hand with which the reins of government
are held; they respect the Dutch, because these treat
them with greater severity.   Under President Maclean
the Krobo troubles would have been settled in six weeks,
now they have lasted four years.*   These shortcomings

---

* Krobo is a protected territory, a mass of highlands about 10
miles west of the Volta, and 45 from its mouth.   There are two main
divisions of the mountain, eastward or near the river, including Kpong
(Pong) and Mámyá, is under the chief Odonko Azu.   Westward is
Yilau, the capital of the chief Ologu Patu.   The troubles began in
1858, with a turmoil between the rivals, arising, it is said, from a
dance at a festival, in which a neighbouring village interfered, and they

on our part are doubtless owing to the frequency of "gubernational changes," necessitated by the nature of the climate.*

It is not a little curious that on this coast several heathen tribes practise circumcision,† whilst their neigh-

are not settled. Odonko Azu and his principal chiefs were taken prisoners, and kept for nine months in captivity. They escaped from Christiansborg by the unjustifiable carelessness of the officer who had charge of them, and who escaped all injury concerning a transaction which would have cost him in India his commission.

* The following is a list of the governors and the acting governors up to the present time :—

1. Commander Worsley Hill, R.N., made in 1844. Lived to return to England.

2. Dr. Lilly (acting), 1845. Superseded.

3. Commander afterwards Sir William Winniett, 1846. Returned home.

4. J. C. Fitzpatrick, Esq., Jan. 1849. Superseded.

5. Sir William Winniett, Jan. 1850. Died at his post. He was one of the best of governors, and steadily pursued his favourite scheme of making the colony self-supporting, till it was cut short by death.

6. J. Bannerman, Esq. (acting), Oct. 1851. Superseded.

7. Major G. J. Hill, Dec. 1851. Returned to England.

8. J. C. Fitzpatrick, Esq. (acting), June 1853. Superseded.

9. B. G. Cruikshank, Esq. (acting), Aug. 1853. Ditto.

10. Major G. J. Hill, Feb. 1854. Returned home.

11. Henry Connor, Esq. (acting), Dec. 1854. Ditto.

12. Sir Benjamin C. C. Pine, March 1857. Ditto.

13. Col. Bird (acting), 14th April, 1858. Superseded.

14. E. B. Andrews, Esq., 20th April, 1860. Returned to England.

15. W. A. Ross, Esq. (acting), 14th April, 1862. Superseded.

16. Mr. Pine, 20th Sept., 1862. Still there.

Thus it will be seen there have been 16 governors, commanders-in-chief, and vice-admirals in 18 years ; and the almost total disorganisation of the colony, or rather the garrison—for colony it is not—can hardly be wondered at.

† The rite is called Keteafo, or shortening. It is practised by both

bours do not.   A similar circumstance of sporadicity in
the rite is noticed by a late traveller in the Lake Regions
of Central Africa.   Morality, despite the precaution,
appears to be at a low ebb.   The *morbus gallicum* and its
varieties are almost universal in some places, *delirium
tremens* is by no means rare, poisoning is common, and
abortion is generally resorted to, when a woman nursing,
contrary to the custom of the coast and the dictates
of Nature, is threatened with once more becoming a
mother.   There is no difficulty in procuring a temporary native wife, locally called a "consort," by the
week or "by the run," as it is termed.   The principal
diseases are dysentery, fever, and dracunculus.*   Owing

Gá and Adanme tribes, and is in the keep of a certain family, though
not directly connected with religion.   The boys—not the girls, as some
authors represent—are circumcised about 13 years of age.   The missionaries believe this to point out a Hebrew or a Moslem origin; I think
not.   They should bear in mind that the Jews derived the rite from
Egypt, that is to say Africa, where it had been used for ages im-
memorial, and that in the very depths of the Dark Continent, where
Jew or Arab never penetrated, it is practised under a variety of
modifications.

   * The *Vena Medinensis* was called from this coast the "Guinea
worm."   The natives deny that it is produced by drinking impure water,
and they are right.   It is doubtless the product of some animal which
deposits its ova in the skin.   The Gold Coast people say that it prefers
those with sweet flesh, avoiding acid and acrid skins.   The great proof
of its external origin is that the legs and feet are the parts most
affected, cases occur most frequently during the rains, when the lower
extremities are liable to be wetted, and those who sleep on the ground or
on mats are more liable to the disease than those who use cots.   The
people, according to Dr. Clarke, believe in a male and a female Guinea-
worm; the former is the thickness of a crow's quill, the latter of a
stout linen thread.   The only part of the body not liable to dracunculus

to the relaxing nature of the climate, unexciting life, un-
nutritious and unchanged dietary, unwholesome water,
and absence of cold weather, a man once "down"
remains so for a long time.

A rude native smith-craft is the favourite industry at
Accra, where zodiacal rings may be found upon every
one's finger. The gold is first melted and reduced to
proper size; it is polished by a mixture of nitrate of
potash, soda, and water, boiled together in a large
limpet shell (Achatina). The mould is cut out in
the soft part of the dead cuttle-fish, and the ring, when
made, is polished with borax and lime-juice, forming a
weak acid. They also make studs, watch-chains, and
other ornaments, which, to say the truth, are utterly
destitute of artistic beauty. The sonmesi, or black-
smith's shop, as in parts of Europe, is a weird place,
where thieves are detected, wounds healed, and so on.
The land is full of tales and legends of gold-dust and
doubloons buried under trees, and the people are
credulous upon this point as the Hindus.

The Accra English is superior to "Black-man's
mouf" generally. In addressing them it is not necessary to use, for comprehension, the horrid jargon of the
S'a Leone man or the Kruboy. There are, however,

---

is the hairy scalp. Some persons have been known to have 30 Guinea-
worms at the same time. The average time of cure is laid down at
three months, but if the worm be broken, it will last six. Lameness
is sometimes caused by it, the Tendo Achilles and other sinews becoming
permanently fixed and contracted by the inflammation.

many English expressions which no Englishman would at first understand. "Put him in log," means fasten his leg to a log; a "house master" is the proprietor of the house; to "put in fetish," is equivalent to our old excommunication; to "make customs," is to mourn for and wake the dead; and, to quote no more specimens of this quaint and queer old trading English, a "tail-girl" is a young woman whose only dress is a T-bandage, with a long extremity pendant behind. It is, say Europeans, as usual wrongly, a sign of fetish.* All such names of places as Accra or Jamestown, Dutch Accra, Christiansborg, Labaddi, Tassy, and others have their native duplicates in Gá, Kinká, Osu, Lá, and Tesi, and the names are mostly significant; the latter would mean, for instance, "stone land."

The languages, or rather dialects, spoken upon this leeward coast are, like the Fanti, of Hamitic origin, and cognate with the tongues of Ashantee, Dahomey, and Yoruba. As all the family, they have no peculiar character, and they were probably never written till Moslems and Europeans appeared. Of late years speeches, histories and legends, proverbs and tales, of which there are thousands, have been published by mis-

---

* Girls amongst the Accras and eastern tribes are not properly allowed to wear any cloth but a narrow strip. When marriageable, they are taken home, kept from work, highly fed, well dressed, and profusely ornamented. After many ceremonies, they are exhibited in the town by the advertisements of finery, dancing, and playing; thus it is pretty much the same in barbarous Medidsiasikpong (Africa) as in civilised England.

sionaries and others. So extensive is this literature, that the people have a name for a single branch, *e.g.*, Anansesem, or spider-stories.* This insect (*ananu*) plays a principal part in animal fables; it has a bad influence upon children sleeping in the same room, it speaks through the nose like a malignant ghost, and its hobbling gait, and other fancied peculiarities, are correctly imitated by the gestures of the relater.† On moonlight nights, when men, like other animals, feel gay and frisky, they sit in circles, and listen to these wild tales, which are recounted with an appropriateness of gesture, a power of imitation, and an amount of fun worthy of Mathews and Robson. The people are fond of singing, and compose extempore, whilst playing, dancing, or working,—the African can do nothing without a chant,—short songs, often highly satirical, and much relished by the listeners. The children in

---

* See a "Grammatical Sketch of the Akra or Ga Language," by the Rev. J. Zimmerman. Stuttgart : J. F. Steinkopf, 1858. It is a useful publication, but ineffably tedious, as such German "sketches" ever are, and not without a fair share of linguistic arrogance—another Teutonic peculiarity. The spelling is abominable, in parts unintelligible ; but what can be expected from Stuttgart English ?

† There is a large Arachnis upon this coast, which may become of commercial importance. It is black with a broad golden band down the back, and the web is not circular, but in long lines thrown from tree to tree, as if it did not prey upon flies. The thread is a deep yellow, stronger than silk, moreover a single insect easily produces more than the largest cocoon. There is no reason why this spider should not be naturalised in Europe, and though my specimens of spider-silk have hitherto been lost, I still hope to send home sufficient for a veil or a lace shawl.

the Krobo mission schools are said to have extemporised little hymns sung to very sweet native tunes. This shows linguistic powers which few European children possess. Perhaps, however,—I am not prepared to support the thesis,—precocity of intellect, as a rule, results in inferiority in later life.

There are two main languages upon the leeward coast, Gá proper, and its mother tongue, the Adánme ; the general language, however, is called the Gá family, and is spoken by about 100,000 or 120,000 out of 400,000 souls.

The Gá Akpa, or Gá Proper, is the speech of the sea-towns, from the Sakumofio or Secoom, west of Accra, to the town of Tesi, about five miles east of Christiansborg. It is spoken by about 40,000 or 50,000 people, and is bounded on the east by the Adánme, on the west by the Ojí of the Akan tribes.

The Adánme, or Adá-gbe, " voice," or " language of the 'Adá people," extends from Tesi on the west, eastwards, to the Volta ; northwards, its area includes the Krobo country and towns at the foot of the Aquapim mountains : to the north-east, on the Volta's left bank, it is spoken by three towns of the Agotim people. It is used by 50,000 or 60,000 souls; but, though more extensively spread, it is by no means so important a tongue as the Gá, which is the speech of tribes enjoying both moral and political supremacy. The missionaries found their assertion that the language of 'Adá is the mother dialect of the Gá, upon these reasons : it is harder and shorter, purer, and unmixed with Oji—*ergo,* it is more primitive. The difference is described to be as great as that between the Saxon, or High Deutsch, and the German of Switzerland or Suabia.

The missionaries thus briefly state the theology of the Gá tribes. God, called "Nyonmo" and other names, is the highest being, the only one, Creator of heaven and earth. The Fetishes (Wodsi) are spiritual and personal beings, either sub-deities who govern, or demons who disturb, the world. There are such Fetishes —*e.g.* earth, air, and sea—common to all men ; others, as rivers and trees, peculiar to distinct tribes, towns, families, or individuals. A person may possess a Fetish, or δαιμων, and is called Wontse, which is translated by Fetish man or priest. Or he may be possessed by some one, which possession is called Wonmomo, or Fetish-fury.* Besides these there are innumerable things sacred to, belonging to, or made effectual by a Fetish.† Such things are cords (wonkpai) tied about

---

* Cases of this affection are frequently seen even in the streets of Accra. If hysterics denoted possession in modern, as epilepsy did in olden times, what a high development of demonism Europe would present !

† This is poorly explained. The West Africans, like their brethren in the East, have evil ghosts and haunting evestra, which work themselves into the position of demons. Their various rites are intended to avert the harm which may be done to them by these Pepos or Mulungus, and perhaps to shift it upon their enemies. When the critical moment has arrived, the ghost is adjured by the Fetish-man to come forth from the possessed, and an article is named—a leopard's claw, peculiar beads, or a rag from the sick man's body nailed to what Europeans call the

the body or the house, teeth, skins, rings, chains, and
other similar articles, which gave rise to the absurd
belief that the African makes everything, even a rag or a
bit of glass, his god; and the missionaries assert that
"a comparison with religious things"—I presume that is
Stuttgart English for "relics"—"and superstitions in
the heart of Christendom, would have fully explained the
matter, without casting the Africans together, no more
with men, but with brutes." *

I am ready to concede that the people of the Gold
Coast have emerged from the utter atheism which
characterises the so-called Kafirs and other tribes of
Eastern Africa. But as yet their ideas are too vague,
and connected with material objects, to rank them with
deistical peoples. They have neither a personal and local
Deity like the heathens, nor the atomic gods of Epicurus.
"Nyonmo" is their word for the Almighty, but the
same means the sky, the rain, and even thunder and
lightning; thus they say God drizzles or God knocks,
i.e., it thunders. The missionaries explain this by the
people considering God to be the "spirit or soul of
heaven, or heaven the face or outward appearance of

"Devil's Tree,"—in which, if worn about the person, the haunter will
reside. It is technically called Kehi or Keti, a "chair" or "stool."—
See "Zanzibar and two Months in East Africa," Blackwood's Magazine,
February, 1858, pp. 220, 221.

* The preceding note will illustrate the difference between the two
absurdities, the African Fetish-chain and the European relic. It must
ever be borne in mind that the former is haunted by an evil influence,
whereas the latter carries with it a blessing.

God." This, however, sounds much like applying German metaphysics to the absurdities of heathen fable. When men associate in language and idea the material with the immaterial, the former is the real thing worshipped. Thus we also find "Sikpon," earth, considered a personage, and adored as well as "Nyonmo," sky, perhaps with more reason, as the former exists, whereas the latter does not. There is the usual African tradition to account for the superiority of Japhet over Ham. God, say the people, made two men, one white, the other black. To these he presented for choice a calabash full of writing materials, and another full of gold—it is needless to say how the selection was made, and what the results were. For this reason the people of the Gold Coast always consider the precious metal their peculiar property, and resent all attempts on the part of foreigners to work it without some royalty. And they mightily despise the mulatto—the "white blackman," they say, is silver and copper, not gold.

In the land of the Akan and Gá races there is a curious dawning of a belief, not in metempsychosis, but in transmigration, not of soul, but of life. The 'Kla or 'Kra* of a person is the principle which animated a

---

* The word is better known as Okla or Okra, which some authors write Occro or Ocro, and translate Fetish or Sanctified boy. It is a slave chosen by his master to be his companion in this life, and to be sacrificed over his grave, that he may accompany him, not in the world to come, but in that state in which man exists—if I may use the word —after death. Most Africans are real Swedenborgians as regards "continuation." I cannot but reflect with horror upon our future

relative or other person before dead. When parents have lost several children, they sometimes cast the body of the child that died last into the bush, any congenital deformity or defect in the next infant, which they believe to be the same child whose corpse is thrown away, is attributed to injuries received from wild beasts or other influences in the jungle. Hence, children born with supernumerary fingers or toes, have been strangled or burned alive. When one or two infants have been lost by death, they mark the next born by making one indelible cut on each cheek. If that fails, they make one vertical and three transverse incisions, and so on. The pregnant woman always visits the Fetish-priest, and asks the 'Kla of her child that is to be; the priest summons it, listens to its voice, and answers her question. A man's 'Kla is considered partly himself and partly not; it is a being like the demon of Socrates, who gives him good advice, and receives thanks and thank-offerings as a Fetish. Moreover, every person has two 'Kla, male and female, the former of a bad, the

prospects, if we are to be for ever liable to a summons from Mr. Hume, if we are doomed to communicate with friends by rapping, and if we are, like Shakspeare and Milton—in their ghostliness—to rap out the feeblest nonsense imaginable. *Revenants* in Africa are at any rate dreaded. In Europe the " spirit " becomes a thoroughly contemptible being, whose knuckles must supply the want of tongue, and who has apparently a mania for prophecy despite perpetual self-stultification.

After all, superstition, like happiness—of which perhaps it is a branch—is equally divided amongst men, and the civilised, generally, have not a tittle of right to deride the most ignorant or the most barbarous of their brethren.

latter of a good disposition. This recals to mind the Jewish and Muslem Kiram el Katibin, the two mysterious beings who, sitting upon man's right and left shoulder, whisper their virtuous or vicious suggestions into his ears. For El Islam, despite the sublimity of its truths and the higher law of unselfishness, which is its real spirit, has retained—as all of human must—some old leaven of superstition, directly derived from man's earliest dawn of belief in things unseen—Fetishism.

The Yara, or funeral customs of the Gold Coast are not less barbarous than those of their neighbours. They consist of washing, dressing, and providing necessaries for the corpse, which is then interred by the burial women, or "Klageweider" (Keeners). Weeping and lamentation, singing and dancing, all accompanied with copious rum drinking, are kept up sometimes for weeks together, and at certain stated periods are repeated. Formerly 'Klas and wives were slaughtered on the graves of people of importance — a custom almost universal amongst barbarians from the days of Homer downwards. So the ruffian Achilles, addressing the ghost of Patroclus, promises him that—

Δώδεκα μεν Τρώων μεγαθύμων υἔας ἐσθλους
Τους ἁμα σοι παντας πῦρ ἐσθίε.

It is now as difficult and dangerous a ceremony as a Sati in Hindostan; yet it is secretly practised whenever found possible.

The principal festival in the year is the Yams Custom, which Europeans call native, or black Christmas. It is

celebrated at the end of August or the beginning of
September, and at the same time their New Year's Day
occurs. The first eating of that vegetable is connected
with many ceremonies; the Fetish must begin, then
the king, and so on.* This is called Yereyelo. Follows Homowo, literally the "outcrying" or "mocking of
hunger;" a harvest-home, celebrated on the coast with
gun-firing, singing, dancing, music, eating, drinking,
and merrymaking, in the interior with the human sacrifices now familiar to Europe.

I proceed now to discuss the three great obstacles to
improvement on this coast,—the presence of the Dutch,
the peculiar style of taxation, and the use of a military
instead of a police corps.

The forts and stations of the British and Dutch govern-
ments closely intersect one another from Apollonia to
Accra, and this causes endless troubles. Our Nether-
landish neighbours have not much improved since the
days of Jonathan Swift; they are still—in Africa at
least—the most selfish and obstinate of colonists. If
the English place a duty of 2 to 2·50 per cent. upon
the invoice price of landed imports, the Dutch establish
a free port. Overtures have, it is said, been made to
give up our windward for their leeward territories;
though heavily in our debt, they have turned a deaf

* The custom has been explained as a hygienic measure ; and Fetish
law generally is resorted to when some measure beneficial to the commonwealth is to be strictly carried out ; such as the prohibition of
eating pork, cutting down trees, or collecting gold.

ear to all our proposals, and have even prepared to re-occupy their deserted posts. Whilst the English make 7000*l*. per annum, and expend nearly 30,000*l*. a year—a little more than the Maynooth grant—upon their possessions in this quarter of the world, the Dutch, defended by the moral influence of our squadron and troops, require only two officers, commanding 200 negroes in "blue baft," and including their civil department, maintain themselves for 6000*l*. to 8000*l*. per annum. Free trade would evidently not dislodge them.

At Accra, where the British Jamestown and the Dutch Kinka are dovetailed into one another, only an imaginary line separating St. George and Tricolor, the workings of the two systems become apparent. After Dutch Accra had been captured by us, the Netherlands were allowed as a favour to rebuild their factory, but not to appoint a commandant. When old Mr. Hanson, originally Hansen, a Danish mulatto, who at one time had charge of both factories, died, our rivals began to exercise jurisdiction, and we "let it slide." At present they claim almost all Jamestown, except a few houses near the fort, because Kajjo, the king of Dutch Accra, is king over the kinglets of Gá, Osu, Krobo, Akim, and Aquapim. They keep a commandant, a sergeant, and four to six men. English ships are charged 3*l*., and foreign bottoms 3*l*. 18*s*. 4*d*. for wharfage at British Accra. The Dutch take 12*l*., but there is neither wharfage due nor import-tax; ships therefore naturally prefer the Dutch roads.* Our merchants are charged even for imported machinery, here more wanted than in America : it is a suicidal policy.† Of course they are unable to compete with their Dutch rivals, whose free ports are frequented by Akims, Ashantees, and the inland tribes generally, who would rather travel a month than waste a dollar. They have even rejected all proposals to co-operate in the imposition of duties, and they are contented to remain a thorn in our side, and to collect occasionally a heavy fine, as $12,000, which was lately imposed on the occasion of a manslaughter.

Were the Dutch to be removed, even at the price of 100,000*l.* our deficit of 23,000*l.* would soon change to a surplus of 50,000*l.* The duties on rum, spirits, arms, and ammunition might gradually be raised to 50 per cent. : a measure a hundredfold more beneficial to the natives than even to ourselves, and gold exploiting might commence in real earnest.

And now for taxation. In April, 1852, a council of British officials and native chiefs was assembled at Cape Coast Castle, to " take into consideration the advantages

---

* The Dutch roads, however, are not so safe as the English. South of Fort James, according to the Directory, there are eight or nine fathoms water with very soft clay, which requires a light anchor, as a heavy one could not be drawn up from the ground.

† There are men who object to using labour-saving contrivances in Africa, because these would foster the indolence of the people ; the idea appears to me exceedingly absurd. Methinks it is better that men who will not work much, should work a little rather than not work at all. But possibly this is not an "elevated view " of the case.

which the country derives from the protection afforded
to it by Her Majesty's Government, by submitting, from
time to time, to pay such taxes as may be determined on
by the majority of chiefs assembled in council with His
Excellency the Governor." Hence the poll-tax on families, of which the " house-master," or the pater-familias,
was made responsible for each member—after the fashion
of Mahommed Ali in Egypt. It began with the Good
Intentions which are said to pave the way to a Certain
Place. "The revenue derived from the tax, after paying
the stipends of the chiefs, and other expenses attending
its collection, shall be devoted to the public good, in the
education of the people, in the general improvement and
extension of the judicial system, in affording greater
facilities of internal communication, in increased medical
aid, and in such other measures of improvement and
utility as the state of the social progress may render
necessary." A poll-tax collector at Christiansborg informed Mr. Consul Hutchinson ("Impressions of
Western Africa"), that he had received in 1855 about
337 ounces of gold, at the rate of a shilling a head, and
that in the Akim districts the people would pay more if
they received for it value in protection or information.

As our fine words buttered no parsnips, the natives
began to murmur. In the earlier Italian railways there
was little to gain because of the impossibility of finding an
honest *employé*. So on the Gold Coast, the poll-tax was
collected, but instead of going to judges, schoolmasters,
and roads, it restored bankrupts to wealth and position.

Letters upon the poll-tax and taxation in general appeared in the local papers, headed with the safe but not novel reflection on the part of a writer, who signs himself, "Yours obediently, an African," "a nation is only the aggregate reflex of 'the man's a man,' the minutial agglomeration of a nation." It—"Lord Grey's pet tax"—is described to be an "oppressive, invidious and ill-managed impost, signifying thraldom and oppression, causing children to be sold or pawned." As regards the promises of the local Government, they are stated to be "false and deceptive as moonshine." The consequence, however, of the "dwarfish demon convention" was that the native towns of Christiansborg, Labaddi and Tesi were demolished by bombardment in 1854; that in 1855 Accra was threatened with the same fate, because she also would not pay; that in 1856 a commissioner, sent to inquire into the state of affairs, reported that although Kajjo (Cudjoe), King of Kinka, and his subject chiefs, were all loyally disposed towards our Government, they would not pay poll-tax, and that in 1857 a mob plundered the French factory at James Town.

However presumptuous may be the supposition, one is almost disposed to think that our Wilsons and Laings, so admirable in the algebra, have not mastered the elemental arithmetic, of tax-gathering. Mr. Wilson left his home, after enunciating in many a postprandial oration the farcical sentiment, that "what is good for England is good for the world." Mad as a hatter, he gave India an income-tax and a flood of paper money.

No subaltern in a native corps would have made such a blunder. Peace to his manes, for

> " To his natal shore,
> Enriched with knowledge, he returned no more,"

dying just in time to escape seeing the failure he had made.

The true art of taxation, allow me to say, is honestly to speak out what you want, and less to regard the theoretical excellence of the tax than the practice which the people have had in paying it. For taxation shows the genius of a nation quite as much as its ballads : what men have imposed upon themselves, they will prefer to the political economy of the stranger, however cunning. There are those who like indirect taxation, which to others seems the dealing of a vampire that sucks your blood whilst you sleep. In my humble opinion, the main, if not the only, injury which American Secession has done to the world, is that it has prevented the trial on a gigantic scale—in a highly civilised and commercial people—of direct, and the total abolition of all other, imposts. In the meantime the items must be sedulously studied and subjected to the local popular system. The Hindu, I have said before, will contribute half his income in the familiar forms of poll-tax, succession dues,"benevolences," and local imposts raised in the Pergunnahs. The African will pay fifty or perhaps cent. per cent. upon imports of arms and ammunition, salt and tobacco, whilst rum is his incense and his eucharist, without which the necessaries of worship cannot be supplied to him.

To conclude with police considerations. I will not insult the reader's understanding by treating upon the inapplicability of soldiers to police purposes under an English Government. Two companies of any West Indian regiment would be amply sufficient for the general military wants of a colony like this; besides which, the police corps might be armed, drilled, and trained to working the guns of the several forts. The present expense of the Gold Coast Artillery, including all charges, cannot be less than 20,000*l.* per annum. For this we have seventeen European officers and 300 men, who are worse than useless for protection duties. Being regularly enlisted soldiers, it is difficult to punish them, and the jealousy of rival departments has enabled them to show a bold front to the Colonial Secretary, who on this coast stands next in rank to the Governor. The officers who fail in securing civil appointments naturally prefer a sick certificate for England or Tenerife to living a wretched, starveling life at Cape Coast Castle or Accra; and though the warrant under which they obtain promotion requires them to serve three years on the Gold Coast, it is generally considered enough to have served for that period in the Gold Coast Corps.

The following distribution of, and estimate for, a police corps of 355 officers and men was drawn up by a friend whose judgment and experience justify my introducing it to the public.

The distribution would be as follows :—

Stations.	Head Constbls.	Constables.	Sub-constables.	Policemen.
1 Dixcove	1	1	3	30
2 Cape Coast Castle .	1	2	6	90
3 Annamaboo . . .	1	1	3	20
4 Winnebah . . .	0	4	6	25
5 Accra, &c.	1	3	6	90
6 Addah	1	4	6	35
Total . . .	5	15	30	290-300

A grand total of 355.*

At five of these stations—Cape Coast Castle does not
require one—there would be commandants acting as
magistrates and collectors of customs. Addah has been
included, because it now equals Whydah in slave expor-
tations. There are shiploads hid in the town, even
within cannon-shot of our cruisers. It is a pity that this
fine port is not taken up by some English company; it
is the only point from which a future can be expected.

The annual estimate for the commandants and the
police force would be as follows :—

	£	s.	d.
1 Chief Civil Commissioner, including table allowance .	600	0	0
Ditto, ordinary travelling allowance . . .	150	0	0
5 Commandants (each 350*l.* per annum) . . .	1750	0	0
Ditto, ordinary travelling allowance (each 75*l.*)	375	0	0
5 Head Constables (each 30*l.* per annum) . .	150	0	0
15 Constables (each 18*l.*)	270	0	0
30 Sub-Constables (each 13*l.* 10*s.*) ˙ ; . .	405	0	0
300 Policemen (each 9*l.*)	2700	0	0
Clothing, at rate of three suits each man .	1000	0	0
House rent	100	0	0
Total	£7500	0	0

* In these sickly climates there must always be supernumeraries : I
allow, therefore, five extra officers and ten men.

For complete efficiency this police corps should be placed entirely under the civil power, which has ample jurisdiction to punish those offences—plundering the natives and living upon threats of accusation—which are now committed with all impunity on the outstations. The five commandants should transmit monthly estimates for the pay of their establishments to the Chief Civil Commissioner; the latter, after checking and signing them, would forward them to the Colonial Secretary, who, in his turn, would submit them to the Governor. This functionary should not, of course, be commander of the corps, as he is Commander-in-chief of the Coast, but he should be charged with drawing up a code of regulations for the force.

I am certain that by such happy changes order would soon grow out of confusion and misrule upon the Gold Coast.

*   *   *   *   *   *

At Accra we left our Spaniard, who, suffering severely from sea-sickness, appeared nothing loth to quit us. He was a gentleman fond of his bed and also of his Madeiran wicker-work arm-chair. He read a little; but, when excited, which was rare, he would declaim loudly against the practice of "lecture" as worthless, touching the main enjoyments of human life—eating, drinking, visiting friends, and attending the theatre. According to him the *summum bonum* of human life was to lie upon his back smoking cigarettes and looking at the moon or at all the stars. He once, but only once, gathered energy to sermon me upon the subject of over-curiosity. I had remarked that the thermometer stood unusually high. "To me," quoth Don ——, "it is hot when I am hot; it is cold when my body feels cold. What do I want to know more?" Perhaps that Don was not so far wrong.

As the "Blackland" steamed along the coast we could see a long succession of open grassy savannahs backed by dark curtains of bush and forest, and many a tongue of land, forming by its gentle rise little valleys which would become swamps during the rains. About three to four miles beyond Tesi, on the eastern end of a little ledge, stands a small black boulder—Greenwich Rock : it transported us in thought far enough north of the Gold Coast. During the night we passed Cape St. Paul's, the western boundary of that ill-omened region the Bight of Benin. And whilst sleep sealed our eyes, the indefatigable ship—how superior is her continual diligence to the best of travelling even by railroad—was bearing us past the infamous regions of Little Popo, Great Popo, and Whydah.

CHAPTER X.

A DAY AT LAGOS,

WHERE

"In July you must die,
August go you must ;
In September remember,
October it's all over."

Old Rhyme describing Rainy Season.

FORMERLY the great centres of the export slave trade from Africa were these three :—

1st. The Semiticised and often Moslem negroes, extending from the Gambia and Senegal, as far inland as Takrur or Sokotu. They were principally Mandengas, Jolofs, and that pseudo-punic tribe of Africa whom men have derived from the lost Cyrenaican Psylli or Psulloi, and called by a variety of names Peul, Púlá, Puloh, Fulá, Phúlá, Pulbe or Fulbe, Felatah and Felláni.* All these people drove the heathen negroes of the Sudam to the coast, although they did not sell or enslave their brother religionists.

* M. Koelle ("Polyglotta Africana") calls the language Pulo, and the people Pula, which is properly an adjective, "yellow," or "brown." Fulbe is the plural of Pulo ; Fuláni is the plural of the Hausa name Fuládsi, and Fulatah is Bornuese. The original home of this people is said to have been near Futa Toro, and in the eighteenth century they moved to Hausa, and built Sokotu.

2nd. The despotisms of Ashantee and Dahomey, Yoruba and Benin, large pagan states, which maintained standing armies well armed and disciplined, and used chiefly for the purpose of forays and slave commanders; all, except Dahomey, have fallen from their former power, and Dahomey will, by self-exhaustion, if not by a foreign blow, follow their example.

3rd, and last. The whole coast about the mouth of the Kongo River, one of the great African four, the others being the Nile, the Niger, and the Zambezi, and without any exception the most neglected. Known to the natives as‧ the Zaire, its name is to be traced, I believe, in Claudius Claudianus, himself an African, born at Alexandria, and who wrote about A.D. 400.

> " *Gir*, ditissimus amnis
> Æthiopium simili mentitus gurgite Nilum."
>> De Laudib. Stilich. lib. i. v. 252.

For dit- some read not- —" notissimus,"—but not so correctly; at any rate, it is far from being the superlative of " notus " now. The name again occurs in a Latin form.

> " Domitorque ferarum
> Guirræus, qui vasta colit sub rupibus antra,
> Qui ramos ebeni, qui dentes vellit eburnos."
>> Idyl. iv. v. 20.

And be it further remarked that the Zaire still gives the best ebony—a tree which does not extend beyond 4° north latitude : thus rendering the common theory which identifies it with the Νίγειρ or Νίγιρ, untenable— that river notoriously wanting ebony. Pliny (Nat. Hist.

lib. v. 10) makes the Nile, after an underground march of twenty days, spring again from the source called Nigris, and form the limit between Africa and Ethiopia. He adds : "cui quoque etiamnum Giris, ut ante, nominatus per aliquot millia, et in totum Homero Ægyptus aliisque Triton." A modern .writer identifies Giris or Gir, with Wed Mzi or Djidi of the Sahara, but nothing can be more unsatisfactory than his remarks.* The negroes on this part of the coast are savage and degraded, and, as in northern Guinea, are settled in small independent communities of 1000 to 5000 bodies. The first treaty between England and Portugal restricted our squadron to the north of the equator, and enabled the export trade, assisted by an admirable waterway, to recruit itself from the very heart of the continent.

These three great centres are now reduced to two, which, separated by a long interval, are incapable of mutual support. The first is the Bight of Benin, still

---

* I allude to the Rev. Mr. Tristram's "Great Sahara," appendix I., p. 262. Barbarously as eastern languages are treated, the exceeding cruelty of this gentleman's practice beats belief. Who could believe that Beni Yssou could mean Beni Isa, sons of Jesus ? When the Arab "looked sadly disconcerted" at his hearer's want of sympathy, and his assurance that *Inglez mafish hinné arrhua*—"that the English never would come here"—the expression of countenance must have been that of utter despair. What would even an English guide understand by "English there is none eer (for here) I go away ? " And so throughout the book, the names of animals : *e.g.*, Nemeur, for Nimr, a leopard ; and el Guett' há, for Katá, a sand-grouse ; and hundreds of other horrors are perpetually offending ears and eyes. Had not the reverend gentleman a spare hour for submitting his cacography to any one who has read Arabic for a few months ?

appropriately termed the Slave Coast, and extending from the Cape of St. Paul's to the Nun outlet of the Niger, a coastal length of 350 miles. The root of the evil lies between Little Popo and Whydah, which are separated by not more than thirty miles. Public attention has been drawn to it, and it is now in a fair way of being extirpated. During the last year steps have been taken in the right direction, the bombardment of Porto Novo, and the annexation of Lagos with its old dependency, Badagry. The next year, I hope, will see the submission or the capture of Whydah and the two Popos.* The Kongo river still awaits modern exploration, and the difficulties thrown in the way are so great, that without assistance from Government it would be vain to attempt it.

The slave coast offers peculiar facilities for shipping cargoes. Low, marshy and malarious, it could hardly be held by foreign garrisons. The dreadful surf which beats upon the shore defends the barracoons from land

---

* At Great Popo there is an inlet which leads up the lagoon to Whydah direct. If it be proved—the point, however, is not yet settled—that there is a beach between the Victoria Lagoon of Lagos and the water that passes Whydah, this entrance, distant only ten hours from the great slave market, will be the best line of attack.

Whydah is perfectly protected from the sea by a strip of land half a mile broad, and it lies north of the lagoon, which is here four feet deep. It is within shot. The people show as Fetish a cannon-ball, fired by a British cruiser seventeen to eighteen years ago, and embedded in earth. Shipping must lie outside the sand-bank when the surf is very heavy. The town is described as poor and squalid, and the people suffer from intermittent fever.

attack, and can be safely braved in canoes only. The bush and jungle conceal the movements of those on land, and the succession of lagoons forming natural canals along the seaboard, enables the trader in human flesh and blood to ship his cargo where and when least expected. The French and English, Spaniards, Portuguese, and Brazilians established themselves there in old times, and by rich presents persuaded the " tyrant " of Dahomey to supply them with the fruits of his annual raids. In 1842, Captain Broadhead saw "thirteen vessels lying in the roads of Whydah at one time." Of late years the vigilance of the cruisers has tended materially to check the traffic, and nothing can now be done openly. Still shipments take place. But lately a large vessel, the " African," carrying 500 to 700 negroes, ran the gauntlet of the coast-guard, passing the African steam-ship " Armenian." Her captain politely raised his hat to his agent, M. Soarez, who, the late Lt. Hollingworth told me, was so delighted with the

---

* Her Majesty's Commissary Judge, Havana, writing in February, 1861 (Class A. "Correspondence with the British Commissioners "), estimates that the safety of one adventure amply repays the loss of ten empty, or five full ships. These are the figures :—

Cost of vessel and provisions . . .	$25,000
Cost of 500 negroes at $50 . . .	25,000
Ten per cent. mortality	2,500
Wages and presents to master and crew .	30,000
Expenses of landing 450 slaves, at $120 each	54,000
Total	$136,500

present prospect of 100,000*l.*,* the normal profit of a full cargo, that he offered to "stand champagne" to all on board.

The English and Dutch had formerly fortified factories, which still await our return to Whydah. Some years ago the French restored their establishment, and used it as a palm-oil store. They have missionaries there,* and according to our Frenchmen, the King of

Brought forward	.	$136,500
Add one year's interest, ten per cent. .	.	$13,650
Total expenditure	.	$150,150
Sale of 450 slaves, at $1200 a head .	.	$540,000
Profit on the adventure . .	.	$389,850

The loss of an empty slaver is estimated at $27,500 only, the cost of the ship, provisions, and interest thereon ; the wages, &c., being contingent on success. If the negroes are on board, it would amount only to $55,000, These figures perfectly account for the continuance and persistency of the traffic.

* "Annales d'Afrique," Nos. XI. and XII., of November and December, 1861.—Lettre de M. François Borghero, supérieur de la Mission de Dahomey, à M. Planque, supérieur du Séminaire des Missions Africaines, à Lyon. "Whydah, 28th April, 1861.—We learn that the reverend fathers were well received by what they call the Jevoghan (Yavogar) of Whydah, and celebrated their first mass on the 21st inst., in the long-abandoned Portuguese Fort, before a hundred men." An old steeple with two bells, and ornamented statuettes in the sanctuary, showed that Fetishism had not quite won the day. The people of Whydah were estimated at 20,000, of whom 300 have been baptised ; but they live in utter ignorance, ' Quomodo audient sine predicante ? ' The snake-worship is well described, and it will be remarked that whilst the men of Whydah worship, those of France curse 'l'abominable animal.' May not the poor serpent, when he speaks, exclaim with Friday—

' Je n'ai mérité
Ni cet excès d'hommage ni cette indignité.'

Dahomey had sent two of his "sons" * for education to Marseilles.

About midday on Saturday, the 21st of September, we were off Porto Novo, sixty miles distant from Lagos, and separated from the sea by the lagoon and sandbank. This town and the little province around are called "Ajáshi:" properly speaking "Newport" is the name of a factory, barracoon, and village built upon the shore by the celebrated, or rather the notorious successor of Da Souza, who died in 1849, the Brazilian, Domingo José Martinez, who used to receive at times from the King of Dahomey a present of 600 negroes, a bakshish worth a "plum." The town itself was founded on the south-east frontier of Dahomey, by Huenbomu, a younger brother of Takudumu, the first recognised Dahomian King, and the

At Great Popo, we are told, the boa, like the Irish pig, is allowed to eat small children. Poison is said to be profusely used. Of the "roi Badou"—*i.e.*, Badohong, the present king—a great truth is told, "Quand nous lui demanderons de permettre à ses sujets d'embrasser le Christianisme, nous aurons autour lui les féticheurs, *devant lesquels le roi lui-même doit se courber.*" The King of Dahomey has no more power to prevent human sacrifice than the Prince of Wales has to forbid morning service on Sunday. These customs are admirably described by the superior as "usages consacrés par des siècles, fondés sur des croyances réligieuses, et soutenus par un puissant hiérarchie—d'imposteurs." On the other hand, the number of victims is ridiculously estimated to be 3000, from which at least one 0 ought to be struck off.

* The King's sons, in African parlance, probably means some of his slavelings. In Europe they will doubtless become "African princes" by the blessings of the black skin. The "princess" is also an institution on this coast : two friends of mine have married princesses.

capturer of Abomey, who loved the senior as little as
such junior usually does. It is distinctly despotic,
orderly, and subordinate, even when surrounded by the
turbulent semi-republics of Lagos, Badagry, and others.
The people prostrate themselves in the streets when the
messenger, bearing the king's cane, passes. The land
is of fine soil, rich, loamy, and well filled for agriculture,
and the natives are fond of fishing and trade. The
population is estimated at 12,000 to 20,000. It was
attacked by Abeokuta in 1839; and in 1840 the Eglas
again assaulted Adu, a Popo town, tributary to Porto
Novo, and lying on the road between the two capitals.
Hence the old enmity between Dahomey and Abeokuta,
which ten years afterwards resulted in the destruction
of Ishagga, and in the crucifixion of the S'a Leone missionary Doherty.

The coast about Porto Novo showed a strip of land,
backed by a thick bush. A single house or barracoon,
with a flag flying, against the higher lands, marks the
situation; and the town, which is some distance from the
beach, is denoted by a grove of tall trees, appearing
through an opening in the foreground.

It is said that Great Britain is never without her little
war; as far as West Africa is concerned, this dictum is
certainly true. And why not? She can no more expect
to be at peace with her thousand neighbours, than a man
of 50,000*l.* per annum in landed property, to be without a dispute or lawsuit. These little wars cost less
than Aldershotts, and are ten times better schools for

soldiering; the military nations of Europe, France and
Russia, always keep up their tilting-lists, Africa and the
Caucasus.   These considerations arise from the view
of a place where lately was fought the battle of Porto
Novo.   It happened after this wise : —

The late lamented Mr. Foote, Her Majesty's consul at
Lagos, in February, 1861, visited, in H.M.'s S. tender
"Brune," Lieutenant Stokes, R.N., commanding, the
town of Porto Novo, where oil belonging to British subjects had been seized.   The object of the consul was to
add a few more stringent clauses to the already-existing
treaty of 1852; but the King "Soji," backed, it is supposed, by Dahomey, behaved with great insolence, refusing to come on board or to treat upon the subject of
slavery, which ten years before he had stipulated to abolish.
After some *va-et-vient*, "Brune" fired a shot, first over,
then into, the town.   The people replying with energy,
the crew of Krumen sensibly betook themselves to the
coal-bunks and behind the paddle-boxes, whence they
were with difficulty removed by their energetic commander Lieutenant Stokes.   The gun-boat found it
necessary to retire upon Badagry.   The Porto Novians,
after African fashion, danced, drank, sang out their
"strong names," and swore that if she ever appeared
again, they would convert her into a war-canoe for their
king.   The European population of Lagos, mostly
veteran slave-traders, condemned by hard times to such
grovelling work as selling palm-oil, exulted over our
retreat, and fondly hoped to see the operation repeated.

From Badagry, Mr. Consul Foote, who could obtain no concessions from the king, applied for assistance to a "big brother," and this time things were better arranged. On the 26th April, Commodore Edmonstone, of H.M.S. "Arrogant," then commanding the West African squadron, accompanied by Mr. Foote in the "Brune," and followed by the hired steamer "Fideliter"—the "Bloodhound," drawing too much water, found herself aground—proceeded with two divisions, of five boats each, armed with howitzers and rockets, up the Ossa River, or Victoria Lagoon, whose mouth is nearly opposite Lagos. Above Badagry they were stopped by a barrier composed of two rows of stakes and floating green islets between—showing that the Porto Novians had not been idle. The work of six weeks, however, was demolished by the "Fideliter" and the boats in two hours and a half, and the fragments threatened to injure the navigation of the lagoon. Then appeared the vaunted Isso canoes, and their fighting owners, who, according to the croakers of Lagos, were to eat up the Englishmen for breakfast. Each long, narrow, and shallow barque carries two fellows, one paddling or poling with a spear, the other occupied with a bunch of shillelaghs and javelins, that are placed at his feet. They hurl the club, and when the adversary "ducks" his head, he is then transfixed with the assagai. The Isso are a tribe subject to Dahomey, and are located to the west of Porto Novo. They acted as a contingent against Badagry in 1851—1854. They are a fierce and

lawless brood, originally, it is said, fugitives from Dahomey, and joined by kindred ruffians, the kidnappers and
pirates of the coast.   Their villages, which are mostly
on the sea-side of the Lagoon, are described as embryo
Venices, huts of bamboo and grass thatch, perched upon
poles four to five feet above the level of the tide, and
forming a boat-house below.   They are remarkable for
nothing but their teeth, blackened with snuff.   They act
as fishermen in peaceful times, and, like the Arabs of
maritime Oman, they plunder when they can.   A few
rockets easily dispersed these braves, who preferred
paddling into the rushy shore to standing up in the open.

At 7 A.M. on the next day the flotilla reached Porto
Novo, which had never seen such an armada before.
After a hot, but harmless, shower of balls, which all
dropped short, both divisions replied with shot, shell,
and rocket, doing awful damage.   The Porto Novians,
especially the Moslems, were no cowards; there were
men in white turbans—here called " white-cap chiefs "—
but I believe no Russians amongst them ; they fought only
too well, willing to be slain in the vain hope of killing
some whites.   The brave Isso retired beyond gunshot, and
philosophically contemplated the disasters of their friends.
After an hour or so, the town and the king's palace
were on fire, the flames rising high.   Captain Raby, V.C.,
of H.M.S. " Alecto," and commanding one of the boat
divisions, landed in his gig, with two men, and spiking
a gun, caused it to explode, singeing his face.   It is
curious how often experienced men will try this green

trick : when you nail up a gun, please do not place your
nose within a few inches of the touch-hole. The Commodore then sent, under command of Captain M'Arthur,
of the Marines, and A. T. Jones, of the "2nd West"—
a promising young officer, now, unhappily, deceased—
some fifty blue-jackets and small-arms men, to fire the
well-built houses which were still standing. This proceeding, on his part, won for Captain Edmonstone the
lasting resentment of certain Europeans at Lagos, who
deferred a proposed picnic, because they wanted no such
smashing guest.

After this harmless little brush, the heroes, fasting, re-
embarked at 11.30 A.M., to became heroes full. Dinner
being over, at the German hour of 1 P.M., and fresh
ammunition having been served out to all hands, Captain
Raby's division formed in line within twenty yards and
abreast of a point where the natives had made an am-
buscade. These negro strategists expected us to land,
another verdant trick, often tried by Englishmen, even
where guns can be brought to bear. An action which
begins with artillery, which proceeds with infantry
charges, and which ends with a rush of cavalry, has
never been unsuccessful in India. Victory under such
circumstances being inevitable, we can hardly wonder
that the plan has not been universally adopted, common
sense being uncommon. Finding themselves discovered,
the natives, who were in force, kept up a brisk fire from
the reeds and rushes. They were soon mowed down by a
feu d'enfer of grape and musketry, case and canister,

rockets and howitzer-shells, and many fugitives were killed whilst retreating. Captains Raby, M'Arthur, and Jones then landed, spiked another gun, carried off a white flag ; and the West Indian shot with his revolver the only man killed in the hand-to-hand fight. The firing afterwards became desultory, and when the place was destroyed,—even the metal heads of the king's canes were melted,—the flotilla disappeared, and the men rejoined their ships outside Lagos bar. Thus ended the battle of Porto Novo, in which we lost but one seaman, of the "Alecto," killed by a shot through the brain, and had five or six others slightly wounded. The number of the enemy was estimated at 10,000 well-armed soldiery, and their casualties, which were ridiculously exaggerated, were doubtless numerous : an officer present in the action old me that he had counted twenty bodies lying within a few yards. It was rumoured that a white man was found amongst the slain, and that another had been seen directing the operations of the enemy. 'Perhaps these might have been Brazilian mulattos, whom the King of Dahomey—it will be observed, that this great bugbear never killed a white man, nor did his father—occasionally orders to his capital rolled up like cigars, or, if recalcitrant, walking barefooted. But there is no folly which excited eyes will not see, and cause others to see, and of late years it has been the fashion to report the presence of hostile white men from China to Morocco. On the 13th June the king reluctantly signed the treaty permitting to all Porto Novians free trade with the

British. The town people were, as usual, middlemen
between the merchant and the producer, consequently
they are ever opposed to extension of traffic. Old Soji's
palace had suffered the most, and all his property was
lost. His people confessed to having had a bellyful,—
the African, unlike the Asiatic, will own to a "thrashing,"
—although he says, with some truth, that the English
cannot fight on shore, and promised to be for the future
a good boy. Mr. M'Coskry, Acting-Governor of Lagos,
kindly promised to procure for him new sticks. The destruction of this noted slave depôt has already borne fruit.
Other towns—for instance, Adu—wavering between Dahomey and Lagos—they are all nests of slavery—now
request permission to "come in," and treaties are being
prepared for them. Thus, by degrees, the black Spartans
of "Dah's Belly" will be shut out from the sea,—the
greatest calamity that can befal an African power,—and
will be broken up by foreign attack, or will abandon
their annual breaches of the peace. Finally, the gallant
members of the little expedition had the high honour of
being grossly abused by a portion of the Manchester
press, from which officers and gentlemen have nought to
fear save praise.

Mr. Consul Foote died before he heard of this
"crowning mercy." A most energetic and useful
officer, he had seen long and hard service in the tropics,
India, China, the Mosquito Coast, Greytown, and Salvador. After passing—

"Per varios casus, par tot discrimina rerum,"—

he was appointed to the Slave Coast in September, 1860, on the death of Mr. Consul Brand. Lagos seems to claim a good man and true every year. Like many others that have passed safely through pestilential lands, he imagined himself fever-proof. He who wants to live, so far from waxing careless, will gain at every step increased respect for the sun, the dews, and the night breeze. Mr. Foote entered without delay upon a course of bodily and mental work, most trying to new comers in these regions. The "Brune" grounding in the lagoon above Lagos, he set out, though unwell, in an open canoe to reach his post in time for writing by mail, exposed himself to the night air and the rain, and sank under a complication of fever and dysentery on the 17th May, 1861.

Mr. Foote was presently followed by Captain Jones, of whom more at a future time.

Along the straight dull coast we steamed eighteen miles, from Porto Novo to Badagry. By lagoon it is reckoned forty, and may be done in six to eight hours. Travellers usually avoid the sun by starting at night, and thus lose the beautiful scenery of the Ossa River, or Victoria Lagoon. This breakwater is one of the many that extend from the Volta, the westerly end of the Bight of Benin, to the Bonny River, in the Bight of Biafra. They form a huge reservoir, into which the streams from the upper country discharge themselves, and during the rains they burst through the sand embankments, which at other seasons defend them from the Atlantic. As a rule, they are river-like streams, rather brackish, and therefore garnished with mangroves. In places there are depressions in the land, causing widenings of the bed, with larger lakes; such are, beginning from the west, the Avon waters, the Denham waters,* and the Ikoradu, so called from a mart north of Lagos, and by us corrupted into Cradoo. I reserve a more particular description of these lagoon streams till we find ourselves upon one of them.

There is no landmark to show the position of Badagry save the mound which appears as a pyramidal clump of bushy trees. There were but three canoes and three merchant ships lying off this once lively, now dull and deserted place, where the landing is detestable and where the surf never seems to rest. It was founded by refugee Popos in 1727, when the King of Dahomey had conquered Whydah. It is therefore not directly mentioned by Bosman, who also ignores Dahomey,† whilst he dwells at length upon Fida, our Whydah, and upon Ardra, which Mr. Lamb calls Ardah. It was the landing-

---

* Captain Denham, who gave his name to one lagoon, in chart xv. places on it " City of Styche," probably a mistake, or a misprint for Stakes (fishing).

† In Letter twenty, however, Bosman speaks of a " potent kingdom farther inland," which uses certain customs of war well-known in Abyssinia, and " strikes such a terror into all the circumjacent negroes, that they can scarcely hear it mentioned without trembling ; and they tell a thousand strange things of them." This must be Dahomey, whose king Takudumu, Chief of Fohi, captured the present capital about A.D. 1700. The intercourse between the Dahomians and Europeans is supposed to have begun in 1724.

place of the two Landers, who, in 1830, made their
celebrated discovery of the Niger's true mouth.   The
picturesque narrative of what reception they met there,
of King Adooly, of the tetrarchy of Mr. Hutton of Cape
Coast Castle, and of the terrible Fetish tree, which caused
the traveller to fall senseless into the arms of "Jowdie,
his faithful slave," are fresh in the memory of this generation.   Presently Badagry became so unsafe for Europeans, and kidnapping in the sandy streets,—when the
victim was noiselessly seized, gagged, or garotted, and
carried off to the canoe,—became so common, that in
1843 Mr. President Maclean and Commodore Foote
thought right to hoist the British flag for the protection
of the English.   About that time Badagry became a
large missionary establishment ; and in 1861 it under-
went the fate of Lagos at the hands of

> The web-footed lion that swims ev'ry sea.

*   *   *   *   *

Evening placed us in the roads of Lagos.   A mild
evening : the wind was hushed, and the heat oppressive.
It is said to average 10° Fah. hotter at this place than
in Lagos town.   Against the purple-black surface of the
eastern sky the bar was smoking forth a white vapour,
as if afraid to break, and we could hear from afar the
muffled roar of the sullen surf.   We and our fellow-
sufferers, six or seven merchantmen, lay broadside on,
with a monotonous ceaseless roll, which seems to drive
comfort out of a ship.   Many must pass months in
this most unpleasant swing-swong till they have taken

in cargo. We are lying in the French roads,* four miles eastward of the entrance or English roads. As night was near, not a canoe would put off from the shore. I spent my *soirée* in the study of bars.

The bar is a notable formation in Western, as in Eastern Africa. It seems placed by Nature—one of her many contrivances—to favour the pristine barbarity of the people. Many rivers are provided with one, the chief exceptions being the Gambia, the Rokel, the Cacheo, the Rio Grande, and the Kongo. A majestic stream like the latter will not tolerate such puny obstacles; others, on the other hand, like all the rivers between the Brass and the New Calabar branches of the Niger, are rendered useless by them. In riverless places, like Cape Coast Castle and Accra, the surf is sometimes dreadful as the upright walls of water on the Cornish coast, but it will not pile up a bar.

The favourite seat of a bar is at the mouth of a river or an outfall which is liable to be much swollen by the rains. From the inland comes a mass of matter mechanically suspended, and sometimes floating islets, which will trip vessels from their anchors; when the emission meets the tide, deposition takes place, and goes on increasing. Some bars are therefore of mud; others, where the sea has greater power, are sand hard as stone. The heaviness of the ocean swell is attributed by certain writers to distant storms; others, especially Captain Fish-

---

* These names are now obsolete on the coast.

bourne, to a "want of hydrostatic equilibrium." As the
sun shifts its place, the rarefaction of the atmosphere
produces an ascending and relieving movement, inducing
"a wave from the point of greatest to that of least
pressure." This hypothesis is favoured by the general
belief in the exceptional warmth of the air about Lagos
roadstead, but it is hardly borne out by the generality of
the coast. The seas at S'a Leone are worst between
December and April; in the Bights of Benin and Biafra,
from April or May to October or November; and in Ascension from February till June; at the latter place the
rollers cease in September, and in December they come
from the north.

Lagos bar—or rather bars, for, as usual, there are two,
an outer and an inner, the latter of which is little
feared—is the best study on this part of the coast,
with the exception, perhaps, of Benin. It is the bugbear
of the Bights, and really dangerous. The average deaths,
not including whites, are fourteen per annum; in 1858
there were forty-five casualties. This year nine were
drowned in three months; amongst them, an English-
woman, the wife of a merchant-captain, who preferred
risking his life to paying a few dollars by steamer.
Escapes are rare, and yet the Acting-Governor has been
capsized in it three times. The principal danger to a
strong swimmer is the shark. It is not every squalus
nor every tiger that will attack a man. I have seen a
sailor picked up unhurt from amongst a school of them
in Suez harbour. This plague is not—others say rarely

—found in the waters off Badagry and Porto Novo. But in places like the sacred Dwarka in Western India, where dead Hindu pilgrims are cast into the bay, and at Lagos, where the corpses of slaves are allowed to float down the river, the shark never hesitates to seize a live man. The crocodile and alligator are to be beaten off by gouging or " purring," as the Lancashire inventors of a practice, supposed to be purely Transatlantic, call the operation. The shark, here at least, is far more terrible ; even when he wriggles himself up to the beach sand, apparently for the purpose of scratching off parasites, all the people run away from the glare of his dull, ferocious, pale-blue eye, whilst the beast, as if conscious of power, never thinks of retiring till the desideratum has been leisurely completed. Few men survive a shark bite, and when seized, they usually lose their hands by snatching mechanically at the limb first hurt. I spare the reader some horrid cases which have come under my immediate notice. There is a small blue shark, which, when young, is eaten by the people. They do not, however, like the Arabs of Sur and Maskat, relish a tough old patriarch, whose taste is something between bull beef and tunny. To end with the shark, this evil might be diminished by spearing and poisoning the animals, and especially by rendering it penal to throw a corpse—night is the favourite time—into the Ossa. And the little " Advance " has already, it is said, done much towards frightening them from their haunts.

Lagos is the largest permanent break in the long line

of coast between the Volta and the Benin Rivers, and
the greater part of the waters collected during the rains
find their way in a tumultuous current through the sand-
spit that parts the lagoon from the Atlantic.   The
safest months are December, January, and February,
when at times it is smooth as glass.   The most dangerous are those of the rainy season—it begins to be
bad in March, and it wages war from May to October.
The epochs of the vernal and autumnal equinoxes according to some, the days when the mail arrives according to others, are the worst; some declare that the
new moon, others that the moon at her full and change,
exasperates the bar.   One may always expect bad bars
during the violent rains in June, July, and August, when
the struggle between the inner inundation and the outer
surf is tremendous, closing ingress and egress sometimes,
though rarely, for a fortnight.   High tide is the safest
time for attempting passage; then half-tide; and the
worst of all is low water.   "The African Pilot"* reckons
the rise of the tide five to six feet at the full and
change on the bar, and says that within the river one foot
must be allowed in the dry and three in the rainy season.   The people of Lagos assert that three to four feet
is nearer the truth, and that there is little difference
between the inside and the outside of the bar.   The
capricious and treacherous rollers will curl in five
fathoms and break in three, and even four fathoms, on

* P. 175.

the radius of a mile from the middle of the entrance. The height of the wave may be fifteen feet when the surf is bad, and it breaks when perhaps you least expect it. The shifting sand of the bar is ever changing place and dimensions. On the 26th July H.M.S. "Prometheus" found but eleven feet under her bow off the eastern spit, where she had most unadvisedly been run : to-day we hear that there are eighteen feet, and that the spit has been nearly washed away; and this time next year there will be a hollow, bounded by a dwarf sandbank upon the place where the good old ship was reported to have broken her back. For the same reason the breadth of the entrance is ever varying; the "African Directory (1855)" gives it from 500 to 600 yards; the "African Pilot (1856)," half a mile from point to point. When I first saw it the width was not more than half a mile, but soon afterwards it greatly increased. The length is calculated to be 300 yards. The outer or sea bar is separated from the inner by a distance of six cables; both are of the hardest sand.

Across this pleasant formation there are three high ways:—the canoe passage, which hugs Le Greslie or the eastern point; it is very dangerous, but sometimes practicable when the other entrances are not. The perils of the Calemars or Raz de Marée, however, are greatly increased by the strong easterly current, which often carries small craft down the dangerous and inhospitable coast. The boat or central passage comes next: many accidents have happened from the use of gigs

manned by Krumen, who drop their oars and are ready
to spring on board the moment there is a chance of
swamping. Why the Masoolah surf-boats used at Madras are not introduced here I puzzle my brains to
conceive. Large ships lay at Beecroft or the western
point abreast, and then turning to the north-north-east,
make for the entrance. The landmarks, however, of
course change with the bar every year, and without a
pilot no one but a madman or those interested in barra-
try would attempt to run in. Usually the entrances are
two, the ship or western, and the canoe or eastern
passage.

No one seems to visit Lagos for the first time without
planning a breakwater. About three years ago an
American company proposed to make floating break-
waters, upon the condition of receiving the harbour dues
for twenty years; Jonathan, however, was refused. But
as from Ningo on the Gold Coast to Camaroons, there
is hardly a pebble upon the loose sands, and no stone
for many miles inland, the construction will probably
keep till the wealth of the place enables it to afford a
floating work. It is dangerous to meddle with such
formations. About 1856, a little iron steamer from
Benin sank whilst attempting to raise the guns which
had been thrown overboard by Her Majesty's steam-sloop
"Hecate;" and the bar, it is said, became worse in consequence. Walling the sides, especially the eastern, with
a small "stone fleet," might be tried, but the measure
would probably do no good; the outpour, strengthened

by narrowing the mouth, would soon cut a new channel. The experiment, tried at Charleston, is said to have improved the passages there: here there are other forces at work. Some have tried landing upon other parts of the coast, but they have generally fared worse from the heavy breakers on the shore; consequently, the bar has become a necessary calamity. The merchants of Lagos were much pleased when they heard that a harbourmaster had been appointed, expecting to see buoys laid down; at the end of the year, however, they had to congratulate themselves only upon a perch stuck in the sands of Beecroft Point. Loath, however, to break through a time-honoured custom, I venture to propose a system of "camels," by which the violence of the breakers would be greatly broken. We turned in early, hoping that the morrow would not prove a rainy day.

Betimes on Sunday morning we were visited by the "Advance," an iron steamer owned by Mr. McCoskry, now acting as Governor. Built as a tug for the Clyde, her tonnage is 120 tons, she draws six feet, with horse power variously estimated at 80 to 160, and her cost was 6000*l*. The mails no longer require to be headed up, an operation which recalls to mind the now classical English pipe-office. She is nearly lost about once a year, and the engineers cannot be kept alive even by drink. Still she makes shift to ply for papers and cargo whilst other vessels cannot. The tender "Brune" lost her funnel shortly after our departure; the "Handy" is pronounced unhandy to cross.

the bar; and the "Investigator" does not appear to relish the process of investigating. Besides which, the former is a "screw," and when these craft show their stern keels to the sky, the violent jerk almost always injures the gear. So the stout "Advance" is really in advance of Admiralty ships, and is a great boon to those who visit Lagos.

After breakfast the consul and I prepared to land by the ship passage. The "Advance" steamed steadily on, under the hands of two helmsmen; the wheel is on the bridge, the favourite station for travellers who do not like the look of the sea from the quarter deck. After getting the direction and breasting the smooth waters outside, we prepared for the run in. This time the much-dreaded bar disappointed me; on certain subsequent occasions it did not. The rapids of the St. Lawrence must be grand enough in an Indian "birch," which shows the wonderful ridge of waters cylindrically piled up in the centre of the stream. Nothing can be tamer when looked down upon from the first floor of a large floating-house river-steamer. I can imagine their emotion—men with a triple coat of brass round their præcordia—who first attempted this bar in the dingy of a caravel or in a wretched cutter. Indeed, even from the vantage ground of the bridge, where we stood high raised to see and sketch, we looked up as it were at the light-green foam-fringed waves swelling, rising, and towering like a concave wall about to tumble in and poop us, whilst the send of the break drove us forward as if

lifted in strong men's arms, and required all the force of
the helmsmen to prevent, as the seas combed under the
quarter, the little steamer broaching broadside on—
the great danger when crossing a bar. The background
to this fierce ocean was a black and lowering surface of
younger breakers, the nearer rushing like the waters
above Niagara to the fray, and the more distant sub-
siding into the surface of a horizon where the slaty
heavens mingled with the leaden-coloured sea.

After shuddering and staggering over the first bar,
which is about 900 feet long, and enduring the normal
break of three—which may be thirty—seas, the brave
little " Advance " fell into deep water, four fathoms or
so, and I did not condescend to sketch the second or
inner, which outlies the entrance. And now the settlement, before veiled by smokes, as fogs in these regions
are called, began to appear. Upon Le Greslie, or
Eastern Point, a low sandy formation, capped with
stunted bush and bearing a few palms, stood a few out
factories, looking very like negro barracoons. Twenty years
ago boats floated over this Clifton of the Slave Coast. A
flag was hoisted to inform the town that the bar was
practicable. Two tide gauges had been set up, one at
Le Greslie Point, the other inside the river, opposite
the house of a M. Carrena, that the maximum rise might
be indicated by signal. As we passed Beecroft Point,
where curlews and plovers rose screaming wildly, and
passed alongside of the shrimp stakes, the town came
up to full view. It was a striking illustration of the

difference between the pro-pyroskaphian and the epi-pyroskaphian settlement; no fort, no gothic hall, no big house, nothing but the plain bungalow built for an inn, not for a house. Here, as at Zanzibar, flagging appeared to be the custom; every factory flies a bit of bunting, and some fly two.

The site of the town, four miles from the entrance, is detestable; unfortunately, there is no better within many a league. It occupies the western side of an islet about three miles and a half long from north-east to south-west, by one broad from north to south; it is formed by two offsets from the Ikoradu (Cradoo) coast, namely, the Ossa River, opposite, and Five Cowrie Creek behind the settlement.

The first aspect is as if a hole had been hollowed out in the original mangrove forest that skirts the waters, where bush and dense jungle, garnished with many a spreading tree, tall palms, and matted mass of fetid verdure rise in terrible profusion around. The soil is sandy, and in parts there are depressions which the rains convert into black and muddy ponds; the ground, however, is somewhat higher in the interior, where the race-course lies. The gap of the Ossa or Badagry Lagoon, is nearly opposite the town; and on the other side there is low, swampy ground, a clay formation, which retains the water, and which adds something more to the evils of the place. The thin line of European buildings that occupy the best sites, fronting the water, are, first, the French *comptoir*, prettily surrounded with gardens; then a large pretentious building, white and light yellow, lately raised by M. Carrena, a Sardinian merchant—it is said to be already decaying; then the Wesleyan Mission-house; the Hamburghers' factory; the Wesleyan chapel, with about five times its fair amount of ground; the British Consulate, like that at Fernando Po, a corrugated iron coffin or plank-lined morgue, containing a dead consul once a year; the Church Mission-house, whose overgrown compound caused such pretty squabbles in days gone by, and which, between whiles, served as a church; another Sardinian factory; a tall whitewashed and slated house, built by Mr. McCoskry; and at the furthest end, another establishment of Hamburghers, who at present have more than their share of the local commerce : these are the only salient points of the scene. They are interspersed with tenements of less pretensions, " *suam quisque domum spatio circumdat,*" a custom derived by the Anglo-Indians through the England and the Germany of Tacitus's day; and the thin line is backed by a large native town, imperceptible from the sea, and mainly fronting the Ikoradu Lake. Some of the houses extend their grounds to the back, and the cumbered sands are alive with impurities; the Acting Governor, however, has wisely determined to have one decent walk. He persevered in clearing a broad line along the water, fitted for riding or driving, despite the insolent opposition of sundry liberated or rather licensed Africans. One fellow who calls himself Captain, upon the strength of having bought a condemned hull, has gone so far as to drive away the workmen : he has been threatened with a special constable, in the shape of a fighting doctor, and as usual with these people, who have got to produce their John Hampden, he subsided. The only ships inside the bar are H.M.S. " Prometheus,"— *Prometheus Vinctus* now—the tender, " Brune," and a small Hanoverian steamer. The two former are required to defend the new occupants, and the town is in a considerable state of excitement.

For Lagos was born in the British family, the youngest member of her colonies, on the 6th day of August, A.D. 1861. • Commander Bedingfeld, R.N., after a hard bumping on the bar off the east spit, had by high direction entered into a palaver with Docemo, King of Lagos, and after " jamming heads"—excuse the phrase, but the " Captain," as the earnest and Rev. M. Monk* insists upon calling him *usque ad nauseam*, piques himself exceedingly upon a very moderate knowledge of the coast—informed him that permanent occupation (a nicer word than annexation) was determined upon, and that he, Docemo, was to be pensioned, and become one of the many kings lately "retired from business." That barbarous person, curious to say, was not delighted by the intelligence. In fact, he made some difficulties. He proposed to meet Her Majesty's consul, " the Captain," and all the British merchants at Palma, a French station some thirty miles east of Lagos, where

---

* See prolegomena to Dr. Livingstone's letters, and ask " the Captain " what he thinks of them.

he probably intended to give them something more than
a bit of his mind. They politely declined a trip so far
out of the range of the Promethean fire. The caboceers
and chiefs also demurred, and foreseeing an embargo
upon their bribes and presents, waxed surly. At the
bottom of the discontent were the liberated Africans,—

"Sharp rogues all, both great and small,"—

as the Cape Coast Castle song hath it. The worst by far
were the S'a Leonites ; they were in debt to the natives,
and debt under English is a very different thing from debt
under native rule. Besides which, all of them had slaves,
and most of them, when occasion served, were slave-
dealers. Mr. Consul Foote, shortly after his arrival,
had summoned before him some of these pets of philanthropy. When the nice point of domestic slavery was
mooted, and they were asked touching their nationality,
the popular answer declared King Docemo of Lagos and
the Alake of Abeokuta to be their sovereigns. They
at once began to make mischief at another of our pets,
Abeokuta—how can learned Professor Kingsley in
" Westward Ho ! " call it " Christian Abeokuta," when
it numbers barely one " professor " to 500 heathen ?
They hinted, not obscurely, that wherever an Englishman plants his foot—the people of Scinde said the same
when they pelted off Sir Alexander Burnes—he makes
the land his own. Abeokuta took the hint with all the
readiness of the suspicious African. Distant but sixty
miles from the sea, she once wanted a road ; presently

she became curiously incurious about any communication more direct than the winding but defensible river; and she ended next year by violently expelling a British vice-consul, threatening if he followed the example of "Monsieur Qui-se-Leve," that they would "burn the house about his ears," or its African equivalent.

So matters ran till the 5th of August, when a flag-staff was slipped and rigged near the British consulate, and Commander Bedingfield landed with his marines. A crowd of people and some chiefs were assembled at the palaver-house. The king, when civilly asked to sign away his kingdom, consented and refused, as the negro will, in the same breath. On the next day he affixed his mark, for of course he cannot write; and there is no African king who will not, in full view of a gallon of rum, "put his name for book," no matter what that book may be, provided that he ignores its contents. In so doing he of course concludes that a bit of paper so easily cut through with a pair of scissors can have no binding force, and a few hours afterwards he will tell you that he can tear it to pieces. Without awaiting, however, the ceremony of signature, possession, nine-tenths of the law, was at once entered upon. The "Captain" read out an English proclamation, very intelligible to the natives, confirming "the cession of Lagos and its dependencies"—a pleasantly vague frontier. Then followed a touching scene. One Union Jack was hoisted in the town, another on the beach. 'Prometheus Vinctus" saluted with twenty-one guns.

The marines presented arms, three hundred fetish, or sanctified boys, as the convert people call them, sang a hymn, headed by their missionaries. It was not

" Dies iræ, dies illa, &c."

And as we Englishmen must celebrate every event with a dinner—I believe that if London were to follow Lisbon's suit, Londoners would dine together amongst the ruins of " Willis's " or the " Tavern "—forty-four Oyibos, Europeans, and Africo-Europeans, officials and merchants, sat down to meat upon the quarter-deck of the " Prometheus," and by their brilliant speeches and loyal toasts added, as the phrase is, *éclat* to the great event. Thus Lagos—rose.*

* The following is the official announcement of

THE CESSION OF LAGOS.

" Foreign-Office, Sept. 19.

"Earl Russell, Her Majesty's Principal Secretary of State for Foreign Affairs, has received a despatch from Mr. McCoskry, the Acting British Consul at Lagos, dated the 7th of August, enclosing a treaty concluded by him and Commander Bedingfeld, R.N., commanding Her Majesty's sloop 'Prometheus,' with Docemo, King of Lagos, for the cession of the isle and port of Lagos to Her Majesty. The treaty is as follows :—

" 'Treaty between Norman H. Bedingfeld, Commander of Her Majesty's sloop " Prometheus," and senior officer of the Bights Division, and William McCoskry, Esq., Her Britannic Majesty's Acting Consul, on the part of Her Majesty the Queen of Great Britain, and Docemo, King of Lagos, on the part of himself and chiefs.

" ' ARTICLE I.

" ' In order that the Queen of England may be the better enabled to assist, defend, and protect the inhabitants of Lagos, and to put an end to the slave-trade in this and the neighbouring countries, and to prevent the destructive wars so frequently undertaken by Dahomey and

King Docemo was persuaded, on the next day, by a
guard of marines, who grounded arms with a most
ominous rattling in his presence, to be duly mediatised.
He was also assured of a pension amounting to something less than 2000*l.* per annum. This sum is

others for the capture of slaves, I, Docemo, do, with the consent and
advice of my council, give, transfer, and by these presents grant and
confirm, unto the Queen of Great Britain, her heirs and successors, for
ever, the port and island of Lagos, with all the rights, profits, territories, and appurtenances whatsoever thereunto belonging, and as well
the profits and revenue, as the direct, full, and absolute dominion and
sovereignty of the said port, island, and premises, with all the royal-
ties thereof, freely, fully, entirely, and absolutely. I do also covenant
and grant that the quiet and peaceable possession thereof shall, with all
possible speed, be freely and effectually delivered to the Queen of Great
Britain, or such person as Her Majesty shall thereunto appoint, for her
use in the performance of this grant ; the inhabitants of the said
island and territories, as the Queen's subjects, and under her sovereignty, crown, jurisdiction, and government, being still suffered to
live there.

" 'ARTICLE II.

" 'Docemo will be allowed the use of the title of king, in its usual
African signification, and will be permitted to decide disputes between
natives of Lagos, with their consent, subject to appeal to British laws.

" 'ARTICLE III.

" ' In the transfer of lands the stamp of Docemo affixed to the document will be proof that there are no other native claims upon it ; and
for this purpose he will be permitted to use it as hitherto.

" ' In consideration of the cession, as before mentioned, of the port
and island and territories of Lagos, the representatives of the Queen of
Great Britain do promise, subject to the approval of Her Majesty, that
Docemo shall receive an annual pension from the Queen of Great Britain
equal to the net revenue hitherto annually received by him : such
pension to be paid at such periods and in such mode as may hereafter
be determined.

[Here follow the signatures.]

" 'Lagos, Aug. 6.' "

equivalent to his annual revenue, but it is subject to
revision. He ungratefully forwarded, *on dit*, an expos-
tulation to Europe; so did his chiefs. On the other
hand, the merchants of all nations were highly pleased
with the result. Thirteen of them, foreigners as well as
Britishers, signed a petition praying the "Prometheus"
to remain inside the bar, for the protection of English
life and property. She was nothing loath: her copper
had been scraped off, her deck had an interesting but
suspicious convexity about the middle region, and the
divers brought up some tubes nearly sixteen inches
long, with which the *Teredo navalis* had lined his dwel-
ling-place. She was subsequently reported not sea-
worthy; an obstinate man, Mr. Master Scudamore,
thought otherwise, and she reached home safely, where
she will die of a respectable old age. The "Captain"
took a lively interest in the baby colony, and perhaps
cherished an idea that his various merits might promote him to the proud position of being its nurse.
Calumny declared him guilty of a plebiscite, but I can
hardly believe this. He was disappointed in this *coup
d'état*, but he was duly promoted, as every man who
loses, or who nearly loses, his ship ought to be. A
French naval officer presently entered the harbour, and
when he heard of the cession, departed in a pet, which
was not *raisonnable*. The decennial treaty with our old
rivals, in which the "high contracting powers" pledged
themselves to refrain from picking and stealing further
territory in Africa, expired in 1855. The Gaul will, it

is reported, lay *main forte* upon the Benin River.
Tant mieux! The civilisation of the coast, or rather its
redemption from a worse state than the merest savagery,
can be effected only by its passing into the hands of
Europe. Japhet must not only live in the huts of
Ham, he must gird his loins for a harder task than he
has ever dreamed of in the idle tents of his brother
Shem.

Before landing at the dwarf pier in front of the Consulate—no mean precaution where the crocodiles are so
uncommonly " spry,"—we accompanied poor Hollingworth on ·board the " Prometheus," for a visit of
ceremony. We were received with that condescension
which sits so gracefully upon the shoulders of Greatness,
and hurried off to the shore. The ship had enjoyed
remarkably good health under an experienced and active
surgeon ; only three men out of her hundred whites had
died during the last year. We little guessed, however,
that of those sturdy fellows only sixteen would be left—
all the rest had been carried off by fever (twenty actual
deaths), or had been sent sick to Ascension—at the end
of March, in four months. Thus, after long indemnity,
she eventually found herself no exception to the rule of
the Coffin squadron. Mr. McCoskry was fortunately at
home, and I had the pleasure of making an acquaintance
which I hope may become a friendship.

After an excellent dinner, in which the presence of
palm-oil chop argued the old " African," I was shown a
symbolical letter, which, on August 24th, had found its

way from Dr. Baikie's camp at Mount Patta, near
Laird's Town, and opposite Igbebe, at the confluence of
the Kwara and the Binue.* This style of writing has
been described by Mr. Crowther as being common on
the Lower Niger, and Miss Barber, of the "Coral
Fund," has obliged the public with a sketch of it. It
is inferior to the Mexican symbols, the rudest form of
correspondence, showing a great gulf between the
African mind and that of the lowest Asiatic. The
"letter" consisted of two pockets from an old pair of
Calico pantaloons, and a "flap," from which the buttons had been removed; it was empty, and significant
enough. There was a little bundle of twine, European
and native wound together, to show that white and
black, even in their poverty, were not divided. An Arab
Taawiz, or talisman—here barbarously called Grigri,—
hinted that the bearer was a Moslem, and little pellets
of paper containing writing, and whipped round with

---

* I would propose to brother Fellows that the river below the confluence retain the classical name, Niger—Joliba is Park's name for the
upper waters, and its extension; that the western influent be called, as
by the Kanuri named, Kwara; and the eastern, Binue, a term well
known to the Hausas. "Chadda," founded only upon the misconception that the stream drains Lake Chad, should be formally dismissed
from our vocabulary. Lake Chad, like the Tanganyika, the Caspian,
and many others, receives many tributaries, and sends forth none—evaporation does all the work of drainage. This is hard to instil into the
mind of the theorist, who determines, despite the direct evidence of
Lake Chad, that all such formations, if undrained, must be salt. The
natives have, of course, no general name for the stream, save Water,
or Great Water, which, as usual in such cases, varies with every dialect.

string, showed that the path was dangerous. Three broken cowries, loose and scattered, insinuated that the sooner a fresh supply was sent the better; half a Malaguetta pepper, or Cardamom, gave comfort, showing that the traveller's heart was still warm. The thing had all the savage ingenuity that goes to making an assagai and a war-club. Whilst upon this subject it may be as well to state that the confluence of the Kwara and the Binue is distant only twenty days of quiet marching from Lagos, without running the risk of climate and the now hostile villages that fringe the banks below the apex of the Delta. It will be the favourite route of explorers. At present the Egbas are fighting one of those ridiculous fights—they almost put to shame the earlier Yankee battles—with the Ibadans, their northern neighbours.

The afternoon was devoted to inspecting the town, which is native to the last degree. Is is said to be five miles in circumference, and containing 30,000 inhabitants, of whom 700 to 800 are Moslems. Like the people of Badagry and Porto Novo, the Lagosans are of Popo race, and many of them are originally Beninese. The eastern is here the " west end," and there have been the usual quarrels for frontage, each factory and mission-house wishing to secure for itself as much, and to leave its neighbour as little, as possible. The native town, which is divided into sundry quarters, Okofája, Obebowo, Offí, and Eggá, which contains the palace of the now destitute Docemo, is to the west of the

"Garden Reach," and stretches over the interior of the island. The streets want only straightening, widening, draining, and cleaning. Ibrahim Pasha's excellent means of confiscating a house that would not keep its environs clean should be applied here at once. There are irregular buildings—intended for market-places, and called, I suppose, squares,—into which the narrow lanes abut; they are dotted with giant heaps of muck and mixen, and in hot weather wooden pattens are required. The houses, not the factories, are of switch or puddled clay, built in courses, and fished out of the river: apparently they are all roof, a monstrous thatch, like that of Madagascar, making, as it were, the brim too broad for the face. These things burn like tinder when Shango the fire-god pays a visit to Lagos; so fast, in fact, that little harm is done to the interior. Europeans prefer, for the same reason, slates and tiles. Even the garden-walls must be protected by a weather-thatch of palm-leaves, or they would be washed away. Everything has the squalid, unclean look of an idle people, and what can be expected from men to whom Pomona has been so indecently kind, whose bread and butter, whose wine and oil, grow for them in the trees around? The redeeming feature was the mixture of country with town, the *vestigia ruris*, which all admire. Like Jericho, it is a city of palms: the cocoa grows almost in the salt water; the broad-leaved bread-fruit, introduced from the far Polynesian lands, has taken root like an indigen; and in the branches of the papaw nestle amadavats, orioles, and

brilliant palm-birds. The people struck me as being of a
lower caste than those of the Gold Coast, more approaching the typical genuine nigger of the Southern republic.
They suffer much from cutaneous complaints, krakra,
yaws (*frambœsia*), lepra, elephantiasis, and a phagœdenic
ulcer common at Fernando Po, and from which even Europeans have no immunity.* The other diseases are fever,
dysentery and dracunculus; they have not yet had an
attack of true vomito, but it is gradually on its way down
from S'a Leone. This yellow fever differs but little in
quality from a violent bilious remittent, and the peculiar
feature from which it derives its Spanish name, seldom
appears till dissolution approaches : the course is rapid,
fever, delirium, cramp, convulsions, emetism, death. At
times the place becomes a charnel-house. This mangy
people appeared to me a merry race of pagans; even at
this early hour I saw a man sitting upon the little raised
step of clay, the East Indian chabutarah, and shamelessly
making himself drunk with "hashish." The instrument is a calabash with tubes and clay chillam or head,
and, as usual, the leaf is inhaled through water. This
smoking Diamba or Liamba, as the local European
name is, is a practice which has probably spread from
the East — Egypt and her neighbours. There are
travellers who contend that in Western Africa cannabis,

---

* It is often fatal. Amputation must be resorted to, and the patient,
who has probably suffered from dysentery and other debilitating diseases,
cannot support the shock : sometimes there is an oozing of blood from
the cut bone.

or bhang, never grows wild, and that, like the lotus, it is an exotic which, without much care, would die out. This may be true touching the lands about the Gaboon River's mouth ; the plant, however, is certainly an indigene of the African continent,—the Moroccans have their fasukh, the Hottentots their dakha, the Eastern people, mbangí, and the Western, diámbá.

An unexpected pleasure was in store for me. Lagos contains, as has been said, some 800 Moslems, though not yet 2000, as it is reported. Though few, they have already risen to political importance; in 1851 our bravest and most active opponents were those wearing turbans. Among these are occasionally found "white Arabs." One had lately died at Ekpe, a village on the " Cradoo waters," where the ex-king Kosoko, lives, and, though a pagan, affects the faith. I was presently visited by the Shaykh Ali bin Mohammed El Mekkáwi. The reverend man was fair of face, but no Meccan; he called himself a Maliki, as indeed are most Moslems in this part of El Islam, and I guessed him to be a Morocco pilgrim, travelling in the odour of sanctity. He was accompanied by the Kazi Mohammed Ghana, a tall and sturdy Hausa negro, with his soot-black face curiously gashed and scarred : he appeared to me an honest man and good Moslem. The dignitaries were accompanied by a mob of men in loose trousers, which distinguished them from the pagan crowd ; one of them, by trade a tailor, had learned to speak Portuguese in the Brazils.

Very delightful was this meeting of Moslem brethren,

and we took "sweet counsel" together, as the missionaries say. The Shaykh Ali had wandered from Tripoli southwards, knew Bornu, Sokotu, Hausa, and Adamáwá—the latter only by name, and he seemed to have suffered but little from a long journey, of which he spoke favourably. He wished me to return with him, and promised me safe conduct. I refused, with a tightening of the heart, a little alleviated, however, by the hope that Fate may spare me to march at some future day through Central Africa homewards. And in that hope I purified my property by giving the Zakat, or legal alms, to the holy man, who palpably could not read nor write, but who audibly informed his followers that "this bondsman" is intimately acquainted with *kull'ilm*—*omnis res scibilis.*

The Shaykh then presented me with a handful of kola nuts,* which have been called the African coffee. They are the local " chaw," the succedaneum for tobacco, betel nut, mastick, and sweet earth. The tree, which grows everywhere in the damp and wooded regions of the tropical seaboard, and on the islands of West Africa (where, however, the people ignore its use), is a kind of sterculia, in leaf not unlike the magnolia, but a stunted scrubby tree ; the flower is small and white, with a polypetalous corolla, and the fruit is a large pod, like a mis-shapen cucumber. The edible parts are the five or six beans, which are compared to Brazilian nuts, and to horse

---

* The Kola (Sterculia acuminata) is written in many ways—Cola, Colat, Khola, Gura, Goora, and Gooroo ; the latter three are the names given by the older travellers.

chestnuts; they are covered with a pure white placenta, which must be removed with the finger-nails, and then appears the rosy pink skin—some varieties are yellow—which gradually becomes rusty by exposure to the air. The nut is easily divided into several, generally four sections, of which one is eaten at a time. The taste is a pleasant bitter, and somewhat astringent. Water drunk "upon it," as the phrase is, becomes, even if before offensive, exceptionally sweet. It must be a fine tonic in these relaxing climates. I am not aware of an extract having been made from it: if not, it would be as well to try. Travellers use it to quiet the sensation of hunger and to obviate thirst. In native courts eating kola nuts forms part of the ceremony of welcoming strangers, and the Yorubas have a proverb: "Anger draweth arrows from the quiver: good words draw kolas from the bag." It is held to be aphrodisiac—of these half the African, like the Asiatic, pharmacopeia is composed—and like the betel to be

"A detergent, and a kindler of Love's flame that lieth dead."

A powder, or an infusion of the bark and leaves, promptly administered, is used on the Gold Coast as a cure of snake bites. There, also, kola powders finely ground are drunk in a wineglassful of limejuice by those who do not wish to become mothers. And a decoction of the leaves, like the terebinthinate palm vine, acts as a substitute for copaiba.

On the morning of the 23d September the fair-weather flag was not hoisted at the beach: to go or to lose one's passage became the serious question. In due time, however, the bit of bunting flew up, and the "Tender Brune," Lieut. Forrest, R.N., was under steam. After taking a temporary leave of our kind host, we transferred ourselves on board, and ran merrily down the Lagos waters, past the tide-rip of the influent Badagry Lagoon, and past the three salient points—Bruce, Beecroft, and Le Greslie. The bar was like that of yesterday, half angry, but it is easier, methinks, and safer to front these formations than to turn back upon them. Although the wind was dead ahead we shipped only four seas, of moderate dimensions—the danger is of their putting out the fires—and the soundings were never less than eleven feet.

At Lagos we dropped our Frenchman—a typical Frenchman in all points but one, he avoided all mention of the fair sex. A Gascon and a Jesuit, bound for the Whydah mission, he represented himself, for what reason beyond "keeping his hand in" no one knows, as a clerk in the establishment of Messrs. Regis & Co., Marseille. A thorough miso-Albion, he was our favourite butt. Being of a serious turn of mind he dwelt long and loudly upon the revolting selfishness of the British Government; the unscrupulousness with which it carries out even its plans of philanthropy, and the grinding tyranny inflicted upon the wretched Roman "Cats." He said it was a horror that priests were not paid like *les ministres Protestants,* by *le Government,* and that Ireland is not permitted to send members to *le Parlament.* French tobacco was superior to English, French

manufactures beat the world; *la France* was the cream
of creation, and Paris was the cream's cream. *Monsieur*
had travelled *beaucoup* and knew the world; he had even
visited Switzerland, and therefore, as in the case of the
"Fall of Kars," he could tell you all about China.
Londres was *le plus sale endroit* that he had ever seen,
and as for *Liverrepoule*—he would only exclaim with
M. de P——, "Ah! bah! poof!" He wore one shirt
apparament from Madeira to Lagos; he never removed
his hat or cap in the *salon*—probably to show his contempt for *ces Anglais*—and he walked the quarter-deck
bareheaded. We parted, however, on the best of
terms; he promised me *un diner* in case of my visiting
Whydah, and I, as the Yankee saith, "re-ciprocated."

At Lagos, too, we parted with another queer lot—our
slavers. They are dark, but European or Brazilian; they
speak Portuguese, travel under *aliases*—to-day Soarez,
to-morrow Pieri—and they herd together. One claims
to have been a lieutenant in some royal navy. They
have visited England to lay in a further stock of money
for the next cargo of *casimir noir*, and with a view to
medical assistance. They are worn out by excessive
devotions at the shrine of Venus, and they seem to live
chiefly on tobacco smoke. Part of their game is to
supply naval officers with champagne and excellent
cigars; to ask them to dinner, and to affect equality
with them, as if both were of the same trade. The new
comer on the coast sometimes associates with them,
thinking he will discern their secret, whilst they are

reading his, and are persuading the natives that he is in league with them. I should strongly exhort officers to be very wary of such society, and certainly not to trust themselves to a dinner on shore, where a cup of coffee would materially assist the departure of a cargo. As for the fiction that they are to be treated like gentlemen, whilst plying a trade which our law makes felony, it is easily disposed of. The pickpocket or the burglar might, with equal reason, claim equal respect for his "profession."

About midday we found ourselves on board the "Blackland," and we entered slowly upon the short stage of about 100 miles which separated us from our next station, the Benin river.

Lagos, according to native tradition, was founded by a body of Beninese warriors, sent by their king, who claimed suzerainty over these parts, to reduce the rebels of Ogulata, or Abulata, a place on the mainland north of the islet. Their leader—whose name is not quoted— having failed in his enterprise, and fearing to return, settled upon the then desert bit of sand, made friends with European travellers, and rejected all promises of pardon. Islands in Western, as in Eastern, Africa are ever the favourite places of settlements; they are defended by the sea, and the habit of fishing raises a generation of canoe-men who have many advantages over the inland peoples. Presently the Ogulata people recognised the chief, and the King of Benin made Lagos a dependency, with annual tribute, which ceased when the slave dealers had strengthened it to resist the mother city. Hence the island's native name, Aonin, or Awáni, corrupted to Oni by Europeans, alluding to its connection with Ini, Bini, Ibini, or Benin. There is another name, Daghoh, mentioned by the slave Abubeko; but is probably a native corruption of "Lagos" —the Lakes—a name given by the Portuguese, probably in memoriam of their Lusitanian home. The old chart-names for the islands Curamo and Ikbekou are not to be met with here. The town is known to its population and throughout Yoruba as Eko, of which some make Ichoo. The settlement must be modern : it is not mentioned by Bosman in 1700.

The great development of the slave trade at Lagos took place about the beginning of the present century. In 1839-41, emigrants to Abeokuta, 265 in number, were plundered and maltreated by the people. In August, 1845, Kosoko (Coçioco), cousin of the King, a powerful slave-trading chief, after twenty-four days' fighting, drove out the liege lord Akitoye, who favoured the English, and murdered, in the market place, his brother Letida and two of the Chief Aduli's sons. Akitoye, a weak man and a foolish, fled to Abeokuta, but the great warrior Shodeke was dead, and the encampment at the town of Adú was broken up. Several missionaries remained at Badagry, the road to Abeokuta, their destination, being unsafe. The first who entered "Understone" was the Rev. T. B. Freeman, on Sunday, the 11th December, 1842, and he was not followed until the 27th July, 1846, when Messrs. Townsend and

Crowther were enabled to reach it. A coalition between Lagos and Porto Novo, backed by Dahomey, threatened the British establishments at Badagry. Under Kosoko, who ruled at Lagos for six years, an attack was actually made upon the place; it was, however, beaten back by the Egbas and their General Shomeye, who afterwards became principal captain of war at Abeokuta. This outrage, which took place in June and July of 1851, led to reprisals.

On the 25th November of the same year, a force of 260 men, in twenty-three boats, under the command of the late Commander Forbes, Her Majesty's ship "Philomel," preceded by the late Mr. Beecroft, carrying a flag of truce, entered the river. About 5000 armed men were assembled, they kept up a sharp fire from behind the houses and trees. Our men landed; but they were soon compelled to retreat, with the loss of two killed and several wounded. The Rev. Mr. Bowen ("Central Africa"), who was near the scene, and shows scant regret at the English being "whipped,"—we were risking our lives for the pretection of him and his,—describes it as a pretty considerable (John) Bull's run.

Being somewhat more enthusiastic about slave-trade matters in those days, we determined effectually to scotch the serpent at Lagos. On the 26th and 27th December, 400 men, from four ships, and headed by the commodore, Captain R. W. Bruce, Her Majesty's ship "Penelope,"—his name is preserved in Bruce Island (Iddo), a green spot in the "Cradoo Waters" to the north of the town,—attacked the place. Kosoko had prepared it with stockades, cannon, and all the material for a determined resistance. The principal fighting was a little beyond the house occupied by Mr. M'Coskry; here the walls of vegetation enabled the defenders to fire unseen upon the assailants. We lost sixteen men killed and seventy-one wounded, a fair proportion out of 400; the destruction of the natives was much greater. Kosoko and his party, after doing their best to no purpose, fled to Ijebu, where he remained four years, and his cousin Akitoye was reinstated. The latter was not fated to live without troubles. In July, 1853, two slave chiefs—Aginia and Pellu—rebelled, and joined their master Kosoko; and on the 5th of August was fought a drawn battle, during which the English Branch Mission and School House was burned. In September of the same year Akitoye poisoned himself at midnight, in the presence of two slave boys—the local custom when the King ceases to give satisfaction to his subjects.

Through the influence of the late Mr. Campbell, Her Majesty's Consul, Docemo succeeded his father in 1853, to the prejudice of Kosoko. This fine old chief eventually took up his abode at Ekpe, upon the Ikoradu Lagoon, and at periods filled the mind of Lagos with a panic. In 1852, the English residents at Badagry, conquering their alarm, visited Lagos, and were followed in a few weeks by the Church and the Wesleyan Missions, the Baptists remaining to till the field. In 1855, most Europeans believed that a plot had been made to murder the Consul and all opposed to the slave trade. Docemo, however, proved himself superior to his father, and not unfriendly to the stranger. But the wheel of Fate revolves at Lagos as elsewhere; kings' heads, according to the Arab saying, now touch the stars, then are under the stones. Docemo was dethroned on the 6th of August, 1861, and Kosoko, for years the horror and *bête noire* of Consul Campbell and the missionaries, is again growing into favour; it has even been thought of readmitting him to his country.

As late as the year of grace 1851, when Mr. M'Coskry first came to Lagos, there were thirty Portuguese, and but four English: not one of the whole number, save himself, survives, or at least has remained here. Those were merry days; the slavers had nothing to do but sleep and smoke, with an occasional champagne tiffin on the beach. The trade-man made all the bargains; the doctor examined the " contrabands;" they were shipped off by the captain and crew, and in due time came a golden return. Then followed, in 1851, the palmy days of palm-oil. Ten gallons were then bought for two and a half heads of cowries = five shillings, and sold per ton of 300 gallons at 40*l.* Every year the price has increased, owing to concurrence, jealousy, and want of combination among the traders, who enjoy "cutting one another's throats," as the phrase is. The oil has now risen from 2·5 to 10 heads, and threatens to rise still higher.* The Lagos oil

---

* The cowrie currency, assuming the dollar at 4*s.* 6*d.*, its normal price in these regions, is as follows :—

is celebrated as the best and clearest upon the West African coast, and the tree extends to at least sixty miles in the interior. The "puncheon" is not, as in the "Oil Rivers," of a fixed size; it may be anything, from a breaker upwards. The amount of oil exported from Lagos this year is about 3,800 tons, worth (at 40*l.* per ton) some 152,000*l.*, and here, as elsewhere, the trade is only in its fitful infancy.

Lagos is a young and thriving place. Its position points it out as the natural key of this part of Africa, and the future emporium of all Yoruba, between the Niger and the sea. It cannot help commanding commerce: even under the wretched management of the native princes, it attracted the whole trade of the Benin country. In proper hands it will be the sole outlet of trade from Central Guinea and the Sudan,* lands teeming with various wealth—palm-oil, cotton, shea-butter, metals, native cloths, sugar, indigo, tobacco of good quality, and ivory; in the neighbourhood of Ilorin, about eight days' journey north of Abeokuta, it is not worth their while, on account of the heavy tolls, to export their tusks. At present the bar is an obstacle to im-

---

40 cowries = 1 string = 3 farthings to 1*d.*
5 strings = 1 bunch = 3*d.* to 6*d.*
10 bunches = 1 head = 1*s.* 9½*d.* to 2*s.*
10 heads = 1 bag   = 18*s.* to $4 = 16*s.* 8*d.*

The bag contains 20,000 cowries, and the rates are exceedingly various.

* Sudan properly means negroes : it is an ellipsis for Bilád el Súdán, *i.e.*, negroland. Moslem nations call the negroes of the interior, the Sudan : thus the negroland of Egypt lies south, and that of Lagos north.

provement ; time, however, will remedy that. The roads require attention, but they are hardly so important to Africa as people at home suppose. In these prairie lands a path is easily cut, and soon becomes a rut impracticable to an Englishman or a horse, but perfectly fitted for the African. Were you to give him the finest highway in Europe, after a year he would have worn a deep track by marching in Indian file, and the rest would be a bright expanse of verdure. These remarks will apply to the special fund of £200, of which an advertisement, " Aquapem Mountain Road," appears once per month in the " African Times," a methodistical publication, whose tone and spirit, venerable cant, and worn-out declamation, take us back to the days of A.D. 1800.

I should like to see, but have very little chance of seeing, Lagos (now that she has become part and parcel of the empire upon which Dan Phœbus must be somewhat weary of gazing) become a model colony. We have learned " what to avoid " in West Africa : as the subjoined extract from the returns of expenditure for the year ending December 31, proves, S'a Leone barely pays itself, whilst Gambia shows a deficit of one-third, and the Gold Coast of nearly half.

PAYMENTS FOR SLAVE AND TONNAGE BOUNTIES.

		£	s.	d.	£	s.	d.
To officers and crew of H.M.S. Viper	-	4,223	10	0			
,,	,, Spitfire -	2,574	10	0			
,,	,, Pluto -	4,382	0	0			
Carried forward -	· · ·				11,180	0	0

	£	s.	d.	£	s.	d.
Brought forward - - - -				11,180	0	0
To officers and crew of H.M.S. Archer -	2,007	10	0			
,, ,, Triton -	5,609	10	0			
,, ,, Arrogant	946	0	0			
,, ,, Alecto -	1,375	0	0			
To Colonel Hill, Sierra Leone - -	1,610	0	0			
To Mr. Pike, harbour master, Ditto -	170	0	0			
Transferred to Civil Contingencies in repayment of advances on account of votes for the service - - -	8,698	10	0			
				20,416	10	0
				31,596	10	0
Paid for support and conveyance of captured negroes -				19,388	18	11
Paid to Commissioners for suppression of the slave trade, including Commissioner at Loando, 1,300*l.*; arbitrator, 800*l.*; clerk, 400*l.* - - - -				10,750	0	0
Total expenses of slave suppression -				£61,735	8	11

COLONIAL REVENUE AND EXPENDITURE, 1860.

	£	s.	d.	£	s.	d.
Sierra Leone—Expenditure - - -	29,146	0	0			
,, Revenue - - -	29,912	0	0			
Gambia—Expenditure - - -	15,273	0	0			
,, Revenue - - -	10,190	0	0			
Gold Coast—Expenditure - - -	9,558	0	0			
,, Revenue - - -	5,004	0	0 ·			
Total expenditure over revenue - - -				8,871	0	0

SPECIAL SERVICE.

	£	s.	d.	£	s.	d.
Niger—Dr. Baikie, salary - . -	500	0	0			
Expenses at the Confluence - - -	1,000	0	0			
				1,500	0	0

ESTIMATE OF CONSULS' SALARIES, &C., FOR THE YEAR, 1862.

	£	s.	d.	£	s.	d.
Lagos—Consul (allowance, 200*l.*) -	500	0	0			
Abeokuta—Consul (allowance, 100*l.*) -	400	0	0			
Fernando Po—Consul (allowance, 20*Cl.*)	500	0	0			
Sherbro—Consular agent - - -	250	0	0			
Quillimane—Consul - - • -	500	0	0			
				2,650	0	0
Grand Total - - - - - -				£74,756	8	11

It wants a Civil Governor, who should be a military or a naval man; a secretary ditto, ready to act as principal when necessary; a staff surgeon, with a relief ready at home when required; a harbour-master—a lieutenant R.N., if possible; a surveyor; and, without ambition of shining as a politician, a civil engineer to lay out the town; three police magistrates; but, in the name of all that is nameable, no civil courts, no courts of appeal, no "regular lawyers," no lawyers' clerks. The one thing needful is a military force, sufficiently strong, not for offence, but to back our authority, and to keep the peace amongst a number of petty, quarrelsome tribes around. A force of 200 men has been proposed; it is about one-third of what is required. Some have advocated Sepoys, who would not live here a month; what is unhealthy to the European would be doubly so to them. Hindus of caste would die on the voyage; Moslems shortly after arrival. Chinese would be excellent, but their day on this coast has not yet come; we are only beginning to learn their value as soldiers in their own land. Others advocate West Indians, the refuse of Jamaica and S'a Leone, fellows little calculated to resist climate, and despised by the black people because of themselves; their conduct in camp is complained of, and only the bravery of their officers enables them to behave even tolerably in the field. The Hottentots might be tried, but, as Captain Speke's imprudent example shows, they are not to be relied upon out of their own country, and little even there. The best men would be from the Gold Coast mixed with Moslems from the north, Ilorins, Fulas, and Gambari, or Hausamen : the greater the mixture and the further the soldier's country, the better. The military establishment requires one small troop of horse artillery, armed with rockets and Blakeley's guns; another troop of eighty cavalry, and a weak regiment of 400 infantry. The latter would be divided into half companies, and besides mere drilling and parading, should fortify the place and make military roads; so shall we escape the sight of those soldier-drones that now infest the colonies. The error to be avoided lies in the multitude of officers : the forces should be irregulars, with a commandant, a second in command, an adjutant, a quartermaster, a full surgeon, and an assistant surgeon—no captains, lieutenants, nor ensigns; if these are wanted they might be kept at home as duplicates.

The custom-house officers would be two in number and the taxes at once changed. To the present time the only impost levied by the King has been export duty of 2·5 per cent. on ivory and oil; and of these the place, probably never exported more than 180,000*l.* per annum, whilst now, in consequence of the protracted war, it exports still less. This is a truly suicidal proceeding : the only possible tax for the present is 2·5 per cent. on imports, which, assuming them at 190,000*l.* per annum, already realises 4797*l.* a year,* without causing the

---

* Mr. Consul Campbell reported in 1858 that Lagos exported 4,612 tons of palm oil (184,480*l.*), 5,776 lbs. of ivory (1,500*l.*), and 2,108

natives to feel it. The Gold Coast has warned us against a poll-tax, and though the whole seaboard is virtually in our hands, it would hardly be prudent as yet to lay a duty of fifty per cent. on arms, ammunition, and alcohol, a consummation which I most devoutly desire may become universal in Western Africa. We might, however, begin with ten per cent.

The town of Lagos is certainly one of the most unhealthy spots on these malarious shores, but the climate may be mitigated. As the people do not bury in their ground-floors, it is here easy to remove a house. Broad streets, admitting free currents of air, and perfectly drained, should run the whole length of the settlement parallel with the Lagoon, and at right angles to these, cross ways from the water side to the interior would supply ample ventilation. The site has a good slope towards the flowing stream which is a ready-made *cloaca maxima,* and very little cutting would draw off the rains, which now stand long upon the stiff hardened sand. Another abuse calls loudly for correction. The town is filled with deep holes, from which the sand mixed with swish for walls has been dug —Clapperton found Sokotu in the same state; these become favourite stores for offal and rubbish, and the

---

bales—weighing 263,500 lbs.—of cotton (5,912*l.* 10*s.*) The total of export in that year was, therefore, 191,892*l.* 10*s.* Although shea-butter had appeared in the market, the native chiefs had organised a powerful opposition to the palm-oil trade, hoping a return to the old state of things. In 1859 the deficiency in the whole export trade of palm oil from the Bight of Benin was expected to reach at least 10,000 tons.

hot weather fills them with putrefaction. And, finally, the natives should be taught, or rather forced, to learn something like purity in their habits.

With this little establishment, and with such simple precautions, I am certain that Lagos, when ten years old, will be able to provide for itself, and that in ten more it would become the emporium of the great and rich Yoruba and Dahomian countries, whose natural adit and issue it is.

CHAPTER XI.

"Ye banks and braes o' Bonny ——"
Burns.

24TH SEPTEMBER, 186—.

IT is September, and one whole month from home—
how short a time, and how great a change! Within
that limited period we have passed through summer,
autumn, winter, and spring, and now we are in the
brumal season once more. A cold and drizzling Irish
rain, driven by the wind across decks, makes everything comfortless. As yet, however, we have been
unable to complain of heat. The "unapparent fount of
glory" is shorn of his beams by the gaseous steamy air,
which fends off the heat from earth. So different is ra-
diation in the dry air of the desert, that, after an experience of Scinde and Aden, the consul declared he had
not yet felt a hot day; the climate is that of Naples
during the sirocco. Touching the four seasons which
we have endured within the last thirty days, it is usual
to make in West Africa a very different distribution of
the year, little intelligible to the pure European, *e. g.*,
the dries, the tornadoes, the early rains, the little dries,
the later rains, the later tornadoes, and the smokes. Yet,

by minute inspection, he can discover something of the
mechanism of the European year. The decay of old, and
the substitution of new growths, even in a land of ever-
greens, show a distinct demarcation. Spring opens with
its thunder-storms in October and November; the hot
dry summer lasts till May; and from June till late in
September, autumn and winter fill up the year.

At 8 P.M. on Tuesday, the 24th September, we find our
pop-guns off the mouth of the Benin river, or Great
Rio Formoso, conspicuous by its high north-western
bank. The vessels were rolling in the long surf, which is
here worse than even at Lagos. We took in two passengers, Doctor and Mrs. Henry—little thought we at
that time that she was destined to an untimely death !
As the steamer never touches here on her way home,
passengers from Benin must perforce endure a long and
dangerous week's trip round the " Oil Rivers." Benin
assumes the dignity of almost classic ground. It was
visited in 1485 by the Portuguese Affonso de Aviro,
who returned home, bearing a demand for Christian missionaries on the part of the King. Fernão de Poo, after
discovering the " Beautiful island " which has taken his
name, sailed up the " Great River Beautiful," which he
probably so named from the family likeness of the
scenery : he founded a settlement at Gwato, and it
speedily numbered one thousand converts. According to
Barbot, who takes, as will be seen, the story from
Merolla, the King of Great Benin City offered, for the
very small consideration of a white wife, to drive all his

subjects into the pale of the Church. At the island of San Thomè, "a strong appeal," to use Mr. Wilson's words,* "was made to the Christian feeling of the sister-hood, one of whom had the courage to look the matter in the face, and actually accepted the hand of his sable Majesty. She ought to have been canonized, but it is not known that this deed of self-sacrifice ever received any special notice from the Father of the Church." I may add, that if the then King was as fine-looking a negro as the present occupant of the " Stool," which here is synonymous with the " Throne," the young lady lost little by exchanging him for an ex-sanguined white of San Thomè.† Here, however, the matter ended, the country was found unwholesome, and at last, after many a struggle, Christianity died out. Benin was visited by Captain Thomas Wyndham in 1553, and in 1823,

---

* " Western Africa," p. 192.

† Bosman, Letter XX., calls San Thomè the Dutch churchyard, and attributes the excessive mortality to three causes : the scorching heat, the "thick and stinking mists," and, thirdly, the " excessive phle-botomy of the Portuguese ; " adding, " they have recourse to this on the very least occasion, some of them letting blood above five times in a year, and this it is which I believe makes them look more like walking ghosts than men ; and this practice, the longer continued, must necessarily the more weaken the constitution, for the nature of the country is not such as to supply them with hasty recruits of new blood." Captain Owen (" Narrative of Voyages," Vol. II. p. 383) asserts that during his whole experience on the African coast, there was not one instance of perfect recovery after a liberal application either of the lancet or of calomel—" decidedly the most deadly enemies in a tropical climate." And yet, in the same page, he recommends these two destroyers, the one as a preventative, and the other as a restorative. "I pray you avoid them."

Belzoni of the Pyramids left his bones near its banks. The lowlands are rich in palm-oil; a little gold is found in the uplands, despite the theory which limits the precious metal to the Secoom river, west of Accra, and the interior exports a few ivories; piper cubebs and Malaguetta pepper grow wild, and the soil might be taught to bear coffee and cocoa, indigo, sugar, and cotton. At present it is a mere waste.

I had no opportunity of entering the Benin river. At the time piracy and murder had been reported, the people of Fishtown had slaughtered a Kruboy or two, belonging to the Messrs. Harrison. A cruizer was hourly expected by the natives to "break town," and they had prepared for it by running all their valuables into the bush. The fault, as usual, lies with the traders, who will not " pull together." There is no " king"— Africanicè for "head native"—in the lower river. Benin was in old times divided into two separate states, Benin Proper and Wari (Warree). The royal family of the former place becoming too numerous, divided, and settled at the latter, which was of course tributary and dependent, till the Portuguese persuaded it to throw off the yoke. Some years afterwards, one of the Wari family, or according to others, a slave of the King of Benin, founded a town on the Jakwa (Jackwaw) creek, which also, in due time, became independent. Alusa, the King of Wari, died in 1848; Jambrá, the present sovereign of Benin, has little power, and " Governor Jerry," of Jakwa, is an effete old man. The state of the river is that of perfect anarchy. Some Europeans sigh for the order and the responsibility of a single ruler—others, and they are in the majority, prefer not to pay the comeys or customs which royalty would demand and enforce.

I inquired of an intelligent fellow-passenger concerning the Joemen, or Ijomen, to whom Mr. Consul Hutchinson has given, by hearsay, so vile a reputation. Next to the tribes of Fernando Po, they are the best abused race in this part of Africa, and both deserve a better fate. Lieut. Forbes* calls them the Joh pirates, and makes them the chief carriers of the human cargoes exported from the Beninese interior to Lagos. A reference to Mr. Henry, of Benin, enables me to deny that Mr. Henry had ever asserted that the "Ejoemen" had eaten two Kruboys, that had deserted from a Liverpool ship. It has not been proved that the Ijos ate the two young officers of Captain Denham's ship, who imprudently boated up the river without sufficient force. Nor can it be established that the West Indian, Carr, who in 1841 (Second Niger Expedition) was returning to Aboh, on the Niger, *viâ* Bonny, was "killed by these people, or King Boy, an Ejoeman."† He was most probably murdered by the Ibos, at the suggestion of some Christian trader.

Cannibalism is an interesting, though somewhat morbid subject. Once, all anthropophagous tales were greedily swallowed; they are now fastidiously rejected. The pages

---

* "Dahomey and the Dahomians," chap. 1.

† "Ten Years' Wanderings among the Ethiopians," chap. 5.

of many African travellers show so much hearsay and little eye-sight, they supply, moreover, such ridiculous details, that the public is justified in doubting anything but personal evidence. But to deny, as some very silly philanthropists of the Ethnological Society have denied, its existence in West Africa, is to maintain, like the old African, the impossibility of water becoming hard because he had never seen it so.

After leaving Lagos, the low lands become a "false coast," the gift of the Niger, whose western branches extend as far as our new colony. Eastward, the furthest limit is the Bonny, and possibly its eastern neighbour the Andoni River, and the Ahombola (Humballah) creek, an inlet not named, though placed, in our charts.* Nothing is more simple than to sketch the view as seen from the sea. Above, an azure space based upon a band of dull and bright greens, resting upon a thin line of golden sand, and in the foreground a little deeper ultramarine than in the air. In the rainy season, change the blue above to a heavy mass of clouds, reposing upon the land, and the blue below to a brown olive. Where a river gap exists it will be denoted by an uneven notch in the land, and as a rule the proper right point, that is to say, the western, will be somewhat higher than the other. The apparent continent will be found divided into islands, and sub-divided into islets, by river-like

* The direct connection of the Bonny River with the true Niger is still a subject of geographical speculation : I hope to solve the problem, despite all its difficulties.

mangrove-haunted creeks, which I prefer to describe when upon them.

About noon, on the 24th of September, we were off the " Escravos," Slave river, corrupted to "Escrados," the first stream lying southward of the Benin : it has a bad bar, and is shallow, fit only for the humbler sort of slavers. Next to it is the Rio dos Forcados " of Galley-Slaves,"*—a bathos—it is called by our pilots, with scanty reason, the " Warree river." With a bar that carries thirteen feet at low water, some say twenty feet, and with a very narrow slope, this noble estuary is wholly neglected. Its next neighbour is the Ramos, or Bough river, which has twelve to fifteen feet on the bar. Up this stream there are fine clay banks, raised twenty to twenty-five yards above the water, and bearing noble trees; the people, contrary to the usual habits of the "Creekmen," cultivate the ground. Of the Dodo I could hear nothing, and will not quote the Directory. Next in order is the Pennington river, so called from the young officer of Her Majesty's ship "Avon," surveying the coast under Captain Denham, in 1846, who was treacherously murdered by the aforesaid Creekmen. The Middleton is as unimportant and little known as the Dodo; it was christened after the assistant-surgeon of the " Avon." The next is the Winstanley outfalls, so called from another murdered man—here, as in the prairies of North America, death

---

* These descriptions, as far as the Niger, are mere hearsay : I have not visited the mouths of the above-mentioned streams.

seems to be the only thing that can be recorded of localities—belonging to the "Avon": the people probably supposed her to be a slaver, awaiting opportunities of capture, and fought accordingly. It was too late for vision when we were off the Sengana, or Sengma, the westernmost direct outlet of the Niger, and it was midnight before we steamed across the mouth of "Blacklands' Nile."

The obvious projection of the land at the base of the immediate delta, has been called by old travellers, whose eye for beauty appears to have been keen, "Cabo Formoso;" with us it is "Cape Formosa," upon the principle that the *prima donna* is ever saluted with Bray-*vo*, and geographers differ as to whether it is to the east or to the west of the river's mouth. The Nun, or Non, was possibly so called by the Portuguese, who seem to have denoted by a negative the several *ne plus ultras* of their course from Lisbon to Australia.* It was promoted to the dignity of principal outlet within our memory; the last century and the first quarter of the present, held four theories touching the course and issue of the mighty Niger.

1. The ancients,† who, unlike the moderns, made their chief explorations by land, and not by sea, held

* Cape Non, in Morocco, may be derived from the Arabic Ras Nun —of Fish—as Jonah is called Zu'l Nún, master of the fish.

† Pliny shows a certain knowledge of the Nigir, Nigeir, or Nigris, its divergence into many streams (ἐκτοπας, as Ptolemy says), and its rise, like the Nile, after tropical rains. Ptolemy adds some remarkable details, which, if mere coincidences, deserve to be considered marvellous.

that the Niger flowed from past the centre of the continent to the eastward, losing itself in a great central reservoir, like the Caspian Sea, called Wangara, or Ghana,* where it was lost in the sands or evaporated by the sun. This theory became popular after the first journey of Mungo Park, whose very short experience had only taught him that the course of the Niger was easterly. This theory had one merit, it anticipated the discovery of the Lake Regions of Central Equatorial Africa, concerning which the geographical world is now so curious.

2. Others opined that the Niger terminates in the White Nile, which D'Anville had then traced to the south-south-west of Senaar. Mr. Grey Jackson, of Moroccan celebrity, published the interesting fact, that in 1780, seventeen native travellers from Tinbuktu reached Cairo by water the whole way in eighteen months, passing 1200 towns and cities. Major Rennell, by a comparison of Mr. (Darfur) Browne's altitudes, found this to be physically impossible.

3. Mr. George Maxwell, an experienced African trader, who had lived long at the mouth of the Kongo, and who had planned a boat exploration of the river, persuaded Mr. Park—contrary to his better judgment, we must hope —that the Zaire, or Kongo river, is the mouth of the Niger.† Many objections were raised to this theory, *e. g.*, that it would make the stream cut the "Kong Moun-

---

* In Captain Tuckey's map the Zaire, or Kongo, is also made to issue from a great marsh.

† Park, writing to Sir Joseph Banks, makes his Kasson guide state

tains "—which it does—and give the Niger a course of
4000 miles, or 500 longer than the Amazon. The theory,
however, led to the fatal expeditions of Park and Tuckey.
4. The two latter were pre-eminently English and erroneous opinions; the fourth was French, and correct.
M. Reichard ("Ephémerides Géographiques," Weimar,
1808) was sanctioned in 1813 by the great Malte-
Brun ("Précis de la Géographie Universelle," vol. 4, p.
635), in opining that the Niger falls into the Gulf of
Guinea by a great delta, the Rio del Rey being the
eastern, and the Great Rio Formoso, or Benin,* being
its western, limits. This remarkable hypothesis, right
in the main, whilst wrong in detail, and characterised at
the time as " hazardous and uncertain," was probably
suggested by native testimony, the coasts of the Gulf of
Guinea being well known to French traders. It is hard
indeed to comprehend how an intelligent sailor could
pass by these shores without suspecting them to be the
delta of some great stream. Caillié, the much-abused
discoverer of Tinbuktu, wrote in 1828 these remarkable
words—" If I may be permitted to hazard an opinion as
to the course of the River Dhioliba, I should say that it

that the Niger, after passing Kashna, runs directly to the right hand,
or southwards, and that he was certain that it did not end anywhere
near Kashna or Bornu. This shows a glimmering of light.

* I quote the above memoriter. If correct, the limits of the
Nigrotic delta thus given are totally incorrect. The Rio del Rey is
wholly unconnected with the Niger ; even the nearer Calabar and Cross
rivers do not flow from it. The same is the case with the Benin river :
its source was placed by Mr. Beecroft in the highlands to the westward
of the Niger.

empties itself by several mouths into the Gulf of Benin." In 1829—*longo intervallo*—Mr. Macqueen, after collecting a large amount of evidence on the subject, recommended a careful examination of the rivers between the Rio Formoso and Old Calabar, neither of which, by the bye, are directly connected with the Niger.

I have given below * a summary of northern West

* In 1553, Capt. Thomas Wyndham, the Portuguese Anes Pinteado, entered the Benin river.

In 1558, Mr. Thompson reached Tenda by the Gambia, and was followed there in 1620 by Robert Jobson.

In 1637, Jannequin ascended the Senegal.

In 1670, Paul Imbart attempted Tinbuktu *viâ* Morocco.

In 1698, the Sieur de Brue visited Galam on the Senegal.

In 1715, M. Compagnon reached Bambúk *viâ* St. Louis de Senegal.

In 1723, Stables reached Bambúk *viâ* the Gambia; the same journey was repeated by Moore in 1731.

In 1742, M. de Flandre reached Bambúk by St. Louis, and he was followed in 1749 by the celebrated M. Adanson.

In 1748, M. Follier reached Bambúk by the Cape Nun Coast.

In 1785, MM. Sanguier and Brisson made the same journey.

In 1786, M. Ruband reached Galam *viâ* St. Louis.

In 1786-7, M. de Beauvois explored Benin and Wari.

In 1787, M. Picard struck Futa Toro *viâ* St. Louis.

In 1791, Major Houghton ascended the Gambia river, and died at Jarra in Ludamar.

In 1794, Messrs. Yates and Winterbottom reached Timbo by the Rio Nunez.

In 1795-7, Mungo Park's first journey to Silla on the Joliba or Kwara river.

In 1804, Mr. Nicholls died in the interior of Old Calabar.

In 1805, Mungo Park's second expedition : all his 44 companions, including Lieut. Martyn, and Messrs. Anderson and Scott, died.

In 1809, M. Roentgen reached Busa *viâ* Mogador.

In 1810, Robert Adams, *alias* Benjamin Rose, an American, was carried prisoner to Tinbuktu.

African, including Nigritic, exploration, brought down
to the present date. The reader may see, by casting his

In 1815, Mr. James Riley, another American, master and supercargo
of the brig "Commerce," reached Tinbuktu by the western coast.

In 1816, Capt. Tuckey, R.N., accompanied by Lieut. Hawkins, Mr.
Fitzmaurice, master and surveyor, Dr. McKerrow, with petty officers
and marines, besides supernumeraries ; Professor Smith, botanist ; Mr.
Cranch, zoologist ; Mr. Tudor, anatomist ; and Mr. Lockhart, gardener ; visited the lower Kongo ; of his 54 white men, a party of 30
set out on the land journey beyond the cataracts, and of these only
nine returned home.

In 1817, Major Peddie and Capt. Campbell reached Kakondi *viâ* the
Nunez river.

In 1817, M. Bandia reached Panjikot *viâ* Egypt.

In 1817, P. Rouzié travelled into the interior.

In 1818, M. Mollien reached Timbo *viâ* St. Louis.

In 1818-19, Capt. Gray, Royal African Corps, reached Bulibani, the
capital of Bondu.

In 1819, M. Dochard reached Yamina *viâ* the Gambia.

In 1819, Mr. Bowdich visited Kumasi in Ashantee.

In 1820, M. Cachelot reached Wad Nun by the west coast of Africa.

In 1822, Major Laing reached Falaba *viâ* Sierra Leone.

In 1822-5, Major Denham and Lieut. Clapperton explored Mandara
and Sokotu of the Sudan, losing Dr. Oudney and other Europeans.

In 1825-6, Captains Clapperton and Peace and Dr. Morrison lost
their lives in penetrating from the Bight of Benin ; Richard Lander
being the sole white survivor.

In 1827-8, Réné Caillié visited Tinbuktu and returned *viâ* Morocco,
and in the same year Major Laing was murdered on his way from
Tinbuktu.

In 1830-1, Richard and John Lander entered Africa *viâ* Badagry,
and discovered the embouchure of the Niger.

In 1832-4, the first, or Liverpool merchants' expedition, under the
late Messrs. Laird and Oldfield, and accompanied by Richard Lander,
ascended the Kwara to Rabba, and the Binue (Chadda) to Dagbo. Of
the 49 European crew in the steamers Qworra and Alberkah—the latter
is Anglo-Arabic for a blessing—only nine lived to return. Richard
Lander was shot with a bullet in the groin, by some people of Anjama,

eye upon the map, that discovery has but begun. At
present, as in Arctic travelling, there is a lull, but it cer-

in the Oru country, as he was descending the river in a canoe full of
cowries, and died at Clarence, Fernando Po.

In 1836, 1840, and 1845, the late Mr. Beecroft, under Mr. Jamieson
of Liverpool, ascended in the "Ethiope" the Benin, Wari, Niger, Old
Calabar, and Cross rivers : he reached within 30 miles of this side of
Busa.

In 1841, the Government expedition under Captain the late Admiral
H. D. Trotter, in the "Albert," and Commander W. Allen in the
"Wilberforce," accompanied by the "Soudan," Commander B. Allen,
ascended to Egga, 150 miles above the confluence, losing in 64 days (the
"Soudan" remained only 40) 48 out of 145 white men. The late Mr.
Consul Beecroft ran up the river in the "Ethiope," and succeeded in
saving the "Albert," conveying her to Fernando Po.

In 1845, the late Mr. Duncan visited Abomey.

In 1852, the African Steam-Ship Company was formed, and in 1856-
57 an intercolonial steamer was sent to promote the establishment of a
regular steam communication between Fernando Po and the confluence
of the Kwara and Binue rivers.

In 1854, the Chadda mixed expedition, sent by the late Mr. M.
Laird, who received 5000l. from the Admiralty for the expenses of the
voyage, under Dr. Baikie, R.N., the senior Government officer after the
death of Mr. Consul Beecroft, Mr. D. J. May, master R.N., Dr. Hutchinson, Mr. Taylor, afterwards vice-consul at Abeokuta, representing
Mr. Laird (the reader has probably perused Dr. Baikie's "Journal"),
explored — in the little steamer "Pleiad," built by Mr. J. Laird,
on the lines of the yacht "America"—150 miles of virgin ground, and
remained in the river 118 days, with 54 Europeans, of whom not a man
died ; a new era in African exploration.

In August, 1857, the Niger mixed expedition,—missionary, scientific,
naval, and commercial,—began under Dr. Baikie, Mr. D. J. May, master, Lieut. Glover, Dr. Davis, Mr. Barter, botanist (dead), and Mr.
Dalton, zoologist.   In opposition to this Government party was Mr.
Laird's commercial venture, Captain Alexander Grant (died at Benin),
supercargo, Mr. Howard (dead), purser, and Dr. Berwick.   The "Day
Spring," which carried them, was lost on a ledge near the Jebba rock,
16 miles above Rabba.   Her commander, by means of his steward,

tainly will not last. The Niger, as has been well observed, is not a lottery in which men may win for-

Selim Agha, returned overland to Lagos in February, 1858, recruited outfit, and once more made the camp.

In 1858, the African Steam-Ship Company's ship "Sunbeam," Capt. Fairweather, went to Fernando Po. Lieut. Glover made a second over-land journey to Lagos, and finding the ship to draw nine feet of water, despaired, and once more returned to the camp. The "Sunbeam" was successfully taken up to Rabba, in July, 1858, by Capt. Fairweather and Mr. May, master R.N., an excellent officer. At the end of September, 1858, came out the African Steam-Ship "Rainbow," Capt. M'Nivan, and the latter returning home, she was commanded by Capt. Walker, whose interesting narrative may be found in the Blue Book of 1861.

In April, 1859, Dr. Baikie and Mr. Barter, followed during the next month by Mr. Dalton, Lieut. Glover, and Selim Agha, rode up to Rabba, and descended the Niger in the "Rainbow" and the "Sun. beam " to the Confluence, where Dr. Baikie has remained ever since.

In Nov. 1859, Lieut. Glover, during the "battle of the depart-ments," left the Niger, having "differed in opinion" with, or been differed with by, every other in the river.

In 1860, Mr. Macgregor Laird, the main-spring of the Niger move-ment, died ; he had not reaped where he had sown, and his executors have, it is said, resolved to end the present expedition before the spring of the year 1862. Meanwhile there is little doing. Dr. Baikie is still at the confluence, and his only white companion, Mr. Dalton, was preparing to return to England ; the "Sunbeam," Capt. Walker, was also about to leave ; H.M.S. "Espoir," Commander Douglas, is said to be hard and fast near Tuesday Island, about 80 miles from the mouth, and *on dit* H.M.S. "Bloodhound," Lieut.-Commanding Dolben, though drawing 10 feet of water, will be sent up with supplies for her.

It is to be hoped that Dr. Baikie will not remain unsupported. Knowingly or unknowingly he has adopted the true plan of civilising Africa, by abandoning the deleterious and impracticable coast to mis-sionaries, and by settling in the interior. He has collected a large town around him, and with a constitution which seems proof against any hardship, privation, or fatigue, he remains there, maturing fresh plans for opening up the African interior.

Without entering into lengthy details touching the produce of the

tunes, but a field of labour in which they may earn them. It is directly connected with the twenty or thirty

Nigerian regions, I may be allowed to quote the following list of the Central and Western African articles sent by him and others to the Exhibition of 1862, extracted from the Catalogue :—

AFRICA, CENTRAL.

Under Staircase, near Central Entrance to Horticultural Gardens.

Baikie, Dr. W. Balfour, R.N.—

1, 2. Striped men's cloth, from Hausa.

3, 4. Cloth made of fibres of the wine-palm and cotton, from the right bank of Kwarra.

5. A tobe, poorest quality, made in Nupe.

6. A tobe of finer quality.

7. A white tobe with plaits, from Nupe.

8. Striped trowsers, Nupe or Hausa make.

9, 10. Common cloth, for women from Bonu.

11. A woman's wrapper, made in Nupe.

12. A woman's wrapper, from Nupe.

13. A woman's wrapper, not made up, called "Locust's tooth."

14. A wrapper containing red silk, called Maizha'n baki, or "red mouth."

15. An inferior wrapper, from Nupe.

16. Blue and white cloth, from Nupe.

17, 18. Cloth made in Yoruba.

19, 20. Cloths from Nupe.

21—25. Cloths from Yoruba.

26. Small cloth for girls, from Nupe.

27. Bag from Onitsha.

28. Mat, from right bank of Kwarra.

29. Tozoli (sulphuret of lead), applied to the eyelids.

30. Man's wrapper, from Ki, in Bonu.

32. Woman's head-tie, or alfuta, from Nupe.

33. Bags for gunpowder, from Onitsha.

34, 35. A calabash and ladle.

37. Red silk, or "Al harini," of Hausa.

38. Sword hangings, or "Amila," made at Kano, in Hausa.

39. Siliya, or red silk cord, from Kano.

40. Rope, from Onitsha.

41, 42. Bags.

millions of people in the Sudan; the centres of trade
are upon the stream, yet the long and terrible caravan

43. White cloth, or fari, made in Nupe and Hausa.
44. White cloth, from below the confluence.
45. A white tobe, from Nupe.
46. Four calabashes, for pepper, &c.
47. A small calabash and lid, for food.
48, 49. Pinnæ of leaves of the wine-palm, dried and used for
thatching.
50. Fruit of a leguminous plant, which buries its fruit like *Arachis hypogœa.*
51. Grass cloth, of wine palm.
52. Two cloths, from Okwani.
53. White cloth, from below the confluence.
54. White perforated cloth, from the Ibo country.
55. Mats from Onitsha.
56. Large man's wrapper, from Nupe.
1. A white mat of leaves of the fan-palm, from Bonu.
2. Mats of the fan-palm, from Bonu. Fan-palm mats, called guva,
or, "Elephant mats."
3. Fine mats and hats, of leaves of the *Phœnix spinosa,* dyed.
Circular mats of the same material, used by chiefs, from Nupe.

AFRICA, WESTERN.
Northern Courts, under Staircase, near Central Entrance to Horti-
cultural Gardens.
Commercial Association of Abeokuta.

1. Oils : Of beni seed, obtained by fermentation and boiling. 2. Of
Egusi, from wild melon seed. 3. Of palm, for home consumption ; 4.
for exportation, obtained by beating, pressing, and boiling the fruit.
5, 7. Of palm nut, for home consumption ; 6. for exportation. 11.
Shea butter. 10. Egusi, or wild melon, fruit. 8. Beni seed. 9. Fruit
of the Shea butter tree.
1. White cotton thread ; 2. Dyed ; 3. Blue. 4. Fine spun cotton.
5. Coarse strong spun cotton, called "Akase." 6. Akase cotton,
cleaned and bowed ; 7. In seed. 8. Seed itself of Akase cotton. 9,
10. Ordinary native cotton. 11, 12, 13. Ordinary green, black,
and brown seeded cottons. 14. Silk cotton. 16. Country rope of bark.

march of four months still supplies articles more cheaply
than we can afford to sell them, *viâ* the Niger.   Hitherto
all has been mismanagement.   Government favoured the
African Steam-ship Company, which excited the jealousy

17. Palm fibre. 18. Red dyed native silk, from Illorin. 20. Fibre used
for native sponge. 23, 24, 25. Native silk, from a hairy silk-worm at
Abeokuta. 26. Leaves of the cotton tree. 27. Pine-apple fibre. 29.
Bow-string fibre. 30. Jute.

15. Long black pepper. 22. Senna. 21. A sample of native anti-
mony, from Illorin.

Sundry native manufactures.

N.B.—Cotton is obtainable in any quantity, and is now grown
extensively throughout the Yoruba country, especially to the east and
north.   Great quantities of cotton cloths, of a strong texture, are
annually made, finding their way to the Brazils, and into the far
interior.   To obtain a largely increased supply of cotton, it is only
necessary to open roads, and bring money to the market.   Upwards of
2000 bales have been exported this year, and the quantity would have
been doubled or trebled if the country had been at peace.   The present
price is 4½d. per lb.   The other fibres are not at present made for
exportation, though, doubtless, some of them—jute, for instance—
would be, if in demand.   Of the native manufacture, the grass cloths,
made from palm fibre, and the cotton cloths, are most prominent.
Very nice leather work is done.   The art of dyeing Morocco leather
different colours has been introduced from the interior.   Indigo is
almost the only dye which can be obtained in considerable quantities.
The natives manufacture all their own iron implements, and the
quality of the metal is considered good.

2. McWilliam, the late Dr. C. B.—1. Cloth, from the Confluence of
the Niger and Tchadda. 2. Raw silk from Egga. 3. Cotton from
the confluence. 4. Fishing spear, used by the natives of Kakunda.
5. Spoons, from Gori market. 6. A curved horn for holding galena,
used to paint the eyelids. 7. Cloths, from towns on the Gambia. 8.
Grass mat, from Angola. 9. Grass mat, from Binguela.

3. Walker, R. B. *Gaboon.*—A collection of mats, fibres, commercial
products, skins, native arms, musical instruments, &c., of the Ba Fan
tribes.

of others, especially the traders of the Brass river, who urged the villagers in the lower course to acts of direct hostility. The last 4000*l.* a year, however, have been granted, and a much larger subsidy, say 9000*l.* or 10,000*l.*, should take its place. Mixed expeditions have been sent out only to fail : where naval officers, missionaries, and mercantile men are all urging their several interests, success can hardly be expected. The quarrels between the members of the last expedition completely crippled it : moreover, it was managed on Exeter Hall principles. Captain Trotter frightened his sailors to death by chalking up, it is said, "PREPARE TO MEET THY GOD," and similar consolatory recipes, in the largest letters, all about the ship. The next exploration allowed the Krumen to rob what they pleased, and the lieutenant who managed naval matters is said to have encouraged slaves to desert from their masters—a proceeding sufficient to account for any failure,

We shall never drop the Niger : the main artery of Western Africa north of the Line must not be neglected. All agree that it will pay pounds, where pence are now collected, though people differ as to the means of making it pay. After many a long "talk" with those whose opinions are worth most, I propound the following as the directest way of opening up the stream. A large armed hulk, manned by Krumen, under military or naval law, and carrying an outfit like that sent to the Brass river, would be stationed at Akassa, within the Nun bar. The next measure would be to make treaties with

the hostile chiefs of the delta, settling a certain Comey
upon them: the want of this is the principal cause of
disturbances. The great requisite would be a commander ready to act with energy, and not "mickonary;"
two gunboats would be safer, in case of grounding, than
one, and they should not enter the river later than the
first of June. After making or forcing a peace, postal
and intercolonial steamers might begin plying; they
should visit the river every month or six weeks, and
steam as high as the Confluence, where they could run all
the year round, if built after the American fashion, flat-
bottomed, drawing two to three feet, with stern wheels,
and with walking-beam engines; the furnaces should be
able to burn wood, the bulwarks high and musket-
proof, and the armament wall-pieces, and a few culverins.
After the steamers would come depots and trading-
houses, at the five following points :—

1. Anjámá, at the head of the lower delta.
2. Aboh, at the head of the upper delta.
3. Oricha, midway between the sea and the Confluence.
4. Idda, between the Onicha and the Confluence.
5. Ibegbe, or the Confluence of the Kwara and Binue.

Thus, and thus only, can considerable collections of
cotton be made upon the Niger; and thus the traffic of
the Great Artery, which injured, it is to be feared, the
fortunes of the intrepid explorer, will, after a few years,
become of importance to England.

On the morning of the 25th September I inspected,
en passant, what is supposed to be the "Beautiful Cape."

To the leeward, or eastward, is "Cape Filana," by the English called Palm Point, a fine clump of feathery trees springing from a thin line of the blondest sand. Here was the old Portuguese town of Akassa, long since in ruins : it is said that a tomb was lately found there, bearing the date A.D. 1635. If this be the case, the Portuguese must have known the upper Niger centuries before we did, and must have kept it a mystery as profound as the Kongo is in the year of grace 1861. Point Trotter, a blue line of tree-clad bluff, rises within Filana, and opposite the latter, or to the westward, is Cape Nun, which we know as "West Point." The bar is said to be one of the best on this coast : it has shifted, however, since the date of the last chart.

We are now fairly inside the Bight of Biafra, or Biaffra, an English corruption from the Portuguese Rio de Maffras, a name which they gave to one of the rivers. It is the innermost part of the Guinea Gulf, extending from Cape Formoso, or the Delta of the Niger, in N. lat. 4° 16′ 17″ to Cape St. John, in N. lat. 1° 9′ 7″. A straight line, uniting both these promontories, and passing near Prince's Island, would measure about 450 miles ; along the coast about 650. It is divided into two very distinct sections by the mass of mountains called the Camaroons. The country to the north of that glorious pile is a false coast, a succession of continental islands and land in a state of formation. The expanse of mud and mangrove forms a fit habitation for the iguana and crocodile, with flats and fetid lagoons haunted

by crabs and craw-fish; whilst a few villages, at long
intervals, lurk at the bottom of blind channels and tidal
inlets, where they can preserve themselves by fight or
flight.   The creeks and rivers, outspread as a network
over the mass of dense and rotten vegetation, are kept
in loco by the strong and steady tides which dredge the
beds without sweeping away the mangroves that hedge
them in.   A glance shows you that all around is literally
a young country, which, perhaps, in ages to be may constitute a Nigrotic empire.   To the south, beginning even
at the Camaroons river, there is a change : the banks
are high and clayey, the palm-oil tree (Elæis Guineen-
sis) becomes rarer, yielding in traffic to ivory, and
the people are, though wilder, a finer race than those
of the Delta.   This gradual improvement continues
through the Gaboon river to Angola, where provisions
are procurable, horses will live, and human life has some
enjoyment.   The southern section of the Bight of Biafra
contains, also, two little coves, known in charts as the
Bights of Pannavia and Bata; the words, however, are
now little used.   Pannavia lies to the north of the
Batanga country, whose river, the Elobe, forms its
southern extremity.   The Bight of Bata is between the
Campo and the Benito rivers; it is the seat of those
remarkable foundations—the Seven Hills or Sisters.

   Of the twenty-five streams which discharge themselves
into this great Bight, there are six Oil Rivers—viz., the
Nun, or Niger, the New Calabar, Bonny, Old Calabar,
Camaroons, and Malimba: those to the south are visited

for ivory, gum-elastic, and timber, especially ebony, African cedar, and mahogany, cam-wood and dye-wood. As yet nothing is known of the interior.

At 7 A.M. on the 25th September we found ourselves off the Brass river.* In this part of the coast every stream appears to have received, from its christeners— Diego Cam, or Fernão de Poo—as many names as that Portuguese hidalgo to whom, as the old Spanish story relates, the innkeeper refused to open his gates, stating that he could not accommodate so many people. The Brass is called Second River, because in old times ships bound for the New Calabar and Bonny estuary used to coast down the six rivers, along the 60 to 70 miles eastward from the Nun or Niger. It is also known to the English as St. John; to the Portuguese as Rio Bento; and some books call it the Oddy, Fonsoady, and Malfonsa.

The land is mangrove, the sky cloudy—nimbus and cumulus disposed meridionally, as they love to be in the tropics, flecking patches of a pale milk-and-water blue— and the dangerous bar chafes and seethes across a dwarf indent, whose bluff and wooded banks open like portals into the azure region within. The next, passed at almost an equal distance—ten to eleven miles—with surprising regularity of shelve, one fathom of depth representing one mile of distance off shore, is the St. Nicholas, Filana or Tilana, Sempta or Lempta,† Juan Diaz, or Third

---

* It was so called from the then favourite object of traffic—"Neptunes" or brass pans.

† Some apply the last two names to the Fourth River, the Santa Barbara.

River; its double bar, which breaks right across, was afterwards crossed by the Consul and Lieutenant Dolben, H.M.S. "Bloodhound," under direction of the late Captain Alexander Grant; they found this stream to be a branch of the Brass river, and there is a well-known creek which threading the " Mosquito Country," as it is called, leads into the New Calabar. Leaving the St. Nicholas, whose coast projects somewhat seawards, we made the broad Santa Barbara, Meas, or Fourth River, another fine study of a bar. The Consul and Lieutenant Dolben were nearly swamped in an attempt to cross it, but escaped, much to the regret of certain gentry on board H. M. S. "Bloodhound," who would willingly have quitted the Bights and the Oil Rivers for the " South Coast Station."

It was almost too far to distinguish the gap of the half-way stream, Rio San Bartolomeo, or the Fifth River. The glass, however, showed us from the southwards an island in mid-channel, formed by two narrow arms ; and the bar was seen bursting with rollers, whose " wall-like sides and hairy heads" looked peculiarly unprepossessing. Then came the Rio Sombreiro, also called the Rio dos Tres Irmãos,—of the Three Brothers— and Sixth River : the first name is derived from a patch of trees on the bluff western entrance, resembling a priest's shovel-hat ; they have of course disappeared long ago. Another seven miles took us to our present destination, the broad estuary of the New Calabar, or Kalabar, *alias* Rio Real, *alias* Calbarine, *alias* Neue Calborgh, *alias*

Calbary.* The brother stream, Bonny, or Grand Bonny, is at least as rich in nomenclature.† Its present popular English name is doubtless derived through the native word "Obani." The contrast between name and nature must have rendered the easy corruption a fashionable pleasantry—nothing can be more categorically unbonny —and possibly the foul sky, fouler water, and foulest land, may have reminded some irate Scotchman of Bonny Dundee, thereby giving so *débonnaire* a sound to so ungodly a hole. "Grand" it is—in abominations, moral and physical.

The approach to the Bonny from the west is denoted by Fouché, or Foché, Gap, a deep indentation in the wooded seabank, three miles to westward of the estuary. Then comes the village and the Point Fouché. Barbot calls the former Foko, and says that the Dutch named it "Wyndorp," on account of its abundance of palm wine: he places it on an island and numbers 309 houses. Dr. Daniell reckons above 300 souls, pilots and fishermen. They are under King Amakree, of New Calabar (from

---

* The name is said to date from almost two centuries back, when one of the Ephraim Duke family from old Calabar settled here.

† Barbot, 1678-1706, calls it Bandy, or Great Bandy river. The people's own word is Okoloma ; the Ibos call it Obani, Ibani, and Okoloba ; and the Abo tribe of Ibos call it Osiminika.

All is changed since 1826, when H. M. S. "Barracouta" surveyed it. Sualo Island, east of New Calabar mouth, is now covered with trees, and is growing to be part of the main land. Monkey Creek and Young Town are not laid down at all ; Breaker Island is laid down as a mere shoal—it is now overgrown with vegetation, and is rapidly rising from the sea.

whose rule, however, they would willingly escape), and they want a lesson, as do most of the negroes in these parts; but, ten to fifteen years ago, the "Juju-king" Awanta was deported to Ascension Island for firing upon ships' boats. We passed the mouth of the New Calabar, about one mile broad, and divided from the Bonny by the Middle Bank, or Calabar Flat. We then crossed over, passing by Breaker Island in the centre to near Rough Corner, the east end of the estuary: Barbot places his Bandy Point four leagues east of Fouché Point; it is usually reckoned seven miles across.

The proper Bonny mouth is two to three miles broad, bounded by Rough Corner, which from its clump of trees the Portuguese called Fanal, or the Lighthouse, and Breaker Island, a low sandy bushy patch, distinctly above high water, and commanding a fine view of the outer bar. Portuguese Channel and Man-of-War Channel being unbuoyed, are left to starboard; they are never used by the mail steamers. There are three chief banks, the Western, the Baleur, connected by a sandpit with the former, and separated by deep water from the third or Portuguese Bank. The shifting of the swash-ways and channels makes this river, even with the best of lead and look-out, a place of cold perspiration to ship-owners; and so it will remain, until some acute official fines the negroes 100 puncheons, and buoys the entrance. The A. S. S. Company is most unwise in stationing its large steamers within this river, whose adit presents more dangers than all the rest of the voyage together, whilst the salt water affects the ships' bottoms, and materially interferes with their rate of progress.

At 1 P.M., when we prepared to run in, the amphitheatre of bar and breakers—roaring, foaming, and bursting everywhere ahead of us, and on both sides—looked uncommonly threatening. We followed, however, the usual rule, avoided the Baleur bank, by keeping Peter Fortis, or Peterside, a village on the river's right bank, a sail's breadth open from Juju Point, a projection of the left shore. The buoys were in good order; we left the outer one on our left, the "Red Nun" and the "Black Can" —a little bucket-like affair—on our right, and we looked vainly for the Black Beacon of the charts. We carried five feet of water clear over the outer bar, which is not so long as that of Lagos; and the inner, here, as in all other African rivers, presents no terrors. Rough Corner is known by an unwhitewashed framework, representing the fanal. A native house or two subsequently added represent embryo defences against possible Yankee pirates. When troubles with America were expected, the supercargoes proposed raising a battery at Rough Corner, to command the run in; the clear way was, however, nearly three miles broad, and would require at least a floating battery. The bar was not unduly violent: perhaps the annual little girl had just been sacrificed to it.* Behind the low, jagged line of trees, called Breaker Island,

---

* According to Dr. Madden (Parliamentary Report, 1842), this barbarous custom was kept up as late as 1840, and it is more than probable that the sacrifice is still privately performed.

a giant cloud, purple with wrath, usurped one quarter of
the heavens, and threatened trouble.

The Bonny fleet then drew in sight, tall ships that are
pleasant to look at—little profitable, however—and seventeen in number. There were seven or eight hulks, four
of them beached, all whitewashed and thickly thatched
over ; the most conspicuous was the " William Money,"
an old Indiaman, teak-built and Dutch-like; she is about
seventy years old, and now acts coal-hulk to the A. S. S.
Company. The merchantmen rode high up the stream ;
lower down, in the men-of-war anchorage, lay a single
paddle-wheel,which proved to be H. M. S. "Bloodhound,"
Lieut.-Commanding Dolben, bound for the Niger, with a
cargo of two score black missionaries, male and female,
who managed to oust him from his cabin, and to beg
provisions till he had not the heart to refuse. As we
passed Rough Corner on our starboard side we remarked
the excessive denseness of the bush ; near the framework
of whitewashed scantling that acts landmark, is a small
platform, where it is said sporting skippers have spent the
night, waiting for leopards, here called "tigers." European sailors were seen perambulating the sands ; it was
low tide then; at the flow this "marine parade" is under
water, and decks form the only promenade. Within
Rough Corner, and separated by a mile of bend, or
baylet, lies Juju Point—the white man's grave before the
cemetery was removed to the former place: now it is occupied by witch houses and holy trees. From this point
three giants of the forest, rising side by side, mark the

site of Bonny Town—one smells it, however. Traces of old barracoons are shown on the other side of the creek, which leads up to Juju Town; occasionally a ship's gig, with a white face in the stern, and six Krumen rowing, may be seen stealing along like cat on housetop that way. "The sex" is not fetish at Juju Town, and King Jack is a *bon enfant*, a *Gunjisk i tíldi*, or "Golden Sparrow," as the Persians call it. A little beyond this lies Smoke Town, so called from the curls of vapour that alone denote its existence; there were, however, sundry palms, everywhere in Africa the symbol of population. On the other side of the broad channel is a low dark bank of vegetation, "Deadman's Island," thus grimly called from the feud between the Bonny people and the New Calabars. We pass in succession Tallifer (1000 souls), half hidden by bush; Fishtown, and the village of Peter Fortis, the latter opposite the Bonny creek. But, where is Bonny itself? The experts reply by pointing to a few rugged wash-houses on the beach, and by telling you that the town, being in a hollow, shows only the top of its smoke to the river.

From the sixteenth century almost to the present day, Bonny was the great slave market of the Bights, seldom exporting less than 16,000 souls a year. According to the philanthropic Clarkson ("History of the Abolition of the Slave-Trade"), this river and Old Calabar exported as many "contrabands" as all the rest of the coast together. Hence the "Eboe" (Ibo) woman of the United States. This lasted till 1832, when it came abruptly to an end; from 1825 it had begun to decline. There are still men on the river who can remember the blockade of boats at the mouth, and tell with gusto how the jolly slavers often managed to make a run. The fate of Bonny is now changed. The old slave river has now become the great centre of the palm-oil trade, seldom exporting less than 16,000, and sometimes 18,000, tons per annum, or nearly three-quarters of a million of pounds sterling, to be divided amongst ten or twelve houses.*

An old collier-like craft, painfully bluff, looked sadly misplaced near the noble Bonny fleet. She proved to be the brig "Bewley," Captain Le Marquand (Jersey man), of 184 tons new register, twenty-eight years old, and hardly worth £400. Messrs. Gammon, Sons, and Carter, coal merchants at Ratcliffe, chartered her, with a crew of twelve articled seamen, for the snug sum of £200 per mensem—receiving £900 in advance—to the King Pimento of these Cannibal Lands, who has come to his own again. On the 18th August, 1861, his Majesty reached the river, without a poet-laureate, but accompanied by nine men—a premier, a secretary, an assistant-secretary, three clerks, and one doctor,—who, before leaving home, expressly stipulated that he was to "hold his proper position at court,"—a farmer to trim mangroves, and a valet for the royal person. The salaries varied from £600 a-year, plus £15 for naval

---

* The Bonny puncheon is thirty-eight inches in head, and forty-two in stern, and contains 240 gallons.

uniforms, to £60, and some of these imprudent greenhorns were men with families at home, and perhaps in
want. I regret to say that there were two Englishwomen,—Mrs. Wood, the gardener's wife, who was to
act schoolmistress, and " Miss Mary," a servant girl,
who became maid-of-honour to Eleanor, *alias* Allaputa
Queen Pimento. The *suite,* on seeing the real state of
affairs, became highly indignant; they were half-starved
on board, and when they reached the unbonny
river, the store of doubloons, supposed to be concealed,
was not forthcoming ; nor was the sum of £12,000, owed
by the King of Calabar, paid. One of them was too
glad to compromise a debt of £120 on the receipt of
half-a-sovereign, the only specie in the royal exchequer.
The captain wanted £1829, arrears of pay, and retained
the king's kit, which royalty valued at £1676,—the last
figure removed would probably be nearer truth. Meanwhile there was a scene on board the " Bewley " that
would hardly bear describing; the less said about the
" inner life of an African king," and his *suite* also, the
better.

About eighty or ninety years ago, an Ibo chief settled
with his slaves on the Bonny river. This Opubo, or
Obullo, the "Great Man," was grandfather of the present
chief : his son took the name of Pepper, which he now
spells with a change, and married a woman from the
Abilli (Billa) country, west of the New Calabar river.
Their progeny, the "king," in the African accepta-
tion of the word, also espoused a bush-woman. He

is one of the three free men in this part of the river, the others being Ben Pepple, a half-idiot, and our friend Jack Brown, of Juju Town; this is a small proportion to about 9000 serviles, of whom some few are "Bonny free," but none "proper free."* This population of Ibo slaves speaks the Okoloma, or Bonny language; but all the slave "gentlemen" know a kind of English. On the 21st November, 1848, he made a treaty for the suppression of slavery with Captain Eden, of Her Majesty's ship "Amphitrite," for an annual present of $2000 till 1854. In 1853 a stroke of paralysis, induced by over-indulgence, crippled King Pimento's right side, and from this hemiplegia he has never recovered. Two of his men, Ishakko, *alias* Fred Pepple, and Yanibu, were then appointed as chiefs and regents. On the 23rd January, 1854, Mr. Consul Beecroft, at the request of all the native chiefs and traders, deposed his Majesty, who was ruining the river by his wars with Calabar, and substituted for him Prince Dappa, or Dapho, son of Pimento's elder brother, and therefore rightful heir to the stool. Pepple was carried to Fernando Po, and his protector died there. At last it was resolved by Commodore Adams and Mr. Acting-Consul Lynslager to send the king, with Allaputa, his wife, and his family, to Ascension Island. On the 7th of December, however, he fled into the bush

---

* The population of Bonny is calculated to be 5000 to 6000; of Juju Town, 1500; Tallifer, 1000; and the rest are less. New Calabar numbers some 4000.

à la Charles, and sat under two large trees surrounded
by bushwood. The royal oak, however, was not here,
and Pimento was sent off the next day on board Her
Majesty's ship " Pluto," Commander Clavering, begging
hard that if he died his body might be headed up in a
cask of rum, and sent to lie near his fathers. Since
that time he has enjoyed the memory of Ascension,
which he has learned to call his St. Helena.

Prince Dapho died 13th August, 1855, surgeons say
of inter-susceptio, others of poison, administered by
friends of the ex-king. Fred Pepple and Yanibu were
saved with difficulty from the fury of the mob by Captain Witt, of the " Ferozepore," when a shocking
massacre commenced; 600 to 700 friends of the "king"
were murdered; many blew themselves up; the white
man's house—used by the court of equity, and also as
a chapel—was razed to the ground, and trade was
stopped by the people, because the supposed poisoners
were carried by Mr. Acting-Consul Lynslager to Fernando Po. On the 1st September, 1855, the same
official visiting the river in Her Majesty's ship
" Philomel," Commander Skene, appointed four regents,
viz., Annie (*alias* Ilola) Pepple, Captain Hart (*alias*
Affo Dappa?), Ada Allison,* and Manilla Pepple.

---

* These ridiculous names are taken from English ships. The slave
chiefs have all their own native names, *e.g.*, Manilla Pepple is known
as Erinashaboo. All were the property of old King Pepple, who, when
dying, appointed Annie Pepple as guardian of his son's wealth. He
fought with Manilla Pepple, was beaten, took to drink, and died.
His son is the present Annie Pepple.

Meanwhile, King Pimento was so persevering a petitioner that he was allowed, in November, 1855, to quit Ascension for S'a Leone, where he arrived some time in 1856.   After another bout of correspondence he reached London in 1857 ; there he resided four years, was baptised, and became a temperance man, sitting under the great George Cruikshank.   He abandoned his favourite dish, a boy's hand-palms, and was admitted to the Upper House, where doubtless he graced *les nobles lords* as much as Sir Jung Bahadur does the Christian Knights of the Bath.   He became very pious; he begged £20,000 to raise a missionary establishment —the traders declare it is the one thing wanted for total ruin to the river,—and he roughed it in champagne and sherry.   The application for a mission was celebrated by a missionary periodical in some fearful verse, beginning with—

"Oh, who shall succour Bonny's King ?"

He seemed to me, however, to have a little neglected his English.   The answer to my question touching her sable majesty's health, was " He lib !" meaning thank you, she is quite well.

Pimento, permitted to return home, arrived in the Bonny river on the 18th of August.   Instead of landing at once, as expected, he lingered coward-like on board till the 15th of October, although several of the supercargoes had offered to accompany him.   Instead of going to the Juju-House,—it fell, by-the-by, a terrible bad omen, on the day of his disembarkation—he used to send for supercargoes to read the Scriptures to him. By way of contrast, he despatched his assistant-secretary and chief clerk, in naval uniforms, swords included, to invite the four regents and chiefs on board the " Bewley." The influential slave, Ilola, *alias* Annie Pepple, whose father was a confidential chattel of the former king, whose body is buried in his house, and Affo Dappa, head slave to the late Prince Dapho, and one of the four regents, steadily refused.

After two or three meetings, King Pimento sent his ship's captain, with the same gentlemen—one of these had been twenty-eight days in Paris, vainly trying to negotiate a French treaty—armed with revolvers, to fetch Ilola by force, if necessary. Seven of the Manillas were combined against Pimento, about seventeen for him, and by striking this blow at Ilola, all would have been brought round. The white men went to the black man's house, and offered a document for signature, which was refused. Presently a pistol dropped out of a certain pocket. About fifty negroes had assembled, but Ilola quietly promising to return, left the house and quitted the town. He had hemiplegia of the left side shortly afterwards, and died, probably poisoned.

When King Pimento landed, all his whites were dismissed. The unhappy doctor, who had stipulated about his "position at Court," was only too glad to take a free passage to Fernando Po, and his majesty was with difficulty persuaded to pay the fare. The supercargoes most kindly contributed 10*l.* to remove the unfortunate

Englishwomen from the pollution of such a position. " Miss Mary " left in October, on board the " Golden Age." Mr. Wood and his wife followed a month afterwards, in the " Star of the Sea," and the premier, the head secretary, and the last of the clerks disappeared in December. The wretched valet was the only one permanently left, a rosy-faced English William ; he had died of semi-starvation and discomfort. Yet Pimento has done nothing towards recovering power. Perhaps it is better he should not ; he has learned a trick or two in Europe, and he only awaits his opportunity ; he threatens with the lawyer or the missionary on all occasions. He lately asked permission to establish a consul for Bonny in London, at a salary of 500*l.* : and he gave as a reason for the indulgence, that he had always permitted Her British Majesty's consul to visit his dominions in the Bights of Benin and Biafra. This is not bad for an individual who dares not stir a cannon shot from his townlet, and whose name and fame amongst his fellow chiefs are about equal to the area of his territories. Of course the strings of this poor old black puppet are pulled by gentlemen *" qui font l'industrie "* nearer home.

The African Steam Ship " Blackland," was to remain two days at Grand Bonny, we therefore took the opportunity of visiting its celebrated Juju House. Taking heart of grace, and stuffing our noses with camphored cotton, we rowed up the river ; it was neap tide, and the waters had left a terrible sight of bare mud and naked slime. The stream runs apparently north

and south; it is foul and feculent as Father Thames of
the Tom cats, and the atmosphere around it forms a
bouquet d'Afrique, worse than that of a London ball-
room, which I had hitherto believed to be the *ne plus
ultra* of supportable decomposition, animal and vegetable. Reaching a creek about four miles from the
mouth, and connected with the Andoni, corrupted from
San Antonio, and the Kom Toro, or Kom river, whose
place is marked in our hydrographic charts, but remains
nameless,* returned to the east, and fronted the town of
Bonny, or as the people call it, Kalomi. It was rising
from its ashes, having been burned down about one month
before. This is the north or west end, the site is best described by a former observer to be "all water, mud banks,
and mangroves—mangroves, mud banks, and water."
The houses are Africanised models of the Swiss cottage,
the sharpest gables, the most acutangular ridge roofs,
with all the exaggerated goniology of the last Neo-
Gothic. The roofs are of dirty thatch, sometimes with
a misplaced glass window half way up, and the sides
are smeared with a sickly yellow clay taken from the
creek. There were some fine canoes, matted over against
the sea and rain, and provided with a sand hearth
for fire, when cold is felt. Some of them are sixty to
seventy feet long, and easily carry twelve puncheons of
palm oil; there may be 100 pull-a-boys, or paddlers, of
whom fifty will be fighting men, and the sides bristle

---

* In old maps the Andoni is called Rio de San Domingo, Loitomba,
or Laitomba : the Kom Toro (or Kan Toro) is called Rio.

with swords, falconets, and wall pieces, whilst a long
carronade is lashed to strong cross-pieces in the bow.
We turned into a much smaller back-water, which leads
a few yards to the south ; at low water it will be a sheet
of putrifying slime, in which a man would sink knee
deep, and in places women and boys were washing themselves with their waist clothes, which they will presently
wring out and restore. It was the most squalid of
sights ; no relieving feature but a few large cotton-trees
and masses of parasites, which hem in the other side of
Bonny. Nothing easier than to find a better site for
Bonny, but it is " Bonny fash " to stick to Bonny.
We forced the boat upon this sewer, and soon reached
the landing-place, a rude scaffold of rough round tree-
trunks lashed to uprights, and leading up the slippery
clay embankment. After this spectacle of filth, I resolved to avoid even the 'Nda, or Bonny salmon, of
which writers speak so highly.

Landing, we observed the effects of the fire, which has
been highly beneficial in removing scorpions, centipedes,
and whip-snakes, the myriads of mosquitoes and sand-
flies, which, too minute almost to be seen, cannot be
guarded against. The houses were rising rapidly. The
chiefs collect, on such occasions, their families and
dependents, and dividing them into companies, apply
them to different work in rebuilding. Some cut
stakes in the bush, others sharpen and plait them with
withies and wattles, others apply the dab, whilst the
rest prepare beams and thatching for the roof, or

break up old boxes to make doors and shutters.
The floor is of tamped earth. Small houses have
but three compartments, kitchen, salon, and Juju-room,
or private chapel. Great men have most intricate establishments, all a congeries of rooms, *oubliettes, culs de
sac,* and passages, more like a labyrinth than a dwelling-
house. The outer entrances and the interior doors—
which must serve as chimneys—are fortified with strong
staked thresholds, eighteen inches high. They are possibly intended to keep out animals; the "housemaster"
is fond of sitting there, and if you cross the step whilst
he is so doing, he will have a sickness, and complain of
"poison for eye," that is, you have bewitched him. The
women's and the men's apartments are distinct, and furniture, such as it is, is always either of the commonest
kind or broken by the awkward slaves. The wealthy
make their houses Old Curiosity Shops, everything, in
fact, from gold cloth to a penny print. The greater
part of their wealth, however, is packed up in boxes,
huddled into a lumber room, or buried, so that it never
lasts long. The bed is a grass mat, and a fire of embers
enables men to dispense with bedding. Every gentleman must have his "Juju-room," and every little
rentier his altar. The Lares and Penates are anything
between a sheet of Punch and a tobacco pipe. This private chapel is a favourite place for stowing away things,
especially rum, as no one will then steal it. Kings
and chiefs are buried in the grand Juju-houses.

After walking through the rising town, we pursued

our way towards the "Grand Juju." Nothing worse
than the streets, narrow, filthy, pool-dotted paths, that
wound between the houses and the remnants of rank
bush. Some of the people there met, were curiously
fair, when compared with the coal-black Ejo men, and all
were scantily clad, even adult girls had not a trace of
clothing. The slaves wore a truly miserable appearance, lean and deformed, with krakra lepra and fearful
ulcerations. It is in these places that one begins to
feel a doubt touching the total suppression of slavery.
The chiefs openly beg that the rules may be relaxed, in
order that they may get rid of their criminals. This is
at present impossible, and the effects are a reduplication
of misery—we pamper our convicts, Africans torture them
to death. Cheapness of the human article is another
cause of immense misery to it. In some rivers a canoe
crew never lasts three years. Pilfering—"Show me
a black man and I will show you a thief," say the
traders—and debauchery are natural to the slave, and
they must be repressed by abominable cruelties. The
master thinks nothing of nailing their hands to a water-
cask, of mutilating them in various ways—many lose
their eyes by being peppered, after the East Indian
fashion, with coarsely powdered cayenne—their ears are
cut off, or they are flogged. The whip is composed
of a twisted bullock's or hippopotamus's hide, sun-dried,
with sharp edges at the turns, and often wrapped with
copper wire; it is less merciful even than the knout,
now historical. The operation may be prolonged for

hours or for a whole day, the culprit's arms being tied to a
rafter, which keeps them at full stretch, and every fifteen
minutes or so, a whack that cuts away the flesh like a
knife, is administered. This is a favourite treatment for
guilty wives, who are also ripped up, cut to pieces,
or thrown to the sharks. If a woman has twins, or
becomes mother of more than four, the parent is
banished, and the children are destroyed. The greatest
insult is to point at a man with arm and two fingers
extended, saying at the same, *Nama Shubra, i.e.,* one of
twins, or a son of some lower animal. When a great
man dies, all kinds of barbarities are committed, slaves
are buried, or floated down the river bound to bamboo
sticks and mats, till eaten piecemeal by sharks.

The slave, as might be expected, is not less brutal
than his lord. It amazes me to hear Englishmen plead
that there is moral degradation to a negro bought by a
white man, and none when serving under a black man.
The philanthropists, doubtless, think how our poorer
classes at home, in the nineteenth century, would feel
if hurried from liberty to eternal servitude by some
nefarious African. But can any civilised sentiments
belong to the miserable half-starved being, whose one
scanty meal of vegetable per day is eked out with
monkey and snake, cat and dog, maggot and grub;
whose life is ceaseless toil, varied only by torture, and
who may be destroyed at any moment by a nod from his
owner? When the slave has once surmounted his dread
of being shipped by the white man, nothing under the

sun would, I believe, induce him willingly to return to what he should call his home. And as they were, our West Indian colonies were lands of happiness compared with the Oil Rivers; as for the " Southern States," the slave's lot is paradise when succeeding what he endures on the west coast of Africa. I believe these to be facts, but *tant pis pour les faits.* Presently, however, the philanthropic theory shall fall, and shall be replaced by a new fabric built upon a more solid foundation.

The Juju-house, now a heap of ruins, was a wattle and dab oblong of 30 to 40 feet. At the head of the room rose a kind of altar, with mat eaves to throw off the rain, and concave, bulging out behind. Across the front, underneath the roofing, in lines impaled together, were fleshless human skulls, often painted and decorated : one had a thick black imitation beard, doubtless a copy of life. Between these two rows were lines of goat's heads, also streaked with red and white, whilst an old bar shot, probably used as a club for felling the victims, hung from a corner. Near the ground there was a horizontal board, striped like the relics, and a sweep of loose thatch from below it formed a base to the altar, and left a central space in which was a round hole, with a raised rim of clay, to receive libations and the blood of victims. There were scattered skulls and spare rows of crania, impaled like Kababs, and planted with their stakes against the wall. As there had been no prisoners of late, I saw none of those trunkless heads "which placed on their necks, with their faces towards the Juju-house, present a dreadful and appalling appearance, as of men rising from the ground." To a small framework of sticks outside, were nailed those relics which the Abyssinians prefer as trophies. The foul iguana, as appropriate to this land as is the shark to these waters, crawled about all this wreck of humanity with perfect fearlessness. Some years ago the monkey was Juju, but he was degraded for theft, a battue took place, and all were "chopped." So these people not only eat each other's gods, but, like certain Christians, their own god. The iguana has since been in favour, and the stranger who maltreats one would be roughly handled. White cloth is also Juju, and the Fetishman's caprice can invent as many other such ordinances as the religion of the place may require.

There is apparently in this people a physical delight in cruelty to beast as well as to man. The sight of suffering seems to bring them an enjoyment without which the world is tame ; probably the wholesale murderers and tor-turers of history, from Phalaris and Nero downwards, took an animal and sensual pleasure—all the passions are sisters—in the look of blood and in the inspection of mortal agonies. I can see no other explanation of the phenomena which meet my eye in Africa. In almost all the towns on the Oil Rivers, you see dead or dying animals fastened in some agonising position. Poultry is most common, because cheapest—eggs and milk are Juju to slaves here—they are tied by the legs head down-wards, or lashed round the body to a stake or a tree, where they remain till they fall in fragments. If a man be unwell, he hangs a live chicken round his throat, expecting that its pain will abstract from his sufferings. Goats are lashed head downwards tightly to wooden pillars, and are allowed to die a lingering death; even the harmless tortoise cannot escape impalement. Blood seems to be the favourite ornament for a man's face, as pattern-painting with some dark colour like indigo is the proper decoration for a woman. At funerals numbers of goats and poultry are sacrificed for the benefit of the deceased, and the corpse is sprinkled with the warm blood. The headless trunks are laid upon the body, and if the fowls flap their wings, which they will do for some seconds after decapitation, it is a good omen for the dead man. When male prisoners of war are taken, they are brought home for sacrifice and food, whilst their infants and children are sometimes supported by the middle from poles planted in the canoe. The priest decapitates the men—for ordinary executions each chief has his own headsman—and no one doubts that the bodies are eaten. Mr. Smith and Dr. Hutchinson both aver that they witnessed actual cases. The former declares that when old Pepple, father of the present man, took captive king Amakree, of New Calabar, he gave a large feast to the European slave-traders on the river; all was on a grand scale, but the reader might perhaps find some difficulty in guessing the name of the dish placed before his Majesty at the head of the table. It was the bloody heart of the King of Calabar, just as it had been torn from the body. He took it in his hand and devoured it with the greatest apparent gusto, remarking, " This is the way I serve my enemies ! "

Shortly after my first visit, five prisoners of war were brought in from the eastern country. I saw in the Juju-house their skulls, which were suspiciously white and clean, as if boiled, and not a white man doubted that they had been eaten. The fact is that they cannot afford to reject any kind of provisions, and after a year or two amongst the people, even a European would, I suspect, look somewhat queerly upon a fat little black boy. Living at Bonny is exceedingly expensive, and at the end of the season a cloth worth 3*s.* has been known to fetch only three small yams. Of course if a stranger asks about their anthropophagy they will invariably reply *anemea*—I don't know !

The climate of the Bonny is exceedingly debilitating ; like that of Baghdad and Zanzibar, it is celebrated for developing latent diseases. The Harmattan, or dry season, locally called *Ikringa*, begins in early December, and lasts three months; old stagers usually find it the most un-healthy ; it is invigorating, however, to the stranger, who admires the cool grey look of the sky, and the sensation of dry cold which reminds him of the north. March, April, and May are the healthiest months, calm and serene, with pleasant breezes, and highly fitted for travelling. The rainy season sets in about latter May, and continues till the end of September ; during July and August it rains almost incessantly, except for an hour or two in the middle of the day. September is a fine month, and in October and November begin the tornadoes, which continue till the Harmattan sets in.

The Bonny, like all regions on this coast, is subject to periodical epidemics, which clear off almost all the white population. Such a year has just happened. The tornadoes had been scanty, and it was observed that the land wind had taken the place of the sea breeze. A typhus, which was rather a yellow fever, soon developed itself. The first case happened on the 14th March, 1862, and was speedily followed by a crisis in May. The last cannot be said to have occurred. Yet, between the middle of March and July, out of a total of 278 to 300 Europeans, there died six supercargoes, five doctors, five clerks, and 146 men, a total of 162. One ship, the "Osprey," lost all her crew—sixteen to seventeen men— except the master. During that fatal year the vomito, of late confined to Northern Guinea, Gambia, and Sierra Leone, descended the West African coast as far as Fernando Po, and extended northwards to Tenerife. It was not confined to Europeans, the Bonny men died by hundreds. The "coffee-grounds" and the yellow colour of the corpse showed what the disease was. And in some places it was followed by a typhus of exaggerated type, the patient sinking at once, and dying after a few hours of low muttering delirium.

The usual Bonny working day is simple. The "gentleman" comes on board as early as possible after daylight, and begins the usual process of "round trade," chaffering and dodging with all his might, now "ryling up" the agent, then sawdering him down, but never going to extremes. He breaks his fast when he can, lounges about, sitting as if at home, using tobacco, and occasionally begging for this, that, and the other thing. After the forenoon thus profitably and energetically spent, he disappears about midday, and is seen no more till the morrow.

The holiday is one of unmixed laziness: the gentleman dozes till late in front of the dead fire that went out before "Cockerappeak." Sending back his night companion to the women's apartments, he passes into a court, sits upon the high threshold and enjoys an air bath, chewing the while pieces of fibrous wood or the plantain fibres, called sápo in the dialect of the Gold Coast. This is followed by the tooth stick, now becoming used in England; it has the advantage over the brush that every separate tooth obtains a careful attention, inside as well as outside. Whilst thus cleansing mouth and throat from the hesternal fumes of tobacco and palm wine, he cracks his joints and—equivalent to European stretching—he twists his neck as much as possible without dislocation.

The whole fabric of society is naturally founded on polygamy. Some of the head chiefs have as many as fifty wives—all, as usual, under the head wife or queen, who is usually the daughter of some great house. There is the customary anxiety for a numerous offspring; yet, contradictorily enough, there are many ways of limiting propagation, such as for instance the destruction of twins, and the banishment of the too prolific mother.

The gentleman presently steps into his bathing room, and undergoes, in the hands of his favourite wives, a thorough soaping from head to foot. The apartment has usually a strong floor of raised rafters, which allow the water to drain off, and the seat is an empty box or a block of wood. There are neither baths nor tubs; calabashes of cold water are poured upon the head, after the fashion of the East Indian "Ghara," and hands are used as flesh brushes to rub the back. He then indulges in a practice popularly known as "wash um belly." During these operations audiences are given to favourites and other persons coming on business.

After being duly scrubbed the gentleman proceeds to his robing court, where sundry large boxes, like sea chests, contain his dresses and ornaments. He is extremely fastidious about the choice of his toilette, opening, and perhaps tying on, a dozen cloths before one suits his fancy. He will kiss it in token of admiration or respect if it has belonged to his ancestors. A silk pocket handkerchief is then folded triangularly and passed through a loop in the knife scabbard—like the British sailor they are abandoning the clasp knife for the bowie form—which is thus attached to the right side. His skin is then polished up with a little palm oil, and his neck, wrists and ankles are adorned with strings of coral or beads, and substantial metal or ivory rings, sometimes decorated with his English name cut out, or "fixed" in various coloured tacks. Finally, his wool is carded, with a comb made of bamboo, whose three or four long prongs are fit only for a horse's mane, and a casquette of broadcloth supplants the scarlet night-cap, fashionable in former days. The kerchief intended for hand use is hung, cravat or scarf-like, round the neck or wrist. Here, as in the Highlands, pockets are wanting.

The toilette being thus finished, breakfast is served. It is a little dinner, ordinarily consisting of obeoka, nda, fufu, fulu and tomeneru,—*Anglicé,* fowl, fish, mashed yam, soup *i.e.* (the liquid in which the stews have been boiled), and tombo, or palm-wine, the latter, however, hard, tasting like soapsuds, and very intoxicating. The cooking is excellent, when English dishes are not attempted. All families have some forbidden meat,— which Captain Owen and Dr. Livingstone call motupo and Boleo ki bo,—such as fowl or fresh beef. The race, however, is carnivorous, eating, when wealthy, fish, poultry, goats, deer, elephant, tortoise and crocodile, the two latter of which are said to be not unlike turtle. Most of the dishes are boiled, and copiously peppered with cayenne and green chili pods to induce thirst. There are many savoury messes of heterogeneous compounds, fish, fresh and dried, oysters, clams, and cockles, poultry, goat and deer, salt beef or ship's pork, yams, plantains, and palm oil. Smoked shrimps are pounded in a wooden pestle and mortar, with mashed yam for consistency, and are put into the soup like forcemeat balls.

The meal always concludes with an external application of soap and water.

After the breakfast tombo is drunk, the warm and savoury nature of the food requiring copious draughts. It is a diuretic, and promotes perspiration, so many a gallon will disappear in the course of a day. When the natural appetite fails, they suck slices of the acid lime, or chew kola nut, or eat ossessossa, a tasteless yellow berry, with a large stone and little pulp, which is said to increase intoxication. When half-drunk the gentleman retires to a cool room, where, fanned by young girls in a state of nature, he sleeps away the sultry hours of noon.

After the siesta he receives or pays visits to his friends, being careful not to appear without armed slaves carrying his large Juju and his snuff-box. He does not dip finger and thumb into the latter, but pours it into the palm of the hand, and leisurely makes up a pinch. Whenever he meets a white man he shakes hands, or rather cracks fingers, holding the crackee's index between the forefinger and thumb of the right hand,—the left is devoted to another purpose,—and loosing snaps them together. It is a knack somewhat difficult to acquire properly. The inferior chiefs and upper slaves are devoted to gambling; all cheat when they can, and a man after losing his supplies, which represent coin, will

part with his beads, armlets, and anklets, next follow his
knife, red nightcap, and loin cloth, and lastly his wives,
relations, and himself.   Some of them have proved adepts
at European games, especially draughts.   When the
gentleman stays at home, he performs upon some native
instrument, grinds a barrel organ, or enjoys a musical
box, a throng of his wives and children peeping through
the doorway.   Or he looks at conjuring tricks, and perchance jokes with his jester, some slave, whose dry
humour, sharp tongue, salt wit, and power of mimicry
have made him a favourite.   Africans are uncommonly
keen in perceiving and in caricaturing any ridicule; they
have never, however, attained the dizzy height of Art in
the days of Thespis.

A dinner similar to breakfast is eaten at 4 to 5 P.M.
Soup and stews are the favourite *ménu*, and mashed
yam acts substitute for bread.   It is also made into a
spoon by a deep impression of the thumb, and thus it
carries a thimblefull of soup with every mouthful of yam.
The evening is passed by the aid of music, chatting with
the women, and playing with the children.   It is wound
up by smoking and drinking tombo, to which, however,
at this hour, the "damned distillation" is preferred, and
the gentleman turns in drunk at midnight.

The women and children pass their day in a far
humbler manner : they begin at dawn by washing in
the creek; they then repair to the artistess who performs
the mysteries of body painting.   The favourite colour is
blue, red, however, is also used.   The tints are the indi-

genous indigo and dye wood, laid on with a hard, flat, sharp-pointed stick. They do not, as our sailors do, depict ships, animals, or figures; they prefer the chequer pattern, and the arabesque, curves and scrolls, beginning and ending with the finest hair strokes, and swelling out, leech-like, to half an inch in the middle. The head woman, whose face and body, arms and legs, have thus been decorated, dresses herself in beads and shawls, or fine cloths, and sallies out after breakfast to see her friends. Sometimes she is received with a nautch, than which no cancan can be grosser : the more literal it is, the more she enjoys it. Men and women prance promiscuously, and the children look on with uncontrollable delight.

Women of the poorer sort pass their time in making nets, hats, fishing-lines, and little mats. During the greater part of the forenoon, and again in the afternoon, they sit in the market-place, selling rum, yams, and plantains. Those who are trusted by their husbands are put in charge of the villages on the banks of the river, and of the " small countries," eight to ten miles in the interior, where superfluous goods and valuables are kept, beyond the reach of bombardment or fire. Sometimes the King invites white traders to his " seat," for the purpose of shooting bullocks that have run wild. The sport is exciting, but as there are no riding animals over-fatigue will probably induce fever. There are, it is said, horses a few days' journey in the interior, and beyond that point they are used as beasts of burthen.

Once a year every great house with its chief repairs to the bush, and makes a surround of men and boys to trap gazelles and antelopes; at times they catch a tartar, in the shape of a leopard, and as few are armed with anything but clubs, a hole is opened in the human ring-fence, allowing it to pass. The evening of the *battue* is spent in devouring its proceeds and in hard striving with strong drinks.

Ladies who are not favourites with the lords their husbands, and all wives of poor men, perform servile work, fetching water, cutting and carrying fuel, fishing with seines, and smoking and drying the proceeds. The younger children are kept at home; after a certain age they resort for education to the streets, or accompany their fathers on business, and when ten years old they are as wise, touching most things and one thing in particular, as their parents.

After this hurried but by no means exaggerated sketch of Bonny Town and the Bonnymen, the reader will perhaps join me in admiring the 'cuteness (Dred, p. 17) which has laid open " the wonderful and beautiful development locked up in the Ethiopian race."

*   *   *   *   *

The A. S. S. " Blackland," left this African Styx precisely at her contract time, 4 P.M. on the 26th September. Early on the next morning, when we appeared on deck, all eyes were turning towards the beautiful Peak of Fernando Po, which, after the dull swampy scenery through which we had passed, appeared of giant dimensions. Separated by a narrow channel of nineteen miles from its still more glorious sister, the Camaroons, or, as the savages more poetically call it, the "Mountain of Heaven," it forms the western staple of a Gate that stunts to a nothing the columns of Hercules. The distance-dwarfed grassy cone, superimposed upon the huge shaggy shoulders of the towering ridge, glowed sweetly rosy in the morning sun, and night still brooded in the black Caldera, or chauldron, which, sheer falling for thousands of feet, breaks the regularity of the ascent on the north-eastern side. Upon the flanks, where dark and umbrella-shaped trees rose tier by tier in uninterrupted succession from the base to the foot of the highest crater-cone, heavy white mists, gently rising in the morning air, clung like flocks of cotton to a quickset hedge. We are now entering the tornado season, when the views are almost without atmosphere, and consequently without distance; one supposes the Peak three or four miles off; by directest route it is a good dozen.

I had eyes for little else that morning. The " Blackland " lay in Clarence Cove, a small semicircular bight, with a brace of islets at the mouth, and a perpendicular seabank of stiff yellow clay, ninety-eight feet, ascended by a double and diverging Jacob's ladder, and showing to the sea front a scattered line of about a dozen whitewashed and thatched bungalows. The background was a glorious host of palms, with cotton woods and African cedars, the noblest of their noble family.

Enfin we are here. This is our destination; the Ilha

Formosa, or Beautiful Island, afterwards called after its Portuguese discoverer, Fernão de Poo, and lately known as the " Madeira of the Gulf of Guinea," or the " Foreign Office Grave." It is vain to attempt fixing its locality in the public brain. The secretary of the Hakluyt Society is perhaps capable of telling you that it is a modern discovery. Sundry friends asked the new Consul how he liked the prospect of the Pacific Coast of South America ; he was puzzled, till he remembered that as all have read Robinson Crusoe so all must have heard of Juan Fernandez. I may add that the name is infamous in civil and military examinations ; when a *coup de grace* has to be administered, young Bœoticus is questioned touching Fernando Po. He returns " plucked " to his papa, who, equally perplexed, employs himself for that day in asking his friends, " Who the deuce is Fernando Po ? " to which the natural answer comes—" How the devil should *I* know ? "

So closed my voyage outward-bound. Arriving in these outer places is the very abomination of desolation. I drop for a time my pen, in the distinct memory of our having felt uncommonly suicidal through that first night on Fernando Po. And so, probably, did the Consul.

THE END.

A CATALOG OF SELECTED
DOVER BOOKS
IN ALL FIELDS OF INTEREST

A CATALOG OF SELECTED DOVER
BOOKS IN ALL FIELDS OF INTEREST

CONCERNING THE SPIRITUAL IN ART, Wassily Kandinsky. Pioneering work by father of abstract art. Thoughts on color theory, nature of art. Analysis of earlier masters. 12 illustrations. 80pp. of text. 5⅜ x 8½.　　　　　　　23411-8 Pa. $3.95

ANIMALS: 1,419 Copyright-Free Illustrations of Mammals, Birds, Fish, Insects, etc., Jim Harter (ed.). Clear wood engravings present, in extremely lifelike poses, over 1,000 species of animals. One of the most extensive pictorial sourcebooks of its kind. Captions. Index. 284pp. 9 x 12.　　　　　　　　　　　　　23766-4 Pa. $12.95

CELTIC ART: The Methods of Construction, George Bain. Simple geometric techniques for making Celtic interlacements, spirals, Kells-type initials, animals, humans, etc. Over 500 illustrations. 160pp. 9 x 12. (USO)　　　　　　22923-8 Pa. $9.95

AN ATLAS OF ANATOMY FOR ARTISTS, Fritz Schider. Most thorough reference work on art anatomy in the world. Hundreds of illustrations, including selections from works by Vesalius, Leonardo, Goya, Ingres, Michelangelo, others. 593 illustrations. 192pp. 7⅛ x 10¼.　　　　　　　　　　　　20241-0 Pa. $9.95

CELTIC HAND STROKE-BY-STROKE (Irish Half-Uncial from "The Book of Kells"): An Arthur Baker Calligraphy Manual, Arthur Baker. Complete guide to creating each letter of the alphabet in distinctive Celtic manner. Covers hand position, strokes, pens, inks, paper, more. Illustrated. 48pp. 8¼ x 11.　　24336-2 Pa. $3.95

EASY ORIGAMI, John Montroll. Charming collection of 32 projects (hat, cup, pelican, piano, swan, many more) specially designed for the novice origami hobbyist. Clearly illustrated easy-to-follow instructions insure that even beginning papercrafters will achieve successful results. 48pp. 8¼ x 11.　　27298-2 Pa. $3.50

THE COMPLETE BOOK OF BIRDHOUSE CONSTRUCTION FOR WOODWORKERS, Scott D. Campbell. Detailed instructions, illustrations, tables. Also data on bird habitat and instinct patterns. Bibliography. 3 tables. 63 illustrations in 15 figures. 48pp. 5¼ x 8½.　　　　　　　　　　　　　　　　24407-5 Pa. $2.50

BLOOMINGDALE'S ILLUSTRATED 1886 CATALOG: Fashions, Dry Goods and Housewares, Bloomingdale Brothers. Famed merchants' extremely rare catalog depicting about 1,700 products: clothing, housewares, firearms, dry goods, jewelry, more. Invaluable for dating, identifying vintage items. Also, copyright-free graphics for artists, designers. Co-published with Henry Ford Museum & Greenfield Village. 160pp. 8¼ x 11.　　　　　　　　　　　　　　　　　　　25780-0 Pa. $10.95

HISTORIC COSTUME IN PICTURES, Braun & Schneider. Over 1,450 costumed figures in clearly detailed engravings–from dawn of civilization to end of 19th century. Captions. Many folk costumes. 256pp. 8⅜ x 11¾.　　　23150-X Pa. $12.95

CATALOG OF DOVER BOOKS

THE INFLUENCE OF SEA POWER UPON HISTORY, 1660–1783, A. T. Mahan. Influential classic of naval history and tactics still used as text in war colleges. First paperback edition. 4 maps. 24 battle plans. 640pp. 5⅜ x 8½. 25509-3 Pa. $12.95

THE STORY OF THE TITANIC AS TOLD BY ITS SURVIVORS, Jack Winocour (ed.). What it was really like. Panic, despair, shocking inefficiency, and a little heroism. More thrilling than any fictional account. 26 illustrations. 320pp. 5⅜ x 8½. 20610-6 Pa. $8.95

FAIRY AND FOLK TALES OF THE IRISH PEASANTRY, William Butler Yeats (ed.). Treasury of 64 tales from the twilight world of Celtic myth and legend: "The Soul Cages," "The Kildare Pooka," "King O'Toole and his Goose," many more. Introduction and Notes by W. B. Yeats. 352pp. 5⅜ x 8½. 26941-8 Pa. $8.95

BUDDHIST MAHAYANA TEXTS, E. B. Cowell and Others (eds.). Superb, accurate translations of basic documents in Mahayana Buddhism, highly important in history of religions. The Buddha-karita of Asvaghosha, Larger Sukhavativyuha, more. 448pp. 5⅜ x 8½. 25552-2 Pa. $12.95

ONE TWO THREE . . . INFINITY: Facts and Speculations of Science, George Gamow. Great physicist's fascinating, readable overview of contemporary science: number theory, relativity, fourth dimension, entropy, genes, atomic structure, much more. 128 illustrations. Index. 352pp. 5⅜ x 8½. 25664-2 Pa. $8.95

ENGINEERING IN HISTORY, Richard Shelton Kirby, et al. Broad, nontechnical survey of history's major technological advances: birth of Greek science, industrial revolution, electricity and applied science, 20th-century automation, much more. 181 illustrations. ". . . excellent . . ."–*Isis*. Bibliography. vii + 530pp. 5⅜ x 8¼. 26412-2 Pa. $14.95

DALÍ ON MODERN ART: The Cuckolds of Antiquated Modern Art, Salvador Dalí. Influential painter skewers modern art and its practitioners. Outrageous evaluations of Picasso, Cézanne, Turner, more. 15 renderings of paintings discussed. 44 calligraphic decorations by Dalí. 96pp. 5⅜ x 8½. (USO) 29220-7 Pa. $4.95

ANTIQUE PLAYING CARDS: A Pictorial History, Henry René D'Allemagne. Over 900 elaborate, decorative images from rare playing cards (14th–20th centuries): Bacchus, death, dancing dogs, hunting scenes, royal coats of arms, players cheating, much more. 96pp. 9¼ x 12¼. 29265-7 Pa. $11.95

MAKING FURNITURE MASTERPIECES: 30 Projects with Measured Drawings, Franklin H. Gottshall. Step-by-step instructions, illustrations for constructing handsome, useful pieces, among them a Sheraton desk, Chippendale chair, Spanish desk, Queen Anne table and a William and Mary dressing mirror. 224pp. 8⅛ x 11¼. 29338-6 Pa. $13.95

THE FOSSIL BOOK: A Record of Prehistoric Life, Patricia V. Rich et al. Profusely illustrated definitive guide covers everything from single-celled organisms and dinosaurs to birds and mammals and the interplay between climate and man. Over 1,500 illustrations. 760pp. 7½ x 10⅛. 29371-8 Pa. $29.95

Prices subject to change without notice.

Available at your book dealer or write for free catalog to Dept. GI, Dover Publications, Inc., 31 East 2nd St., Mineola, N.Y. 11501. Dover publishes more than 500 books each year on science, elementary and advanced mathematics, biology, music, art, literary history, social sciences and other areas.